The Brazilian Sound

Samba, Bossa Nova, and the Popular Music of Brazil

The Brazilian Sound

Samba, Bossa Nova, and the Popular Music of Brazil

Chris McGowan
and Ricardo Pessanha

New Edition

Temple University Press
Philadelphia

Temple University Press, Philadelphia 19122

Copyright © 1998 by Chris McGowan and Ricardo Pessanha. All rights reserved

Published 1998

Printed in the United States of America

♾ The paper used in this book meets the requirements
of the American National Standard for Information Sciences—Permanence
of Paper for Printed Library Materials, ANSI Z39.48-1984

Text design by Anne O'Donnell

A Note on the Translations
All song lyrics, most of the interviews with Brazilian musicians
and critics, and all quotations from books in Portuguese were
translated by the authors. The translations of the song lyrics, in
particular, reflect the authors' emphasis on literal accuracy rather
than poetic license.

Library of Congress Cataloging-in-Publication Data

McGowan, Chris, 1956–
     The Brazilian sound : samba, bossa nova, and the popular music of
Brazil / Chris McGowan and Ricardo Pessanha. — New ed.
          p.   cm.
     Includes bibliographical references (p.   ) and index.
     Discography: p.
     ISBN 1-56639-544-5 (cloth : alk. paper). — ISBN 1-56639-545-3
(paper : alk. paper)
     1. Popular music—Brazil—History and criticism.   I. Pessanha,
Ricardo.   II. Title.
ML3487.B7M4   1997
781.64'0981—DC21   96-52587

Contents

Preface

After the first edition of *The Brazilian Sound* was published, something very important happened: the fledgling marketing category of "world music" grew wings and took flight. Suddenly it was possible in better U.S. record stores to find at least a small selection of the music of Brazil and other non-English-speaking countries. The situation still leaves much to be desired, but there has been a marked improvement in the availability of "the world's music."

In terms of Brazil, many excellent collections, reissues, and contemporary albums were released in this decade. The labels Verve, Hemisphere, Tropical Storm, Milestone, Concord, Luaka Bop, Rykodisc, One Globe, Triloka, Nimbus, Blue Jackel, Tech Records, and World Pacific greatly expanded the catalog of Brazilian sounds for sale in North America. "The Girl from Ipanema" is no longer the only option. Of course, Brazilian jazz has been around since the bossa nova days, but now one also finds *samba, maracatu, forró, mangue, choro, frevo,* and *axé* music in the bins of progressive independent stores and major chains.

These welcome changes have coincided nicely with the emergence of many important new Brazilian artists and musical styles in recent years. Accordingly, for this edition we have added information about these events and doubled the size of our discography to include more than one thousand titles. We also greatly expanded our coverage of axé music and doubled the length of the chapter on Bahia. Our intent with this edition, as it was with the first *Brazilian Sound,* is to provide

an interesting and reliable introduction to Brazil's twentieth-century popular music, with an emphasis on major genres and artists of the past fifty years.

We have tried to present the most thorough and accurate historical and musicological information possible, and to make the music and artists come alive through anecdotes, descriptions, and biographical details. As our base, we conducted first-hand interviews with leading figures in Brazilian music (see the Acknowledgments), critics, and music-industry executives. We supplemented this with quotations and information from published works by Mário de Andrade, Oneyda Alvarenga, Luis da Câmara Cascudo, José Eduardo (Zuza) Homem de Mello, Vasco Mariz, Sérgio Cabral, José Ramos Tinhorão, Tárik de Souza, Antonio Risério, John Storm Roberts, David Appleby, Charles Perrone, and other leading musicologists and critics.

Of course, Brazil is a huge country and its music is a vast subject. Trying to cover it all would be like trying to encompass all of the music of the United States in one book. Therefore, there are some areas—such as música sertaneja, Amerindian music, and traditional music in the South and Central-West—that we could touch on only briefly. Those subjects will have to be left to another volume, or to other writers.

We hope *The Brazilian Sound* will inspire the reader to listen to more music from the Southern Hemisphere and that it will serve as a useful guidebook for new musical journeys.

Acknowledgments

We would like to thank Andrew Fisher, Paul Mahon, and our editors Doris Braendel, Joan Vidal, and Debby Stuart for helping to make this second edition possible. Monica Braga Ferreira, Linda Yudin, and Bruce Gilman offered invaluable suggestions, and Alda Baltazar supplied us with essential information on many contemporary artists.

We also appreciate the help given along the way by David Bartlett, Ana Maria Bahiana, J. Emilio Rondeau, John Ii, Dexter Dwight, Sérgio Mielniczenko, David Glat, Antonio Moraes Ribeiro, Luiz Badarô, Bahiatursa, Embratur, Lígia Campos, Charles Perrone, Cristina Portela, Terri Hinte, Lisa Urgo, David Heymann, Paul Winter, Herbie Mann, Viola Galloway, Denise Romano, Francisco Rodrigues, Aretuza Garibaldi, Cecilia McDowell, Cacaia, Edna Duarte, Dayse Sacramento, Edgard Rocca, Paulo Guerra, Zilah Araújo, Cláudio Vianna, Ben Mundy, Carlos de Andrade, Lila Pereira, Victor Kenski, Antonio Duncan, Mário Aretana, Ioná Zalcberg, Zico, Luana, Marcelo, Luis Antonio, Marv Fisher, Don Lucoff, Judith Wahnon, the late Márcio Ferreira, Andrew Seidenfeld, João Parahyba, Karl Garabedian, Valerie Garabedian, Marcus Lima, Ivan Cordeiro, Josh Schiffman, Tay McGowan, Nancy Ott, Ana Paula Macedo, Clesio Ferreira, Neusa Ferreira, and Layra Pessanha.

We wish to thank all our interviewees, most especially Antonio Adolfo, Alcione, the late Laurindo Almeida, Carlos de Andrade, Leny Andrade, Mario de Aretana, Geraldo Azevedo, Ana Maria Bahiana, João Bosco, Carlinhos Brown, Charlie Byrd, Oscar Castro-Neves, Dori Caymmi, Gal Costa, Hermínio Marques Dias Filho, Djavan, George Duke, Dexter Dwight, Engenheiros de Hawaii, Gilberto Gil, Don Grusin, Tim Hauser, Rildo Hora, the late Tom Jobim, Josias of Salgueiro, Rita Lee, Téo Lima, Ivan Lins, Lobão, Herbie Mann, Lyle Mays, Mazzola, Zuza Homem de Mello, Sérgio Mendes, Margareth Menezes, Andre Midani, Sérgio Mielniczenko, Airto Moreira, Milton Nascimento, João Parahyba, Flora Purim, Paulo Ricardo, João Jorge Rodrigues, J. Emilio Rondeau, Lulu Santos, Bezerra da Silva, Simone, Toquinho, Alceu Valença, Herbert Vianna, Paulinho da Viola, Paul Winter, and Linda Yudin. All nonattributed quotations in the book come from our interviews with the above.

The Brazilian Sound

Samba, Bossa Nova, and the Popular Music of Brazil

(Northern Brazil)
BOI-BUMBÁ

CARIMBÓ
LAMBADA

BUMBA-MEU-BOI

(Northeast Brazil)
BAIÃO   FORRÓ
COCO   XOTE
EMBOLADA   XAXADO

RORAIMA

AMAPÁ

AMAZONAS   PARÁ   MARANHÃO   CEARÁ   RIO GRANDE
· Manaus   São Luis   DO NORTE
                                              · Fortaleza
                    Belém   PARAÍBA
                                        PIAUÍ   · Recife
ACRE   PERNAMBUCO
                                                    ALAGOAS
        RONDÔNIA   TOCANTINS   BAHIA   SERGIPE

                    MATO GROSSO   GOIÁS   · Salvador

(Central Brazil)   · Brasília
MÚSICA SERTANEJA   MINAS GERAIS
CATERETÉ
                                        Belo Horizonte   ESPÍRITO
(Southeast Brazil)   MATO GROSSO   SANTO
JONGO   DO SUL   SÃO PAULO   · Três
CALANGO   Pontas
CAXAMBU   São Paulo ·   RIO DE JANEIRO
TOADA   · Rio de Janeiro
MÚSICA SERTANEJA   PARANÁ

                    SANTA CATARINA   AXÉ MUSIC
                                              SAMBA-REGGAE
(Southern Brazil)   · Porto Alegre   AFOXÉ
MÚSICA SERTANEJA   RIO GRANDE   SAMBA   SAMBA DE RODA
CHULA   DO SUL   CHORO   CAPOEIRA
BOI-DE-MAMÃO   MAXIXE
VANERÃO   MARCHA
                                  BOSSA NOVA
                                              FREVO
                                              MARACATU
                                              MANGUE

BRAZIL
Important Brazilian musical
genres and categories, and the
areas in which they first arose
or with which they are most
associated.

Introduction

In Brazil, music is everywhere. You can find it in a complex rhythmic pattern beaten out by an old man with his fingers on a cafe table, in the thundering samba that echoes down from the hills around Rio in the months prior to Carnaval, and in the bars where a guitar passes from hand to hand and everyone knows all the lyrics to all the classic Brazilian songs played late into the night.

Music is part of the Brazilian soul, and rhythm is in the way people speak, in the way they walk, and in the way they play soccer.

In Rio de Janeiro, after the national team has won an important soccer game, fireworks explode in the sky and samba detonates in the streets. On sidewalks and in city squares, the celebration begins. Impromptu percussion sections appear, made up of all types of Brazilians, rich and poor, black and brown and white. As participants pick up instruments—a drum, a scraper, a shaker—an intricate, ebullient samba *batucada* (percussion jam) builds. Each amateur music-maker kicks in an interlocking rhythmic part to create a groove that would be the envy of most professional bands in other parts of the world. The singing and dancing inevitably go on for hours.

Music is a passport to happiness for Brazilians, an escape from everyday frustrations and (for

Rio de Janeiro. *Courtesy of Embratur.*

Musical notes in a sidewalk in Vila Isabel, a neighborhood in Rio known as the home of many great samba composers and musicians. *Photo by Ricardo Pessanha.*

the ballad singer. Second, a high level of poetry is present in the lyrics of much Brazilian popular music. And last, vibrant Afro-Brazilian rhythms energize most Brazilian songs, from samba to baião.

Brazilian music first grabbed international attention with the success of the dance-hall style *maxixe* in Europe between 1914 and 1922. The public was captivated by this vivacious and provocative song and dance, much as Europeans were taken with *lambada* in the summer of 1989. The 1940s saw the first exportation of samba, as songs like Ary Barroso's marvelous "Aquarela do Brasil" (known to most of the world as simply

most) a hard and difficult material life. "There's an amazing magical, mystical quality to Brazilian music. Their music is paradise," says jazz flutist Herbie Mann.

In the twentieth century more than a little of this paradise reached the outside world, and Brazil arguably had more of an impact on international popular music than any country other than the United States. It was successful abroad for as many reasons as there are types of Brazilian music. Just as the United States has exported a wide variety of musical genres, so too has Brazil, even though very few countries speak its national language, Portuguese.

Most Brazilian music shares three outstanding qualities. It has an intense lyricism tied to its Portuguese heritage that often makes for beautiful, highly expressive melodies, enhanced by the fact that Portuguese is one of the most musical tongues on the earth and no small gift to

Two youngsters in Rio playing the tamborim. *Photo by Ricardo Pessanha.*

Elba Ramalho. *Photo by Livio Campos. Courtesy of BMG.*

"Brazil") reached North America. Barroso's tunes were featured in Walt Disney films and covered in other Hollywood productions by a playful, exotic young woman who wore colorful laced skirts, heaps of jewelry, and a veritable orchard atop her head. Her name was Carmen Miranda and she sang catchy sambas and marchas by many great Brazilian composers in a string of Hollywood feature films. For better or worse, she would symbolize Brazil to the world for decades and become a cultural icon in North America and Europe, a symbol of fun and extravagance.

Samba became a fundamental part of the world's musical vocabulary. It would get another boost when one of its variations, a sort of ultra-cool modern samba called *bossa nova*, entered the world spotlight through the 1959 movie *Black Orpheus*, which won the Cannes Film Festival Grand Prize and the Academy Award for Best Foreign Film. In North America, a bossa craze was ignited by the 1962 smash hit album *Jazz Samba*, recorded by guitarist Charlie Byrd and saxophonist Stan Getz.

Jazz artists also helped globally popularize the new sound, which had a breezy syncopation, progressive harmony, and a deceptive simplicity.

Gilberto Gil. *Courtesy of Tropical Storm/WEA.*

Bossa nova was the big pop-music trend of the early 1960s, until it was supplanted by the English rock invasion led by the Beatles.

Bossa, like samba, is now a solid part of the international repertoire, especially in the jazz realm. Bossa's leading figure, Antonio Carlos Jobim, is one of the most popular songwriters of the century, and his stature rivals that of George Gershwin, Duke Ellington, and other great composers of Western popular music. Bossa nova initiated a widespread infiltration of Brazilian music and musicians into North American music.

Beginning in the late 1960s, Brazilian percussion became an essential element of many jazz and pop recordings. A new generation of talented Brazilian musicians began a long-term interchange with jazz artists that would put Americans on dozens of Brazilian albums and Brazilians on hundreds of American albums in following decades. Airto Moreira and Flora Purim were two of these artists, and they performed on groundbreaking albums that helped establish the new subgenre called "jazz fusion."

At the same time that Brazilian music was influencing jazz in the Northern Hemisphere, a remarkable new generation of singers and songwriters was coming to the forefront in Brazil in the late 1960s and 1970s. They fashioned original sounds from an eclectic variety of sources in and outside of Brazil. Milton Nascimento, Gilberto Gil, Caetano Veloso, Ivan Lins, João Bosco, Djavan, Gal Costa, Maria Bethânia, Elba Ramalho, Alceu Valença, Chico Buarque, and others created and performed songs that came to be referred to as MPB (an acronym for *música popular brasileira*), a new catch-all category. Their superb integration of

rhythm, melody, harmony, and lyrics resulted in one of the richest bodies of popular music ever to come from one country.

At the end of the 1980s yet another Brazilian song and dance—the sensual lambada—gained international currency. Although lambada was of more commercial than artistic merit, it became part of an important musical movement sweeping Salvador that decade and the next. *Axé music* became the name for *samba-reggae* and other updated Afro-Brazilian styles performed by Olodum, Carlinhos Brown, Timbalada, Daniela Mercury, Ara Ketu, Luiz Caldas, and Margareth Menezes, among others. Elsewhere in Brazil, many other notable artists also established careers during this time, including Marisa Monte, Chico Science, Skank, and Chico César.

Today, as in past decades, Brazil's popular music can lay claim to a dazzling variety of song forms and musical traditions. There are the troubadours who strum guitars and trade improvised stanzas back and forth, each trying to top the other, in traditional *desafio* song duels. There are accordion virtuosos who lead their bands in rollicking syncopated *forró* music. There are ritualistic *afoxés*, festive *marchas*, frenetic *frevos*, and the leaping instrumental improvisations of *choro*. And there are the walls of sound and waves of color that are the *escola de samba* (samba school) parades during Rio's Carnaval. Each escola's rhythm section, comprised of some three hundred drummers and percussionists, works in perfect coordination with thousands of singers and dancers to create an awe-inspiring musical spectacle, the greatest polyrhythmic spectacle on the planet.

Whether manifested in these or other forms, Brazilian music above all has a profound ability to move the soul. In its sounds and lyrics, it reflects the Brazilian people—their uninhibited joy or despair, their remarkable capacity to celebrate, and the all-important concept of *saudade* (a deep longing or yearning).

To best understand Brazil's rich musical heritage, we must first journey back several hundred years, to where Brazil and its music both began.

CARTE DU BRÉSIL.

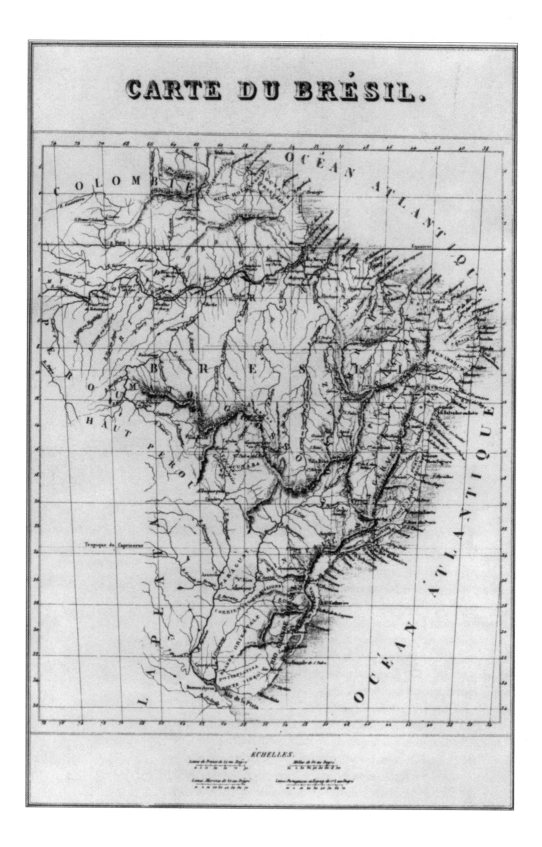

ÉCHELLES.

Five Centuries of Music

In Brazil, the first world and the third world exist side by side. Brazil is highly industrialized in some areas and absolutely medieval in others. It is wealthy and miserable, chic Ipanema and mud-and-stick hut, high-tech engineer and Stone Age Indian, computers and bananas. As a common joke goes: if there were no Brazil, someone would have to invent one.

Another argument for Brazil's singularity is that nowhere else on earth do different races, cultures, and religions coexist as peacefully as they do there. That is partly because intermarriage has been common in Brazil for centuries, creating a truly mixed society: most everyone has ancestors from two or three continents. There is prejudice among Brazilians (more on this later), but it is rare to encounter overt racial or religious hatred of the kind that is common in many other countries. A good example of Brazilian tolerance can be seen in the commercial district in downtown Rio called *Saara* (Sahara). There, Brazilians of Jewish, Lebanese, and Syrian descent all go to the same *botequins* (bars) at the end of the workday for a beer, a chat, and, on Fridays, a little samba. Brazil has been a real melting pot for centuries, not a mixed salad like the United States. As such, a person in Brazil of Lebanese or Yoruba or Japanese ancestry usually identifies himself or herself first and foremost as *Brazilian*.

The First Brazilians

Brazil's national character and its rich musical tradition both derive from the profound mingling of races that has been going on since April 1500, when the Portuguese explorer Pedro Álvares Cabral stepped onto the lush tropical coast of what would later be southern Bahia.

Of course, Cabral was not the first human to arrive in Brazil, and long before his foot touched

Bahian sand, a long musical tradition had been at play for thousands of years. The ancestors of today's Brazilian Indians migrated from Asia to the Western Hemisphere somewhere between twelve thousand and forty thousand years ago and eventually made their way down to South America. When Cabral first came to Brazil, the indigenous population probably exceeded two million. In their music, they sang songs solo and in chorus, accompanying themselves with flutes, whistles, and horns. They beat out rhythms with hand-clapping, foot-stamping, rattles, sticks, and drums.

Their music did not, however, play a major role in the development of Brazilian popular music. In part, this is because so many tribes were devastated by Portuguese invaders, and the Indians that survived often lost their cultural traditions when they left their native homes and went to live in cities and towns. There is Indian influence in some Brazilian popular music, as seen in songs by musicians like Egberto Gismonti and Marlui Miranda, instruments like the *reco-reco* scraper, and traditions such as the *caboclinho* Car-

A simple house in Maranguape, Ceará, in the Northeast of Brazil. *Photo by Chris McGowan.*

naval groups. But generally one must journey to the remote homelands of the Yanomâmi, Bororo, Kayapó, and other indigenous groups to hear their music.

The Portuguese Conquest

Cabral encountered a land of great geographic diversity that is now the world's fifth largest nation in terms of land mass. Brazil is a tropical country, situated largely between the equator and the tropic of Capricorn. It possesses some forty-six hundred miles of coastline, as well as the vast Amazon River basin, home to the largest rain forest on the planet. While parts of that humid region can receive up to 150 inches of rain a year, Brazil's arid, drought-stricken Northeast has areas that may go years with no rain at all. Other regions include a savannah-covered plateau in central Brazil, grassy plains in the South, and a lush coastal belt that was once covered by Atlantic rain forest.

Cabral sailed back to Portugal and the court of King Manuel I, bearing monkeys and parrots but—to everyone's disappointment—carrying no jewels, silks, or spices. However, royal expeditions that returned to the new continent shortly

thereafter discovered something quite valuable: plentiful stands of brazilwood, a tree that yielded a useful red dye and that gave the country its name. Handsome profits from the brazilwood trade soon increased the number of visiting Portuguese and French traders; naturally, the Portuguese crown decided to expand its exploitation of Brazil and get rid of the French interlopers. In 1532 the first settlement, São Vicente, was established near present-day Santos in São Paulo state. The first sugar mills were constructed there and farther north, in Pernambuco.

Some respectable Portuguese settlers came with their families to Brazil. But for the most part, writes E. Bradford Burns in *A History of Brazil*, "the Portuguese monarchs customarily sent out on their global expeditions a combination of soldiers, adventurers, and petty criminals condemned to exile. Women were excluded. The Portuguese female was noticeably rare during the first century of Brazilian history. Her scarcity conferred a sexual license on the conquerors, already well acquainted with Moorish, African, and Asian women and seemingly attracted to dark-skinned beauty." A colony of mixed races was soon in the making, quite different from the civilization that would be created in North America by English

Ángelo Agostinho's depiction of entrudo in Rio in 1880, a rude celebration that was one of the elements of nineteenth-century Carnaval in Brazil. *Courtesy of Agência JB.*

Protestants and their families, who came to settle permanently, kept more of a distance from the natives, and maintained an air of moral superiority with regard to other races.

Whether they were adventurers or settlers, the Portuguese brought their culture to this new land. In the realm of music, this included the European tonal system, as well as Moorish scales and medieval European modes. They also brought numerous festivals related to the Roman Catholic liturgical calendar and a wealth of dramatic pageants such as the *reisado* and *bumba-meu-boi* that are still seasonally performed in the streets. The reisado celebrates the Epiphany, and the processional bumba-meu-boi dance enacts the death and resurrection of a mythical bull. Both are *autos,* a dramatic genre from medieval times that includes dances, songs, and allegorical characters. Jesuit priests introduced many religious autos that eventually took on local themes and musical elements.

In addition, the Portuguese brought many musical instruments to Brazil: the flute, piano, violin, guitar, clarinet, triangle, accordion, cavaquinho, violincello, jew's harp, and tambourine. The Portuguese used a lot of syncopation and brisk, complex rhythms—traits that would help their music mesh well with the music the Africans brought to Brazil—and they had a fondness for lyric ballads, often melancholy and suffused with saudade.

Portuguese song forms included *moda*, a sentimental song that became the *modinha* in Brazil in the eighteenth century; *acalanto*, a form of lullaby; *fofa*, a dance of the eighteenth century; and (later) *fado*, a melancholy, guitar-accompanied Portuguese ballad. And along with their music, the Portuguese brought the *entrudo*, a rude celebration that was the beginning of Brazil's *Carnaval* tradition.

As they settled the new land, planted tobacco and cotton, and built sugar mills, the Portuguese looked on the native peoples as prime candidates for forced labor on the sugarcane plantations being developed in northeastern Brazil. But the Indians were unsuitable—they either escaped to the forest or died from the brutal work. So the colonizers of Brazil looked east, to Africa.

The Africans in Brazil

The first recorded importation of Africans into Brazil occurred in 1538. From that year until the slave trade ended in 1850, historians estimate that four million to five million Africans survived the crossing of the Atlantic to Brazil. (Hundreds of thousands died on route.) This was many times more than were taken to North America. The institution of slavery continued until the Brazilian abolition of 1888.

Three main ethnic and cultural groups made the journey. The *Sudanese* groups (Yoruba, Fon, Ewe, and Ashanti peoples) were brought from what are now Nigeria, the People's Republic of Benin (formerly Dahomey), and Ghana. *Bantu* groups came from Angola, Zaire (formerly the Congo), and Mozambique. And the *Moslem Guinea-Sudanese* groups (Tapas, Mandingos, Fulahs, and Hausa) were taken from Ghana, Nigeria, and neighboring areas.

The African peoples brought their music, dance, languages, and religions, much of which survived in a purer form in Brazil than in North America. In part this was due to the sheer numbers of Africans arriving in Brazil, and the large concentrations of slaves and free blacks in coastal cities such as Rio, Salvador, and Recife. It was also affected by Portuguese attitudes toward their slaves, the influence of the Catholic Church, the existence of *quilombos* (colonies formed by runaway slaves), and other factors.

The Mediterranean world had already experienced great religious and linguistic diversity by the time Cabral first came to Brazil. On the Iberian peninsula Christians and Moors had been enslaving one another for hundreds of years. African influence in Portugal, in fact, predated the settlement of Brazil by several centuries and was quite apparent long after Moorish rule ended in A.D. 1249. Thus, compared with northern Europeans, the Portuguese were relatively more tolerant of, or indifferent to, the native culture of their captives.

The formation of Catholic lay brotherhoods called irmandades, beginning in the seventeenth century, also helped perpetuate African traditions. These voluntary organizations functioned as social clubs and mutual aid societies and were organized along social, racial, and ethnic lines. Thus, because many slaves from particular cultural groups in Africa belonged to the same irmandades when they came to Brazil, they were able to continue their homeland traditions. In many cases, they syncretized elements of their own festivals and ceremonies with those of the Catholic Church.

Many irmandades were located in large cities, which were centers of slave importation and in general provided opportunities for enslaved and free blacks to gather together. "Until 1850," writes Diana Brown in her book Umbanda: Religion and Politics in Urban Brazil, "thousands of Africans per year were still arriving in Brazil, bringing with them fresh infusions of the cultures of their African homelands." "The numbers and density of Afro-Brazilian populations," she continues, "provided favorable conditions for the maintenance of their cultural traditions; in addition, these large cities offered to these groups a relatively greater degree of free time and movement than was true, for example, of rural plantation life. Not surprisingly, it was these cities in which the various regional Afro-Brazilian religions first developed."

In addition, the Portuguese intermarried extensively, partly because most of the early settlers came without wives. A racially mixed population was soon formed by the offspring of the Portuguese, Indians, and Africans, who intermingled at all levels of society. And many wealthy white officials and planters were exposed to African culture as children by playmates and nannies, and as adults by mistresses and wives.

Quilombos, colonies formed by runaway slaves in the interior of Brazil, also helped perpetuate African culture. The largest and most famous of these was Palmares, established in the rugged interior of northeastern Alagoas state in the seventeenth century. The inhabitants of Palmares made an effort to organize a society based in African traditions. It lasted for several decades and had a population in the thousands (some say as high as twenty thousand). To the Portuguese, Palmares was a threat to the established order, not to mention the institution of slavery. Numerous armed expeditions were mounted against it by the Portuguese crown, beginning in 1654. All were unsuccessful until the last major campaign, waged in 1694, which overwhelmed and destroyed Palmares. Zumbi, the quilombo's famed war commander, was captured and killed the following year. The legendary warrior is still celebrated in Brazilian music today, and his birthday (November 20) has been a national holiday since 1995.

African heritage survives in modern Brazil in a variety of manifestations. Brazilian Portuguese has incorporated many Yoruba and other African words. The cuisine in Bahia is quite similar to that of West Africa. And Brazilian music, dance, and culture in general are heavily rooted in Africa. In fact, Brazil has the largest African-descended population outside of Africa. In 1980, Brazil's population was 44.5 percent black or mulatto, according to the government census, and it is obvious that more than half of all Brazilians have at least one ancestor from the mother continent.

Issues of Race in Brazil

Yet, despite generations of racial intermarriage in Brazil, racism persisted in an overt form for many years after the abolition, and the government persistently repressed public displays of Afro-Brazilian culture. By the late twentieth century, racial attitudes had changed for the better, yet today they remain complicated, subtle, and often invisible.

It is certainly true that Brazil is one of the most tolerant countries in the world in terms of interracial dating and marriage, which are commonplace. And it is perfectly ordinary to find people of all colors amiably interacting in the bars, beaches, and streets of cities like Rio. People of different ethnicities are at ease with one another socially, especially in the working class—where racial conflict has often been extreme in other countries. Most Brazilians believe that discrimination in their homeland today is more often tied to one's wealth and perceived social standing than it is to one's skin color.

In speaking of Brazil, it is important to remember how different it is from countries like the United States, which follows a "bipolar" model in which anyone with any degree of African ancestry is considered "black." Brazilians, on the other hand, see racial identity as a fluid continuum. They distinguish between *preto* (black) and *mulato* (mulatto) and have words for a wide variety of skin colors resulting from varying degrees of African, European, or Amerindian heritage. Another difference between the two countries is that African Americans are in the minority in the

United States, while people with at least some degree of African ancestry are the majority in Brazil.

Beginning in the 1930s, influenced by the sociologist Gilberto Freyre and others, "Brazil nurtured the notions that its multiethnic heritage was a source of strength, and that any social inequality that did exist was based not on ethnicity but on class. The national identity of 'Brazilian' was promoted and ethnic identity as 'black' was discouraged," observes G. Reginald Daniel in his essay "Multiethnic Populations in the United States and Brazil."

Yet there persists in Brazil an association, sometimes openly acknowledged and other times subtly implied, of lighter skin with higher status. Magazine and television advertisements regularly feature models who mostly look as if they are from northern Europe. Black Brazilians are conspicious by their overwhelming presence in many *favelas* (slums) and in their marked absence from the elite levels of business, politics, and society. Mulattos and blacks, especially the latter, suffer disproportionately more from poverty and lack of opportunity than do lighter-skinned Brazilians. Mulattos generally have a higher social status than do blacks, but both have been subject to prejudice in the past.

Daniel and other social critics argue that Brazil's "racial democracy" is a myth, and that racism is a serious problem about which most Brazilians are in perpetual denial. Racial issues have often been addressed in popular music. Since the 1980s, Afro-Brazilian pride has been more frequently asserted—and racial injustices protested—in lyrics by artists like Gilberto Gil, Bezerra da Silva, and Batacotô, and in Carnaval songs written for Rio's escolas de samba and Bahia's *blocos afro*. This is a significant change from previous decades, when racial commentary in music usually consisted of jokes at the expense of blacks and mulattos. For example, one of the most popular Carnaval songs of all time is Lamartine Babo's 1932 marcha "Teu Cabelo Não Nega" (Your Hair Doesn't Deny It), in which he sings, "Your hair doesn't deny it, *mulata* / Your color is mulata / But as color isn't contagious / Mulata, I want your love."

The subject of racial slurs in pop songs came to the forefront in 1996 because of lyrics considered offensive to blacks in the single "Veja os Cabelos Dela" (Look at Her Hair) by Tiririca (Francisco Everardo Oliveira), who is himself a mulatto. An activist group filed a lawsuit against the song and a judge in Rio ordered Tiririca's record removed from stores, an unprecedented move that provoked as much controversy as the tune itself. About the situation, *Veja* magazine wrote, "The principal improvement is that it is no longer possible to keep the black in his condition of invisible citizen, without rights—including that of complaining."

Whether one believes or does not believe that racial prejudice is a problem in Brazil, the debate is now fully open.

Afro-Brazilian Religion

While a combination of racism and the Roman Catholic Church resulted in a long-standing suppression of Afro-Brazilian religions, the latter nevertheless became firmly rooted in the national culture and also had a tremendous influence on the development of Brazil's popular music.

The enslaved Yoruba, Ewe, and other peoples brought their animist beliefs from Africa to the New World. These religions are probably thousands of years old, predating Christianity, Islam, and Buddhism. Their belief systems were maintained for millennia, not on parchment or tablets, but as living oral traditions in ritual and music handed down from generation to generation. The Yoruba, who had the greatest influence on Afro-Brazilian religion, came primarily from what is now Nigeria.

An outdoor candomblé ceremony in Salvador. *Courtesy of Bahiatursa.*

Their òrìṣà tradition, carried across the Atlantic Ocean, was transformed in Brazil into candomblé. It became santería in Cuba and Shango in Trinidad. The Yoruba deities, the òrìṣà, are called orixás in Brazil and orishas in Cuba. The anthropologist Migene González-Wippler, in her book Santería, the Religion, estimates that as of 1989 there were more than one hundred million practitioners of Yoruba-based religions in Latin America and the United States. Most of them are in Brazil.

In Haiti, the òrìṣà religion also played a role in the formation of vodun, which incorporates many traditions but is especially dominated by those of the Fon from Dahomey (which became the Republic of Benin in 1975). In the American South, especially Louisiana, vodun became known as voodoo, the subject of a great deal of outrageous legend and misunderstanding by outsiders.

In Brazil, macumba is a common generic name—used mostly by outsiders—for all orixá religions. Candomblé is the closest to the old West African practices, while umbanda is a twentieth-century variation with considerable influence from spiritist beliefs. Xangô, catimbó, caboclo, and batuque are regional variations, with different sects reflecting influences from particular African ethnic or cultural groups—nações (nations). The greatest influence of the Fon, and hence closest similarity to vodun, in Afro-Brazilian religions can be found in the casa das minas religion (or minas) of São Luis, the capital of Maranhão state.

The Afro-Brazilian religions began to take an organized form in the nineteenth century, and ter-reiros (centers of worship) were first reported around 1830 in Salvador and 1850 in Recife. The religions were syncretized in Brazil into new forms by their followers because of government and Roman Catholic repression that persisted into the twentieth century. Devotees secretly worshipped their West African gods during Catholic ceremonies. Blacks who prayed to a statue of the Virgin Mary often were actually thinking of Iemanjá, the goddess of the sea. Saint George might represent Ogun, god of warriors; Saint Jerome could stand in for Xangô, god of fire, thunder, and justice; and Jesus Christ might really signify Oxalá, the god of the sky and universe. Catholicism, with its abundance of saints, meshed well with the orixá tradition and inadvertently sheltered it.

In the Afro-Brazilian religions, a follower always has two different orixás, a male and a female that "rule your head" and are seen as your spiritual parents. For example, you might have Xangô

An umbanda supply store called Bazar Oxalá in Rio. *Photo by Chris McGowan.*

and Iemanjá as the "masters of your head." The head priestess, the *mãe-de-santo* (mother of the saints), typically discovers this and asserts that these two orixás, because of their specific personalities and powers, are the natural guides for you and your life. During the ceremonies, the drums and singing call down the orixás, and they or their intermediary spirits "possess" the bodies of the initiated sons and daughters.

While the traditional sect of candomblé focuses solely on the orixás, umbanda has incorporated many influences from *espiritismo* (Spiritism), a religion that formed in the nineteenth century around the ideas and writings of Allan Kardec, the pseudonym of the French philosopher Léon Hipolyte D. Rivail. Today, candomblé and umbanda are an accepted and integral part of Brazilian culture, with many leading cultural figures counted among their adherents. One notable example is the novelist Jorge Amado, who is a son of Xangô. Many Brazilian musicians praise or refer to Afro-Brazilian

deities in their song lyrics, and some have included invocation songs for the orixás on their albums.

Although Brazil is said to be 90 percent Roman Catholic, at least half of its population also follows Afro-Brazilian religions. Rio, for example, has hundreds of umbanda supply shops that sell beads, candles, dried herbs, and plaster-cast figures of spirits and saints. Offerings of food for an orixá can often be found beside flickering candles late at night alongside a road. And every New Year's Eve, millions of Brazilian men and women dress in white and throw flowers and other gifts into the sea as offerings to the goddess Iemanjá. Each orixá is called by a particular rhythm and song, and these rituals have kept alive many African songs, musical scales, musical instruments, and rhythms.

The wide assortment of African-derived instruments still played in Brazil today include the *agogô* (a double bell struck by a wooden stick), *cuíca* (a small friction drum), and *atabaque* (a conical single-headed drum). The African influence also reveals it-

Ceremonial umbanda drums and figurines in the Bazar Oxalá. *Photo by Chris McGowan.*

An amateur musician playing pagode samba in a bar in the Salgueiro neighborhood in Rio. *Photo by Ricardo Pessanha.*

self in Brazil's traditional and folk music (as it does in the rest of the Americas) through the use of syncopation and complex rhythmic figures, the importance of drums and percussion instruments, certain flattened or "falling" notes, the so-called metronome sense of West Africa, the use of call-and-response patterns, short motifs, improvisation, and—perhaps most important—the tendency of music to play a central role in life.

Religious, ceremonial, and festive African music would form the basis of Afro-Brazilian songs and dances that would eventually develop into various musical forms: afoxé, jongo, lundu, samba, maracatu, and more.

The Development of Brazil

Brazil's mixed population today reflects its Portuguese, Amerindian, and African ancestors, and the arrival of numerous German, Italian, Japanese, and Lebanese immigrants since the nine-

teenth century. Tragically, the numbers of Brazil's indigenous Indian peoples have declined drastically over the centuries. Many were slain early on by the Portuguese conquerers or decimated by European diseases. Others were absorbed into colonial settlements, voluntarily or against their will. And a great many intermarried with the Portuguese, adding to Brazil's miscegenation. Today there are perhaps only two hundred thousand full-blooded Indians in Brazil, and their population has continued to decline in recent decades as new settlers push farther into the Amazon rain forest in search of gold and land.

Carnaval in Salvador. *Courtesy of Bahiatursa.*

Naná Vasconcelos paradings with Olodum during Carnaval in Salvador. *Photo by Artur Ikishima. Courtesy of Bahiatursa.*

sor, Dom Pedro II, was overthrown in 1889 and a republic was established. Since the nineteenth century, Brazil has had both authoritarian and democratic governments. It was ruled by a military regime between 1964 and 1985, but since then has been a democracy.

Brazil's economic development was powered initially by trade in brazilwood, then sugar, gold, diamonds, coffee, and rubber fueled the country's growth. Industrialization came largely in the twentieth century, accelerating especially during the Getúlio Vargas regimes (1930–1945, 1950–1954). By the late twentieth century, Brazil had diversified and become an important exporter of soybeans, orange juice, steel, military weapons, airplanes, shoes, and cultural products such as recorded music, movies, and television *novelas*. In some years Brazil had the ninth largest economy in the world, and by the mid-nineties its population surpassed 150 million people.

After the colonization began, Portugal ruled Brazil until 1822, when Dom Pedro, heir to the Portuguese throne, declared Brazil's independence and became its first emperor. His succes-

But the "economic miracle" that followed the military coup of 1964 and greatly modernized

Sambista Paulinho da Viola (*left*) and rocker Lobão (*right*). *Photo by Cristina Granato. Courtesy of BMG.*

Brazil did not benefit the majority of the population. Perhaps it is true, as Brazilians often say, that soccer, beer, *cachaça* (sugar-cane liquor), and Carnaval are the only things that keep the poor from staging a revolution.

A Musical Melting Pot

Over the course of the last five centuries, Portuguese, African, and—to a lesser extent—Amerindian rhythms, dances, and harmonies have been mixing together, altering old styles and creating new forms of music. One of the most important early Brazilian genres was the lundu song form and circle dance, brought by Bantu slaves from what is now Angola to Brazil, where it began to acquire new influences and shock the Europeans.

The first recorded reference to lundu in Brazil was in 1780. The dance was considered lascivious and indecent in its original form, which included the *umbigada* navel-touching movement, an invitation to the dance that was characteristic of many African circle dances. By the end of that century, lundu had made an appearance in the Portuguese court, transformed into a refined style sung with guitar or piano accompaniment and embellished with European harmonies. By the mid-nineteenth century in Brazil, lundu was performed both in salons and in the streets. As a popular style, it featured sung refrains and an energetic 2/4 rhythm carried by handclapping. Both types of lundu would remain popular in Brazil until the early twentieth century.

Another important song and dance, *maxixe*, was created in Rio around 1880 by Afro-Brazilian musicians who were performing at parties in lower-middle-class homes. The first genuinely Brazilian dance, maxixe was a synthesis of lundu, polka, and Cuban habanera with additional voluptuous moves performed by the closely dancing couple. (Influences from Argentinian tango came later.) Maxixe gave as erotic and scandalous an impression as lundu had one hundred years earlier and lambada would one hundred years later.

Maxixe and other Brazilian styles would be popularized by a native music industry that dates to 1902, with the release of Brazil's first record: the lundu "Isto É Bom" (This Is Good), written by Xisto Bahia and performed by the singer Baiano for the Casa Edison record company. In later decades, Brazil developed a large domestic music industry and began to export its songs all over the world.

Musically, Brazil has continued to reflect the great racial and cultural miscegenation of its history, and to continually absorb and modify new ideas and styles. A good example of this is the long and rich tradition of Brazil's most famous musical form: samba.

Martinho da Vila

Pixinguinha and the Batutas

CENTRO

MANGUEIRA

ESTÁCIO

VILA ISABEL

A samba school's ala das baianas

TIJUCA

Alcione

Paulinho da Viola

Cacique de Ramos

RIO DE JANEIRO

Samba: The Heartbeat of Rio

Chapter Two

He who doesn't like samba isn't a good guy
He's rotten in the head or sick in the feet

Dorival Caymmi
"Samba da Minha Terra"
(Samba of My Land)

On a hot and humid summer night in Rio de Janeiro, a small stage is packed with dozens of musicians holding assorted drums and percussion instruments, engaged in an *escola de samba* (samba school) rehearsal. They are inside a cavernous pavilion that most resembles an airplane hangar and it is crowded with people—black, white, brown—who all have one thing in common: the samba.

Surdos (bass drums) pound out a booming beat, and their incessant drive provides the foundation for the rest of the *bateria*, the drum-and-percussion section that will later parade triumphantly during Carnaval. Snare drums called *caixas* rattle away in a hypnotic frenzy, and above them *tamborins*—small cymbal-less tambourines that are hit with sticks—carry a high-pitched rhythmic phrase like popcorn in an overheated pot. Enter the sad cries and humorous moans of the *cuíca* (friction drum), the crisp rhythmic accents of the *reco-reco* (scraper), and the hollow metallic tones of the *agogô* (double bell). Other percussion instruments add more colors, the ukelele-like *cavaquinho* adds its high-register plaintive harmonies, and the *puxador* (lead singer) belts out the melody.

Dense polyrhythms dance and cross, reinforce and contrast with one another. By now the sound is deafening and it's impossible to talk to the person next to you. Sweat flows, your head spins with the dense sound, and the festive atmosphere carries you away in euphoria. Cares are tossed to the wind. There's no doubt in anyone's mind: samba is what it's all about.

A cold technical definition would never express what samba, and the whole universe that revolves around it, is. For one thing, in a musical sense, there are many varieties of samba—from dense, thundering *samba-de-enredo* played by the escolas de samba during Carnaval to melodious, sophisticated *samba canção* to earthy, exuberant *pagode samba*. And, if

A member of a samba school pounding out the rhythm on a surdo during Carnaval in Rio. *Photo by Lidio Parente. Courtesy of Embratur.*

21

we ask an average Brazilian (especially a Carioca) what samba is, the answer is generally subjective and doesn't always refer to music. "It's something that runs in my veins, it's in my blood," say many samba musicians and devotees.

It is common for Cariocas to say, rather ironically, that everything ends up in samba. If things go wrong there's always samba to lift one's spirits. Samba is solace, celebration, escape and abandon, and it is culture, philosophy, and tradition. Samba is a musical form largely created and sustained by the black and mulatto working classes in Rio, but all types of Brazilians draw vitality from it, and most of the country dances to it during Carnaval. Almost every Brazilian musician—whether from the area of MPB, of jazz, or even of rock—records a samba at some point in his or her career.

Samba's Roots

Samba coalesced into a distinct musical genre in Rio de Janeiro in the early twentieth century. The exact course of samba's early evolution is unknown, but there is no shortage of theories about its origins. The word *samba* appears to have come from Angola, where the Kimbundu word *semba* refers to the *umbigada* "invitation to the dance." Some scholars believe that samba and the other Afro-Brazilian circle dances that feature or once featured the umbigada are all variants of the same theme.

There are those who argue that lundu, in Brazil since the eighteenth century, was the true musical parent of samba. Others theorize that a primitive type of samba, or at least its essential elements, was brought to Rio from Bahia more than one hundred years ago. In *Brasil Musical* (edited by Caúrio) journalists Roberto Moura, Tárik de Souza, and Rita Cáurio cite "Moqueca Sinhá" (a lundu), "Laranjas da Sabina" (Sabina's Oranges), and "A Morte do Marechal" (Marechal's Death), from 1870, 1888, and 1893, respectively, as early examples of songs that "tended rhythmically towards samba."

The mystery of samba's roots is complicated further by the fact that the word *samba* was used in the late nineteenth century both as a synonym for various Afro-Brazilian dances and to designate parties held by slaves and former slaves. But it was certainly in Rio that samba was developed, embellished, and transformed into a distinct genre.

Many slaves and former slaves emigrated to Rio, the nation's capital, in the late nineteenth century because of a decline in the fortunes of tobacco and cocoa plantations in Bahia state, and because of two important acts: the Law of the Free Womb in 1871 (which declared free all children born to slaves), and the abolition of slavery in 1888. The immigrants worked at the docks, as street vendors, and as domestic servants, struggling to make a living any way they could. They brought with them African and Afro-Brazilian batucadas (percussion jams) and dances, both usually referred to by the generic name of *batuque* prior to the twentieth century. Many of the new arrivals settled in a central area of Rio called Praça Onze.

Praça Onze and the Birth of Carioca Samba

Such was the influx of Bahian—and hence Afro-Brazilian—culture that by 1915, Praça Onze (Plaza Eleven) was called "a true Africa in miniature." Here, many of these immigrants and their children gathered together in their leisure time to make music, dance, and worship the *orixás* (Afro-Brazilian deities) at the homes of old Bahian matriarchs, respectfully called *tias* (aunts). Neo-African culture had survived to a greater extent in Bahia than in other parts of Brazil, in part because of the large black population in Salvador and the

Praça Onze, a historical site in the history of samba. *Courtesy of Agência JB.*

ongoing trade between that city and ports in Nigeria and Dahomey. And it was kept alive in Rio by the tias, once they had immigrated from Bahia.

Near Praça Onze, an important site in samba's evolution was Rua Visconde de Inhaúma, number 177, the home of a woman nicknamed Tia Ciata (Hilária Batista de Almeida, 1854–1924). Born in Salvador, Tia Ciata was renowned in Rio as a maker of sweets and as a party hostess. Her house was a point of encounter and party site for expatriate Bahians and members of Carnaval groups, and bohemians, journalists, laborers, and middle-class professionals. Tia Ciata was a daughter of Oxum, and devotees worshipped the orixás in her backyard. The parties at her house were enlivened by the inspired music-making of several gifted young men who would alter the course of Brazilian popular music.

In the early years of the twentieth century, the now-legendary Pixinguinha, Donga, João da Baiana, Heitor dos Prazeres, and Sinhô gathered at Tia Ciata's house. There they played lundus, marchas, choros, maxixes, and batuques in jam sessions that must have been incredible to watch. These men were talented instrumentalists and part of Rio's first generation of professional songwriters. Together, they discussed music, created songs, and began to shape the urban Carioca form of samba that we know today.

The emerging style gained influences from polka, habanera, and the lively genres of marcha and maxixe. From this rich matrix emerged samba, a vibrant musical form distinguished by its responsorial singing and percussive interplay and a less formal sound than either maxixe or marcha. Technically, samba has a 2/4 meter, an emphasis on the second beat, a stanza-and-refrain structure, and many interlocking, syncopated lines in the melody and accompaniment. The

main rhythm and abundant cross-rhythms can be carried by handclapping or in the percussion (the batucada), which may include more than a dozen different drums and percussion instruments. Samba is commonly accompanied by instruments such as the guitar and four-string cavaquinho and—less frequently—brass.

The authors of *Brasil Musical* and the series *Nova História da Música Popular Brasileira* (edited by Navarro) cite Alfredo Carlos Brício's "Em Casa da Baiana" (In the Baiana's House), released in 1911 by Rio's Casa Faulhaber, as the first samba ever recorded. However, the consensus among the majority of Brazilian musicologists is that "Pelo Telefone" (On the Phone), created at Tia Ciata's house, deserves that distinction. The melody was a collective creation and the words were Mauro de Almeida's, but Donga registered it as his alone in December 1916, under the designation of "samba." The song was released in 1917, performed by Banda de Odeon.

The commandant of fun
Told me on the phone
To dance with joy

At the time, the differences between maxixe, samba, and marcha had not yet completely crystallized. Thus, Ismael Silva, one of the founders of the first escola de samba, complained to Donga that "Pelo Telefone" was not a samba but a maxixe.

"What's samba then?" asked Donga rather angrily.

" 'Se Você Jurar,' " answered Ismael, citing one of his own successes.

" 'Se Você Jurar' is not a samba. It's a marcha," replied Donga.

The debate went on for years, and in fact some musicologists today refer to "Pelo Telefone" as a samba-maxixe. But it was a hit Carnaval song that year, and samba took its place alongside marcha as a preferred Carnaval musical style in Rio and much of Brazil.

Pixinguinha (Alfredo da Rocha Vianna, Jr., 1898–1973) stood out as one of the most important of samba's founding fathers and was also renowned in the choro and maxixe genres (see Chapter Eight). He was a virtuoso flutist (later adding saxophone) with superb technique and improvisational creativity. Pixinguinha was also an original arranger who enriched the harmony of samba, and the leader of Os Oito Batutas (The Eight Masters), an all-star band that included Donga and performed Brazilian music before European audiences in 1922. Besides this, Pixinguinha composed more than six hundred tunes. Some of his more famous sambas are "Teus Ciúmes" (Your Jealousies), "Ai Eu Queria" (How I Wanted It), and "Samba de Negro" (Black's Samba).

Pixinguinha's contemporary Sinhô (José Barbosa da Silva, 1888–1930) was a dance-hall pianist and fellow habitué of the musical sessions at Tia Ciata's. His many Carnaval hits earned him the title of "king of samba" in the twenties and made him the most popular of the first sambistas. Accusations of plagiarism directed toward Sinhô by Heitor dos Prazeres triggered a longstanding feud between the two, with former friends Pixinguinha and Donga taking Heitor's side.

Sinhô was a regular in every bohemian spot in town, and he wrote sambas, marchas, and love songs that were chronicles of nocturnal city life. Sinhô gained attention in 1918 with "Quem São Eles?" (Who Are They?) and achieved his greatest popularity in the 1920s with marchas such as "Pé de Anjo" (Angel's Foot) and sambas such as "Jura" (Swear It) and "Gosto Que Me Enrosco" (I Like It Bad). The last song was co-written with Heitor dos Prazeres and explored the consequences of late-night carousing.

> **One shouldn't love someone if he's not loved**
> **It would be better if he were crucified**
> **May God keep me away from today's women**
> **They despise a man just because of the night life**

Together and apart, these former visitors to

Pixinguinha and the Batutas in 1919. *Top row (left to right):* José Alves, Pixinguinha, Luis Silva, Jacó Palmieri. *Seated (left to right):* Otávio Viana, Nelson Alves, João Pernambuco, Raul Palmieri, Donga.

Early Sambistas

Donga (Ernesto Joaquim Maria dos Santos, 1891–1974), the son of Tia Amélia, started playing music with Pixinguinha and others at Tia Ciata's house in 1916. He co-composed "Pelo Telefone," as well as the hits "Passarinho Bateu Asas" (The Little Bird Beat Its Wings), "Cantiga de Festa" (Party Song), and "Macumba de Oxossi." Adept with cavaquinho and guitar, he played with the rancho Dois de Ouro, the Grupo de Caxangá, and the Oito Batutas.

João da Baiana (João Machado Guedes, 1887–1974) was the grandson of slaves and the son of the Baiana Tia Prisciliana. At the age of ten he also paraded with Dois de Ouro and with the rancho Pedra de Sal. He is credited with introducing the *pandeiro* as a samba instrument. The police are said to have stolen João's pandeiro when they were cracking down on batucadas in 1908, but Senator Pinheiro Machado gave him a new one. He was invited to tour Europe with Pixinguinha and Os Batutas but never made the trip. He composed the tunes "Mulher Cruel" (Cruel Woman), "Pedindo Vingança (Asking for Vengeance), and "O Futuro É Uma Caveira (The Future Is a Skull).

Donga (*left*) and Pixinguinha (*right*) at the bust of Heitor Villa-Lobos in 1968. *Photo by Jacob. Courtesy of Agência JB.*

Heitor dos Prazeres (1898–1966), adept with the cavaquinho, composed the famed samba "A Tristeza Me Persegue" (Sadness Follows Me) and was active in the formation of Portela and other escolas de samba.

Caninha (Oscar José Luis de Morais, 1883–1961) was one of Sinhô's principal competitors for the title "King of Carnaval" in the 1920s. Caninha is famous for writing such songs as "Me Leve, Me Leve" (Take Me, Take Me), "Seu Rafael" (Mr. Rafael), and—with Heitor dos Prazeres—"É Batucada" (It's Batucada).

Tia Ciata's home—Sinhô, Pixinguinha, Donga, Heitor dos Prazeres, and João da Baiana—popularized samba, started developing its structure, and set it on its course toward becoming one of the world's great musical genres.

Estácio

Nearby Praça Onze was the Estácio neighborhood, now known as "the cradle of samba." Today, it looks much as it did in the 1920s: narrow streets lined with old, decaying two-story houses and the small simple bars called *botequins* where the locals spend hours drinking, talking, and singing.

From Estácio came such now-legendary sambistas such as Bide, Ismael Silva, Nilton Bastos, and Armando Marçal. They took the fledgling samba genre and clearly differentiated it from maxixe and marcha, introducing longer notes and two-bar phrasing, and making the tempo slower, in contrast to the maxixelike sambas composed by Sinhô and Donga. The form they codified became the standard reference of samba, to which sambistas always return. The other major historical contribution of these pioneers was that in 1928 they created the first escola de samba: Deixa Falar (Let Them Talk).

Ismael Silva (1905–1978) was the most important composer of the Turma do Estácio (Estácio Gang) because of his melodic creativity and sophisticated modulations. His often-ironic lyrics created strong poetic images out of simple, common themes. In "Meu Único Desejo (My Only

Ismael Silva. *Photo by Antonio Teixeira. Courtesy of Agência JB.*

When Armando died, his family kept the music alive. His son, Nilton Marçal, was a famous percussionist and a *mestre de bateria* (percussion conductor) for Portela. Nilton's son, also named Armando, is a superb percussionist as well, highly respected in Brazil and known to North American fans for his work with the Pat Metheny Group.

The musical language elaborated by the Estácio masters was an important form of expression for the Carioca lower classes in the early twentieth century. Samba became a voice for those who had been silenced by their socioeco-

Desire), Silva's sly verse speaks of unrequited love.

> **You've returned the photographs**
> **My letters and my presents**
> **I didn't accept them**
> **There's only one thing I really want**
> **To have you return**
> **All the kisses I gave you**

His many famous sambas include "Se Você Jurar" (If You Were to Swear), "Nem É Bom Falar" (It's No Good Talking About It), and "Antonico." He also co-composed many songs with Nilton Bastos, Noel Rosa, and Lamartine Babo and had a profound influence on later Brazilian composers like Chico Buarque.

Two other Estácio stalwarts were Bide (Alcebíades Barcelos, 1902–1975) and Armando Marçal (1902–1947), a powerful songwriting team in the 1930s and 1940s who co-wrote warm, flowing samba masterpieces including "A Malandragem," "Sorrir" (To Smile), and "Agora É Cinzas" (Now It's Ashes).

Ataulfo Alves. *Courtesy of EMI.*

nomic status, and a source of self-affirmation in society.

Crooners, Composers, and Malandros

At the height of the radio era in the 1930s, many of the great songs of the Estácio songwriters reached a wide audience through the interpretations of vocalists Mario Reis, Francisco Alves, Chico Alves. and Carmen Miranda, among others. An especially successful crooner from this era was the singer-songwriter Orlando Silva (1915–1978), who became known as "the singer of the multitudes." Silva made his debut on Radio Cajuti in 1934 and initially recorded under the pseudonym Orlando Navarro. He was the first vocalist to record Pixinguinha's "Carinhoso" (Affectionate) and the first singer to have his own show on Radio Nacional, and he appeared in movies such as 1938's *Banana da Terra* (Banana of the Earth). His many hits included "A Jardineira" (The Gardener) and "Lábios Que Beijei" (Lips That I Kissed). In the late thirties and early forties, he was the most popular singer in Brazil.

Two other important samba composers who supplied hit songs for the above vocalists were Ataulfo Alves and Assis Valente. Alves (1909–1969) married lyrical laments with long, slow musical phrases, a songwriting style that may have been influenced by his youth in slow-paced, bucolic Minas Gerais. Some of his most popular songs were "Ai, Que Saudade de Amelia" (Oh, How I Miss Amelia), "Pois É" (So It Is), and "Mulata Assanhada" (Restless Mulata).

Assis Valente (1911–1958), one of the most popular songwriters of the 1930s and 1940s, wrote lyrics that were witty snapshots of the times in which he lived. He also had an almost naive preoccupation with glorifying what he considered authentically Brazilian, as shown in the song "Brasil Pandeiro" (Brazilian Tambourine).

> **Uncle Sam wants**
> **To know our batucada**
> **He's been saying Bahian spices**
> **Improved his dishes**

Carmen Miranda recorded many Valente compositions, including the samba-choro "Camisa Listrada" (Striped Shirt), "Recenseamento" (Census), and "Fez Bobagem" (You Were Foolish).

An important samba singer from this era was Moreira da Silva (born in 1902), who sang sambas when not strolling the boulevards. He invented an original way of performing sambas: he would stop the song, use spoken dialogue to dramatize the situation described in the lyrics, then continue. It was called *samba de breque* (break samba). His most famous song in this style is "Acertei no Milhar," written by noted samba composers Wilson Batista and Geraldo Pereira and recorded by da Silva in 1938. It tells the story of a man who dreams he won a fortune in a lottery and tells his wife all that they will do with the cash windfall. Da Silva continued performing this song into his nineties. He was a colorful figure who personified the lifestyle of the *malandro*, a type of hustler or layabout that was a romantic bohemian ideal for some in Rio in the 1930s and 1940s. Malandros did not work. They made their living exploiting women, playing small confidence tricks, and gambling. They liked to dress fine, typically in a white suit and white hat, and were proud of their lifestyle. A great cinematic portrait of

Noel Rosa as pictured on one of his albums.

these characters may be seen in Ruy Guerra's *Ópera do Malandro*, a 1987 film musical based on Chico Buarque's stage play.

Samba-Canção

In more upscale neighborhoods in Rio in the 1930s, a brilliant new generation of middle-class samba and marcha composers also came of age. The most famous among them were Noel Rosa, Braguinha, Lamartine Babo, Ary Barroso, and Dorival Caymmi, and they composed sambas that emphasized the melody more than the rhythm, added more complex harmonies, and had more sophisticated lyrics—usually tied to sentimental themes. It was a kind of cool, softened samba, later labeled samba-canção, and it popularized the genre with the middle class. They wrote both Carnaval songs and "middle-of-the-year" songs (as the non-Carnaval compositions were known) and set the trend for Brazilian music until the advent of bossa nova in the late 1950s.

Noel Rosa and Braguinha

Noel Rosa (1910–1937) was born in Rio and is so popular today that he has a statue on the main street of Vila Isabel, the Carioca neighborhood where he lived. Rosa was known for Carnaval

songs like his first big success, "Com Que Roupa?" (With Which Clothes?), released in 1931. He composed melodies that were harmonically rich and pioneered the use of colloquial language and social criticism. Rosa died at an early age from tuberculosis but left more than two hundred songs for posterity. Some of his tunes were collaborations with others, including many fine sambas co-written with the pianist Vadico (Osvaldo Gagliano, 1912–1962). Rosa's masterpieces include "Conversa de Botequim" (Bar Talk), "Três Apitos" (Three Whistles), "Palpite Infeliz" (Unfortunate Suggestion), and "Onde Está a Honestidade" (Where's the Honesty?). His song "Último Desejo" (Last Desire) demonstrates the raw emotional power of Rosa's lyrics. It is a melancholy coda to a romance that had ended.

> **Our love that I can't forget**
> **Began at the festival of St. John**
> **And died today without fireworks**
> **Without a photograph and without a**
>   **message**
> **Without moonlight, without guitar**
> **Near you I'm silent**
> **Thinking everything, saying nothing**
> **I'm afraid of crying**
> **I never again want your kisses**
> **But you can't deny me**
> **My last desire**
>   **If some friend of yours asks**
>   **You to tell her**
>   **Whether or not you want me**
>   **Tell her you adore me**
>   **That you cry and lament our separation**
>   **The people that I detest**
>   **Always say I'm worth nothing**
>   **That my home is a saloon**

That I ruined your life
That I don't deserve the food
That you bought for me

For some time Noel Rosa played guitar and sang with a group called Os Tangarás. One of the members of this group was Carlos Braga (born in 1907), who was also from Vila Isabel. Since Braga was the son of a rich man and in those times being a popular musician was not considered something honorable, he invented another name for himself: João de Barro. Also called Braguinha, he became one of the greatest Carnaval hitmakers, writing light-hearted and lively sambas and marchas with lyrics that featured good-humored and apt social criticism.

Braguinha composed classic songs such as "Touradas em Madrid," a hit in the Carnaval of 1938 and known in the United States through the recordings of Carmen Miranda, Dinah Shore, and Xavier Cugat. Like Noel Rosa, Braguinha was an intuitive musician who never studied music. He played a little guitar but composed his songs whistling. Besides samba, he also excelled in children's songs, celebration songs for Junina (festivities honoring Saints John, Peter, and Anthony), and even *repentes* (a northeastern style with improvised verses). Other successes include "Chiquita Bacana," "Balancê," "Yes! Nós Temos Bananas" (Yes, We Have Bananas), and "Copacabana" (recorded by Dick Farney and considered a precursor of the bossa nova style), all composed with partner Alberto Ribeiro (1902–1971).

Another important figure from that era was Lamartine Babo (1904–1963), who composed the standards "Teu Cabelo Não Nega" (You Hair Doesn't Deny It), "Eu Sonhei Que Tu Estavas Tão Linda" (I Dreamed You Were So Beautiful), and "Moleque Indigesto" (Indigestible Urchin).

Ary Barroso. Photo by Campanella Neto. Courtesy of Agência JB.

Ary Barroso

Ary Barroso (1903–1964), a legendary composer of Carnaval marchas and samba-canção tunes, wrote one of the most famous Brazilian songs of all time, "Aquarela do Brasil" (Watercolor of Brazil), internationally known as "Brazil." Born in Uba, Minas Gerais, Barroso studied classical piano as a youth and played for dance-hall orchestras after moving to Rio in 1920.

Barroso only decided to write Carnaval songs because he wanted to get married and the only way he could think of to make enough money for his wedding was to have a Carnaval hit. So he wrote "Dá Nela" for the 1930 Carnaval. It won Casa Edison's annual Carnaval song contest and was the most popular marcha that year. From then on, he was a successful composer whose many beautiful sambas were known for their elaborate harmonies. For many years, he was also the host of a radio show that showcased new singing talent.

In 1934, Ary took a trip to Bahia and became deeply inspired by the beauty and atmosphere of Salvador. As a result, he composed several of his most popular tunes, all of them recorded by Carmen Miranda: "Na Baixa do Sapateiro," "No Tabuleiro da Baiana" (On the Baiana's Tray), "Quando Penso na Bahia" (When I Think of Bahia), "Boneca de Piche" (Tar Doll) with Luis Iglesias, and "Como Vaes Você?" (How Are You?).

In 1939, Ary wrote his famous "Aquarela do Brasil," which popularized a new subgenre, *samba exaltação*: songs that praise the beauty and richness of Brazil.

> **Brazil, Brazil**
> **For me, for me**
> **Oh! These murmuring fountains**
> **Where I quench my thirst**
> **And where the moon comes to play**
> **Oh! This brown and beautiful Brazil**
> **You are my Brazilian Brazil**
> **Land of samba and tambourines**
> **Brazil, Brazil, for me, for me**

A Dorival Caymmi album cover. *Courtesy of EMI.*

"Aquarela do Brasil" received international exposure in the 1940s. Walt Disney heard the song on a trip to Brazil in 1941 and chose to include it in his 1942 animated film *Saludos Amigos* (called *Alô Amigos* in Brazil), which starred Zé Carioca, a Rio malandro in cartoon parrot form.

Ary also contributed the song "Rio de Janeiro" to Disney's 1944 film *Brazil*, and he received an Academy Award nomination for it. Another Disney animated movie, *The Three Caballeros* (1945), included Barroso's "Na Baixa do Sapateiro" (renamed "Baia" [sic] in the film) and "Os Quindins de Iaiá" (Iaiá's Coconut Candies), sung by Aurora Miranda, Carmen Miranda's sister.

"Aquarela do Brasil" would be remembered for years to come and be recorded a few hundred times by musicians within and outside Brazil. And decades after its first film appearance, "Aquarela" would be used as the theme song for Terry Gilliam's 1985 black comedy *Brazil*, the music representing a vision of beauty and freedom to the protagonist, trapped in a futuristic totalitarian society.

Dorival Caymmi

Another key figure in the history of samba is Dorival Caymmi, born in 1914 in Salvador. He contributed many samba-canção standards as well as *toadas*, *modinhas*, *canções praieiras* (fishermen's songs), and *pontos de candomblé* (invocation songs for orixás). His tunes "Samba da Minha Terra" (Samba of My Land), "Gabriela," "É Doce Morrer no Mar," "Marina," "Saudade de Itapoã," "Das Rosas" (English title: "Roses and Roses"), "João Valentão," "Requebre Que Eu Dou um Doce," "Rosa Morena," and "Oração da Mae Menininha" have become part of Brazil's musical heritage.

Caymmi was the son of a public functionary who played guitar and mandolin. At the age of twenty-four, he decided to seek his fortune in Rio and left for the big city aboard a ship that traveled slowly down the Brazilian coast. The young man had inherited his father's musical ability, and at night a group of passengers would gather on the deck to listen to Caymmi play guitar and sing in his deep, smooth, often dolorous voice.

Once in Rio, he found work as a graphic artist with the magazine *O Cruzeiro* and began studying for the law school entrance exam. But soon he switched his efforts to his music and rose to the top with astonishing speed. Composers Assis Valente and Lamartine Babo took him to the Radio Nacional station, where he was given a chance to sing "Noite de Temporal" (Stormy Night), a canção praieira that mixed elements of samba and the capoeira rhythm. He was a success and was contracted by Radio Tupi, where he first performed his samba "O Que É Que a Baiana Tem?" (What Is It That the Bahian Woman Has?). That same year, 1938, the producer Wallace Downey was arranging songs for the movie *Banana da Terra*, which would star, among others, Carmen Miranda. One scene was to feature Miranda wearing—for the first time—what would become her trademark: the turban, skirt, and ornaments of a *baiana* (a Bahian woman).

Downey planned on using Ary Barroso's "Na Baixa do Sapateiro" for the scene, but Barroso wanted more money than Downey was willing to pay and the song was dropped. It was then that Miranda remembered a young composer at a radio station who had one shown her a song about Bahia. Downey tracked him down and Caymmi was on his way. The film debuted in 1939. "O Que É Que a Baiana Tem?" was a huge success and in-troduced into the national vocabulary the Bahian word *balanganda* (an ornamental silver buckle with amulets and trinkets attached). It also set the style for Miranda's costumes. She would steadily exaggerate and embellish her Bahian outfit, often to the point of absurdity, in the years to come.

Miranda recorded that song and "A Preta do Acarajé" in duet with Caymmi on an Odeon single. Next came Miranda's recording of Caymmi's "Roda Pião" and his own solo recording debut with "Rainha do Mar" (Queen of the Sea) and "Promessa de Pescador" (Promise of a Fisherman). Caymmi's more urban material was perfect

Carmen Miranda with no fruit atop her head, from the 1944 movie *The Gang's All Here. Courtesy of Museu Carmen Miranda.*

for the radio era, and he subsequently wrote numerous hit songs. Many were harmonically progressive with altered chords and other innovations. "I arrived here [in Rio] with an unusual way of playing guitar for that time," he was quoted in *Nova História*. "I always had the tendency of altering the perfect chords. There were two soloists who did approximately the same thing as me, but with a difference: they were studious musicians and I wasn't. They were Anibal Sardinha [Garoto] and Laurindo de Almeida."

Along with using unusual harmonic touches, Caymmi had an important influence on Brazilian lyric writing with his poetic use of colloquial language from Bahia and natural simplicity in storytelling. His urban sambas and evocative folkloric songs have been recorded by Miranda, Angela Maria, Dick Farney, João Gilberto, Gilberto Gil, Caetano Veloso, Gal Costa, Paul Winter, Andy Williams, Richard Stoltzman, and Caymmi himself. His guitar playing and compositions are credited by many as being an important influence on the bossa nova generation. And beyond that is another legacy: his children—singer Nana, guitarist-composer Dori, and flutist-composer Danilo—have made important marks on Brazilian music as well.

Carmen Miranda

In the 1940s, Carmen Miranda was the personification of Brazil for many people in other countries. She was a beautiful woman who wore bangles on her arms, heaps of jewelry adorning her curvaceous body, and tropical fruits atop a turban. She danced on clogs with outrageously high heels, sang with enthusiasm and playfulness, and illustrated each stanza with expressive hand gestures. Although few outside of Brazil are aware of it, Miranda (1909–1955) was a samba star in Brazil in

the 1930s before journeying to the United States to capture Hollywood's imagination.

Miranda was not entirely Brazilian. She was born in Março de Canavezes, Portugal, but at the age of one moved with her family to Rio de Janeiro. A charming singer and exuberant performer, she conquered Brazil in 1930 with "T'ai," a marcha written by Joubert de Carvalho. A string of hit records followed, as she interpreted sambas and marchas by Dorival Caymmi, Ary Barroso, Assis Valente, Lamartine Babo, and other leading samba-canção-era songwriters.

In 1939, thanks to help from her friend Sonja Henie, the Olympic ice skater, and her American agent, Lee Shubert, Miranda made her Broadway debut, wearing an exaggerated, embellished version of the colorful Bahian dress that she had worn in *Banana da Terra*, and singing catchy songs like "South American Way" and "Mamae Eu Quero." Exotic, merry, and vivacious, Carmen took Manhattan by storm. Soon her face was everywhere, on magazine covers and billboards. Saks Fifth Avenue sold her exclusive line of turbans and costume jewelry, and she appeared in advertisements pitching Rheingold beer.

During concerts, Miranda was backed by the Bando da Lua (Band of the Moon), a superb group led by Aloysio de Oliveira, who would later play a major role in helping launch bossa nova. Miranda soon got a call from Hollywood, and she acted and performed musical numbers in many films in the 1940s, including *Down Argentine Way, That Night in Rio, Weekend in Havana, The Gang's All Here, Greenwich Village*, and *Copacabana*. She also recorded numerous singles, including the now-famous choro "Tico Tico no Fubá" in 1945.

Along the way, her outfits became steadily wilder and more colorful, inspiring many Carmen Miranda impersonators. One of the first was

Mickey Rooney, in the 1941 film *Babes on Broadway*, and decades later Miranda continues to be a popular character for costume parties. She is still seen by many as the personification of fun and extravagance.

Samba from the Morro

In the 1930s, as Carmen Miranda was crooning radio hits and the samba-canção songwriters were hitting their stride, the central area of Rio de Janeiro underwent great changes. Hundreds of houses were razed to make way for new streets and avenues. Suddenly the area where the poor blacks who had created samba lived became too expensive for them, and they had to move. Some relocated to the outskirts of town, but most preferred to make new homes in the *morros*, the hills that surround Rio. Samba may have had its birth in Praça Onze, but within a few decades it was perfomed there only once a year, during Carnaval.

By the 1950s the commercially popular samba-canção style had been diluted by contact with boleros, fox-trots, and cha-cha-cha. The musical quality declined and some dissatisfied young musicians, mostly middle-class, made their own revolution: bossa nova. But up on the morros, in the *favelas* where many of the poor people now lived, the samba pioneered in Estácio had survived and continued its own evolution, while sticking to the traditional instruments of cavaquinho, pandeiro, and tamborim. At the time, the media labeled this classic style of samba *samba de morro* (to distinguish it from samba-canção and offshoots such as *sambolero* and *samba-lada*). In its almost purely percussive form it was sometimes called *samba-de-batucada*.

By the late fifties, samba de morro was too strong a cultural manifestation to stay in Rio's ghettos. It invaded the city and then the entire country. Cartola, Nelson Cavaquinho, Clementina de Jesus, Monsueto, Silas de Oliveira, and Mano Décio da Viola, Zé Keti, and others led the charge.

Zé Keti (José Flores de Jesus) was one of the great samba de morro figures of the time. Born in 1921, Keti wrote songs such as "A Voz do Morro" (Voice of the Hill) and "Opinião" (Opinion). Along with romantic songs, he wrote outspoken sambas with melancholy and fatalistic lyrics. They denounced the sad poverty in which the majority of Brazilians seemed doomed to live and lamented the fact that so many died needlessly. One such song was "Acender as Velas" (Light the Candles).

> **When there's no samba**
> **There's disillusion**
> **It's one more heart**
> **That stopped beating**
> **One more angel that goes to heaven**
> **May God forgive me**
> **But I'll say it**
> **The doctor arrived too late**
> **Because on the hill**
> **There are no cars to drive**
> **No telephones to call**
> **No beauty to be seen**
> **And we die without wanting to die**

When Cartola (Angenor de Oliveira, 1908–80) became identified with samba de morro, he was already a veteran sambista who in 1929 had helped found the most traditional escola de samba in Rio: Estação Primeira de Mangueira. In the 1930s he composed many hit sambas, including—with frequent partner Carlos Cachaça—"O Destino Não Quis" (Destiny Didn't Want It). Cartola's songs were acclaimed for their artful melodies and poignant lyrics.

João Bosco and Clementina de Jesus. *Photo by Ricardo Pessanha.*

In the early 1960s, he and his wife, Zica, ran Zicartola, a restaurant that became a point of encounter between the bossa nova crowd of the Zona Sul (southern Rio) and the samba de morro artists of the Zona Norte (northern Rio). There it was easy to find, in the audience or on stage, names like Tom Jobim, Ismael Silva, Paulinho da Viola, João do Vale, Zé Keti, Dorival Caymmi, Clementina de Jesus, and Nara Leão.

Cartola's career had a resurgence in the early 1970s, when many well-known singers covered his songs and popularized them throughout Brazil. Nara Leão recorded "O Sol Nascerá" (The Sun Will Rise), whose lines included "I intend to lead my life smiling / Because I lost my youth crying"; Gal Costa covered "Acontece" (It Happens); and Beth Carvalho released "As Rosas Não Falam" (The Roses Don't Talk), which became an instant classic. In 1973, at sixty-five, Cartola finally got a chance to record his first album, on the Marcus Pereira label.

Two other noted sambistas also had late-blooming commercial success: Clementina de Jesus and Nelson Cavaquinho (Nelson Antonio da Silva, 1910–1980). The latter was nicknamed for his facility with the cavaquinho during his early days of playing choro music. Later he switched to guitar, on which he developed his own technique of playing with only two fingers, pinching the strings, and creating original chords. That, together with his

harsh, weary voice, made commercial acceptance of his music even more difficult than it had been for Cartola. Alone or with his frequent partner Guilherme de Brito, Nelson Cavaquinho wrote more than two hundred songs. But his lyrical sambas had to wait until 1965 to achieve public acclaim, when singers like Nara Leão, Elizeth Cardoso, and Elis Regina started recording them. That opened the doors for Nelson to release his own record in 1970. Among his classics are "Rugas" (Wrinkles), "Luz Negra" (Black Light), and "A Flor e o Espinho" (The Flower and the Thorn).

Clementina de Jesus (1902–1987) had to wait even longer to achieve mass acclaim. When she was sixty, Clementina was "discovered" by the writer and impresario Hermínio Bello de Carvalho, who arranged concert appearances for her. Clementina was something of a living musical archive, singing old lundus, *jongos,* and *sambas do partido alto* that had fallen into obscurity. She recorded her first album when she was sixty-eight: "Clementina, Cade Você?" (Clementina, Where Are You?).

While samba-canção ruled the Carioca airwaves, many great sambistas from the morros had composed and performed in relative obscurity. But by the late 1950s, the tide had turned. The escolas de samba were expanding into large and formidable institutions. They gave samba de morro a stronger and more elaborate rhythmic force and presented it in a new, grandiose form, with thousands of singers and dancers, and hundreds of drummers and percussionists.

From the days of "Pelo Telefone" and ever after, samba would be intimately tied to Carnaval. It would transform Rio's Carnaval into one of the greatest popular festivals in the world. And the annual need for Carnaval songs to sing and parade to would in turn accelerate the development of samba.

The bloco Cacique de Ramos parading in 1970. *Photo by Antonio Teixeira. Courtesy of Agência JB.*

Carnaval

A poor man's happiness resembles
The grand illusion of Carnaval

Tom Jobim and Vinícius de Moraes
"A Felicidade" (Happiness)

Carnaval, disillusion
I left pain waiting for me at home
And I sang and danced
Dressed up as a king
But on Wednesday the curtains always fall

Chico Buarque de Hollanda
"Sonho de Carnaval" (Carnaval Dream)

Every year, seven weeks before Easter, Brazil stops. It is Carnaval time. For four days, from Saturday through Tuesday, as a climax to the Southern Hemisphere summer, the country sings and dances in dance halls and clubs, on the streets and beaches, or wherever there are people and music. In cities like Salvador, the celebration may go on for seven or eight days.

The music may be provided by a three-hundred-piece escola-de-samba drum section, a horn-and-percussion band, or a spontaneous group of people beating cans and bottles. Some wear special outfits for the occasion, some don't. You'll see clowns, pirates, sheiks, Indians, and lots of men dressed up as women. On display are as many different costumes as the imagination can conjure. Women dress in sophisticated costumes or in very little at all—sometimes just shoes, miniscule bikinis, and some body paint. Carnaval is a hedonistic party in which all that counts is joy and pleasure. As an office clerk told us, "During Carnaval the devil is on the loose. Nobody belongs to anybody."

Not every city in Brazil has an intense street Carnaval. In some all you'll find are relatively well-behaved indoor balls. People with less "carnavalesco" souls use the holidays to travel to places where they can relax far from the drums during the day and, if they feel like it, go dancing at night. But between New Year's Eve and Carnaval nothing really important is decided in Brazil. Quoting a popular Chico Buarque song, most people will say, "I'm saving myself for when Carnaval comes." The weather is hot, people become more outgoing, and sensuality is in the air. But amidst all the craziness and frivolity, Carnaval serves the important purpose for Brazilians of maintaining cultural traditions—encoded in the music, dance, and costumes of the celebrations across the country.

Carnaval is a pre-Lent celebration (like Mardi Gras in New Orleans and Carnival in many Spanish-speaking countries) that has its roots in pre-Christian festivities held by the ancient Greeks, Romans, and others. Around the sixth

A cartoon by Ângelo Agostinho depicting the death of the entrudo tradition during Carnaval. *Courtesy of Agência JB.*

century B.C., the Greeks held spring festivals in honor of Dionysus, the god of wine and the power of wild nature. Often, merrymakers would parade down the streets of their towns, sometimes with floats. The Romans carried on the seasonal celebration, expanding it into *Saturnalia*, wherein slaves and masters would exchange clothes and engage in orgiastic behavior, and *Bacchanalia*, drunken feasts in honor of Bacchus, the Roman version of Dionysus. It was, and is, a time to make merry, to drink, dance, and be crazy. The normal social order is turned upside down and mocked, and anything goes.

Despite their pagan origins, these festivities were assimilated into the traditions of Roman Catholic countries in Europe. There, as Carnaval evolved, it retained some of the characteristics of the ancient celebrations, such as the use of masks and the time of year—generally February—but started losing its orgiastic features. It remained an important societal safety valve, a time to vent pent-up frustrations.

Entrudo, Zé Pereiras, Cordões, and Ranchos

Carnaval arrived in Brazil in the form of the chãotic Portuguese entrudo, in which celebrants would go to the streets and throw mud, dirty water, flour balls, and suspect liquids at one another, often triggering violent riots. The first masked Carnaval ball

in Rio took place in 1840 at the Hotel Itália, with waltzes and polkas as the music of choice. Out in the streets, a young Portuguese shoemaker named José Nogueira Paredes had the idea in 1848 of entering a Carnaval parade and beating a big bass drum. In the following years many *Zé Pereiras* (a name that possibly was a distortion of José Paredes) filled the city with their songs and drums. The first European-style parades appeared in 1850, and these would become competitive events with horses, military bands, and adorned floats, often sponsored by aristocratic groups called *sociedades*.

Around this time, Rio's poor people, who could not afford tickets to the expensive masked balls, and who were bored by the orderly parades, formed *cordões*, male-only groups that celebrated violently in the streets and paraded to African-based rhythms. This Afro-Brazilian influence increased after 1870, when the decline of the coffee plantations in northern Rio de Janeiro state forced a great number of

Chiquinha Gonzaga. *Public domain image.*

slaves and former slaves to emigrate. Many came to Rio, the capital, looking for work.

From cordões came *ranchos*, a more civilized type of cordão that includes women. They made their first organized Carnaval appearance in 1873 and are important in the history of Carnaval for their introduction of themes to their parades. Like moving theater pieces, ranchos today still tell stories, even though their space in Carnaval has largely been taken by the escolas de samba. Ameno Reseda, Flor do Abacate, and other famous ranchos parade now on the Monday of Carnaval's four days. They have maintained their elegance of past years and dance to *marcha-ranchos*, slow and more melodically developed variations of the marcha.

The Marcha

In 1899, the cordão Rosa de Ouro asked composer Chiquinha Gonzaga (1847–1935) to write a song for their parade. She composed a tune that incorporated a boisterious rhythm that she had heard cordões parading to as they passed by her house. The result was "Ô Abre Alas" (Make Way), the first registered marcha as well as the first song to be written specifically for Carnaval. It was also an enormous popular success, having just what it takes to be a successful Carnaval song: a contagious rhythm and simple, easy-to-memorize lyrics.

> **Hey, make way**
> **I want to pass**
> **I like parties**
> **I can't deny that**

In the 1920s, the *marcha* (or *marchinha*) began taking over Carnaval celebrations, especially the indoor ones. It was based on the song form developed by Gonzaga but gradually added influences from ragtime and the North American one-step. Today, marcha is a happy, festive style. It has a strong accent on the downbeat, lots of horns and drum rolls on the snares, and simple, humorous lyrics that often contain some kind of social criticism.

The 1930s were the golden decade of Carnaval songwriting. Innumerable marchas and sambas written then are classics today. The generation of composers that became popular around that decade—Noel Rosa, Ary Barroso, Lamartine Babo, Braguinha, and others—are legendary and their songs are still sung during Carnaval and frequently recorded by contemporary artists. Other famous and successful Carnaval songwriters of the 1930s and 1940s include Caninha, Eduardo Souto, Haroldo Lobo, Joubert de Carvalho, Benedito Lacerda, Antônio Nássera, Romeu Gentil, and Wilson Batista.

Samba has been the most popular Carnaval music in Rio since the early sixties. But even though marchas have taken second billing ever since, the old standards from decades ago are still performed every year during Carnaval time, especially at indoor balls. And *bandas*, which pass through Rio's streets with crowds trailing behind, primarily play marchas. Bandas have drums and a brass section and are informal in their structure, with some people wearing costumes or T-shirts with the banda's name, and others dressing as they wish. In many ways, bandas have brought back the spontaneity of Brazil's old street Carnavals. Almost every neighborhood and suburb of Rio has its own such group now, following the example of the pioneering Banda de Ipanema, founded in the 1960s.

Another type of celebration in Rio's Carnaval comes from *blocos de empolgacão*, great masses of people wearing the same costume that parade in one solid block, dancing very enthusiastically. To see a big bloco like Cacique de Ramos, whose members always dress up like Indians, or Bafo da Onça (Jaguar's Breath), with their six to seven thousand members coming down the street, is an unforgettable sight as they dance to thundering *samba de bloco*, played by the bateria that closes the parade. Samba, of course, is also the mainstay of Rio's most important Carnaval institution, the escolas de samba (samba schools).

The Escolas de Samba

Since their beginning in 1928, the escolas de samba have been an integral part of Rio's Carnaval and have evolved into a grand spectacle, an overwhelming experience for both participants and observers. The parade of the escolas encompasses dazzling floats, outlandish costumes, thousands of dancers, and veritable symphony orchestras of rhythm. It is like a giant popular opera, with so much happening, musically and visually, that you can't possibly take it all in at once.

The first escola de samba, Deixa Falar (Let Them Talk), was founded on August 12, 1928, in Estácio by Ismael Silva, Bide, Armando Marçal, Nilton Bastos, and others. Apparently, the name "samba school" was an ironic reference to a grade school across the street from where the group met. Deixa Falar was more like a club or a fraternity, dedicated to making music and parading during Carnaval.

At the time, however, the police discouraged the *blocos* (Carnaval groups) of blacks and mulattos from celebrating downtown. This wasn't unusual, because the police were still repressing many manifestations of Afro-Brazilian culture at the time. In defiance, Deixa Falar went out for a small parade during the Carnaval of 1929 in Estácio and Praça Onze, where also appeared blocos from Mangueira, Oswaldo Cruz, and other neighborhoods. Deixa Falar was short-lived: by 1933 it was defunct. But a seed had been planted, and other samba schools were soon created.

On April 30, 1929, the members of several blocos formed an escola that ultimately proved to be the most traditional and longest-lived of them all: Estação Primeira de Mangueira (Number-One Station of Mangueira), whose founders included famed composers Cartola and Carlos Cachaça. Mangueira made its debut as a samba school in the Carnaval of 1930 and has since attracted many illustrious songwriters and singers, including Nelson Sargento, Elza Soares, Alcione, Leci Brandão, and Jamelão.

Another milestone came in 1935, when Paulo da Portela (Paulo Benjamim de Oliveira), Heitor dos Prazeres, and others created Portela. The new escola had its roots in the bloco Baianinhas de Oswaldo Cruz, which was founded in 1923 and later turned into Vai Como Pode. Portela was the most innovative of the escolas for many decades.

The 1990 version of the annual *Sambas de Enredo* album, a compilation of the year's Carnaval songs from the sixteen samba schools in Group A. *Courtesy of BMG.*

Also in 1935, the Getúlio Vargas federal administration stopped discouraging Rio's escolas and officially recognized their parades. Consequently, the festivities moved from Praça Onze to the wide avenues of downtown Rio. Every year grandstands were assembled, drawing large audiences, generating big expenses, and creating terrible traffic hazards. This problem was solved in 1984 when the city built the Passarela do Samba (Samba Path), on Rua Marquês de Sapucaí. Cariocas call it the Sambódromo. Designed by the famous architect Oscar Niemeyer, it is a seven-hundred-meter-long pathway flanked by concrete stands that seat ninety thousand people. At its end is the huge, aptly named Praça da Apoteose (Apotheosis Square).

Over the past few decades, the escolas have grown to become vital cultural institutions, and their importance stretches far beyond just staging parades. By 1990, there were fifty-six officially registered escolas de samba in Rio de Janeiro and dozens more in other Brazilian cities. Today, there are also several dozen informal samba schools and blocos located in countries such as Germany, Japan, Great Britain, the United States, and Finland.

Although some escolas in Rio are located in middle-class neighborhoods, many are in favelas or working-class areas, with mostly low-income people as their members. For them, the escolas are a source of pride and in some cases the center of the community in which they are located. They are often social and recreational clubs, and some sponsor schools and nurseries and provide medical assistance and other services to their members. The money for all this comes from members' donations, and income from dances, record sales, open rehearsals, and performances all over the world. The escolas are also supported by the rich, including many engaged in questionable activities such as illegal lotteries and drug dealing.

The parade during Carnaval is a ninety-minute climax, around which life in an escola revolves the whole year. "The parade is the realization of people. They feel like kings for a day," says Hermínio Marquês Dias Filho, director of the Arranco do Engenho de Dentro escola de samba.

A samba school parade in Rio.
Photo by Lidio Parente. Courtesy of Embratur.

Much of the passion Cariocas display toward their escola's presentation is generated by the event's competitive nature. Parade presentations are judged on music, theme, costumes, and other criteria. Those parading at the Sambódromo vie to remain or become one of the sixteen samba schools showcased in the select "Group A," which is the focus of the media's attention. Each year, the two lowest-scoring escolas are demoted to "Group B," while the two highest-ranked "B" units are promoted, and they will parade with the top group at the next Carnaval.

The Parade

Mounting an escola-de-samba parade is a vast undertaking that involves tens of thousands of people, including musicians, dancers, craftsmen, costume-makers, and other contributors, but its basic format is always the same. To begin with, every parade must have a theme, the *enredo*, which might be political or historical or a tribute to a particular person. Until 1996 the enredo had to be related to Brazil. It is chosen by the *carnavalesco*, a type of art director who is responsible for the visual aspect of the escola. After the enredo is approved by the board of directors, the carnavalesco writes a synopsis of it, describing the message he wants to visually convey in the parade. Then, around June, this synopsis is distributed among the escola's composers so that they can begin writing sambas on the theme. Such a samba is called a samba-enredo.

When the composers have their sambas ready, they submit them to the directors, who choose the best ones. Around September, rehearsals begin in the escola's headquarters, where musicians play old sambas and the contending samba-enredos. The reaction of the members to the new sambas will be decisive in the picking of the samba-enredo for the parade. On a certain night, usually at the end of October, the escola chooses the winner from the finalists.

It is a very special night. The escola-de-samba headquarters is noisy and crowded, and the composers organize groups of rooters who

The ala das baianas. *Photo by Lidio Parente. Courtesy of Embratur.*

dance and sing loudly, carrying flags adorned with the name of their favorite samba. The competing sambas are sung in sequence, and at the end of the night the escola's president announces the winning song. The result is not always welcome and fights can break out. The tension is understandable: the samba-enredo is crucial for a good parade and also generates money for the winning songwriters. The samba-enredos from the escolas in Group A are included in an annual album that usually sells more than a million copies.

For Carnaval in 1988, Mangueira's samba-enredo was "100 Anos de Liberdade: Realidade ou Ilusão" (One Hundred Years of Freedom: Reality or Illusion), commemorating the centennial of Brazil's abolition of slavery in 1888 and protesting the proverty of many blacks in the country. The lyrics, written by Hélio Turco, Jurandir, and Alvinho, included an allusion to Ary Barroso's "Aquarela do Brasil."

Today, in reality, where is freedom
Where is that which nobody has seen
Little boy, don't forget that the Negro also
**   built**
The riches of Brazil
Ask the Creator who painted this watercolor
Free of the plantation's whip
Imprisoned in the misery of the favela

Vila Isabel's samba-enredo that year also explored Afro-Brazilian history. "Kizomba, Festa da Raça" (Kizomba, Festival of the Race) sang of Zumbi, the famous leader of the Palmares *quilombo*, samba singer Clementina de Jesus, and numerous aspects of African-based culture. In contrast, other escolas in 1988 took themes such as Brazil's deepening economic crisis, Rio's worsening problems, the magic of cinema, and the highly popular Tra-

palhões comedy troupe. In any year, some samba-enredos are celebratory, while others are serious protests. And by the time Carnaval comes around, most people in Rio know many of that year's samba-enredos by heart, having purchased the annual album (recorded and released before the parades), or having heard the most popular enredos played over and over on the radio.

After an escola's samba-enredo is chosen, all energy is focused on preparations and rehearsals for the parade. By this time, the carnavalesco has already designed and ordered the costumes for the *alas*—the parade units into which escolas de samba are divided. Each ala wears a different costume and plays a specific part in the development of the theme. A big escola like Mangueira has sixty-five alas with an average of eighty members each—more than five thousand participants. Most have to buy their costumes from the escola, and many do so by making small monthly payments (some costumes are inexpensive; others are quite elaborate and costly). Sometimes wealthy contributors pay for the outfits of poor but loyal members.

Two alas are mandatory. The *ala das baianas*, introduced by Mangueira in 1943, includes older women dressed Bahian-style who wear turbans and broad, long-laced dresses. It recalls the Bahian tias who practiced candomblé and participated in the blocos that merged to form Mangueira. The other obligatory ala is the *comissão de frente* (front commission), a group that usually wears costumes related to the enredo. They open the parade, walking solemnly or performing a slow choreography.

Practically every Brazilian can dance to samba, but few master its specific steps. Those men and women who do are called *passistas*. The most important passistas in the escola are the *porta-bandeira* (flag-bearer), always a woman, and the *mestre-sala* (master of ceremonies), a man. These characters made their first appearances with the nineteenth-century sociedades. Dancing elegantly, the porta-bandeira carries the escola flag, while the mestre-sala dances around her, providing symbolic protection.

In between alas come the *carros alegóricos*—huge decorated floats that depict important aspects of the enredo. These floats are true pieces of art, mixtures of sculpture, architecture, and engineering. On top of them stand the *destaques*—men and women wearing either luxurious, expensive costumes or almost nothing at all. The making of the floats employs hundreds of people for at least six months. Seamstresses, sculptors, carpenters, smiths, and painters work busily together like a colony of ants up to the last minute so that everything is ready for the February parade.

Each big escola typically has from four thousand to more than five thousand members who perform in its parade. To organize this many people is extremely complicated. That is what the *diretores de harmonia* (harmony directors) are for. They do not have fun. They just work. Hours before the escola enters the Sambódromo, the harmony director begins organizing the parade in an outside area, the *concentração* (concentration), putting the arriving ala members in their proper places and setting the alas in the right order.

Some time before the parade, the *puxador* (main singer) in the sound float begins to sing the samba-enredo. He is responsible for keeping five thousand voices in time with the drum section, the bateria. He will sing the same song for almost two hours and must make no mistakes. Slowly the members start singing with him, stimulated by the harmony director, who also takes care of keeping the energy high during the parade. After the whole escola has sung the samba two or three times without accompaniment, the most exciting moment in the parade preparation occurs: the musical entrance of the bateria. Anyone who has witnessed this moment will never forget it. Some three hundred percussionists under the command of the *mestre de bateria* (percussion conductor) start playing perfectly in synch with the singing, coordinated by the mestre's whistle—which serves as his baton.

The Bateria

The number and type of percussion instruments used varies from escola to escola. Arranco's Her-mínio gives the following as a typical line-up for a large bateria, by instrument and number of musicians playing that instrument: surdo (30), caixa (40), tarol (40), repique (40), tamborim (70), pandeiro (15), prato (10), cuíca (20), frigideira (20), agogô (20), reco-reco (20), and chocalho or ganzá (40). But each escola has its own mix. For example, in 1997 Mangueira used only surdos, caixas, repiques, tamborins, cuícas, agogôs, reco-recos, and chocalhos.

There are three types of surdos usually used by the baterias. The most important is the *surdo de mar-cação* (marking surdo), also called the *surdão*, *surdo de primeira*, or *surdo maracaña*. It is the heaviest surdo,

Surdos (biggest drums), repiques, and caixa played during a rehearsal for the bloco afro Orunmilá (a Carnaval alternative to the samba schools). *Photo by Ricardo Pessanha.*

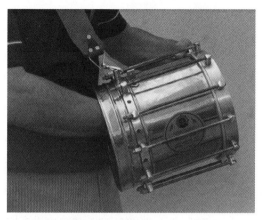

Cuíca. *Photo by Ricardo Pessanha.*

João Parahyba playing a ganzá. *Photo by Ricardo Pessanha.*

the one that plays on the second beat of the 2/4 samba. The surdo de marcação holds the rhythm and is the base for the whole bateria.

The second largest surdo is the *surdo resposta* (answering surdo). As its name suggests, it answers the surdo de marcação by playing on the first beat, though less forcefully than the latter. The *surdo cortador* (cutting surdo) is the smallest surdo, and it plays on the beats and off-beats, "cutting" the rhythm and adding syncopation. In small samba groups, the percussionist uses one surdo to play all three parts by himself—Airto Moreira provides an example of this technique on the samba-based song "Dreamland" on Joni Mitchell's album *Don Juan's Reckless Daughter.*

The conductor has a truly educated ear: during rehearsals he is able to spot one percussionist making a mistake among thirty playing the same instrument and a hundred playing others. He goes up to the erring musician and shouts instructions or tells him to stop and listen. And he must be able to keep all the percussionists synchronized in complicated *viradas* (changes in percussion patterns) and *paradinhas* (full stops), in which a bateria ceases playing during the parade so that everyone can hear other members carrying the rhythm with only their voices. Then the playing resumes. This operation is the musical equivalent of stopping a jumbo jet's take-off at the end of the runway and then getting it to take off again, but they do it.

A bateria percussionist is, together with the composers, passistas, destaques, baianas, and directors, part of the elite in a escola de samba. It's challenging to be one of them. Lobão, a rock drummer and singer who has played tamborim for Mangueira, says, "I took a test to enter, a very hard one. The technique is very sophisticated. You've got to be very precise with a tamborim. You play together with seventy others, but everybody's got to play at the same time. You've got to hear only one beat. If not, the effect is lost."

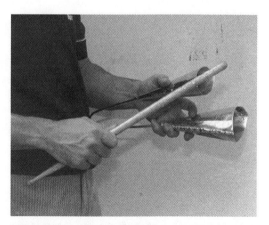

Agogô. *Photo by Ricardo Pessanha.*

Chocalho. *Photo by Ricardo Pessanha.*

A metal reco-reco. *Photo by Ricardo Pessanha.*

of the jury. There, the drummers and percussionists play before the judges, while the second half of the escola passes. Then, the bateria, following the last ala, closes the parade. By this time the next escola is preparing to enter the Sambódromo.

The jury gives grades from one to ten for theme, samba-enredo, harmony, comissão de frente, mestre-sala and porta-bandeira, costumes, evolução (dance performance of the escola), bateria, baianas, and carros alegóricos. The results are known on Ash Wednesday. The winning escola celebrates in its headquarters, stretching Carnaval for one more night.

One big escola parade can cost more than a million dollars. It may seem absurd for poor people to spend so much money on something that lasts just ninety minutes. But what moves them is passion. Just as they are crazy about soccer, people in Rio love their escolas de samba. People do not say, "My favorite escola is Mangueira" or "I like Vila Isabel." People say, "I am Salgueiro" or "I am Portela." It's part of them. It's in their blood. It's in their souls.

Although today's escolas are comprised of

In the concentração, when the bateria starts playing, the energy level rises incredibly. As Lobão puts it, "The sound is twice as loud as a heavy metal band." Excitement takes over. Everything is ready for the parade.

Right before the gates open and the clock starts running, fireworks explode in the air. Then the comissão de frente steps into the Sambódromo, greeting people and asking permission to pass. One more parade has begun.

The bateria follows the first half of the escola into the passarela. They pass in front of thousands of spectators, and along the way come to a space set off to the side for the bateria to play in front

João Parahyba with the tamborim. *Photo by Ricardo Pessanha.*

people from all races and social classes, they remain vital strongholds of Afro-Brazilian culture. As a standard-bearer from a São Paulo escola told us, "Candomblé and escolas de samba are the twentieth century's quilombos."

Television Coverage and Growth

In the early 1960s, the escola Académicos de Salgueiro hired Fernando Pamplona (born in 1926), who became the first outside professional designer to be a carnavalesco and design an escola's float and costumes. When Salgueiro, with Pamplona in charge, won the samba school parade in 1963, it was indicative of how the role of carnavalesco and the ambitiousness of each escola's presentation had both expanded greatly. From that point on, the parades became increasingly theatrical and grandiose. This trend coincided with the growth of the Brazilian television industry, and since the 1960s the parades have been televised live every year, from start to finish.

The parades were generating huge amounts of money, but at first the samba schools received very little of it. Riotur, the state tourism agency, had a lock on the ticket sales and broadcast rights income and handed out only a small percentage of the profits to the escolas. Then in 1988 the major samba schools formed an association and demanded a new deal. They got it: 40 percent of Sambódromo ticket sales and a one-million-dollar contract with TV Globo (of which Riotur received 10 percent). The escolas also formed their own record company to release the lucrative annual compilation album of samba-enredos.

The samba parades are now of an enormous scale and technical sophistication that would have been inconceivable in 1928 to the founders of Deixa Falar. They are also vital to Rio's tourist business and generate huge sums through broadcast, record, and video rights. Not everyone has

been happy about the transformation of the escolas into giant artistic and commercial enterprises. Paulinho da Viola, a major samba figure of the last four decades, left Portela for many years because he felt that the escolas had become overly commercialized and bureaucratized, a common complaint in the 1970s and 1980s.

Paulinho da Viola feels that something got lost along the way. "Nowadays commercial interests are more important than cultural ones," he told us. "What was spontaneous has become official. An escola de samba now has an average of five thousand members. You can imagine the fights there are to choose the suppliers for all these people who will need shoes, costumes. That has attracted people to the escolas who don't belong to that cultural environment." And, what is worse, the funding needs of the samba schools has made many dependent on the financial largesse of drug lords and gangsters who run the *jogo de bicho* (animal game) lottery. But, despite having suffered some high-profile defections, venerable escolas like Portela and

Paulinho da Viola, with his cavaquinho. *Photo by Walter Firmo. Courtesy of BMG.*

Mangueira continue to mount ever more ambitious and lavish parades each year.

The Major Escolas de Samba

Portela has been responsible for setting most of the patterns that the others have followed. Its founder, Paulo da Portela, and his associates introduced into the parade such now-obligatory items as the enredo (theme), the comissão de frente (front commission), and the carros alegóricos (decorated floats). In addition, many famed composers and singers have been associated with Portela, including Zé Keti, Paulinho da Viola, Candeia, João Nogueira, and Paulo César Pinheiro.

Portela is located in the neighborhood of Madureira, as is another historically important escola, Império Serrano. Composers Silas de Oliveira (1916–1972) and Mano Décio da Viola (1908–1984), singers Jorginho do Império (Mano's son) and Roberto Ribeiro, and Ivone Lara, the first woman to have one of her compositions sung by an escola, are among those associated with Império during its history.

While Salgueiro set the precedent for ever more ostentatious parades, Beija-Flor has taken this tendency to its extreme and is now famous, though occasionally criticized, for its visually glittering and luxurious presentations. Fittingly, Joãozinho Trinta—who worked under Pamplona at Salgueiro—was Beija-Flor's carnavalesco in the 1970s and 1980s; he later moved to Unidos do Viradouro, which was champion in 1997. Aside from its audacious floats and costumes, Beija Flor has also had talented singers such as Neguinho da Beija-Flor, a puxador who has recorded several best-selling samba albums.

Mocidade Independente, another major force, is famed for the perfection of their bateria, generally conceded to be the most synchronized and precise of any escola. One of its past conductors, Mestre André, was the inventor of the immensely difficult, aforementioned *paradinha* maneuver.

Today's escolas have a faster, more uniform *batucada* than in the days of old, in large part because of time constraints. If a samba school takes longer than ninety minutes for its parade, it loses precious points in the final judging. Before the events were so organized, the samba schools played slower, mellower, and more melodic samba-enredos. Nowadays they are faster, jumpier, and less musically differentiated. Still, there are clear differences between the escolas. For example, Mangueira sounds different because traditionally all of its surdos play only on the second beat of each bar. Salgueiro displays a heavier use of *cuícas*, which adds more flavor to the general sound and lessens its percussive impact. And Império Serrano's extensive employment of *agogôs* gives its sound a more metallic texture.

Escolas de samba have many talented members, old and young, traditionalists or revolutionaries. They exemplify the creative power of a Carioca population that, in general, lives in very poor socioeconomic conditions. The escolas are often their community center, and samba itself their spiritual sustenance.

Other important samba schools include Unidos do Cabuçu, Unidos da Tijuca, São Clemente, Estácio de Sa, Vila Isabel, Imperatriz Leopoldinense, Caprichosos de Pilares, Lins Imperial, Acadêmicos de Santa Cruz, Império da Tijuca, Grande Rio, Unidos da Ponte, and União da Ilha.

The Modern Samba Era

Paulinho da Viola, whom we mentioned above, is someone whom music critic Sérgio Cabral considers "a legitimate heir of the Estácio sambistas," meaning that he follows in the footsteps of innovative composers such as Ismael Silva, Bide, and Marçal from the Estácio neighborhood, the "cradle of samba." Paulinho is a defender of samba in its traditional form, as it was created by the Estácio composers. Paulinho does not accept samba mixed with bolero or diluted with other pop currents, and he likes playing it with the traditional instruments: guitar, cavaquinho, pandeiro, tamborim. Paulinho comments in *Nova História*, "It seems absurd that I have attached myself to these formulas that are considered of the past, but I like them very much. To me the most important thing is the feeling, and this form of music moves me more."

Paulinho combines modern arrangements and a subdued, elegant vocal style. His songs are especially known for their clear, clean lyrics that are full of feeling but avoid sentimentality. Born in Rio in 1942, Paulinho (Paulo César Batista de Farias) has a guitar-playing father, César Farias, who was and still is a respected choro musician. Every week Jacob do Bandolim and his choro group, Epoca de Ouro, got together at César's place to make some music. That made little Paulo decide to learn how to play the guitar and instilled in him a love for traditional samba.

His first contact with escolas de samba was with a small one—Unidos de Jacarepagua—but in 1963 he was admitted to the *ala dos compositores* (composer's wing) from Portela. The samba that opened the door for him was "Recado" (Message), written with Casquinha. Today it is a classic.

> **Take this message**
> **To she who only did me wrong**
> **Tell her I'm better the way I am**
> **In the past I was a sufferer**

He also composed Portela's unofficial hymn, "Foi Um Rio Que Passou em Minha Vida" (There

A Clara Nunes album cover. *Courtesy of EMI.*

was a River That Passed Through My Life). Paulinho joined Zé Keti's group, A Voz do Morro, and the group's two albums in 1965 included five of Paulinho's sambas and were critically acclaimed. The next year, he recorded an album with his partner and friend, Elton Medeiros, *Na Madrugada* (Late at Night). That LP featured excellent sambas like "Arvoredo," "Quatorze Anos" (Fourteen Years), and "Momento de Fraqueza" (Moment of Weakness). In 1969 came Paulinho's first big hit, "Sinal Fechado" (Red Light), with which he won TV Record's music festival.

The tune is considered a masterpiece, a perfect metaphor for that closed, dark dictatorship era. It is a dialogue between two friends who have not seen each other for a long time, as by chance they stop side-by-side at a traffic light.

> **I had so much to say**
> **But it vanished in the dust of the streets**
> **. . . I also have something to say**
> **But I have just forgotten it**

Paulinho also frequently explored the choro genre, recording songs in the style, such as "Abraçando Chico Soares" (Hugging Chico Soares). After "Prisma Luminoso" (Luminous Prism) in 1983 came a six-year silence from Paulinho in terms of recording. "I wouldn't get

Beth Carvalho. *Courtesy of BMG.*

An Alcione album cover. *Courtesy of BMG.*

strong promotion from the record companies. It was a time when they had decided that only rock would sell," he commented. Paulinho's comeback 1989 record was called "Eu Canto Samba" (I Sing Samba), a clear statement of his musical beliefs and of the purity of his art.

Clara, Beth, and Alcione

Three names stand out among female samba singers who achieved popular success during the last three decades: Clara Nunes, Beth Carvalho, and Alcione. All three fully explored all the stylistic evolutions and permutations undergone by samba in the twentieth century, carrying the genre's history in their collective albums.

Clara Nunes (1943–1983) was the best-selling samba vocalist of the 1970s, her success propelled by an impassioned, sensual voice and a generally strong choice of material. Her big breakthrough came in 1974 with her *Alvorecer* (Dawn) record, the first LP by a female singer in Brazil to sell more than five hundred thousand units (a staggering figure at the time).

From then on, all of Nunes's releases went gold or platinum. She was also an international success, who toured Europe and Japan. Her innumerable hit songs covered not only contemporary pop and samba tunes but also old-guard compositions (by Ataulfo Alves, for example) and songs that explored her Afro-Brazilian heritage. "A Deusa dos Orixás" delved into candomblé mythology, while "Ijexá (Filhos de Gandhy)" used the Bahian *ijexá* rhythm.

Singer Beth Carvalho (born in 1946), who helped launch the pagode movement in the early 1980s, has had a knack for picking the best work of Brazil's samba songwriters. She has also helped preserve Brazil's musical heritage by recording songs in a variety of genres. For example, her 1987 release *Ao Vivo—Montreux Festival* (Live at the Montreux Festival) included renditions of *partido alto* ("Carro de Boi"), *samba de bloco* ("Cacique de Ramos"), *pagode samba* ("Da Melhor Qualidade," "Pé de Vento"), a folkloric *jongo* ("A Vovo Chica"), a *pagode* sendup of Jobim's *bossa nova* "Samba do Avião," and an Edil Pacheco and

Martinho da Vila. *Courtesy of Sony.*

Moraes Moreira *afoxé* ("O Encanto do Gantois"). "O Encanto" is a tribute to Mae Menininha, a *mae de santo* (head priestess) of the venerable Gantois candomblé in Salvador. Carvalho interprets her selections with a powerful, smoky voice and richly rhythmic arrangements.

Like Clara and Beth, vocalist Alcione (born in 1947) covers a wide range of regional styles on her albums and can switch effortlessly from romantic ballads perfect for a dark nightclub to regional pop styles and folkloric excursions. For example, her 1986 LP *Fruto e Raiz* (Fruit and Root) had pop sambas and ballads, a *bumba-meu-boi* ("Mimoso"), and a *forró* ("Eu Quero Chamegar"). With her robust, commanding voice, Alcione has had numerous hit albums ever since her first smash, 1975's *A Voz do Samba* (The Voice of Samba). "Samba is the principal music of this country," she told us. "It's capable of miracles, it has a power that is magical even for those who don't listen to it throughout the year. When the month of Carnaval arrives, samba can unite all types of persons, from every religion, race, color, musical background, and economic class."

Born in São Luis de Maranhão in 1947, Alcione came to Rio when she was only twenty. But she adapted quickly, joining the Mangueira escola de samba by the early 1970s and later becoming a member of its board of directors. "I don't sing with Mangueira, I *am Mangueira*. My blood is pink and green [Mangueira's colors]."

Martinho

In the Vila Isabel neighborhood, once the haunt of Noel Rosa, the most famous name these days is Martinho da Vila (real name Martinho José Ferreira), a singer-songwriter who was born on a Carnaval day in 1938 in Duas Barras, a small town

in Rio de Janeiro state. His first escola was Aprendizes da Boca do Mato, of which he was the musical director. At the same time, he was serving in the army. In 1965 Ferreira switched his allegiance to Vila Isabel and identified so much with his new escola (and vice-versa) that he became Martinho da "Vila."

Martinho's songwriting would play a role in samba-enredo lyrics becoming shorter and more colloquial. "Carnaval de Ilusões" (Carnival of Illusions), his first effort for Vila Isabel, was revolutionary. At that time samba-enredos had extremely long narrative lyrics and a subdued, mellow tempo. Martinho's 1967 composition, written with Gemeu, was based on partido alto, an old type of samba featuring short, light refrains that the singers must follow with improvised verses. "What I did was to add a story to the partido alto structure," Martinho explains in *Nova História*.

At that point Martinho didn't think he could make a living making music. Then in 1968 came his first big success, "Pra Que Dinheiro?"

Grupo Fundo de Quintal's Bira playing a pandeiro. *Photo by Armando Gonçalves. Courtesy of RGE.*

Grupo Fundo de Quintal's Sereno playing a tan-tan. *Photo by Armando Gonçalves. Courtesy of RGE.*

(Money, What For?). The next few years brought many more hits: "O Pequeno Burgues" (The Little Bourgeoisie); "Iaiá do Cais Dourado" (Iaiá of the Golden Pier), the samba-enredo for Vila Isabel in 1969; "Segure Tudo" (Hang on to Everything); and "Batuque na Cozinha" (*Batuque* in the

Kitchen) among them. Sargeant Ferreira retired from the military in 1971. That decade, Martinho enjoyed enormous commercial success, commonly selling more than a half million copies of each album (big numbers for the Brazilian record market at that time).

Martinho's songs feature his relaxed, subtle, husky voice, which softly and confidently works in and around the intricate, compelling rhythms played by his band. It is a rich sound, one that allows listeners to savor all the rhythmic and textural subtleties of his material. And his songs range across many genres: in albums like *Batuqueiro* (Drummer), *Coração Malandro* (Malandro Heart), and *Festa da Raça* (Party of the Race), he explores *partido alto, congada, bossa, afoxé,* and *pontos de umbanda*. He returned to the top of the charts in 1995 with *Tá Delícia, Tá Gostoso* (It's Delightful, It's Delicious), which sold more than one million copies.

Besides being an innovative sambista, Martinho has a special concern for the black culture. He has been to Angola many times to learn about other aspects of African music, and during the eighties organized Kizomba, a festival of black culture in Rio. But he wants to share his cultural blessings and Afro-Brazilian *axé* (a Yoruba word for "positive energy," "life force," or "peace") with all, as he sings in "Axé Pra Todo Mundo" (Axé for All the World).

> **I, a black Brazilian**
> **Desire this for all Brazil**
> **For all races, all creeds . . .**
> **Axé for all the world**

Pagode Samba

The 1970s were good years for samba, commercially and artistically. Record sales for the category soared and deserving artists like Mart-

Bezerra da Silva singing a samba. *Photo by Ricardo Pessanha.*

inho da Vila and Clara Nunes thrived. Also included in the success were many singers without strong cultural roots who pleased the public with samba-based songs with romantic lyrics. Using this formula, Benito de Paula, Luis Airão, Agepê, and Wando cumulatively sold millions of albums. But more important, a new generation of samba musicians emerged in that decade who would update the genre while also bringing it back to its roots. Their style of samba would gain the label of *pagode,* and it soon became a major musical movement.

It all started in the mid-1970s, when a group of musicians associated with the Carnaval bloco Cacique de Ramos started getting together for a *pagode,* a party where people played samba. Every Wednesday night, Bira, Ubirany, Sereno, Almir Guineto, Neoci, Jorge Aragão, and various other talented musicians united for beer, appetizers, and samba in the bloco's rehearsal space. The samba that they made took the genre back to its roots and added some new instrumental twists.

Sereno introduced the *tan-tan,* a type of atabaque, which replaced the larger and heavier surdo. This was more practical for informal samba get-togethers, as the tan-tan could be more easily carried on buses, the mode of transportation for Rio's working class. Almir Guineto added a banjo, which was louder than a cavaquinho and better for open-air gatherings. Ubirany started playing a hand-held repique, called a *repique de mão,* and dispensed with the usual use of drum sticks. And Bira played the pandeiro in unusual ways. The sound was intimate and earthy with new percussive textures. Their lyrics were unpretentious, focusing on situations from their daily life.

When Beth Carvalho and her producer Rildo Hora heard the new samba, they became tremen-

dously enthusiastic. Carvalho brought the music to the Brazilian public for the first time in her album *De Pé no Chão* (Feet on the Ground) in 1978, which included the compositions and playing of the Ramos musicians. Several of them formed the Grupo Fundo de Quintal (Backyard Group), which—with Carvalho's help—secured a recording contract with RGE and released their debut album *Samba é no Fundo de Quintal* in 1980.

Many big names started recording songs by the group, and the recording companies and press started calling their music pagode. The songs by composers like Aragão, Zeca Pagodinho, and Almir Guineto had catchy melodies, strong rhythms, and a refreshing lack of pop overproduction. Carvalho continued to popularize pagode songs on her albums, and the Grupo Fundo de Quintal's sales increased with each new release. Guineto secured a record deal with RGE and a compilation album called *Raça Negra* (Black Race) introduced Pagodinho, Jovelina Pérola Negra, Elaine Machado, Mauro Diniz, and Pedrinho da Flor to the public. From this point on, many pagode musicians started recording albums under their names, singing their own songs. Around 1985, their careers took off and they started selling millions of records. Within a few years, the commercial success of pagode had peaked, but it had introduced many worthy new artists, added some great songs (like Guineto's "Caxambu") to the list of samba standards, and breathed new life into Brazil's most notable genre.

Bezerra and Dicró

Also important in the 1980s was singer Bezerra da Silva, who interprets sambas that he calls "heavy partido alto," which paint a vivid picture of life in Rio's favelas. Bezerra was born in Recife in 1937 and later moved to Rio, where he established his career. He told us, "The authors of the songs are humble people who live in the *morros*. They write about the day-to-day reality of the morro," including the prejudice and victimization suffered by residents there. "In Copacabana, the police need an authorization to enter someone's house," said Bezerra, "but on the morro, they enter without one, and rob and kill. Everyone thinks that those who live on the morro are all bandits. So these songwriters live there, and they write about the day-to-day reality of the morro."

The words in the sambas Bezerra da Silva sings feature so much slang from the morro that sometimes his lyrics are barely intelligible to the Brazilian middle class. They generally talk about drug dealing, murder, crime, police repression, racism against blacks, and other situations experienced by favela residents. "Bicho Feroz" (Wild Animal), by Tonho and Claudio Inspiração, recorded by Bezerra, has lyrics that are not far afield from those of American gangster rap.

> **When you have a gun**
> **You are real mean**
> **Without it, your walk changes**
> **So does your voice**

Dicró, another singer, runs on the same track as Bezerra, singing lyrics that are a window into favela life. Their style of samba has been labeled by critics as *sambandido* (bandit samba).

Sambalanço

In 1992 a group from São Paulo called Raça Negra that had been performing on the road for ten years finally achieved commercial success, invading the airwaves with their own material and covers of rock and sertaneja tunes sung in samba rhythm. Over the next four years, their albums sold an average of 1.5 million copies each. What Raça Negra created is called *sambalanço*, a new variation of samba that most traditional sambistas do not like. They replaced tan-tans, cavaquinho, and banjo with keyboards, saxophone, and bass guitar and gave their songs what Luiz Carlos da Silva, the band leader, calls "a funky swing" heavily influenced by the soul music of Tim Maia and the Jorge Benjor beat.

Sambalanço was extremely popular in the nineties, with many new groups following Raça Negra's lead. They included Só Prá Contrariar, Molejo, Grupo Raça, and Negritude Junior. Two of the most successful bands at that time were Companhia do Pagode and Gera Samba, which scored the respective hits "Na Boquinha da Garrafa" and "É o Tchan" in the mid-1990s. Both groups were from Bahia and featured a bouncy pop samba sound that included simple lyrics loaded with sexual double-entendres. Their songs are on a completely different track from the other offspring of the music created in Praça Onze and in Estácio, but they are yet another variation of the vast genre that is samba.

The Samba Resolution

In Brazil, millions of people sing, dance, or just listen to samba. Its importance in the maintenance of a relative social peace is hard to measure, but it is evident. One doesn't need to wait for Car-

naval to see how samba brings people from all social classes and races together and keeps them in
harmony. All you have to do is go to downtown
Rio on Friday during "happy hour" after work.
The bars and sidewalks in the center of the city are
full of secretaries, executives, office boys,
bankers—various levels of professionals celebrating the oncoming weekend. They all drink, sing,
and dance together. And the party music is always
samba.

After all, in Brazil everything sooner or later
ends up in samba.

Tom Jobim and Elis Regina

Luiz Bonfá

VICTOR

The New Face
of Bonfá
Luiz Bonfá

TIJUCA

Antonio Carlos Jobim

COPACABANA

LEBLON   IPANEMA

Vinicius and Toquinho

Miúcha, Stan Getz, João Gilberto

Stan
Getz

RIO DE JANEIRO

Bossa Nova: The New Way

Chapter Three

If you insist on classifying
My behavior as antimusical
I, even lying, must argue
That this is bossa nova
And that it's very natural

Tom Jobim and Newton Mendonça
"Desafinado"

"Desafinado" (Off-Key), sung by João Gilberto with his very personal, intimate, whispering style, was an ironic reply to critics who mockingly said that bossa nova was "music for off-key singers."

This negative reaction had been occasioned by Gilberto's previous record, a landmark 78-RPM single with "Chega de Saudade" (written by Antonio Carlos "Tom" Jobim and Vinícius de Moraes) and "Bim-Bom" (by Gilberto himself) that came out in July 1958. Much of the Brazilian public was intrigued by the two songs, but others were offended by their unconventional harmonies, the apparently strong influence of American jazz, and Gilberto's unusual vocals.

The prevailing singing style at that time was an operatic one. Great loud voices were a must for successful crooners. Although singers like Johnny Alf, Dick Farney, and Lúcio Alves already had developed more introspective singing styles, it was only with João Gilberto, the young man from Bahia, that people started noticing that something new was happening in the Brazilian music scene.

As for the criticism surrounding "Desafinado," Tom Jobim said, "Actually it's not an off-key song. It's crooked on purpose. It's tilted. It could be a very square song, except for the endings of the musical phrases that go down unexpectedly. It's a criticism of experts. The guy next door, he's off-key but he's in love with this girl,

and he can say that to her because loving is more important than being in tune. Some people are always in tune, but they don't love anybody."

"Desafinado" was released in November, four months after "Chega de Saudade." It became a defiant but good-humored anthem for the emerging Brazilian musical style of bossa nova, which was casual, subtle, and imbued with an infectious swing.

Bossa would explode in popularity in 1959—in Brazil with the success of Gilberto's album *Chega de Saudade*, and internationally with the release of Marcel Camus's award-winning film *Orfeu Negro* (Black Orpheus), the soundtrack of which featured songs by Tom Jobim, Vinícius de Moraes, and Luiz Bonfá.

Bossa nova was a new type of samba in which the genre's rhythmic complexity had been pared down to its bare essentials, transformed into a different kind of beat. It was full of unusual harmonies and syncopations, all expressed with a so-

João Gilberto's 1959 album that launched bossa nova in Brazil. *Courtesy of EMI.*

phisticated simplicity. Sometimes small combos performed bossa; but it was ideally suited to a lone singer and a guitar. This "new fashion" or "new way" (the approximate translation of "bossa nova") of singing, playing, and arranging songs was born in Rio de Janeiro in the mid-1950s.

Developed by Jobim, Gilberto, and their peers, bossa nova was "off key" only in relation to the Brazilian and international pop music of the time. It had a harmonic richness previously heard only in classical music and modern jazz. For example, the unexpected melodic alterations of "Desafinado" included the use of the "tritone interval" (an augmented fourth), which many listeners found hard to accept in a pop song.

Speaking of Jobim in Zuza Homem de Mello's book *Música Popular Brasileira*, keyboardist-arranger Eumir Deodato explains, "He managed for the first time to popularize songs with a harmonic form that was strange for people to hear." As examples, Deodato cites "Chega de Saudade" and "Desafinado," noting that the latter was "harmonically very elaborate."

The international success of bossa nova was the first large-scale global exposure of Brazilian music and musicians. Bossa achieved a huge success in North America in 1962 following the release of Stan Getz and Charlie Byrd's *Jazz Samba* album (which included tunes by Jobim, Bonfá, and Baden Powell). Other bossa-themed LPs were recorded by Herbie Mann, Paul Winter, and Coleman Hawkins, among others.

Pop and jazz listeners alike were entranced by the cool Brazilian swing and warm lyrical beauty of the "new way." Over the next three decades, bossa nova had a huge impact on jazz and international music, as well as on the next generation of Brazilian composers. The genre provided many enduring tunes of remarkable lyricism,

musical economy, and harmonic sophistication. One of its most famous hits was "Garota de Ipanema" (The Girl from Ipanema), one of the best-known songs in the world in the late twentieth century.

Bossa's Beginnings

Derived from samba, bossa nova had many musical antecedents, especially in progressive samba-canção tunes written by Noel Rosa, Ary Barroso, and Braguinha. Braguinha's tune "Copacabana," recorded in 1946 by Dick Farney (with arrangements by Radamês Gnatalli), was a suave and sophisticated piece that foreshadowed the bossa sound. And the guitarist Garoto (Anibal Sardinha, 1915–1955), who added altered and extended chords to sambas and choros, would be a strong influence on all bossa nova guitarists.

Johnny Alf, who was on the periphery of the bossa movement, had a large impact on many of its composers. Alf (Alfredo José da Silva) was born in 1929 in Rio's Vila Isabel neighborhood. Heavily influenced by George Gershwin, Cole Porter, Debussy, and bebop jazz, Alf could be heard by the early 1950s in clubs around town such as the Plaza, where many future bossa musicians were often in attendance. By then he was already using his sharp harmonic and melodic senses to shape Brazilian songs, such as Dorival Caymmi tunes, in a way that sounded avant-garde to Brazilian audiences used to bolero and samba-canção. His singing was jazzy, with scatting and mannerisms typical of bebop, and his piano attack was heavily syncopated.

In 1953, Alf cut his debut single, "Falsete" (Falsetto), and in 1955 scored his first hit with the single "Rapaz de Bem" (Nice Guy), which

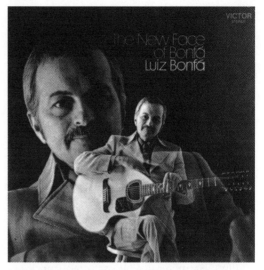

A 1970 RCA release by Luiz Bonfá. *Courtesy of BMG.*

featured new harmonic conceptions and casual lyrics and clearly showed Alf prefiguring the bossa nova style. As the musicians that would form the new movement were getting together in the late 1950s, Alf received an invitation to work in São Paulo. Bad timing, but the money was good and Alf left town for several years. He cut his first album, *Rapaz de Bem*, an instrumental work with a trio in 1961. By the time he moved back to Rio the following year, bossa had already peaked commercially. He had a big hit song, "Eu e a Brisa" (Me and the Breeze), in 1967 but never really received the public attention he deserved.

Guitarist Luiz Bonfá (born in 1922) wrote several songs that foreshadowed the bossa style. Examples include "Perdido de Amor" ("Lost in Love"), a hit for Dick Farney in 1951, and the tunes he wrote in the mid-1950s with Jobim: "Engano" (Mistake), "Domingo Sincopado" (Syncopated Sunday), "Samba não é Brinquedo" (Samba Isn't a Toy), "A Chuva Caiu" (The Rain Fell), and others. João Gilberto, who would one day be called the "pope" of bossa nova, credited both João Donato and Bonfá as important influences on his innovative guitar sound.

João Donato (born in 1934) developed a percussive, harmonically adventurous playing style that struck many listeners as weird. His chords seemed crooked and dissonant, but his rhythmic sense was secure and precise. Donato's sound had points in common with Thelonius Monk's piano playing, and he took a decidedly jazz-influenced approach to Brazilian tunes. He and João Gilberto became good friends and wrote a song together: "Minha Saudade" (My Saudade). But even in the late 1950s, as bossa nova was about to take over,

Donato's oblique piano playing was not welcome in nightclubs. People said he "disorganized the rhythm." Donato toured Mexico with vocalist Elizeth Cardoso (1920–1990), then moved to California, where he lived for thirteen years. But he was not forgotten by those who would gain far-reaching fame from bossa.

Tom Jobim (1927–1995), the most accomplished songwriter of the group, would cite modern classical music, including Brazil's twentieth-century composer Heitor Villa-Lobos, as the major influence on his work. Other bossa composers would draw more from "West Coast" cool jazz, a smooth, relaxed, restrained jazz style of the 1950s that incorporated the melodic and harmonic advances of the bebop style.

In 1956, Carlos Lyra and Roberto Menescal formed a guitar academy in Copacabana, and the two spent a lot of time experimenting with chords influenced by the music of cool-jazz players Gerry Mulligan, Chet Baker, and Shorty Rogers. The academy became a meeting point for future bossa musicians, as did the home of one of their students—Nara Leão. There could be found Lyra, Menescal, and other up-and-coming musicians like Marcos Valle, Edu Lobo, and Ronaldo Bôscoli.

These musicians, along with Jobim, Gilberto, and others, absorbed the rich musical currents flowing through Brazil at the time (samba-canção, jazz, Villa-Lobos) and drew from them to create an economical and colloquial new style of popular music. The rhythm usually came from samba, but on occasion baião, bolero, and marcha were used and transformed by the bossa sensibility. Harmonically, bossa nova tunes included altered chords, inverted chords, and unusual harmonic progressions, as well as unexpected melodic leaps and tonal shifts. Yet, as the bossa songwriters applied complex chords, they were also taking out extraneous notes. The effect was elegant and precise, deceptively simple, and low-key.

This new musical vanguard would find a spiritual and professional center in Rio de Janeiro's most famous neighborhood: Copacabana.

A Cozy Corner and a Guitar

In Copacabana in the mid-to-late 1950s lived the more sophisticated Carioca middle class, which had a taste for jazz, American movies, and other forms of culture from abroad. They often frequented three hip little nightclubs on a narrow side street off Rua Duvivier nicknamed the Beco das Garrafas (Bottles Lane).

Why was it called Bottles Lane? Because Copacabana is a long, narrow strip of tall buildings squeezed between the ocean and the mountains, and sound has only one way to go: up. And a lot of sound did drift up from the Beco das Garrafas, especially since there were often more people milling around outside the small clubs than there were inside. So, sometimes tenants from the adjacent buildings, fed up with the late-night carousing and frequent fighting going on in the

lane, would throw bottles down on the noisemakers.

In these three clubs—Bottles Bar, Little Club, and Baccarat—met the musicians who would make up the core of the bossa movement. They had their own slang and code of behavior, and a way of making music that was unknown outside of Copacabana. Their informal shows sparkled with creativity and lots of improvisation. And they often stayed up all night playing for one other at their homes.

"We did the music because we liked to, nobody was trying to create a movement," recalled guitarist-composer Oscar Castro-Neves. "We just made music and showed it to our friends. We used to go to Jobim's house and we'd leave the place with a fever, because we'd get so excited by the harmonies and everything else."

Often they would end up at the home of Nara Leão, who hosted guitar sessions that lasted until dawn at her parents' apartment on Avenida Atlântica, the avenue that runs along Copacabana Beach. Leão (1942–1989) was a muse to the movement as a teenager and developed into a singer with a cool, gentle style. She would later record many of her friends' songs.

Among those performing and communing in the Beco das Garrafas were Carlos Lyra, Tom Jobim, Roberto Menescal, Durval Ferreira, Luis Eça, Baden Powell, and Sérgio Mendes. One of the most dedicated participants was the poet Vinícius de Moraes, who would become the most prolific and important bossa lyricist. He and his friend Antonio Maria, a journalist and lyricist, would stay in these bars until the very last song and then, after many doses of what de Moraes called "bottled dog" (whisky—man's best friend), they would go to the beach and watch the sunrise.

Nighttime view of Rio de Janeiro's Copacabana Beach, where nearby nightclubs and homes were the headquarters of bossa nova musicians. *Photo by Lidio Parente. Courtesy of Embratur.*

The mood of the bossa musicians reflected that of the Brazilian middle class in the 1950s, especially those who lived in Rio. The future was bright. The country had a popular and democratically elected president, Juscelino Kubitschek, and he was building the new federal capital, the daring and futuristic city of Brasília, on the high plains of Goiás state. Kubitschek's motto was "fifty years of development in five."

Everyone thought Brazil would finally shed its role as the eternal country of the future and become a developed nation. Everything pointed in this direction in the late 1950s and early 1960s. The national soccer team won the World Cup for the first time in 1958, a great source of pride to a soccer-crazed country. Oscar Niemeyer was creating his most famous buildings, including those in Brasília. The movie industry's progressive Cinema Novo movement was emerging. In all the arts, it was a time of effervescence.

Bossa's lyrics reflected this optimism. Most bossa musicians lived in Rio's *Zona Sul* (South Zone) and they sang casually of simple things and their daily environment: the beautiful beaches, waves, sailboats, flowers, blue skies, and, most of all, women. Music-making itself was also celebrated, as in Jobim's "Corcovado": "A cozy corner and a guitar / This is a song to make the one you love happy."

Lyrics in bossa nova were used not only for their meanings but also for their musical sounds. Ronaldo Bôscoli wrote the words for a Roberto Menescal song called "Rio" in which short words with similar sonorities are used to evoke Rio de Janeiro on a hot summer day: "É sal, é sol, é sul" (It's salt, it's sun, it's south). In many bossa songs, especially in the music of João Gilberto, such elemental lyrics and how they were sung were not meant to stand out. Rather, they were intended to blend into the music and contribute to the whole. Harmony was essential, and few understood this as well as Tom Jobim.

Jobim

Antonio Carlos (Tom) Jobim was born on January 25, 1927, in a Rio de Janeiro neighborhood called Tijuca. When he was one year old, his family moved to Ipanema. There, he grew up running in the dunes, swimming in the unpolluted sea, playing soccer on sandy unpaved streets, and contemplating the birds, trees, dolphins, and other aspects of nature that were much more abundant in Rio in the 1930s. When Tom was fourteen, his stepfather bought a piano for Tom's sister Helena; it wasn't long before young Tom

A Sampler of Jobim Standards

Tom Jobim: "Triste" (Sad), "Luiza," "Ela É Carioca" (She's a Carioca), "Samba do Avião" (Samba of the Plane), "Corcovado" (English title: "Quiet Nights of Quiet Stars"), "Vivo Sonhando" (I Live Dreaming; English title: "Dreamer"), "Wave," "Águas de Março" (Waters of March).

Tom and Vinícius de Moraes: "Garota de Ipanema" (The Girl from Ipanema), "Por Toda Minha Vida" (For All My Life), "Água de Beber" (Water to Drink), "Só Danço Samba" (I Only Dance Samba), "Insensatez" (Foolishness), "O Grande Amor" (The Great Love), "Chega de Saudade" (Enough Saudade; English title: "No More Blues"), "Se Todos Fossem Iguais a Você" (If Everyone Were Like You), "A Felicidade" (Happiness).

Tom and Aloysio de Oliveira: "Dindi," "In-útil Paisagem" (Useless Landscape), "De-mais" (Too Much).

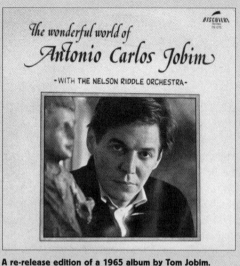

A re-release edition of a 1965 album by Tom Jobim. Courtesy of Discovery Records.

Tom and Newton Mendoça: "Desafinado" (Off-Key), "Samba de Uma Nota Só" (One-Note Samba), "Meditação" (Meditation).

himself was playing it. So his stepfather found him a piano teacher, Hans Joachim Koellreutter.

Koellreutter (born in 1915) was a German who settled in Brazil in 1938. He had studied at the Berlin State Academy of Music and, in Brazil, was a leader of the *música viva* (living music) group, which organized concerts of modern European composers, beginning in 1939. Koellreutter was an enthusiastic advocate of the twelve-tone system of Arnold Schoenberg and an excellent music professor who influenced a whole generation of avant-garde Brazilian pianists.

Tom absorbed a great deal of knowledge about harmony and composition from Koellreutter, but his love for music became a passion when he discovered the works of the Brazilian composer Heitor Villa-Lobos, who had written such masterpieces as the "Bachianas Brasileiras," which merged baroque forms with Brazilian folk-music elements.

As a young man, Jobim at first chose architecture as his occupation. He found a job in an architect's office but soon was disappointed with it. Tom came home every day with the sensation of time lost. So he decided instead to dedicate his life to music.

Jobim studied theory and harmony intensively and drew inspiration from the classical composers he had studied, but he never forgot popular music. He told us, "I could write a piece using the twelve-tone scale, but Brazil, with all its rhythms, was more important. I liked Pixinguinha, Donga, Vadico, and Ary Barroso."

Tom started playing in nightclubs around 1950, but he was married already and money was short. Things started to get better only when he found a job at the Continental record company in 1952, where he transcribed songs for composers who could not write music. The next year he landed a job as the artistic director for the Odeon label.

Meanwhile, he began writing songs with Newton Mendoça (1927–1960), an old beach friend and very good pianist. In 1954 Tom began his career as an arranger and worked on records by Dick Farney, Os Cariocas, and Elizeth Cardoso. He also started collaborating with another partner, Billy Blanco. The pair composed "Teresa da Praia" (Teresa of the Beach) and the ten-inch album *Sinfonia do Rio de Janeiro: Sinfonia Popular em Tempo de Samba*. The latter included vocals by Farney, Cardoso, Os

Foreground: Vinícius de Moraes (*left*) with Toquinho (*right*), a frequent musical partner, in concert in the 1970s. *Courtesy of BMG.*

Cariocas, Lúcio Alves, Doris Monteiro, and others in tune with the nascent bossa-nova style.

Tom was developing his own innovations in regard to Brazilian popular music, adding new twists to the venerable samba and creating a sound that was all his own. He said to us, "I had those new harmonies coming from me only. I was always revolting against the establishment, against normal harmonies. It was a very personal thing. Sure I heard Debussy and Ravel, but they didn't have this African beat we have here."

Jobim was not a great instrumentalist, like Bonfá or Powell, or a charismatic singer, like Lyra or Gilberto. But his compositions would make him the most famous Brazilian musical figure of his time.

By the mid-1950s, Tom had garnered a great deal of prestige in the Brazilian music scene. He had a television show in São Paulo called "Bom Tom" (a pun that means "nice Tom" and at the same time "good taste"). He was writing songs with Mendonça, Blanco, and—by this time—Bonfá, revitalizing the samba-canção. Then in 1956 Tom began working with a brilliant and fast-living poet who would be his most important songwriting partner.

Vinícius de Moraes

Vinícius de Moraes (1913–1980) applied his considerable poetic gifts to writing lyrics for more than two hundred songs, most of which demonstrate a powerful sense of rhythm, sound, economy, and metaphor. Vinícius's lyrics, like those of his bossa contemporaries, often centered on elemental themes, especially love, with a subtlety and profundity that usually elude translation.

Before gaining fame as a bossa lyricist, Vinícius had already established a well-respected place for himself in Brazilian literature, as the author of several books of acclaimed poetry. His poems had evolved from an early formalism—his first book

was published in 1933—to a very personal approach in which he brought the eternal, the cosmic, the inexplicable into the reality of daily life.

He wrote his first song lyrics in 1932 for a foxtrot called "Loura ou Morena" (Blonde or Brunette), co-written with Haroldo Tapajós. But that didn't start a musical career. After penning two more songs in 1933 that were recorded by artists at RCA, Vinícius moved on to other things, not returning to lyric writing until 1952.

During those intervening years, he graduated from law school, studied English poetry at Oxford, and then became a diplomat. He was posted in Los Angeles between 1946 and 1950 and became vice consul at the Brazilian consulate there. Once he returned to Rio, Vinícius worked as a journalist and plunged into the night life again. He resumed songwriting and composed his first samba, "Quando Tu Passas por Mim" (When You Pass by Me).

Vinícius, barely scraping by financially, asked for another diplomatic position abroad. He was lucky: in 1953 he was assigned to Paris. There he met Sacha Gordine, to whom he sold a story for a film: *Orfeu da Conceição.* But the French producer then had problems raising the money for the film. So, back in Brazil, Vinícius decided to stage the story as a play and started looking for a composer to write the music. Then he remembered a young musician he had once seen perform in a nightclub called Club da Chave: Tom Jobim.

Bossa nova was arguably born in 1956, the

João Gilberto in concert in 1987. *Photo by Karl Garabedian.*

year that Jobim and Vinícius met and collaborated on music for the play *Orfeu da Conceição*, as well as the song "Chega de Saudade." In the liner notes for Paul Winter's album *Rio*, Vinícius looks back at his work with Jobim and the early bossa years. He recalls, "I did not know I was giving this young composer from Ipanema a signal to begin a new movement in Brazilian music. About the same time, by a kind of telepathy, other young Brazilian composers like Carlos Lyra, Roberto Menescal, and Oscar Castro-Neves were beginning to compose in a similar style."

The play transplanted the Greek myth of Orpheus and Eurydice into the favelas and Carnaval of modern-day Rio. *Orfeu da Conceição*, with sets by Oscar Niemeyer, opened at Rio's Teatro Municipal on September 25, 1956. It was a big hit and so too was an accompanying record of the score, which included songs by Jobim and de Moraes like "Se Todos Fossem Iguais a Você" (If Everyone Were Like You) and "Eu e o Amor" (Me and Love).

In 1957, Sacha Gordine, finally with financial backing, came to Rio with director Marcel Camus to make the *Orfeu da Conceição* movie. Gordine wanted original music for the French-Brazilian production, to be retitled *Orfeu Negro* (Black Orpheus). The new score included Luiz Bonfá's "Samba de Orfeu" (Samba of Orpheus)

and the lovely "Manhã de Carnaval" (Morning of Carnaval), with lyrics by Antonio Maria. Jobim and Moraes composed new tunes, including the sweetly melancholy "A Felicidade" (Happiness).

> **Sadness has no end, but happiness does**
> **Happiness is like a feather the wind carries**
>   **into the air**
> **It flies so lightly, yet has such a brief life**

João Gilberto

Vocalist Elizeth Cardoso's 1958 LP *Canção do Amor Demais* (Song for an Excessive Love) features João Gilberto's new style of guitar-playing, Jobim and de Moraes's songs, and Jobim's arrangements. Tom recalled, "We were developing our style. You can see it very clearly in this album."

Gilberto's arrival on the scene opened new perspectives with "the rhythm that he brought," according to Jobim in *Música Popular Brasiliera*. The harmonic and melodic part of the bossa equation was already established, but "the beat of bossa nova appeared for the first time on the guitar played by João on Elizeth Cardoso's album. That album constituted a boundary mark, a fission point, a break with the past."

João Gilberto was born in 1932 in Joazeiro, a small city in the interior of Bahia state. Jobim's description of bossa in the *Chega de Saudade* album liner notes also aptly characterizes Gilberto's artistic personality. Jobim writes, "Bossa nova is serene, it has love and romance, but it is restless." Gilberto's singing and playing seem natural now that they have been incorporated into the repertoire of international music, but back in the 1950s they were extremely unusual.

Gilberto's highly syncopated style of plucking acoustic guitar chords—nicknamed *violão gago*

(stammering guitar) by some—introduced a type
of rhythm that resembled a cooled and slowed
samba but was very difficult to play. "He was the
only one who could do that beat at first, said
Brazilian music critic Zuza Homem de Mello.
"After time others could, too."

la Brazilian writer

According to Oscar Castro-Neves, Gilberto's
guitar style was "a decantation of the main elements of what samba was, which made bossa
nova more palatable for foreigners and the
rhythm more easily perceived. He imitated a
whole samba ensemble, with his thumb doing
the bass drum and his fingers doing the *tamborims*
and *ganzás* and *agogôs*. The rhythm was right there
with his voice and guitar alone. You didn't feel
anything was missing."

João's singing was new, too. Both voice and
guitar were simultaneously melodic and highly
rhythmic, as he syncopated sung notes against guitar motifs. "The way he phrases is incredible," said
Castro-Neves. "The guitar would keep the tempo
going and he would phrase in a way that was completely free, atop that pulsating rhythm. The way
his phrases would fall—he would delay a chord
here, put a note there—was very hypnotic.

"And he had a blend between the volume of
his voice and the volume of the guitar. He could
emphasize a note in the vocal and it would be like
completing a chord on the guitar. Suddenly the
voice really complemented the harmonic structure of the chord."

Gilberto sang quietly, subtly, with a low-
pitched, smooth, precise voice without vibrato, as
if whispering an extremely intimate secret only for
the listener (Miles Davis was quoted as saying that
Gilberto "would sound good reading a newspaper"). In the book *Balanço da Bossa*, Augusto de Campos describes how Tom Jobim took João Gilberto
one day to a studio so that some recording indus-

try bosses could hear him sing. After João finished
singing . . . silence. Nobody knew what to say. After some time, one of the guys murmured to the
one next to him, "Tom said he'd bring us a singer
but ended up bringing a ventriloquist."

Gilberto's style was anti–show business, cozy
and conversational, and the music business executives didn't understand it—yet.

The Bossa Boom

Fortunately, Jobim had connections at the Odeon
label, where he had once worked. He was friends
with the artistic director there, Aloysio de
Oliveira, the ex-leader of the Bando da Lua,
which had backed Carmen Miranda in the United
States in the 1940s. Through Oliveira's efforts,
Odeon agreed in 1958 to release Gilberto's first
single, "Chega de Saudade" (the Jobim-de
Moraes song written two years earlier), which
most historians consider the first recorded bossa
nova song. The arrangements were Tom's and the
critical reaction was to a large extent highly neg-

A still from the film *Black Orpheus*, with the stars Bruno Mello
(Orpheus) and Marpessa Dawn (Eurydice). *Courtesy of The
Voyager Company.*

ative. But the album sold well enough that Odeon decided to let João record an album.

In 1959 came the *Chega de Saudade* LP, arranged by Jobim and produced by de Oliveira. The record put the movement on track and is considered the first bossa nova album. Besides the song, the album included "Desafinado" and other tunes by Tom and Vinícius, three Carlos Lyra compositions, and two Ary Barroso classics.

Another major musical event of 1959 was the premiere of the movie *Orfeu Negro*, which put bossa nova on the world musical map. Shot in Rio the previous year, mostly in the hills overlooking the city, it was beautifully photographed and filled with the vivid colors, sounds, and excitement of Rio and Carnaval. The extraordinary Jobim-de Moraes-Bonfá soundtrack featured vocals by Agostinho dos Santos and Elizeth Cardoso, guitarwork by Bonfá, and heavily percussive samba and candomblé ritual music.

The movie won the Grand Prize at the Cannes Film Festival that year (and an Academy Award for Best Foreign Film). Its theme song, Bonfá's "Manhã de Carnaval," a worldwide smash hit, was covered by countless musicians, and its various renditions sold millions of copies. The film's music inspired critical adjectives such as "joyous," "rapturous," "unforgettable." Bonfá and Jobim became internationally famous.

This radical and romantic new sound was a huge success, and during the next four years its beat took over the country. Bossa artists Lyra, Nara Leão, Roberto Menescal, Ronaldo Bôscoli, Marcos Valle, Baden Powell, and many others came into the spotlight. After *Chega de Saudade*, Gilberto recorded two more very successful albums: *O Amor, o Sorriso e a Flor* (Love, the Smile and the Flower) in 1960 and *João Gilberto* in 1961. These albums included both new bossa tunes and bossa interpretations of old stan-

dards by composers like Dorival Caymmi and the sambistas Bide and Marçal.

The new sound was also popularized by many talented groups that played at the Beco das Garrafas clubs and at other Brazilian hotspots (including venues in São Paulo like the Paramount) in the late 1950s and 1960s. Among them were the Tamba Trio (Luis Eça, Bebeto, and Hélcio Milito), Zimbo Trio (which included Luis Chaves and Amilton Godoy), Sambalanço Trio (with César Camargo Mariano and Airto Moreira), Bossa Jazz Trio (with Amilson Godoy—younger brother of Almilton), Bossa Três (with Edson Machado), 3-D (with Antonio Adolfo), Jongo Trio, and the Sexteto Bossa Rio (led by young keyboardist Sérgio Mendes). Other vocalists who performed bossa nova songs during this era included Leny Andrade (who often sang with the Sexteto Bossa Rio), Pery Ribeiro, Maysa, Sylvia Telles, and Alayde Costa.

Baden Powell

Another great Brazilian guitarist who gained fame during the bossa nova era was Baden Powell de Aquino, called simply Baden Powell. Born in 1937 in Varre-e-Sai, a small town in Rio de Janeiro state, Baden has a technical mastery of the guitar and a singular capacity to mix Afro-Brazilian influences with jazz and classical elements. When he performs, Powell weaves a hypnotic spell with his guitar, producing sounds as soft and melodious as a mother singing a lullaby, or as swinging and percussive as any drummer.

Castro-Neves described Baden Powell as "a marriage of a great performer and player. Very charismatic on stage. Baden was influenced by jazz, but filtered it through his Brazilian soul. His solos are very Brazilian, with definitely Brazilian phrasing. And he has fast fingers, the chops, to go with it. The way he does rhythm is very personal,

A Sampler of Bossa Standards

Carlos Lyra: "Lobo Bobo" (Foolish Wolf), "Saudade Fez um Samba" (Saudade Made a Samba), both co-written with Ronaldo Bôscoli; "Maria Ninguém" (Maria Nobody). All three appear on the Chega de Saudade album.

Carlos Lyra and Vinícius de Moraes: "Primavera" (Springtime), "Minha Namorada" (My Girlfriend), "Pau de Arara," "Sabe Você" (You Know), "Samba do Carioca," "Você e Eu" (You and Me), "Coisa Mais Linda" (Most Beautiful Thing), "Marcha da Quarta-Feira de Cinzas" (Ash Wednesday Marcha).

Ronaldo Bôscoli and Roberto Menescal: "O Barquinho" (Little Boat), "Rio," "Você" (You), "Nós e o Mar" (Us and the Sea), "Telefone" (Telephone), "Vagamente" (Slightly), "A Volta" (The Return).

Marcos Valle and Paulo Sérgio Valle: "Samba de Verão" (Summer Samba), "Lágrima Flor" (Flower Tear), "Preciso Aprender a Ser Só" (I Need to Learn to Be Alone), "Viola Enluarada" (Moonlit Guitar).

Durval Ferreira: "Sambop," "Chuva" (Rain), "Batida Diferente" (Different Beat).

Oscar Castro-Neves: "Patinho Feio" (Ugly Duckling), "Onde Está Você?" (Where Are You?).

such as the way he plucks the strings in fast succession. He was extremely influential."

Baden entered the bossa nova scene at a young age. He was twenty-two when he co-wrote "Samba Triste" (Sad Samba) with Billy Blanco in 1959 and over the next two years appeared as a session guitarist on many bossa albums. In 1962, he began collaborating with Vinícius de Moraes. On many occasions, often for days on end, the two would hole up in Vinícius's apartment in Copacabana, to drink whiskey and make music.

Baden and Vinícius composed more than fifty songs together, most with beautiful melodic themes that Powell would elaborate imaginatively on the acoustic guitar. Some were bossas and some were what they termed *afro-sambas*. While Baden was mulatto, Vinícius was white but identified strongly with Afro-Brazilian culture. He was a son of Xangô in the candomblé religion and jokingly referred to himself as "the blackest white man in Brazil." The pair researched Afro-Brazilian music from Bahia and incorporated it into their compositions. The song "Berimbau," for example, was named after the Bahian musical bow used to accompany capoeira. In the recording, Baden plays the berimbau's rhythmic part on the guitar. "Canto de Ossanha," a song for the orixá Ossanha, begins with a simple brooding base-note riff on the guitar that is accompanied by muted plucked guitar patterns and soft percussion. It builds

steadily until the song explodes into a joyful, upbeat guitar-percussion celebration. Many of their best numbers in this vein were gathered together for their 1966 album *Os Afro-Sambas*.

One of their most famous songs, "Samba da Benção" (Blessing Samba) was included in the 1966 Claude Lelouch movie *Un Homme et une Femme* (A Man and a Woman). They also composed tunes such as "Consolação" (Consolation), "Apelo" (Appeal), "Tempo Feliz" (Happy Time), "Deve Ser Amor" (It Must Be Love), and "Deixa" (Leave It).

Once the two split up, Baden moved to Europe. In the years that followed, he has recorded numerous albums, including *Uma Viola na Madrugada* (A Guitar Late at Night), *Baden Powell Swings with Jimmy Pratt*, *La Grande Reunion* (with jazz violinist Stephane Grappelli) and *Baden à Vontade* (Baden at Ease).

Bossa Nova Criticism

Of course, musicians and singers who had nothing to do with the movement also wanted to sing or write bossa nova songs. The term "bossa nova" turned into an adjective for everything modern, surprising. There were bossa nova girls, a bossa nova president, as Kubitschek was called, and even bossa nova cars. There was also a lot of bossa nova criticism.

Many Brazilian music critics, including the well-respected José Ramos Tinhorão, blasted bossa nova as being little more than an imitation of cool jazz. Yet that was far from the truth, and even classifications of bossa as a mixture of jazz and samba are an oversimplification. Jazz certainly influenced most bossa musicians, but the genre's greatest songwriter, Jobim, was most heavily influenced by samba-canção and classical music. In any event, it is clear that bossa nova put together many musical elements in an original way and was something definitely Brazilian.

In Mello's *Música Popular Brasileira*, Jobim comments, "Many people said that bossa nova was an Americanized phenomenon. I think this is entirely false. Much to the contrary, I think what influenced [North] American music was the bossa nova. I received letters and telegrams from various illustrious composers . . . saying that bossa nova had been the biggest influence on American music in the last thirty years."

The North American Invasion

John Coltrane had cut a jazz-samba cover of Ary Barroso's "Baia" (known in Brazil as "Na Baixa do Sapateiro") in 1958 and Capitol had released *Brazil's Brilliant João Gilberto* in 1961, but the American public was not yet ready for bossa nova.

But more seeds were being sown at the start of the 1960s, when American jazz musicians Charlie Byrd, Herbie Mann, Kenny Dorham, Roy Eldridge, Coleman Hawkins, Zoot Sims, and Paul Winter toured Brazil, some of them in connection with a State Department–sponsored visit, and were exposed to the new sound.

When Charlie Byrd returned from Brazil, he brought back with him a Gilberto record and played it for a friend, the saxophonist Stan Getz. Charlie had a natural affinity for the style in part because "I had been studying the classical guitar

for about ten years and playing with my fingers, which is the way the Brazilians play it. And it's the way you can play those rhythms much more authentically than you can with a pick." At that time, recalled Byrd, "there were no jazz guitarists but me who played that way."

Byrd loved the melodies of bossa nova. In the ingredients of what became bossa, he noted, "you can't discount the strength of the tunes by Jobim, Gilberto, and Menescal. It was very strong material, a key factor in making things happen. And I've said it before—I think Jobim is the most significant writer of popular music in the second half of the twentieth century. He is one hell of a songwriter, and he has written in all kinds of styles. His songs have beautiful lyrical lines and he has rhythmically and harmonically constructed them like a fine watchmaker."

When Getz listened to the Gilberto album, he was so impressed with it that he and Byrd decided to record an album together that would feature songs in the new style. They chose songs by Jobim (including "Desafinado" and "Samba de Uma Nota Só"), Bonfá, Baden Powell, Billy Blanco, and Ary Barroso. Getz and Byrd's *Jazz Samba* was produced by Creed Taylor and released by Verve in April 1962.

"Desafinado" made the *Billboard* Top 20 for pop singles and won a "best solo jazz performance" Grammy for Getz. The album did even better: it received a five-star review in *Downbeat* magazine and shot to the number 1 position on the *Billboard* pop chart. It sold hundreds of thousands of copies, remarkable for a jazz record (especially an instrumental one) and stayed on the charts for seventy weeks. It was really jazz-bossa rather than bossa nova, but the new sound had struck a nerve. Byrd quipped, "I knew it was something that would have a lot of public appeal. I didn't know it would inspire bossa nova neckties."

Before the release of *Jazz Samba*, a young saxophonist named Paul Winter had also checked out a Gilberto album (played for him by critic-lyricist Gene Lees), loved it, and then toured Brazil and heard more of the new style. "It was such a breath of fresh air," recalled Winter. "We were hearing a very gentle voice that had the kind of soul and harmonic beauty that we loved in jazz. But as opposed to the very hard-driving bebop that we were playing then, it was astounding to find a very quiet, gentle music that had an equal amount of magic. It was a whole new possiblity for us.

"Guitar wasn't something that was part of our universe and here was someone doing all this subtle magic on the classical guitar. João Gilberto was sort of a new prophet. Following that tour, guitar became an integral part of my musical world," added Winter. That year (1962), Paul's sextet recorded *Jazz Meets the Bossa Nova* in Rio and New York, interpreting tunes by Jobim, Lyra, Menescal, and Dorival Caymmi. It also fell into the area of jazz-bossa but was more "Brazilian" than *Jazz Samba* in that it included Brazilian percussionists who added instruments like the afoxê, reco-reco, and cuíca to the sound. It marked the beginning of Winter's long relationship with Brazilian music.

Do the Bossa Nova with Herbie Mann was another album released in 1962. Flutist Herbie Mann recalled his trip to Brazil the previous year: "I was so totally mesmerized by the country and the music that I realized it was going to save my musical life. Up till that point my success had come from having an Afro-Cuban type jazz band with four percussionists. But Afro-Cuban and African music were so simplistic melody-wise that it really got boring. When I went to Brazil I saw that their music could be as rhythmically involved as other eth-

nic musics were but with it they had these melodic masterpieces. So as a jazz person, it was the best of both worlds—to have great melodies to improvise with combined with these rhythms."

Mann and trumpeter Kenny Dorham flew to Brazil in September 1962 and recorded an album there with Baden Powell, Jobim, Durval Ferreira, the Tamba Trio's Bebeto and Hélcio Milito, and the Sérgio Mendes Bossa Sextet, which Mann described at the time as "like Horace Silver or Cannonball Adderley with a samba beat." *Do the Bossa Nova* was an important meeting of American and Brazilian musicians, as was an album recorded in December of that year: *Cannonball's Bossa Nova*. That LP, released on Riverside Records in 1963, teamed the jazz saxophonist Cannonball Adderley with the Sexteto Bossa Rio. Mann and Adderley, like Byrd and Winter, would extensively record and play with Brazilians for years to come.

On November 21, 1962, at Carnegie Hall in New York, a now-legendary concert was staged by impressario Sidney Frey (owner of Audio Fidelity Records) that further publicized bossa nova. The show presented the Brazilian artists Gilberto, Bonfá, Castro-Neves, and others with American jazzmen enamored of the new style, including Getz, Byrd, Gary Burton, Gary McFarland, and Lalo Schifrin. Despite inclement weather, it was a sellout, with some twenty-eight hundred spectators inside and more than a thousand turned away. The show was disorganized and the sound was terrible, but the concert got recording contracts for many Brazilian artists and marked the growing affinity of American jazz musicians for bossa nova.

Bossa conquered the United States with its fresh sophistication, bridging "mass" popular music and "art" popular music, as John Storm Roberts puts it in *The Latin Tinge*. After the huge success of *Jazz Samba*, magazines and newspapers

Musicians Stan Getz and João Gilberto—whose earlier collaboration *Getz/Gilberto* marked the climax of the bossa invasion of North America—pictured with vocalist Miúcha, João's second wife, on their 1976 album. *Courtesy of Sony.*

Astrud Gilberto, whose vocals on "The Girl from Ipanema" helped begin a Brazilian music boom in the United States in the early 1960s, pictured here on her 1987 Verve release. *Courtesy of Verve.*

were full of articles about bossa nova, and dozens more jazz-bossa albums were released that year and the next. In the early 1960s, Ella Fitzgerald, Al Hirt, Zoot Sims, Vince Guaraldi, Coleman Hawkins, Curtis Fuller, Ray Charles, and Lalo Schifrin all recorded bossa-inspired tunes or al-

bums, as did an abundance of pop musicians. Elvis Presley sang "Bossa Nova Baby" and Eydie Gormé recorded "Blame It on the Bossa Nova."

Getz and Byrd went their separate ways after the *Jazz Samba* success. Byrd would record many Brazilian-flavored albums in succeeding decades, delving deeply into the works of venerable Brazilian composers like Pixinguinha and Ernesto Nazaré.

Getz, Gilberto, and the Girl from Ipanema

Getz grabbed the lion's share of fame from the bossa boom with his next few releases. His second jazz-bossa effort was *Big Band Bossa Nova*, which hit number 13 on the pop charts. He teamed with Bonfá for *Jazz Samba Encore* in 1963 and then—just as the bossa craze seemed to be dying out—joined Gilberto and Jobim for the album *Getz/Gilberto*, released in 1964. On it, João added guitar and vocals, Tom played piano, Milton Banana was on drums, and Tommy Williams on bass. Two numbers featured João's wife, Astrud, who had come to the recording session only to be with her husband. At Getz's insistence, she added English vocals to some songs, because João couldn't sing in English.

One of the tunes featuring Astrud's cool, light, and gentle vocals was the now world-famous "The Girl from Ipanema," the English version (with lyrics added by Norman Gimbel) of the song "Garota de Ipanema," composed by Jobim and Vinícius de Moraes in 1962. With that song, Astrud became an instant international star.

> **Tall and tan and young and lovely**
> **The girl from Ipanema goes walking**
> **When she walks she's like a samba**
> **That swings so cool and sways so gently**

"The Girl from Ipanema" was a duet between João (in Portuguese) and Astrud (in English), and

Tom Jobim, Helô Pinheiro (the real life inspiration for "The Girl from Ipanema"), and Pinheiro's daughter, in the late 1980s. *Photo by Lidio Parente. Courtesy of Embratur.*

it bridged the language-gap with the U.S. audience. The breezy song won a Grammy for best song that year and went to number 5 on the *Billboard* singles chart. More important, it opened the minds of many Americans to the richness of Brazilian music. Its smooth syncopation and graceful lyricism made it into a standard, one of the most recorded and performed songs of its time. Unfortunately, in the 1960s and 1970s it was so overplayed and covered by so many musicians (some great, some good, many bad), that in the United States "The Girl from Ipanema" began to epitomize cocktail-lounge music. Happily, time has dissipated the excesses of commercialization and a replaying of the song's definitive version (with João, Astrud, Jobim, and Getz) is again a delight to hear: cool, seductive, and wistful.

The inspiration of the song was a beautiful, tanned teenaged girl named Heloisa Eneida Pinto (now Pinheiro) who used to "sway so gently" past a bar called Veloso on her way to Ipanema beach. Two regulars at Veloso were Tom and Vinícius, who turned their appreciation of Helô's sexy gracefulness into a song, and an unknowing muse into a pop icon of youth and beauty. The first recordings of the song came in 1963 in Brazil, where it was interpreted by Jobim, the Tamba Trio, and singer Pery Ribeiro. Only after the song became famous was Helô introduced to Tom on the beach. Today the Veloso bar is named Garota de Ipanema after the song. The street it faces, Rua Montenegro, is now called Rua Vinícius de Moraes.

The album *Getz/Gilberto* garnered three other Grammys (Best Album, Best Jazz Performance, and Best Engineering) as well and went to number 2 on the pop charts. It failed to reach number 1 only because the Beatles were making pop music history that year. *Getz/Gilberto* spent an extraordinary ninety-six weeks on the charts, fifty of those in the top 40. Interestingly, just a few years

The former Veloso bar, now renamed for the song that made it famous. The street, also renamed as shown on the sign at the far right bearing tribute to Vinícius de Moraes. *Photo by Ricardo Pessanha.*

later, the Beatles and bossa nova would both be strong influences on a new Brazilian musical movement: *Tropicália.*

Also in 1964 came another excellent jazz-bossa album, when Paul Winter and Carlos Lyra teamed for *The Sound of Ipanema*. Recorded in Rio, it featured Lyra's compositions and included the playing of Sérgio Mendes (piano), Sebastião Neto (bass), and Milton Banana (drums). Winter, in fact, was the only American on it, and he fit very well with the bossa spirit because of his lyrical and open-minded musical sensibility. The album was a smooth and engaging American-Brazilian fusion. Winter then cut the also superb *Rio* in 1965, featuring Bonfá, Roberto Menescal, and Luis Eça.

After the Bossa Boom

While bossa nova was enjoying its heyday in North America, the bright, optimistic era that had begun with Kubitschek and helped create bossa nova was fading. A few years earlier, in 1961, Janio Quadros, the next president, had resigned for reasons that today are still obscure. His cryptic letter of resignation mentioned "foreign" and "terrible" forces that opposed him. The vice president, João (Jango) Goulart, took over. He had a more leftist orientation and faced great opposition from the conservative sectors of society. Artists in general supported the new president, who courted Cuba, reestablished relations with Eastern Europe, condemned foreign economic imperialism, and promised to carry out basic reforms. He also further limited the profits that foreign corporations could send out of Brazil, in response to those who felt that multinational firms were exploiting the country.

Politically, Brazil was torn in two. In 1964, a military coup toppled the Brazilian government and replaced it with an authoritarian, repressive regime. This accelerated the movement of bossa nova's songwriters in different directions. Some bossa artists grew more involved with politics. Carlos Lyra, Nara Leão, Sérgio Ricardo, Marcos Valle, and Paulo Sérgio Valle began to use their song lyrics to protest poverty and social injustice in Brazil. *Opinião* (Opinion) was a protest musical in 1964 that matched singer Leão with sambista Zé Keti and northeastern songwriter João do Vale. A television show called "O Fino da Bossa" (The Best of Bossa) often featured the more socially oriented bossa tunes, which the government was not yet censoring to any great degree.

In 1965 began the era of the Brazilian musical festivals, which would launch a new generation of Brazilian singers and songwriters whose eclectic music came to be known as MPB (*música popular brasileira*). Many bossa figures would be absorbed by MPB, a few continued the bossa line, others moved into jazz and instrumental music, and some traveled to the United States and Europe to establish careers there.

Guitarist Luiz Bonfá moved to the United States in the 1960s and frequently performed there and in Europe in succeeding decades. A vital bossa musician and accomplished classical guitarist, he played an important role in the evolution of Brazilian guitar-playing. "He is an incredible soloist with a lot of technique and a very beautiful and personal quality of sound," noted Oscar Castro-Neves. "You can hear two notes and know this is Bonfá." Musicians continue to cover his "Manhã de Carnaval."

Carlos Lyra (born in 1936) led bossa into its activist phase, adding social commentary and northeastern folk elements to albums such as *Pobre Menina Rica* (Poor Little Rich Girl). Then, because of the political atmosphere, he left for Mexico. He stayed there between 1966 and 1971, writing music for film and the theater. Meanwhile, the Brazilian dictatorship in 1968 began its heaviest phase of censorship and repression. When Lyra returned to his homeland, he found a different country from the one he had left. He made a record in 1973 but only two of its songs passed the government censorship; it was released with old material substituted instead. He did not record again in Brazil until 1996.

Ronaldo Bôscoli (1929–1995) and Roberto Menescal (born in 1937) wrote many bossa successes together and both worked as producers in later years. One of Menescal's production efforts was Leila Pinheiro's beautiful 1989 collection of bossa classics, *Benção, Bossa Nova* (Blessing, Bossa Nova). Singer Nara Leão recorded many bossa standards, then became political and nationalistic, sang samba, and starred in the didactic play Opinião. At the end of the 1960s she made another artistic switch and participated in the brief yet influential Tropicália movement with Gilberto Gil, Caetano Veloso, and others.

Vocalist Leny Andrade was another "Beco das Garrafas" veteran and recorded her first album in 1960, *A Sensação Leny Andrade*. She went on to a long and varied career performing jazz, bossa, samba, bolero, and other styles. Her formidable vocal technique, including skillful improvisation and scat singing, is showcased in her 1988 LP *Luz Neon* (Neon Light).

Composer-guitarist-arranger Oscar Castro-Neves (born in Rio in 1940) settled in the 1960s in Los Angeles. He served as music director for Sérgio Mendes's band for ten years, then worked extensively with the Paul Winter Consort in the 1970s and 1980s as a songwriter, guitarist, and co-producer. Oscar's many other credits include scoring films and television shows, and working as a guitarist, arranger or producer for Jobim, Quincy Jones, Lee Ritenour, Flora Purim, and Hubert Laws.

As for Vinícius, his final important collaborator was Antonio Petti Filho, known as Toquinho, whom he met in 1970. Toquinho (born in São Paulo in 1946) is a singer-songwriter and accomplished guitarist who mixes bossa nova with classical-guitar technique and has absorbed influences from Baden Powell, Paulinho Nogueira, and Oscar Castro-Neves.

With Toquinho, Vinícius rediscovered the joy of making music. They worked a lot together, co-writing dozens of memorable tunes in the bossa nova and afro-samba veins, with Toquinho providing the strong melodies and Vinícius adding his inimitable poetic flair. Sharing vocals and often singing in unison, Toquinho and Vinícius performed in concert and recorded sixteen albums together (some in Italy and Argentina). They were remarkably popular as a duo. Such Toquinho–de Moraes tunes as "As Cores de Abril" (The Colors of April) and "Como É Duro Trabalhar" (How Hard It Is to Work) have become standards, heard wherever Brazilians pick up acoustic guitars to sing songs together. Another of their standards is "Aquarela" (Watercolor), in which they sing:

And the future is a spaceship
That we try to pilot
It doesn't have time or pity
Nor an hour of arrival

Their collaboration lasted until Vinícius's death in 1980. After that, Toquinho recorded many solo albums. One of the best was 1985's *A Luz do Solo* (Solo Light), an excellent retrospective of his career up to that point, featuring songs he had written with Vinícius and other artists.

João Gilberto lived in the United States from 1966 to 1980, when he moved back to Rio. Once back home, the shy and reclusive legend rarely gave concerts or interviews. But he continued to be an inspiration for guitarists and singers around the world, and many are the Brazilian musicians who remember the very day, hour, and place where they first heard that strange new song "Chega de Saudade" coming over the radio.

João and Astrud divorced soon after their success, and he was married for a time afterward to

Sérgio Mendes

Sérgio Mendes (born in Niterói in 1941) was a fixture at a very young age in the Beco das Garrafas, where he added his jazz-influenced piano to the ongoing sessions. Early on, he recorded albums such as *Sérgio Mendes & Bossa Rio* and was a participant on jazz-bossa albums with Cannonball Adderley, Herbie Mann, and Paul Winter. In 1964, he moved to the United States and cut an album called *Sérgio Mendes and Brasil 1965*. His sound mixed bossa, American pop, and MPB in a light, upbeat blend, usually with two female vocalists singing in unison, while a drummer—João Palma and Dom Um Romão were two—layed down a trademark crisp, catchy beat.

The Mendes formula was a huge success, starting with his A&M album *Sérgio Mendes & Brasil '66*, which hit number 7 on the pop charts. It went gold, as did his next three records (*Equinox, Look Around,* and *Fool on the Hill*). Mendes's band scored two top 10 singles at that time, as well as a lesser hit with Jorge Benjor's "Mas Que Nada," sung in Portuguese. Sérgio is a bandleader who has been able to surround himself with top-flight musical talent and translate Brazilian sounds for international ears. His albums marked the first times that many foreigners had heard material by Jobim, Benjor (formerly known as Ben), Ivan Lins, Milton Nascimento, Gilberto Gil, and other leading Brazilian songwriters. Mendes stepped out of his usual mold with *Primal Roots*

Sérgio Mendes in the 1970s. *Courtesy of A&M.*

(1972), which included folkloric styles in the mix, and the Grammy-winning *Brasileiro* (1992), which showcased rising Bahian songwriter Carlinhos Brown and fused MPB and Rio samba with axé music and funk.

Mendes and his bands—in their various incarnations—have done more than any other musicians to popularize Brazilian music around the world. From the late 1960s through the 1980s he was the most consistently successful Brazilian recording artist in the United States, his level of sales rivalled only recently by the rock group Sepultura.

the singer Miúcha, the sister of Chico Buarque. Astrud Gilberto (born in Bahia in 1940) continued the career that grew out of her serendipitous appearance on "The Girl from Ipanema" and was a popular solo artist internationally in following decades. João and Astrud's daughter Bebel also later established a career as a singer in Brazil.

After the success of *Getz/Gilberto* and "The Girl from Ipanema," Jobim became a famous name in North America. He was a guest on American television specials, recorded solo albums like *Wave* (1967) and *Tide* (1970), and appeared on two LPs with Frank Sinatra, *Francis Albert Sinatra & Antonio Carlos Jobim* (1967) and *Sinatra and Company* (1973). Tom's music had a profound effect on fans all over the world. Recalled Jobim, "I got so many letters from people saying things like 'I was going to commit suicide, but I heard your music and decided that life was worth living.' "

Jobim didn't stop developing artistically during the heady days of the 1960s. One of his greatest songs was "Aguas de Março" (Waters of March), first recorded in 1972. It incorporates samba and maracatu influences, and its beautifully crafted lyrics consist of an incredible string of images that are as effective in English (Jobim's translation) as they are in the original Portuguese.

A stick, a stone, it's the end of the road
It's the rest of a stump, it's a little alone

**It's a sliver of glass, it is life, it's the sun
It is the night, it is death, it's a trap, it's a
gun
And the riverbank talks of the waters of
March
It's the promise of life, it's the joy in your
heart**

The images wind on and on, vivid and concrete, evoking the deep mystery of life. Recorded by many artists (including Jobim and Elis Regina in a marvelous duet in 1974), the tune is a lively and wistful, a melodic-rhythmic-poetic masterpiece.

From the 1970s on, Tom's lyrics often reflected his love of nature and concern for ecological problems. Songs like "Boto" (Amazonian Porpoise) celebrated nature, while "Borzeguim" called for the protection of all Amazonian life, including its indigenous peoples.

> **Leave the jaguar alive in the forest
> Leave the fish in the water . . .
> Leave the Indian alive
> Leave the Indian alone**

Jobim's music defied classification. One of his greatest works, the 1976 album *Urubu* (named for the Brazilian Black Vulture) was a meeting of MPB, bossa nova, Brazilian regional music (such as the capoeira rhythm), sounds of nature (including simulated bird calls), and classical music. The instrumental compositions on side two (three by Tom and one by his son Paulo Jobim) were performed by an orchestra and were essentially modern impressionistic tone poems. Produced by Claus Ogerman, the LP featured Miúcha on vocals, João Palma on drums, Ray Armando on percussion, and Ron Carter on bass. Jobim's compositions on *Urubu* are part of a rich body of work that rivals, in sophistication and originality, the music of twentieth-century composers such as George Gershwin, Duke Ellington, and Jobim's idol, Heitor Villa-Lobos.

The legendary composer Jobim in the late 1980s. *Photo by Ana Lontra Jobim.*

The Bossa Legacy

As Jobim argued, bossa nova had a huge impact on American music. In fact, it became a permanent subset of jazz, and countless jazz and pop composers would incorporate bossa melodies, harmonies, rhythms, and textures into their songs over the next few decades. And, the guitar would be reinvigorated as a jazz instrument in part because of the inspired playing of João Gilberto, Baden Powell, Luiz Bonfá, Bola Sete, Laurindo Almeida, Oscar Castro-Neves, and the bossa-influenced Charlie Byrd.

The importance of bossa nova in the evolution of Brazilian music itself was also immense. After its golden days, 1958 to 1964, the bossa nova movement lost momentum, but every musician that came after it fed on its sophisticated harmonies. Young musicians who before bossa nova would look for novelties abroad started looking for them inside Brazil, inside themselves. In the years to follow, many artists, when asked about the beginning of their serious interest in music, would answer, "Well, it all started with bossa nova."

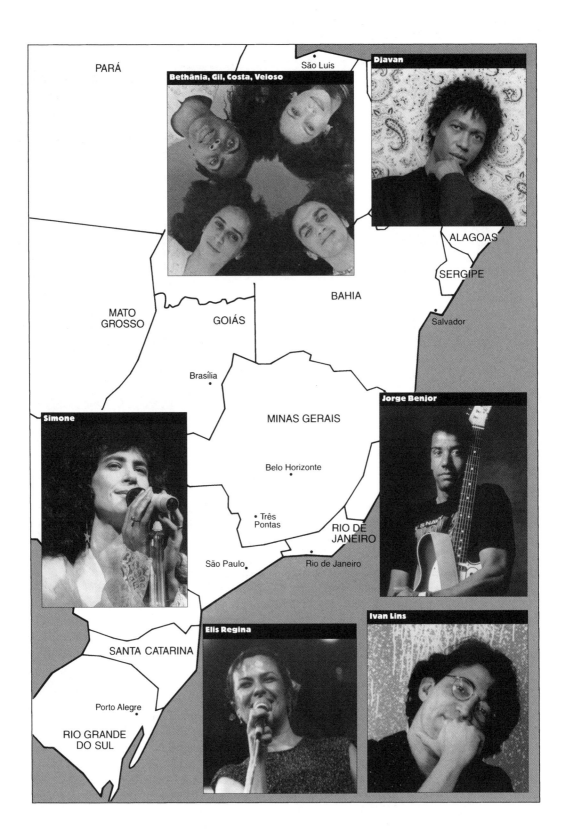

PARÁ

São Luis

Bethânia, Gil, Costa, Veloso

Djavan

ALAGOAS

SERGIPE

BAHIA

MATO GROSSO

GOIÁS

Salvador

Brasília

MINAS GERAIS

Jorge Benjor

Simone

Belo Horizonte

Três Pontas

RIO DE JANEIRO

São Paulo

Rio de Janeiro

SANTA CATARINA

Elis Regina

Ivan Lins

Porto Alegre

RIO GRANDE DO SUL

MPB: A Musical Rainbow

Chapter Four

It could be a fox-trot or even rock
Because on my part there was never any
Prejudice, resentment, or intolerance
I want to be far from those who think like
  that . . .
I prefer Portela with Paulinho's mind
I prefer Elis, Aldir and João Bosco forever
Forever Nazareth, Radamés, and Jobim
I prefer the night with Leni and Luis Eça
After a cold beer, without much hurry

Ivan Lins and Vítor Martins
"Bonito" (Beautiful)

In the late 1960s and early 1970s, a new group of composers and musicians came into prominence in Brazil. Their music was dubbed MPB, an acronym for *música popular brasileira*. It refers to a whole generation of artists such as Edu Lobo, Geraldo Vandré, Elis Regina, Chico Buarque, Milton Nascimento, Dori Caymmi, Simone, Caetano Veloso, Gilberto Gil, Maria Bethânia, Gal Costa, Alceu Valença, Geraldo Azevedo, João Bosco, Ivan Lins, and Djavan.

MPB can refer to Brazilian popular music in general, but it has become a common way to refer to these performers, whose music defies easy categorization. It is intensely eclectic, varying greatly in style from artist to artist, and developed from a collision of bossa nova, regional folk music, protest songs, samba, rock and roll, the Tropicália movement, and other influences. These elements were mixed together in such a way that the final result cannot be placed into any particular genre such as bossa, samba, forró, or rock. Instead, it is a new category, and MPB has proven to be a convenient label for it.

An especially important characteristic of MPB songwriters is their keen ability to combine compelling melodies, rich harmonies, varied rhythms, and poetic lyrics. The popular music that they created from the 1960s through the 1980s is among the best ever produced by one generation in any country in the world. Most of the leading MPB musicians gained national fame in a series of music festivals that began in the mid-1960s and coincided with the early years of a brutal military dictatorship that would rule Brazil for twenty-one years.

The Dark Times

The up-and-coming MPB artists were shaped by the political tumult of the era, which stifled some artists and inspired others. In fact, most MPB stars hit their strides during a time of heavy government repression, and many were exiled, jailed, censored, or otherwise harassed during this time. Theirs was an art sometimes created under great duress.

On March 31, 1964, the right-wing Brazilian military overthrew the government of João (Jango) Goulart. The generals who commanded the takeover said they would stay in charge only for a year, while they "reorganized the country," and then would hold new elections for president. But they ended up retaining power for two decades, until they allowed the Brazilian Congress to elect a civilian president in 1985.

For a few years after the coup there was still some peaceful resistance. However, because the political rights of most union leaders and opposing politicians had been canceled, artists, students, and journalists became the spearheads of opposition. In the streets, students held demonstrations, demanding better universities and democratic elections. The biggest one took place in Rio in 1968 and had over one hundred thousand participants.

75

An early album from Chico Buarque, one of Brazil's greatest songwriters. *Courtesy of RGE.*

Such protests generated a strong and violent reaction from the military, including the invasion of universities and killing of students.

By the end of 1968, the political scene was radicalized to its limit. Fights between rightist and leftist students were frequent. Right-wing terrorist groups like MAC (the Anti-Communist Movement) and CCC (the Communist Hunter Command) had appeared as a counterpoint to leftist demonstrators. In 1968 in São Paulo, CCC members invaded the theater, attacking and beating actors, musicians, and technicians working on singer-songwriter Chico Buarque's play *Roda Viva*.

In Brasília, Congressman Márcio Moreira Alves gave a speech before the chamber of deputies, proposing a boycott against the September 7 Independence Day celebrations. The senior officers of the military considered his words offensive to the armed forces and wanted to put him in jail. Congress, however, denied permission for Alves to be tried. That was the excuse the generals needed for a second and deeper coup. On December 13, 1968, the military implemented Institutional Act No. 5, and Brazil was plunged into the fiercest dictatorship of its history. Congress was closed, all civil rights were banned (anybody could be kept in jail without a trial), and all forms

of press and the arts had to be censored before they reached the public. Acting president General Costa e Silva wielded dictatorial powers.

Politicians, students, artists, and intellectuals were arrested and tortured. Many dissidents "disappeared" and were never found; hundreds or even thousands of citizens were killed—nobody knows the total. Others were forced to leave the country. Many small guerrilla groups rose up to fight the government, but they weren't successful. By 1972 the military had the country firmly in their hands.

Act No. 5 was not revoked until 1978. The following year political prisoners were granted amnesty, marking the beginning of the Brazilian *glasnost* that would only be complete ten years later, with direct elections for president in 1989.

The Festivals Begin: Voices of Protest

Amid the climate of growing fear and repression, the televised music festivals were a vital cultural outlet for many Brazilians. Not only did many musical careers begin there, but for a time (until Act No. 5 in 1968) they were a forum for political dissent—as expressed in song.

The festival era opened in 1965. The first important one was sponsored by the TV Excelsior channel and took place in Guarujá, a beach town in São Paulo state. Generally, at these and later festivals, the television station organized a jury formed of musicians, journalists, and other music industry people. They sorted through tapes sent by applicants and classified those songs that would compete. With the television cameras transmitting, the nominees then performed live before large audiences at arenas and theaters.

The public participated boisterously, cheering for their favorites and booing the others. Audiences responded to songs according to both musical merit and how they related to issues of Brazilian nationalism and politics. The juries picked the winning compositions, and the victorious singers and songwriters were rewarded with trophies, money, and national exposure. First prize at the TV Excelsior festival went to "Arrastão" (Fishing Net), interpreted by a talented young singer named Elis Regina and written by Edu Lobo and Vinícius de Moraes.

Edu Lobo

The young co-author of "Arrastão" was a singer, guitarist, and songwriter. Edu Lobo wrote beautiful, stirring songs that combined regional folk music with bossa nova harmonies. His lyrics protested the injustice and misery of Brazil's Northeast, an area that has suffered more than the rest of the country from poverty and neofeudalism.

Lobo's song "Borandá" (Let's Go), written in 1964 and released on his first album in 1965, was a bossa with a slight northeastern flavor and poignant lyrics bemoaning the terrible droughts in the region.

> **Let's go, the land is dry already**
> **Let's go, the rain won't come**

His 1967 song "Ponteio" (Strumming), written with Capinam, was also a protest song, with words that were a subtle comment on the political repression of the time. "Ponteio," performed by Lobo and Marília Medalha, took first place at the TV Record festival that year.

> **Running in the middle of the world**
> **I never leave my guitar**
> **I'll see new times coming**
> **And a new place to sing**

Born in Rio in 1943, Lobo was proficient in both samba-canção and bossa when he met Carlos Lyra in the mid-sixties. Lobo was impressed by Lyra's new bossa style, which used northeastern musical elements and socially conscious lyrics. Edu began to follow a similar line and— together with singer Regina and the composers Geraldo Vandré and Sérgio Ricardo, among others—he would expand bossa nova's intimate sound into extroverted, epic protest songs that the new military government did not like one bit.

At this time, bossa nova split between the old guard and the new protest singers, and the Brazilian audience became sharply divided in its preferences. Nationalistic music with a clearly Brazilian flavor was set against "foreign" music, such as the rock songs heard on the "Jovem Guarda" (Young Guard) television show in the mid-1960s.

Edu composed many standards: with moviemaker and lyricist Ruy Guerra, Edu wrote "Canção da Terra" (Song of the Earth) and "Reza e Aleluia" (Pray and Say Hallelujah), and with Gianfranceso Guarnieri he composed "Upa Neguinho." Edu's aforementioned "Ponteio," which took first place in the 1967 TV Record Festival, was the last protest song to win a festival. From then on, censorship and the general hopelessness of the country dramatically reduced the number of such tunes performed at these events.

The political climate in Brazil convinced Edu to leave. In 1969 he moved to the United States, where he appeared on Paul Desmond's album *From the Hot Afternoon* (which included four Lobo songs). He returned to Brazil in 1971 and since then has concentrated on writing music for plays, movies, and ballets. After many years, he began to record again, releasing fine albums like *Meia-Noite* (Midnight) in 1995.

Geraldo Vandré

Singer-songwriter Geraldo Vandré, as mentioned above, was another musician who was shaking and stirring the bossa in a radical way. Vandré was the artistic last name of Geraldo Pedrosa de Araújo Dias, born in 1935 in João Pessoa, Paraíba. Geraldo, whose first guitar teacher was João Gilberto, incorporated many folkloric genres into his music, among them toada, frevo, moda, *baião*, and *aboio*. He said he interpreted these styles in a "more ideologic than formal way," meaning he used them to create protest songs that had strong, angry lyrics.

Vandré's "ideological" adaptations had a distinctly progressive edge in part because of the creative virtuosity of his backup bands. In 1966 and 1967, he worked with Quarteto Novo (New Quartet), a now-legendary group that included Hermeto Pascoal on flute, Airto Moreira on percussion, and Heraldo do Monte and Théo de Barros on guitars. Then, in 1968, he was backed by Quarteto Livre (Free Quartet), which included percussionist Naná Vasconcelos and guitarist Geraldo Azevedo. Most of the musicians in Vandré's groups went on to become stars in their own right.

Vandré's songs, performed by others, took first place in two festivals in 1966. "Porta-Estandarte (Standard-Bearer), written with Fernando Lona, captured the TV Excelsior event, where it was performed by Tuca and Airto. And Vandré and de Barros's "Disparada" (Stampede), sung by Jair Rodrigues, tied for first place in the TV Record contest. "Disparada" was a toada that told the story of a northeastern *vaqueiro* (cowboy) who is enraged that he and the other vaqueiros are treated like cattle.

> **We mark, drive, brand**
> **Fatten and kill the herd**
> **But with people it's different**

For his fiery protest songs, Vandré became a national hero, more famous even than Lobo. Armed only with his guitar, he was perceived as a serious threat by the military government.

Vandré's masterpiece, "Prá Não Dizer Que Não Falei de Flores" (Not to Say I Didn't Speak of Flowers), also known by the shorter name of "Caminhando" (Walking), was considered by Brazilian journalist Millôr Fernandes as a "Brazilian 'Marseillaise,' the true national anthem."

> **There are armed soldiers, they may be**
> **loved or not**
> **Almost all of them lost, with guns in their**
> **hands**
> **In the barracks they are taught an old lesson**
> **To die for their country**
> **And to live a meaningless life**

"Caminhando" took second place in Rio's third annual FIC, Festival Internacional da Canção (International Song Festival), in 1968. Vandré's provocative song was subsequently banned by the censors for ten years. In the October 10, 1968, edition of the *Correio da Manhã* newspaper, General Luis de Franca Oliveira presented his reasons for the prohibition of "Caminhando." He cited its "subversive lyrics, its offensiveness to the armed forces, and the fact that it would serve as a slogan for student demonstrations."

He was right. Even after it was banned, "Caminhando" never ceased to be sung wherever there were people who resisted the dictatorship. It was still heard at protests at the end of the 1970s, when Brazilian society started to challenge the government, demanding a return to democracy.

Once Act No. 5 was invoked, Geraldo had to leave Brazil to ensure his personal safety. From 1969 to 1973, he wandered through Chile, Algeria, Greece, Austria, Bulgaria, and finally France—where he made his only record during this time, *Das Terras do Benvirá*. When he returned to Brazil in 1973, he was arrested as soon as he arrived. A month later he was released from jail and appeared on a national news program saying, among other things, that he hoped he could integrate his latest songs with the new Brazilian reality and that the connection made between his music and certain political groups had been made against his will.

This public statement was probably the price he had to pay to be allowed to remain in the country. After that, Geraldo recorded no more new songs and got rid of his stage name, Vandré. After seven albums, Geraldo's short but incandescent career was over. Eventually, there was only Geraldo Dias, the lawyer. Nevertheless he'll always be remembered as the author of songs that make one want to stand and fight for what is right.

Chico Buarque and Elba Ramalho. *Photo by Livio Campos. Courtesy of PolyGram.*

Chico Buarque the Poet

The 1966 TV Record festival ended in a tie for first place between "Disparada" by Vandré and "A Banda" (The Band), performed by bossa nova muse Nara Leão and a newcomer, singer-songwriter Chico Buarque de Hollanda. With his melancholy, nasal voice, Chico sang beautifully crafted, extremely literate sambas and marchas. He soon became very popular and would ultimately be considered one of the greatest lyricists of all time in Brazilian popular music.

Born in Rio in 1944 but raised in São Paulo and Italy, Chico achieved national acclaim when he released his first three albums in the mid-1960s. He was considered an heir apparent to the great samba-canção composers of the 1930s like Noel Rosa, and his popularity was the only thing that almost all of polarized Brazil agreed about: Chico was the man every woman wanted to marry and every man admired. To many he seemed the true defender of traditional Brazilian music against the

furious attack of protest songs, the aesthetical revolution proposed by Tropicália (the musical movement led by Gilberto Gil and Caetano Veloso), and the alien electric guitars in the music of Jovem Guarda rockers Roberto Carlos and Erasmo Carlos.

Chico found his path composing traditional sambas like "A Rita," "Olê Olá," and "Pedro Pedreiro" (Pedro the Bricklayer), and marchas like "A Banda." In "A Banda," Buarque depicts music as a force that rejuvenates and spreads happiness, but only temporarily, while the band plays on.

> **But to my disenchantment, what was sweet ran out**
> **Everything back in its place, after the band had passed**
> **And each back in his corner, and in each corner sorrow**
> **After the band had passed, singing songs of love**

Chico's early lyrics were subtle yet powerful, and

often strongly nostalgic. Short excerpts do them little justice because they were intricately constructed, building themes and ideas over many verses. They almost always told about good things that had already gone by. Maybe that explains his enormous success: the present was so insecure that listening to a talented young musician who praised the past and reverently revived old Brazilian musical genres gave people hope that soon things would return to the good old days. Such songs were very popular. Old or young, rich or poor, communist or capitalist, everybody loved Chico, the nice green-eyed young singer . . . until around 1968.

Chico didn't like being idolized. He felt used and abused, and his answer to his fans' blind devotion came in 1968 in the form of a play: *Roda Viva* (an expression that means "commotion"). The drama tells the story of a young pop star who is devoured by the public. Literally. During the performance of the play, actors offered "pieces" of the star's "liver" to the audience. That caused a scandal, and an extreme backlash from conservatives. In São Paulo, CCC right-wing extremists invaded the theater and beat the actors. In Porto Alegre, after the first night, members of the cast were told to leave the city or they would be killed. Government censors immediately prohibited any further performances. *Roda Viva* marked the death of "nice guy" Chico Buarque.

While Buarque was angering the government with his play, Gilberto Gil and Caetano Veloso were attacking him for the formal conservativism of his music. Chico was no longer the national choice. After the *Roda Viva* debacle, Chico went to Italy, staying there for over a year and playing on European stages with such disparate performers as Josephine Baker and Toquinho.

In 1970, Chico was the first of the exiled MPB musicians to return to Brazil. Although he wasn't arrested, he was a favorite target for the censors. In 1971, only one out of every three songs he wrote was approved by them. Some passed and then were censored later. For example, "Apesar de Você" (In Spite of You) was banned after it became a hit. The censors must have missed the irony in the lyrics that were obviously directed toward the government.

In spite of you
Tomorrow is going to be another day
I ask you where you are going
To hide from the immense euphoria

In 1971, Chico recorded his fifth album, *Construção* (Construction). It was a dramatic record that represented a break in his career. Nostalgic subjects give way to an almost hallucinatory treatment of the disappointments and tragedies of everyday life. Buarque vividly evokes the dehumanization caused by work, marriage, routine, the system.

In the album's title song, blaring, edgy horns build tension and the percussion keeps a steady, ominous "tick-tock" beat. The lyrics describe the last day of a bricklayer who dies in the middle of the road after falling from a window.

He tripped over the sky as if he heard music
And floated in the air as if it might be
Sunday
And ended up on the ground like a timid
bundle
Agonized, shipwrecked in the middle of the
sidewalk
Died on the wrong side of the street
disturbing the public

When they returned from exile in the early 1970s, Veloso and Gil patched up their friendship with Buarque, which had been badly shaken for a time because of aesthetic differences. Soon after, Chico recorded a live album with Veloso and then in 1973 wrote "Cálice" (Chalice) with Gil. Using powerful Catholic religious imagery, the song is a metaphorical comment on the repressive times and the silencing of an entire nation.

> **How to drink this bitter drink**
> **Gulp down the pain, swallow the drudgery**
> **Though my mouth is quiet, my breast**
> **   remains**
> **No one hears the silence in the city . . .**
> **Father, take this cup away from me**

The song's title carries two meanings: "Cálice" translates as "chalice" yet is also a homophone of the phrase *cale-se*, which means "shut up." And that is exactly what the authorities did to Buarque and Gil when they first attempted to perform "Cálice" in public. The police came on stage and turned off the microphones as they were singing. The song was banned, but it became yet another anthem against the dictatorship.

The censors continued to hound Buarque for the next several years, and in 1974 and 1975 practically none of the songs that he wrote met with their approval and made it on record. Brazilians came to regard Chico as a symbol of cultural resistance, even though little of his work actually reached the public. At one point, Buarque apparently gave up trying to get his own material through and instead recorded only covers on his 1974 album *Sinal Fechado* (Red Light). The record included the title song by Paulinho da Viola (which actually was a clever, coded protest) and tunes by Veloso, Gil, Noel Rosa, Toquinho, and an unknown newcomer: Julinho da Adelaide. The press material for the album included a biography for Julinho and described him as a sambista from the morro. His song "Acorda Amor" (Wake Up, Love) had a theme of fear of the police. Trouble was,

Julinho didn't exist—he was an alter ego for Chico and the truth was soon discovered. From then on, any composer sending a song to the censors had to include a copy of his or her identification card.

In the 1980s, the goverment censors became more lenient. Buarque began including formerly banned songs along with new ones on his albums such as 1981's *Almanaque* (Almanac). By this time, Chico had turned into an eclectic composer, writing marchas, fados, waltzes, and even rock tunes, but his main style was still samba. Throughout the decade his songwriting partners varied greatly; he worked with Francis Hime, Gil, Sivuca, Nascimento, Toquinho, and Jobim, among others. Buarque's lyrics continued to use subtle irony and evocative imagery, contrast dreams with reality, and artfully blend the comic with the tragic. Often, he reflected on existential matters, as in "Vida" (Life), from 1980.

> **Look what I've done**
> **I left life's sweetest slice**
> **On the table of men with empty lives**
> **But, life, at that time**
> **Who knows, I was happy**

And Chico also devoted many songs to romantic matters, giving love an ironic, knowing treatment, as in "Deixa a Menina" (Let the Girl Go).

> **Behind a sad man there's always a happy**
> **   woman**
> **And behind that woman a thousand men,**
> **   always so genteel**

Vinícius de Moraes, one of Buarque's greatest fans, said that Chico "is a phenomenon who accomplished the perfect union of both cultivated and popular culture."

Elis Regina

Not all of the artists who gained prominence at the music festivals were highly politicized singer-songwriters. Many were simply talented musicians who delved into controversial material only on occasion, or never at all. An example of the latter was Elis Regina, the young female singer who sang "Arrastão," the winning entry at the TV Excelsior event.

Born in 1945 in Porto Alegre, Elis Regina Carvalho da Costa was only twenty years old when she took first place at the festival. Yet by this time she had already gained some recognition for her appearances on various television programs, where her impassioned singing style was the opposite of subdued bossa nova behavior. The TV Excelsior victory helped propel her to the top, and her contagious energy and strongly emotional interpretations soon made Elis a big star in Brazil.

She recorded bossa, samba, and the new eclectic songs of the emerging MPB composers. She co-hosted the television show "O Fino da Bossa" (The Best of Bossa) with singer Jair Rodrigues from 1965 to 1967 and the MPB television show "Som Livre Exportação" (Free Sound Exportation) with Ivan Lins in 1970 and 1971. She also staged ingenious live shows that harmoniously blended music and theater.

Elis had a remarkable ability to find talented new composers. She was the first to record songs by Lins, Milton Nascimento, João Bosco, and Belchior, all of whom would later achieve great renown. During her very successful career, some of Regina's biggest hits were Lins's "Madalena," Renato Teixeira's "Romaria" (Pilgrimage), Lobo's "Upa Neguinho" (Hey Black Boy), Belchior's "Como Nossos Pais" (Like Our Parents), Bosco and Blanc's "O Bebado e a Equilibrista" (The Drunkard and the Acrobat), and Jobim's "Águas de Março" (Waters of March).

But the charismatic singer's life was cut tragically short by a cocaine overdose in 1982, just as her artistic abilities were in full flower. Most critics and MPB fans in Brazil considered her the most important Brazilian singer of her time. For many years after her death, one could find the words *Elis vive* (Elis lives) in graffiti on the walls of Brazilian cities.

Nana Caymmi and Dori Caymmi

The 1966 International Song Festival (FIC) in Rio was won by Nana Caymmi, a young vocalist who was the daughter of the legendary Bahian composer Dorival Caymmi. She triumphed with the tune "Saveiros" (Fishing Boats), written by Nelson Motta and Nana's younger brother, Dori Caymmi. Nana (born in 1941) is a sophisticated, jazz-influenced singer who has long been a favorite of Brazilian musicians, Nana has a deep, soulful voice that is wonderful for interpretations. A good example of her expressiveness is her

Elis Regina performing at the Montreux Jazz Festival. *Courtesy of Tropical Storm/WEA.*

vocal on "Velho Piano" (Old Piano) on her brother's album *Dori Caymmi*, in which she marvelously captures the shifting tensions, complex modulations, and intricate rhythms in the composition. She has recorded many fine solo albums as well as joint LPs with the rest of the Caymmi family. Among the cognoscenti of Rio and São Paulo, Nana is a cult favorite.

Dori Caymmi (born in 1943) is one of the most accomplished arrangers, composers, and guitarists of his generation. Don Grusin, a composer and producer who often collaborated with Brazilian musicians in the 1980s, said of Dori that "his melodies are my favorite melodies in the world and some of his chords are too." Grusin noted that, on his guitar, Dori often "tunes the top E down to a B, so that he has a double B. Then he makes these cluster chords by putting one finger on the top string and the second finger just one fret off, and he gets minor-second clusters." Grusin observed that such tonal effects were also favored by Ravel and Debussy. "It's a way to make the harmonic basis a lot more interesting."

Caymmi's musical arrangements in the late 1960s reveal his many talents. He arranged the debut albums of Caetano Veloso and Gilberto Gil; had his songs recorded by Nascimento, Jobim, Djavan, Regina, and Maria Bethânia; and wrote scores for movies and plays. Dori's music is a collection of impressionistic images, mixing Brazilian rhythms with influences from Bill Evans, Villa-Lobos, Debussy, and Ravel. "I'm pretty much the guy who looks at nature and makes my portraits. I use my music like a painter," he said.

In 1987, he arranged jazz singer Sarah Vaughan's album *Brazilian Romance*, which featured five of Dori's compositions and was nominated for a Grammy award. With the release in 1988 of *Dori Caymmi*, his first record in the

Dori Caymmi. *Photo by Diego Uchitel. Courtesy of Qwest/WEA.*

United States, Dori earned a wider audience outside Brazil. He sang and played guitar on the album, which was intensely lyrical and richly textured, perfectly expressing Dori's unique style.

Tropicália

As the music festivals entered their third year, they continued to launch new artists. In 1967, it was the time of Gilberto Gil and Caetano Veloso, who used this forum to kick off a radical new musical movement: Tropicália.

By this time, these events had become a national craze. The streets of Brazil would be deserted on festival nights because everybody would be home watching them on television, just as they did when big soccer games took place. The audience behavior at the concerts was also similar to that of soccer fans at stadiums such as Maracaña. Those attending the festivals would go to the theater to support their favorites with banners and applause and try to disturb the "enemies."

When Veloso performed his Tropicália anthem "Alegria Alegria" (Joy Joy) at the TV Record

Caetano Veloso performing at Rio's Canecão arena in 1989. Photo by Livio Campos. Courtesy of PolyGram.

event that year, he was booed. Much of the audience was intensely nationalistic. They revered "authentically" Brazilian music and detested what symbolized U.S. colonialism. To them, "Alegria Alegria" was Americanized because it was a rock song and Veloso was backed by a rock group, Os Beat Boys. Many also didn't respond to its strange, fragmented imagery.

> **Walking against the wind**
> **Without handkerchief, without documents**
> **In the almost December sun, I go**
> **The sun scatters into spaceships,**
>   **guerrillas . . .**
> **Teeth, legs, flags, the bomb, and Brigitte**
>   **Bardot**

Gil's entry, "Domingo no Parque" (Sunday in the Park), received a much warmer response, in part because it wasn't rock and roll. But it was something markedly different. It included a Bahian capoeira rhythm, electric instrumentation, and cinematic lyrics. The song was arranged by Rogério Duprat, a Paulista who had a solid background in both classical and experimental electronic music. He was willing to add his experience as an avant-garde musician to the popular music being made by the Tropicalistas.

The arrangement was influenced by the Beatles' "A Day in the Life" from their 1967 *Sgt. Pepper's* album. When Gil wrote "Domingo," he was listening over and over to the Beatles' song, which he says was "my myth of the time." Gil then created an equally fascinating song, in which Bahia met George Martin (and Rogério Duprat).

At the TV Record Festival, the winning song was Edu Lobo's "Ponteio" (Strumming). The jury put "Domingo no Parque" and "Alegria Alegria" into second and fourth places, respectively. But those tunes had an enormous impact and introduced Tropicália music to the public. In the liner notes of the retrospective *Grandes Nomes: Caetano*, music critic Tárik de Souza wrote about Veloso's performance: "The introduction of electric instruments to Brazilian popular music, until then unplugged, the new costumes, made of plastic, the bristling hair of the performers and the aggressive stage performances, making a stark contrast with the acoustic guitar and the quietude of bossa nova, were elements that changed definitely the course of Brazilian popular music."

When Gilberto Gil and Caetano Veloso—both from Bahia—moved to São Paulo in 1965 and were exposed to the burgeoning, heady arts scene there and in Rio de Janeiro, they developed the idea of creating an iconoclastic mixture of music in which everything would have its space. Luiz Gonzaga, the Beatles, João Gilberto, Chuck Berry, film director Jean-Luc Godard: everything would be cannibalized and put into the stew. Their lyrics would be sometimes poignant, other times surreal, always provocative.

In Tropicália, anything went: rock and samba, *berimbaus* and electronic instruments, folk music and urban noise, the erudite and the kitsch. There had been rock and roll in Brazil since the late 1950s, but this was the first time it was being mixed with native styles (and much else).

Tropicália was not only a musical phenomenon. It was an entire arts movement, which lasted roughly from 1967 to 1969. It manifested itself in music, theater, poetry, and the plastic arts. The word Tropicália came from a 1967 ambient-art piece by Hélio Oiticica. Some of the Tropicalistas' ideas had precedents in the works of the *Paulista* poet Oswald de Andrade, who four decades earlier had created the concept of artistic cannibalism, which he discussed in his 1928 "Manifesto Antropofágico" (Cannibalistic Manifesto). Gil and Veloso took Andrade's ideas to heart, devouring everything—national music and themes and imported cultural elements—and then re-elaborating it all "with autonomy," as Andrade had urged. "Power to the imagination" and "Down with [aesthetic] prejudice" were slogans that inspired Tropicália. Other musicians who participated in the movement included Júlio Medaglia (another classical conductor), Gal Costa, Torquato Neto, Os Mutantes, Capinam, and Tom Zé.

Zé (Antonio José Santana Martins) had studied classical music with the renowned professors Ernst Widmer (a follower of Igor Stravinsky and Béla Bartók), Walter Smetak (who later tutored Uakti in the construction of strange, original instruments), and Hans Joachim Koellreutter (who had taught Jobim). In his own quirky, experimental music, Zé used everyday objects (typewriters, blenders, floor polishers) in his orchestrations and combined avant-garde music with northeastern styles. Years later, in the liner notes for his 1992 album *The Hips of Tradition*, Zé described his music as "a mixture of Schoenberg, Beethoven, and Jackson do Pandeiro."

Musically and lyrically, Tropicalista songs were intelligent and often ironic montages. One of its most representative songs was Gil and Neto's "Geléia Geral" (General Jelly), which mixed *bumba-meu-boi*, a folkloric style from Maranhão, with electric rock instrumentation. In the

song's lyrics, the traditional ("sweet *mulata*," "Mangueira where samba is purer," and "saintly Bahian baroque") was juxtaposed with the modern ("TV," "Formiplac and the azure sky," and "I get a jet, travel, explode").

Rogério Duprat's arrangements punctuated and stressed the contemporary and traditional references. For example, he added tamborim percussion when the samba school Portela was mentioned. To further add to the mix, the word *bumba-meu-boi* was juxtaposed ironically with *iê-iê-iê* (yeah-yeah-yeah), the pejorative name given by Brazilian critics to 1960s rock and roll.

> **In the general jelly**
> **That *Jornal do Brasil* announces**
> **It's bumba-iê-iê-boi**
> **Next year, last month**
> **It's bumba-iê-iê-iê**
> **It's the same dance, meu-boi**

Not all the public understood what Gil and Veloso were doing. Many of them hated it. They didn't like the rock and roll part of it; they didn't like the electric guitars. When Veloso presented his latest outrage in 1968 in São Paulo, during the International Song Festival, he was booed even more loudly than he had been for "Alegria Alegria." He appeared with the rock group Os Mutantes (the Mutants), who were dressed in plastic clothes, and performed "É Proibido Proibir" (Forbidding Is Forbidden). He didn't get to finish the song, but he did give a famous extemporaneous speech castigating his intolerant audience, saying, "You are the youth who will always kill tomorrow the old enemy that died yesterday! You can't understand anything."

Tropicália opened a temporary gap between the political avant-garde and cultural avant-garde, but by the early 1970s its ideas would be quite acceptable. Tropicália songs were aesthetically daring and

Clockwise from bottom left: **Maria Bethânia, Gilberto Gil, Gal Costa, and Caetano Veloso on the cover of their collective LP.**

sporadically brilliant and included a few master-pieces such as "Domingo no Parque." Ironically, the most controversial Tropicália tunes—the ones with the strongest rock and roll influence—were generally the weakest of the bunch. The movement had a brief life (it was over by 1969), but it greatly accelerated MPB's musical experimentation and hybridization and gave all musicians who came after it a greater sense of creative freedom.

Gilberto Gil

The creativity of Gilberto Gil by no means ended once the Tropicália years were over; in the years afterward, he continued to experiment with new musical styles, blending international pop music (rock, funk, reggae) with Brazilian urban and rural music in his own singular extroverted, up-beat style.

Born in 1942 in Salvador, Gil spent his child-hood and adolescence in the small town of Itu-açu, in the interior of Bahia state. There he ab-sorbed a wide variety of influences: Luiz Gonzaga, classical music, polka, Italian music, fado, Celia Cruz, mambo, samba, bolero, Yma Sumac, Duke Ellington, Miles Davis, and Chet Baker. Gil's first instrument was the accordion, then he switched to guitar after hearing a startling new song on the radio: João Gilberto's "Chega de Saudade."

After studying business administration at the federal university in Salvador (where he met Veloso and Bethânia) and working a brief stint for a multinational corporation in São Paulo, Gil be-came a full-time professional musician. His recording career kicked off in 1965 with a single containing the folkish protest tunes "Roda" (Wheel) and "Procissão" (Procession). In 1966, Elis Regina and Jair Rodrigues recorded the Gil–Torquato Neto tune "Louvação" (Praise),

and it was a big success. Gil began to appear reg-ularly on the "O Fino da Bossa" television show and soon proved that he was a charismatic per-former with a lilting voice.

As the Tropicália movement took off in 1967, Gil released his first album, *Louvação*. Gil, Veloso, and the other Tropicalistas succeeded in irritating the military dictatorship, who feared that the movement might sway Brazilian youth toward an alternate lifestyle involving drugs, chãos, and hippiedom. Gil was jailed in 1969 but never charged with a specific crime. "Just for being dif-ferent," recalled Gil, "unexpected, daring, bold, adventurous, unknown, and dangerous." He laughed. "I never considered my lyrics and every-thing as really heavy. Never. My attitude—okay. But my words . . ."

In prison, Gil took up yoga, meditation, and a macrobiotic diet. Once out, he left for England, as did Veloso, and lived there in a self-imposed ex-ile until 1972. When he returned to Brazil, both the government and nationalist-minded Brazil-ians were not as critical of Gil and his Tropicalista peers. Their rock-and-roll–flavored music was no longer seen as subversive by the Right or cultur-ally imperialistic by the Left. It was instead viewed as healthy experimentation.

Gilberto Gil in the 1980s. *Photo by Livio Campos. Courtesy of Braziloid.*

The world was changing and Gil set his sights on the future. In "Expresso 2222" he sang of a train traveling from a Rio suburb to modernity.

The 2222 Express started running
From the central station of Brazil
It goes directly from Bonsucesso
To beyond the year 2000

From that point on, Gil began to delve heavily into his Afro-Brazilian roots and to incorporate them into his global pop fusions. In 1977 he attended the Festival of Black Art and Culture in Lagos, Nigeria; it was an experience that profoundly affected him. In Lagos, Gil met Fela Kuti, Stevie Wonder, and other African descendents from all over the world. "That caused something shaking, emotional, very intuitive, telluric. Like being replanted in the soil of Africa and then being able to flourish as a new tree," he told us.

Gil expanded his exploration of African culture. *Refavela* (Re-Favela) in 1977 included "Baba Alapalá" (an homage to the candomblé god Xangô), the marvelous afoxé "Patuscada de Gandhi" (Revelry of the Filhos de Gandhi), the use of Yoruba words in several songs, and the marked influence of Nigerian musical forms like *highlife* and ju-ju. Gil's self-immersion at this time in his African roots paralleled the rise in Salvador of *blocos afro* (Afro-Brazilian Carnaval groups). His participation in Bahia's "re-

Africanization" helped propel the whole process.

Gil's following albums experimented with a variety of song styles. He blended funk and afoxé in "Toda Menina Baiana" (Every Bahian Girl) in 1978. Numerous tunes were based in reggae, including "Vamos Fugir" (Let's Escape), recorded with the Wailers in 1984. Many songs added Brazilian touches to rock and technopop. Gil's acute lyrics critiqued society, while his rhythmic blends continued to break new ground. Indeed, Gil has been creating what was later labeled "world music" beginning with "Domingo no Parque."

In the late 1980s, Gil became involved in politics, taking two years off from music to serve as the secretary of culture and on the city council for the city of Salvador. After returning to the recording studio, he hit another artistic peak with *Parabolicamará* (1991), a rootsy yet high-tech effort that blends *samba-reggae, samba de roda*, capoeira, and funk. It yielded the joyful tune "Madalena," a huge hit that year in Carnaval.

Caetano Veloso

Caetano Veloso (Caetano Emanuel Vianna Telles Veloso) was born in 1942 in Santo Amaro da Purificação, Bahia. As a singer, he was heavily influenced by his idol, João Gilberto. As a composer, Caetano has had an extrãordinary ability to weave poetry and melody together so seam-

Chico Buarque and Caetano Veloso, in concert on their television show "Chico & Caetano." *Courtesy of Som Livre.*

lessly that it is difficult to imagine them separately. He is always ready to try new musical paths; for example, he was the first Brazilian artist to incorporate reggae elements into a song, which he did in 1972 in a rock tune called "Nine Out of Ten." Yet in his own way, Veloso has been quite nationalistic with regard to music. He is famous for his knowledge of old Brazilian songs and aided in the comebacks of venerable figures like Luiz Gonzaga, the king of baião, who had been forgotten during the sixties.

Throughout that decade and those that followed, Caetano would embrace old styles and create new ones. *Domingo* (Sunday), his debut 1967 album with Gal Costa, was mostly bossa nova, with Veloso obviously following the path of João Gilberto. The collaborative montage of the *Tropicália* LP came the next year. In 1969, he recorded "Atrás do Trio Elétrico" (Behind the Electric Trio), which captured the sound of the musicians who play kinetic frevos atop sound trucks called *trios elétricos* during Carnaval in Salvador.

But the government did not view him as nationalistic in an acceptable sense. Caetano—like Gilberto Gil—disturbed the authorities with his Tropicalista "chaos." He was imprisoned by the regime for four months in 1969, before a two-year exile in London. When he came home, leftists who had neither understood nor liked Caetano during Tropicália tried to adopt him as a symbol of resistance to the government, as they had with Chico Buarque. Caetano destroyed this idea in his first show by dancing on stage like Carmen Miranda, shocking both the Left and the Right. Brazil was not ready for such androgynous behavior. The military kept Gil and Veloso under surveillance. But in the

recording studio Caetano was equally unconventional. His 1972 album *Araçá Azul* combined static, folkloric music, and incidental noise (it was one of the worst-selling albums of all time by a big-name MPB artist). Since then, Veloso's work has ranged freely from iconoclastic compositions to romantic, lyrical ballads. His songs frequently focus on themes of self-renewal and expanded possibilities. The song "O Quereres" (What You Want) from 1984 is quintessential Veloso.

> **Where you want the act, I am spirit . . .**
> **Where you want romance, [I am] rock'n'roll**
> **Where you want the moon, I am the sun**
> **Where you want pure nature, [I am]**
> **insecticide**

"My role is to change people's minds," he has said, and his lyrics are often provocative and discursive, as in "Ele Me Deu um Beijo na Boca" (He Gave Me a Kiss on the Mouth), a 1982 song of many verses that Caetano conceived as an imaginary dialogue with a friend covering life, politics, music, art, spirituality.

> **He gave me a kiss on the mouth and told**
> **me**
> **Life is empty like the bonnet of a headless**
> **baby**
> **Like the burrow of a drunken fox**
> **And I laughed like crazy**
> **And said enough of this talk, this bottomless**
> **well**

Caetano has explored rock, bossa, afoxé, frevo, reggae, and other genres, counterpointing his inquistive words and delicate, Gilberto-influenced vocals. Mass popular acceptance came in the 1980s, when Caetano went from cult figure to full-fledged star in Brazil. He co-hosted a television musical show with Chico Buarque ("Chico & Caetano") and had his songs covered extensively by other artists. Near the end of the decade, he recorded albums such as *Caetano* and *Estrangeiro* (Foreigner) that found him still on his searching, wondering path.

Estrangeiro illustrates Caetano's "turbulent poetry" (critic Stephen Holden's phrase) with the harsh electric guitar of Arto Lindsay and a biting, rock-oriented production by Lindsay and Peter Sherer that often evokes a cold, unsettling mood. One of the songs, "Os Outros Românticos" (The Other Romantics) has a sense of impending apocalypse.

> **They were the other romantics, in darkness**
> **They made a cult of another middle age**
> **Located in the future not in the past**
> **Being incapable of following**
> **The blah blah blah of economics recited on**
> **   television**
> **These irreducible atheists simulated a**
> **   religion**
> **And the Spirit was the sex of Pixote**
> **In the voice of some German rock singer**
> **With hatred for those who killed Pixote by**
> **   hand**
> **They nurtured rebellion and revolution**

There are references in the song to the Hector Babenco film *Pixote* (1980), which is about a homeless boy in Rio and his tragic and violent life. Fernando Ramos da Silva, who played the protagonist, Pixote, was himself living on the streets before becoming an actor; he followed his character's fate when he was killed by police in São Paulo in 1987. *Estrangeiro* won high praise from foreign critics: Stephen Holden and Jon Pareles of the *New York Times* both picked it as one of the top albums of 1989. An in-depth analysis of Veloso's lyrics is provided by Charles Perrone's academic study *Masters of Contemporary Brazilian Song*, which looks at the song texts of several major MPB composers.

Gal Costa

Another participant in Tropicália was singer Gal Costa (Maria da Graça Costa Penna Burgos), born in 1945 in Salvador. Wearing beads, necklaces, and colorful blouses, Gal was the female singer

Gal Costa. *Courtesy of BMG.*

Maria Bethânia. *Courtesy of BMG.*

Roberto Carlos and Erasmo Carlos, Luis Melodia, and Jorge Benjor. In the early years of her career, Gal's naturally beautiful voice could sometimes be raucous and uncontrolled, especially on rock or blues-based numbers. But she worked hard to improve her technique and developed a well-tuned voice that can be poignant or aggressive, gentle or piercing.

Throughout her career, she has recorded in a variety of song styles, including samba, baião, frevo, blues, and rock. She has released thematic albums like 1976's *Gal Canta Caymmi* (all Dorival Caymmi songs), 1988's *Aquarela do Brasil* (Ary Barroso tunes), and 1995's *Mina D'Água do Meu Canto* (material by Veloso and Buarque). One of Gal's most popular songs was her version of the Moraes Moreira–Abel Silva frevo "Festa do Interior" (Party in the Interior), the huge hit of the 1982 Carnaval season and part of the double-platinum album *Fantasia* (which can translate as "costume" or "fantasy"). Later albums saw Gal continue to expand her repertoire, recording tunes by everyone from Cole Porter to Carlinhos Brown.

Maria Bethânia

It should not be surprising that, like Gal Costa, vocalist Maria Bethânia has also been closely linked with Gil and Veloso throughout her career, since she is Caetano's sister. Maria (Maria Vianna Telles Veloso) was the first of the foursome to gain fame. With her eloquent, sensuous voice, she quickly attracted attention as a singer. In 1965, she recorded João do Vale's hard-hitting protest song "Carcará" and became nationally known as an intense, passionate vocalist. That same year she replaced Nara Leão in the famous protest play *Opinião*.

Born in 1946 in the town of Santo Amaro da

most involved with the movement, which she later termed "political" because of its emphasis on transforming behavior. Indeed, in the years afterward, Gal's artistic career and lifestyle were symbols, in a way, of the openness and freedom that Tropicália sought: she was a hippie, a sophisticated torchsinger, a Carnaval celebrant, and an audacious sex symbol.

From the Tropicália days through the 1980s, Gal would work in close collaboration on many albums with Gil and Veloso, her friends from Bahia. In 1967, she made her recording debut with the *Domingo* album with Veloso. In 1968 she appeared on the *Tropicália* collective album and also released her first solo LP, *Gal Costa*.

While Gil and Veloso were living in exile, Gal was their spokesperson and would record their songs in Brazil. She also interpreted tunes by

Purificação, Bethânia was largely a cult figure—like Caetano—until 1978. A small but faithful group of fans would attend her shows, in which she would perform barefoot, walking and running around the stage, reciting poetry and singing theatrically, capturing the hearts and minds of the audience with her magnetism. She did not seem to want stardom and did not even take part in Tropicália. Keeping away from groups, she was nicknamed "Rio's Greta Garbo." But Maria's 1978 album *Alibi* marked a turning point in her career. Her interpretations of romantic ballads by Chico Buarque, Gonzaguinha, and others so pleased the public that the LP eventually sold more than one million copies, the first time an album by a female recording artist had done that in Brazil.

The album's success started a trend wherein female singers became the biggest record sellers: Bethânia, Costa, Simone, Clara Nunes, Beth Carvalho, and others sold million of records in the late 1970s and early 1980s. After that, Maria became the female counterpoint to Roberto Carlos; she was the queen and he was the king of Brazilian romantic music. Appropriately, her 1993 album *As Cançoes Que Você Fez Pra Mim* (The Songs You Made for Me) was dedicated entirely to the compositions of Robert Carlos and Erasmo Carlos.

An artist who started by singing for small, elite audiences, Maria became an idol who sang sentimental songs for legions of fans and provided the background music for many a Brazilian romantic rendezvous. Yet her albums have consistently ventured into interesting new territory, including guest artists such as Carlinhos Brown, French actress Jeanne Moreau, and South African vocal group Ladysmith Black Mambazo.

Jorge Benjor: Rhythm and Samba

Jorge Benjor is another Brazilian artist who has helped bring cultural walls tumbling down, although without being shocking like the Tropicalistas or overtly political like Edu Lobo and Geraldo Vandré. Benjor has simply fused the styles of different countries in his music in a very smooth, nonabrasive way that few listeners can resist. One of Brazil's most rhythmically creative musicians, Benjor creates music with a contagious swing, a transcontinental Afro-groove. The singer-guitarist-composer has been mixing rhythmic elements from North America, Brazil, and Africa since the

Jorge Benjor (formerly Jorge Ben). *Courtesy of Tropical Storm/WEA.*

1960s, and some have termed his music "rhythm and samba."

Jorge (Jorge Duílio Menezes) was born in Rio in 1940. He adopted the stage name "Jorge Ben" (Ben was his Ethiopian mother's maiden name), which he used for almost thirty years. In 1989, he took a new pseudonym: Jorge Benjor. He started performing during the bossa boom years but would hit his stride during the MPB era. His career was helped by appearances in the festivals, notably the 1969 International Song Festival (FIC) in Rio.

Critics who give more importance to harmony and melody than to rhythm have accused Jorge's music of being repetitive. But with Jorge it is rhythm that is most important and that is where his creativity runs free. His songs fuse samba with blues and funk, and sometimes incorporate elements of rock, maracatu, candomblé, and baião. His blends always carry Jorge's unique musical signature and ever present swing.

Jorge's best concerts are like tribal celebrations in which the entire audience dances almost to the point of a trance, propelled by his funky, infectious guitar strumming and the dense rhythms of his band Zé Pretinho (Little Black Jose). The band often features two drum sets and three or more percussionists. Colorful, energetic, and highly syncopated, Benjor's music creates a festive atmosphere.

Like many musicians from his generation, Benjor started to take his guitar playing seriously only after he heard João Gilberto but found it hard to imitate the complicated bossa nova harmonies. So he developed his own style, playing only with the thumb and the forefinger. He used "mostly the bass strings of the guitar, resolving the song in the minor tones. That made bass and guitar clash all the time," bassist Roberto Colossi explains in *Nova História* (edited by Navarro).

Colossi sometimes accompanied Jorge when he was playing bossa nova in the early 1960s.

Back then it was so hard for bassists to play with Jorge that, on some cuts of his first album, the producer decided not to have a bass, leaving it all for Jorge's guitar. Jorge also began ignoring the normal relation of syllables to notes, singing the lyrics in a way that many conservative musicians thought was wrong. Often his words were longer than the musical phrases, which made him stretch the melody to fit his verses. And those verses often pursued unusual themes, such as alchemy, soccer, spaceships, and bandits, as well as love and daily life.

As Jorge Ben, he scored his first big hit in 1963 with the kinetic, irresistible "Mas Que Nada" (Oh, Come On), a light pop mix of bossa and samba that dropped references to macumba and had a soaring chorus. The latter element would be well exploited by Sérgio Mendes, who scored a hit in the United States with "Mas Que Nada" in 1966, with Lani Hall and Karen Philip singing the tune in Portuguese. Herb Alpert, Dizzy Gillespie, and Jose Feliciano would also record Benjor's tunes.

In Brazil, Jorge released more hits, such as "Chove Chuva" and "Bicho do Mato." Many more hits followed in the years to come, including "Pais Tropical," "Que Maravilha" (with Toquinho), "Charles Anjo 45," "Fio Maravilha," "Xica da Silva," and "Taj Mahal," all of which became standards. His repertoire has been recorded by a wide variety of Brazilian artists, including the Paralamas do Sucesso, Biquini Cavadão, Leila Pinheiro, Marisa Monte, Fernanda Abreu, and Skank.

Music fans outside Brazil heard a little of "Taj Mahal," released by Jorge in 1972, a few years later without realizing it. Rod Stewart copied portions of the song in his 1979 hit "Do Ya Think I'm Sexy?" The British rock performer acknowledged the similarity shortly afterward and donated his royalties to the United Nations Children's Fund.

In 1989, Jorge said good-bye to the name Ben and released *Benjor*, which featured Nigeria's King Sunny Ade and Brazil's Paralamas do Sucesso. He enjoyed another surge of popularity in the 1990s and on New Year's Day 1994 drew more than three million people to a free concert on Copacabana Beach.

Ivan Lins. *Courtesy of PolyGram.*

The Decline of the Festivals

Since political themes were never part of Jorge's songs, he did not have problems staying in Brazil during the dictatorship. But by the time the 1970 FIC was staged, Act No. 5 was in full swing and many musicians had already left. The festivals began to lose their vitality, with many stars absent and the shadow of the dictatorship looming ominously. At that year's event, government censors prohibited twenty-five of the thirty-six finalists from performing their songs. Tom Jobim, Chico Buarque, and many other leading musicians signed a petition against censorship. They were arrested.

Benjor's song "Eu Também Quero Mocotó" did go on stage, performed by the singer Erlon Chaves and three female backup vocalists. They were arrested too, because the censors decided the dancing of the women was too lascivious.

By 1972, when Benjor won the FIC with "Fio Maravilha," the festival era was essentially over. There would be other, smaller musical contests held later in the decade, but that year's festival would be the last major event of its kind.

Ivan Lins and Vítor Martins

During the prime of the big televised festivals, many young musicians felt shut out of the FIC, TV Record, and similar contests. In 1968, a festival called Universitário became an alternative. It

was directed toward college students and sponsored initially by Rio's TV Tupi channel. One of those who attracted a lot of attention at the Universitário events was a singer-songwriter who played the piano: Ivan Lins.

American jazz flutist Herbie Mann stated, "Ivan Lins is the genius of lyrical music in Brazil, a magician with harmony. I've recorded fifteen to twenty of his songs and for me he's on the same par as Gershwin, Kern, and Rogers and Hart, as well as Ravel and Debussy." Pianist George Duke said, "He reminds me of a modern-day Michel Legrand, the way his chords move, the way the circle of fifths move around. His chords are complicated, but the melody is so strong it's undeniable."

Born in Rio in 1945, Ivan grew up in its Tijuca neighborhood. As a pianist, he was influenced by Luis Eça and João Donato and performed in a jazz-bossa trio while in college. Ivan also loved the singing of David Clayton-Thomas, the lead vocalist for the American jazz-rock band Blood, Sweat and Tears, and in trying to sing like him developed a hoarse, soulful style. It didn't really sound like Clayton-Thomas, but it intrigued TV Globo executives, who were looking for artists to fill the shoes of exiled stars like Buarque, Gil, Veloso, Lobo, and Vandré. Globo created a show, "Som Livre Exportação" (Free Sound Export), and in-

Gonzaguinha

Singer-songwriter Gonzaguinha (Luiz Gonzaga, Jr., 1945–1991), son of the famed northeastern musician Luiz Gonzaga, also gained visibility through the university music festivals. From 1973 on, with aggressive and ironic lyrics sung atop a mixture of urban and rural Brazilian music, he protested the country's situation and battled government censors (they blacklisted fifteen songs from his debut album). In many ways, Gonzaguinha filled the vacuum that had been created by Geraldo Vandré's departure from the spotlight. In time, after the censorship waned, Gonzaguinha's romantic and good-humored side came to the fore with songs like "Feijão Maravilha" (Marvelous Beans). But he never forgot his desire for a more just society, as expressed in his 1988 samba "É" (Is).

Gonzaguinha and Fagner in concert. *Photo by Conceição Almeida. Courtesy of BMG.*

We want to make our love valid
We want affection and attention
We want the best of everything

---

vited Lins and others from the university festivals to host and perform on it. The program was a great success, and Ivan became a pop star. Unfortunately, he was massively over-exposed, and when the network canceled the show, the young artist went through hard times for several years.

Commercial success returned in 1977 with Lins's record *Somos Todos Iguais Nesta Noite* (We Are All the Same Tonight). By then he was already working with his most important lyricist, Vítor Martins, and had developed his instrumental skills after studying with Wilma Graça, who had also taught Lobo, Nascimento, Francis Hime (Buarque's songwriting partner), and Gonzaguinha (son of Luiz Gonzaga). For the album's title song, Martins protested the military regime with symbolic lyrics.

> **We are all the same tonight**
> **In the coldness of a painted smile**
> **In the certainty of a dream that is over**

Ivan's harmonies had begun to incorporate difficult chords and make frequent use of minor seconds. He noted, "There was a lot of jazz influence, bossa nova, Milton Nascimento, Dori Caymmi, Debussy, and Ravel." Ivan's singing

gradually became more natural and less strained. He scored hits like "Nos Dias de Hoje" (In the Days of Today), "Começar de Novo" (Start Again), known as "The Island" in its English-language version, "Vitoriosa" (Victorious), and "Dinorah, Dinorah."

Vítor Martins's eloquent lyrics, which ranged from romantic verses to anthems, contributed greatly to Ivan's comeback. Martins continued to battle political repression through metaphors, as did many of his MPB peers. In the xaxado "Formigueiro" (Ant Hill), Martins mentions the *repinique* (also called *repique*) and *caixa* drums, the *xique-xique* rattle, and *batuque* (Afro-Brazilian drumming) to stand for the mind control exerted by the dictatorship.

> **Repinique and xique-xique, so many caixas**
> **with repiques**
> **To block our eardrums, to mask our groans**
> **When the batuque ends, another trick**
> **appears**
> **As does another miracle of the type we're**
> **used to**

"Formigueiro" was released on Ivan's 1979 album *A Noite* (The Night), as was "Antes Que Seja

Tarde" (Before It Is Too Late), which included some of Vítor's most stirring words.

> **We must liberate the dreams of our youth before it is too late**
> **Men must be changed before the call is extinguished**
> **Before faith dies out, before it is too late**

At the end of the seventies, Ivan was gaining recognition as a composer outside his country. Paul Winter recorded Lins and Ronaldo Monteiro's "Velho Sertão" (Old Sertão) in 1978, renaming it and using it as the title track for his album *Common Ground*. Jazz guitarist and vocalist George Benson's *Give Me the Night*, produced by Quincy Jones, included Lins's "Love Dance" (English lyrics by Paul Williams) and "Dinorah, Dinorah." In 1981, for his album *The Dude*, Jones recorded Ivan's "Velas" (Sails), which won a Grammy for best jazz instrumental performance.

After this, some of America's greatest jazz artists scrambled to record Lins's compositions, which were coveted for their strong melodies, Brazilian rhythms, and interesting chords. Patti Austin, Herbie Mann, Sarah Vaughan, Joe Pass, Diane Schuur, the Manhattan Transfer, and Ella Fitzgerald covered Ivan's songs, although unfortunately they usually were fitted with new English lyrics that were far inferior to Martins's poetic words.

Ivan sang two of his tunes on Dave Grusin and Lee Ritenour's 1986 Grammy-winning *Harlequin* album, and two others on the 1988 Crusaders LP *Life in the Modern World*. In 1987, jazz singer Mark Murphy released *Night Mood*, an entire album of Lins-Martins tunes. After Jobim, Ivan Lins and fellow MPB artist Milton Nascimento are the most-recorded Brazilian composers outside Brazil in recent times.

João Bosco and Aldir Blanc

João Bosco, one of MPB's most eclectic and imaginative musicians, also gained attention after successful university song festival appearances. Bosco often performs solo in concert, with just an acoustic guitar to accompany his singing. That's more than enough: he is the most self-sufficient of musicians, a band unto himself. He sits on a stool in a venue like Rio's Canecão, wearing a red bow tie and a white silk shirt, easily inspiring the audience to sing along to a beautiful melody. Then he is apt to throw out a funny improvised line to make them laugh uproariously. Plucking the guitar strings with an infectious samba swing or in intricate flamenco patterns, Bosco moves across the musical spectrum from merengue to jazz, Jackson do Pandeiro to Ary Barroso. He'll add a few bars of Gershwin or scat a rendition of Ravel's *Bolero*. He is like a postmodern troubadour, alternating the sublime with the ironic in songs that flow freely through key and idiom and tone.

Born in 1946 in Ponte Nova, Minas Gerais, Bosco has recorded many successful albums and

João Bosco (*right*). Photo by Ricardo Pessanha.

had his songs covered by many of Brazil's leading singers. Until the mid-1980s, almost all of his compositions were written with Aldir Blanc, a psychiatrist who gave up his profession to pen lyrics for Bosco's sambas and boleros. Blanc's words were, in Elis Regina's words, "the most sincere narration of their time."

Blanc (born in Rio in 1946) writes stanzas that can be serious, ironic, surreal, ludicrous, simple, and full of multiple meanings—all in the same song. They are packed with Brazilian cultural references and frequently comment on social manners and life among the working class. In "Bandalhismo" (Good-for-nothing-ism) in 1980, Blanc wittily updated a 1902 poem by Augusto dos Anjos ("Vandalismo"), bringing it into a setting of the modern underclass.

> **My heart has squalid taverns . . .**
> **Where trembling vagabond hands**
> **Beat out samba-enredos on a matchbox**

"Escadas de Penha" (The Steps of Penha) found a killer reflecting on a crime of passion in front of Rio's Penha church.

> **On the steps of Penha**
> **He grieved over the candle stub**
> **He watched the craziness of the flame**
> **And called his guardian angel**
> **He put his remorse in a song**
> **Sang the lie of the black girl**
> **Denied the jealousy that murders**
> **That murdered his samba-school friend**

In more playful lyrics, Blanc may use Portuguese, Yoruba, Tupi, French, English and Spanish words, polylingual combinations, and imaginative puns. Working together, Blanc and Bosco created some of MPB's greatest standards, including "O Mestre-Sala dos Mares," "Bala com Bala"

(Bullet with Bullet), "De Frente pro Crime" (Facing the Crime), and "Kid Cavaquinho." Many of their modern sambas are important contributions to that genre. Bosco's 1984 album *Gagabirô* was a creative tour-de-force that fused Brazilian, African, and Cuban styles and showed off Bosco and Blanc's multifaceted, virtuosic talents. By the end of the 1980s, Bosco and Blanc were no longer writing songs together and had gone their separate ways. Bosco worked with lyricist Antônio Cícero on 1991's *Zona de Fronteira* (Border Zone), while Blanc teamed with singer-songwriter Guinga on 1994's *Delírio Carioca* (Carioca Delirium).

Luis Melodia

In 1975, the TV Globo network tried to revive the by-then nearly defunct festivals. It promoted an event called Abertura (Opening) that as a whole wasn't successful but had the merit of giving larger exposure to a musician who was a cult artist at the time: Luis Melodia.

Samba, rock, blues, funk, and baião—Melodia's musical language uses all these vocabularies. *Bluesamba* might be a good label for his work. His inventive tunes, full of original rhythmic divisions, are intricate and oblique. His lyrics are surprising, somewhat surrealistic, sung in an anguished, very personal voice. But despite being a subtle and moving singer, Melodia is not a big name in Brazil. He is more of a cult figure.

Luis Carlos dos Santos (his real name) is from Rio's Estácio neighborhood, the cradle of samba. Born in 1951, he had his first taste of popularity at the age of twenty, when Gal Costa and Maria Bethânia recorded his songs. Gal sang "Pérola Negra" (Black Pearl), which became an instant classic. In the song, soothing trombone, piano, and bass guitar notes build a bluesy atmosphere in

Luis Melodia in concert in 1988. *Photo by Luis Bettencourt. Courtesy of Agência JB.*

which the instruments tenderly work as a counter-point to Melodia's calm voice tinged with sadness. The melody is slow, recitative, trance-inducing.

Pérola Negra, Melodia's first album, was released in 1973 to critical acclaim and featured a mix of soul music, choro, rock, and samba-canção. In 1975 Luis appeared at the Abertura festival and recorded his biggest hit, "Juventude Transviada" (Youth Led Astray). The following year, he released a second album, *Maravilhas Contemporâneas* (Contemporary Marvels), then left his native Rio to live on Itaparica, an island near Salvador. He spent two years there, fishing, playing the guitar, and writing new songs. When he thought he was ready, he came back to make a new album. Such periodic cycles of stardom and withdrawal have formed the routine of his career. He has not been prolific as a recording artist, but his works have always had a loyal audience that includes many of Brazil's top musicians.

Djavan

The song "Fato Consumado" (Consummated Fact) by Djavan took second place at the same 1975 Abertura Festival where Melodia performed his big hit. Djavan was the last big MPB star to be introduced by the waning festival system.

One of Brazil's most popular musicians in the 1980s, Djavan Caetano Viana is also one of its best-known performers outside the country. His songs, with their radiant melodies and funky, jazzy Brazilian swing, have been covered by many international artists. He is also known for his bright, clear, highly expressive voice, heard by many North Americans on his U.S. albums *Bird of Paradise* and *Puzzle of Hearts*.

Born in 1949 in Maceió (the capital of the northeastern state of Alagoas), Djavan came to Rio at sixteen to try a musical career. He brought with him a guitar and a bag of mixed influences, including Bahian and northeastern music, bossa nova and jazz. Comparing himself to his famous

Djavan. *Courtesy of Sony.*

peers from the Northeast such as Fagner, Alceu Valença, and Geraldo Azevedo, Djavan said, "They make a music that is more regional, mine is more cosmopolitan." With these musical elements, Djavan forged a sophisticated, rhythmically vibrant, pan-American style that is his alone. Djavan has viewed his music as a demonstration of affection toward people. "When I started my career Brazil was a different country already. I don't write protest songs like those that appeared after 1964. I write love songs, and expressing love is a way of protesting against this violent world." Djavan's lyrics might be called minimalist-symbolist. He sparingly uses exact words to convey his messages—sometimes clear, sometimes cryptic—as he explores love, emotion, nature, and mysticism in songs like "Sina" (Destiny),

> **Father and Mother**
> **Gold from the mine**

Simone. *Courtesy of Sony.*

> **Heart, desire, destiny**
> **All the rest, sheer routine**

or "Faltando um Pedaço" (Missing a Piece).

> **Love is a big lasso, a step into a trap**
> **A wolf running in circles, to feed the pack**

After Djavan's third album, *Djavan*, singers like Nana Caymmi, Gal Costa, Caetano Veloso, and Maria Bethânia began to record his songs. In 1982, his album *Luz* (Light), which included Stevie Wonder, Hubert Laws, and Ernie Watts as guest artists, made Djavan a superstar. Small theaters were not big enough for his concerts anymore; he filled arenas all over the country. *Lilás* (Lilac) in 1984 was also recorded in the United States and has a jazzy American accent in the arrangements and instrumentation. Djavan went back to his roots on *Meu Lado* (My Side), recorded in Rio with drummer Téo Lima, bassist Sizão Machado, and keyboardists Hugo Fattoruso and Jota Moraes. It fuses Brazilian and Hispano-American rhythms and includes a beautiful rendition of South African Enoch Sontonga's "Hymn of the African National Congress." Then as now, Djavan has aptly balanced the sounds of three continents in his music.

Simone

The singer Simone, one of Brazil's most popular vocalists, was another great MPB artist who was not introduced by the festivals. Her deep, mellifluous voice has a special quality: it can seduce like a mistress, comfort like a mother, and beckon like a siren. Simone has a stage presence that is elegant, sexy, commanding. About her, Don Grusin commented, "She has a kind of phrasing that I think no one else has. She really is a master of phraseology, as they used to say about Sinatra. When she lays out

Some of the most prominent artists who fall into the broad category of MPB are discussed in other chapters. They include: Milton Nascimento, Moraes Moreira, Baby Consuelo, Pepeu Gomes, Alceu Valença, Geraldo Azevedo, Elba Ramalho, Fagner, Fafá de Belém, Roberto Carlos, and Ney Matogrosso. Other noteworthy MPB vocalists include Joyce (a talented songwriter as well), Tim Maia (godfather of Brazilian soul), Jane Duboc, Tânia Alves, Zizi Possi, Jair Rodrigues, and Emilio Santiago. Also important are singer-songwriter Guinga, and the vocal groups Boca Livre, Quarteto em Cy, and MPB-4.

just a few notes and words and comes to the end of it and her voice turns just a little, it kills me."

Tall, lean, and striking, Simone Bittencourt was born in Salvador in 1949 and was a member of the Brazilian national basketball team before becoming a professional singer. She recorded her first album, *Simone*, in 1973. Like Costa and Bethânia, Simone has interpreted a wide variety of material on her albums, from sambas to romantic ballads, by Bosco and Blanc, Nascimento, Buarque, Tunai (João Bosco's brother), Francis Hime, Moraes Moreira, and Sueli Costa.

Simone has twice performed to more than one hundred thousand fans, in 1981 at São Paulo's Morumbi stadium and in 1982 in Rio's Quinta da Boa Vista park. She is one of Brazil's most outspoken vocalists and on occasion she includes political anthems in her repertoire. In 1979 she gave a now-legendary concert at which she performed Geraldo Vandré's most famous protest song, "Caminhando." This was a courageous act, since the government's Abertura (Opening) policy had only recently curtailed heavy censorship and the military was still solidly in charge of Brazil. A great rustling and excitement could be heard in the audience when Simone began singing the song's first verse, "Walking and singing, following the tune."

The Legacy of MPB

What if the military dictatorship and censorship had not affected the evolution of MPB? Gilberto Gil's answer was, "We don't know. We were just beginning to develop." Singer-songwriter Geraldo Azevedo, who was imprisoned twice by the regime, felt the repression "interrupted a Brazilian cultural cycle." André Midani, former president of WEA Brazil, disagreed. "It didn't kill a thing. On the contrary, I think it was a kind of catalyst. You had your big enemy, you wrote against him and tried to pass your message along in spite of him. But when censorship disappeared, many MPB composers lost their compass; suddenly you could say whatever you wanted."

However one judges the effect of the political climate, MPB's composers and interpreters were a vital part of Brazil's cultural life during the dictatorship. They came of age under brutal repression as their country suffered through the dark years of a military regime, and they spoke for those that had been silenced by the government. MPB singers and songwriters took Western popular music to new heights in the 1960s and 1970s and have continued to produce important work ever since.

Gal Costa and Toquinho accepting "Premio Sharp" awards at a gala in the late 1980s. *Photo by Fernando Seixas. Courtesy of BMG.*

Marisa Monte: MPB's New Diva

Brazilian popular music went in many different directions in the 1980s, and most of the new stars coming to the forefront fell into categories like rock, pagode, músic sertaneja, and axé music. However, singer Marisa Monte, who established her career at the end of the decade, seems a true heir apparent of the MPB artists who preceded her.

Monte (born in Rio in 1967) has a beautiful, versatile voice that can be tender and precise, or slinky and sensuous. Along with her vocal talents, she is also an excellent songwriter. She grew up with two powerful influences that would help shape her formidable musical abilities. Her father was on the board of the Portela samba school, and

Marisa Monte. *Photo by Marcia Ramalho. Courtesy of World Pacific.*

on the weekends samba musicians often jammed in the family's living room. Her mother loved bossa, jazz, and blues, and Marisa herself avidly listened to pop from Brazil, the United States, and the United Kingdom. She began studying music seriously at fourteen, then decided she wanted to be an opera singer and by eighteen was studying *bel canto* in Italy.

But opera wasn't her true calling, and she returned home intent on pursuing a musical path that came more naturally to her, one that would bring together all the styles that she loved. She started performing in bars and small clubs, building a following and attracting the attention of EMI-Odeon. In 1989, when she recorded her debut album *Marisa Monte,* the record company backed her with a prime-time television special and heavy promotion. The album deserved the push: it is a confident work that ranges adeptly through hard rock (from the Titãs), "South American Way" (a 1940 Carmen Miranda number), songs by George Gershwin and Kurt Weill, a reggae version of "I Heard It Through the Grapevine," and Luiz Gonzaga's old hit "O Xote das Meninas." A brilliant new vocalist had clearly arrived, revealing a voice that was both full of feeling and technically flawless.

Her next effort, *Mais* (More) in 1991, was even better. It was produced by Arto Lindsay and features Japanese keyboardist Ryuichi Sakamoto, American saxophonist John Zorn, northeastern guitar wizard Robertinho de Recife, and standout percussionists Naná Vasconcelos and Armando Marçal. The LP is less eclectic than Marisa's previous release but more coherent in its approach. *Mais* ranges from folk-rock to choro to *heavy samba* (samba with hard rock), as Marisa interprets songs written mostly by herself and Titãs alumni Nando Reis and Arnaldo Antunes. Also included are Pixinguinha's venerable choro "Rosa," Cartola's samba "Ensaboa" (Soap It), and the Caetano Veloso ballad "De Noite Na Cama" (At Night in Bed). *Mais* cemented Monte's stardom; fans showered the stage with roses at her concerts and countless young woman sought to emulate her elegant style.

In 1994, she recorded *Verde Anil Amarelo Cor de Rosa e Carvão* (released in the United States as *Rose and Charcoal*). It is a rich, lyrical work that has more songs written by Monte, Antunes, and Reis; the compositions and percussion of axé-music phenomenon Carlinhos Brown; an old samba by Portela legends Jamelão and Bubu da Portela; the swinging Jorge Benjor samba "Balança Pema"; and Lou Reed's "Pale Blue Eyes." U.S. avant-garde musicians Philip Glass and Laurie Anderson also appear on the album, as do Paulinho da Viola and the Velha Guarda da Portela (Old Guard of Portela).

Two years later, Monte's *A Great Noise* offered both studio recordings and live versions of her songs and Brazilian standards. There is an intriguing reading by Monte of an Octavio Paz poem, "Blanco" (White); new tunes by Brown; and inspired covers of "Cérebro Eletrônico" (Electronic Brain) by Gilberto Gil, "Panis et Circensis" (Bread and Circus) by Gil and Veloso, George Harrison's "Give Me Love," Lulu Santos's "Tempos Modernos" (Modern Times), and Paulinho da Viola's "Dança da Solidão" (Solitude's Dance). It is an outstanding effort that showcases Monte's impressive musical range, positions her as arguably the greatest Brazilian vocalist of the decade, and takes the legacy of the MPB generation into the future.

Milton Nascimento

Toninho Horta

TOCANTINS

GOIÁS

BAHIA

MATO
GROSSO

Brasília

MINAS GERAIS

Wagner Tiso

Belo Horizonte

ESPÍRITO
SANTO

SÃO
PAULO

• Três
Pontas

RIO DE
JANEIRO

São Paulo

Beto Guedes

SANTA CATARINA

Porto Alegre

Minas Gerais: Musical Treasure

Chapter Five

I am from South America
I know you won't know
But now I'm a cowboy
I am of gold, I am you
I'm from the world, I am Minas Gerais

**Lô Borges, Milton Nascimento and Fernando Brant
"Para Lennon e McCartney" (To Lennon and
McCartney)**

The rolling green hills of Minas Gerais hide many secrets. Some of these are material, like the impressive deposits of gold and diamonds discovered in the eighteenth century in this Brazilian state, whose name literally means "General Mines." These treasures built the towns of Ouro Preto and São João del Rey, masterpieces of colonial architecture. They also helped bankroll the industrial revolution, as Portugal used gold from Minas to pay for English manufactured goods.

The region also holds secrets of a different kind: those of the heart. Political conspiracies have been plotted here: the Inconfidência, an independence movement led by the dentist Tiradentes, was crushed in 1789 by the colonial government. Mineiros know how to keep quiet about their plans and real feelings. They have a reputation in Brazil for being quiet, complex, mystical, and more respectful of tradition. Such a temperament befits their environment: Minas is mountainous, landlocked, and located on a high plateau to the north of Rio de Janeiro and São Paulo. It has a cooler climate than does the sultry, humid Atlantic coast. Accordingly, its inhabitants, the Mineiros, are much less expansive than the extroverted Brazilians one finds in Rio and Bahia.

The music of Milton Nascimento reflects this difference; in it one can hear the pastoral, spiritual, and contemplative nature of the Mineiro. Nasci-

mento is one of the most accomplished singers and composers that Brazil has ever produced, and many of his musical peers from Minas Gerais—such as Wagner Tiso, Toninho Horta, Lô Borges, Márcio Borges, Beto Guedes, and Fernando Brant—have also made important contributions to their nation's music. Collectively nicknamed the *clube da esquina* (corner club) by the Brazilian press, many of these musicians grew up in the same towns and first played together in cities like Três Pontas and Belo Horizonte, later establishing their careers on the larger stages of Rio and São Paulo.

Their music is generally highly lyrical, full of elaborate harmonies, a rich variety of styles, and a strong lyricism expressive of a yearning imagination. It carries influences from a wide variety of

A church in Ouro Preto, one of the oldest and most historic cities in Minas Gerais. *Photo by Chris McGowan.*

sources: the choir music sung in the baroque churches of Minas, the folk *toadas* heard in the countryside, and the melodic pop-rock of the Beatles. Their songs reflect Minas Gerais, yet have a universal appeal that crosses all boundaries.

Milton Nascimento

Of all the members of the clube da esquina, Nascimento has achieved the greatest critical and commercial success. His music can be melancholy and haunting, or it can be upbeat with catchy melodies and bouncy rhythms. Jazz musi-

Milton Nascimento. *Photo by Márcio Ferreira.*

cians especially revere Nascimento's compositions for their beautiful melodies and unusual textures and harmonies. Milton's songs seamlessly weave together threads of Mineiro toada, bossa nova, Gregorian chants, *nueva canción*, fado from Portugal, Spanish guitar, Andean flute music, jazz, rock, or classical music.

While Nascimento sometimes writes his own lyrics, more often they are penned by his longtime partners, an impressive group that includes Guedes, Brant, Márcio Borges, and Ronaldo Bastos (who unlike the others is a Fluminense, a native of Rio de Janeiro state). Usually, the words are messages of compassion and friendship, expressions of loneliness and the need to love, or statements against oppression.

As a singer, Nascimento has a resonant and remarkably melodious voice that is rich in timbre and infused with emotional power. He has a wide vocal range that swings from a deep masculine sound to a high feminine falsetto, or soars in flights of wordless singing. "I think he's the best singer in the world now and one of the most original composers," Brazilian musicologist Zuza Homem de Mello said to us. He added, "Milton writes music that is apparently simple but in actuality is very difficult. It leaves musicians trying to decipher the secrets of the music when they attempt to play it. He has changes in rhythm in the middle of a song without your being able to perceive it."

In Vasco Mariz's book *A Canção Brasileira*, Milton notes, "I use different divisions in my music: for example a 6/8 within a 4/4. I compose on the guitar and afterwards record. I always have difficulties writing my songs down on paper, because of rhythmic breaks, because of the design of the guitar." He adds that the type of music he makes is a *toada*—a short, stanza-and-refrain song usually with a sentimental melody and narrative lyrics. Nascimento continues, "The toada is different according to the region. That of Dorival Caymmi is maritime. Mine has a connection with the region of Três Pontas. But I don't consider mine regional, as neither my harmonies nor melodies are regional. I was greatly influenced by having grown up in Minas, but I think jazz is also important in my music."

From Três Pontas to Rio

Nascimento was born in 1942 in Rio de Janeiro, the son of Maria do Carmo Nascimento, who worked in the household of Lília Silva Campos, and her husband Josino Brito de Campos. Maria died when Milton was an infant and the de Campos family adopted him. When Milton was three, the family moved to the small rural Minas Gerais town of Três Pontas. Surrounded by mountains, Três Pontas (Three Peaks) has narrow streets and one-story houses whose doors open straight out to the sidewalk. Life is slow-paced and in the late afternoon families put chairs outside their front doors and have a chat before dinner.

Lília and Josino adopted two more children (Elizabeth and Luis Fernando) and had one daughter of their own (Joceline), but Milton was the only black member of the family, and thus the target of malicious gossip. Though he felt mistreated and suffocated by the intolerant Três Pontas mentality of that era, at home he was accepted as a true son. "I'm fascinated by my family," Milton told us. "I couldn't have had more love, education, and freedom with any other family in the world. They shaped my life."

His adoptive father, Josino, was a professor of mathematics at high schools in Três Pontas and also a bank clerk, a director of the local radio station, and an amateur astronomer. He spent many nights exploring Ursa Major, the Southern Cross, and the moons of Jupiter through his telescope,

with his eldest son at his side, who came to know the heavens "like the palm of my hand."

Milton was singing and playing instruments from an early age. "My first instrument was a harmonica my godmother gave me. Then she gave me a button accordion, and when I got it my musical life started." In the backyard, in the shade of mango, guava, and black-currant trees, Milton began conceiving musical theater entertainments for a growing band of neighborhood pals. "It was very easy for me to make up stories, like Walt Disney ones, but my own. I would imitate voices, create songs, dialogues, everything on the spot. This was around age five or six."

When he was fourteen, Nascimento played his first guitar, a steel-stringed instrument. "It was then that I started looking for sounds, discovering chords, all by ear. This was a very fertile time here in Brazil. We used to listen to everything: samba, mambo, rock, bolero, rumba, foxtrots, classical music—influences from all over the world." Milton's favorite vocal artists included Yma Sumac from Peru, Ângela Maria from Brazil, and Ray Charles from the United States. At the same time, Nascimento was absorbing the various regional sounds of his state: its toadas, church music, and songs of the *Folia de Reis* folkloric groups that performed their dramatic dances in the post-Christmas season.

As a teenager, Milton met and became close friends with Wagner Tiso, who lived on the same street. They formed a rock group that had many different names, including Luar de Prata (Silver Moonlight). Milton told us, "We played rock, ballads, foxtrots, Little Richard, every kind of music we knew. We didn't have any musical prejudices, because in small towns we liked what we liked and nobody cared what it was or where it came from. I only discovered that there was such a thing as prejudice in music when I moved to the big city." Tiso would later serve as Nascimento's arranger and go on to became a renowned keyboardist and composer in his own right.

In 1958, Milton heard the João Gilberto single "Chega de Saudade." "I went nuts," he remembered. "This shock with bossa nova opened our minds. We started searching for bossa nova on the radio, changing stations all the time. We didn't have a TV set, and the radio broadcast we received was terrible, with lots of static. So we would listen to a song one day and only listen to it again two weeks or a month later.

"So we had an agreement. Two of us would pick out the melody—usually Wagner and I— and somebody else would get the words. We'd invent our own harmony. Without perceiving it, we created our own style for accompanying those songs. Then when we got to the big city and heard how [other musicians] played those same songs, we said to ourselves, 'Oh, we did it all wrong!' We decided to change everything, but people convinced us not to. They said nobody did it that way and that it was really great. So this was a great stimulus for our creativity."

Milton and Wagner and their band—now called "W's Boys"—began to play dances and travel throughout Minas Gerais, playing rock and bossa. Milton also worked as a disc jockey for the Três Pontas radio station managed by his father and was known for excessively spinning disks by Gilberto and Henry Mancini.

In 1963, Milton decided to move to the capital, Belo Horizonte, to take an accounting job in an office and, as he said, "to see what would happen." Once there, Milton met several like-minded musicians and wrote a letter to Wagner, urging him to come. The two began playing nightclubs like the Japanese bar Fujiama with new friends such as drummer Paulinho Braga and flutist-saxophonist Nivaldo Ornellas. Milton also met his future collaborators Lô and Márcio Borges.

In Belo Horizonte, Milton had his first prolonged exposure to bossa and jazz musicians. The experience was overwhelming: "My first contact with jazz left me speechless. I had never seen anyone play drums that way. I had never seen anyone play bass that way. I simply felt sick. [Afterward] I couldn't sleep well, I couldn't eat. I said to myself, 'What's that? I'll never do anything like these people." But soon he found out that Belo Horizonte's jazz musicians felt the same way about his music. Thus started Milton's interest in jazz, and he listened intently to records by Miles Davis, John Coltrane, Charles Mingus, and Thelonious Monk.

Milton started out interpreting other people's songs. That all changed one day when he and his friend Márcio Borges went to the movie theater to see François Truffaut's *Jules and Jim*. The film's intense imagery and vivid characters had a strong effect on the two young musicians. They arrived in the afternoon and only left late that night after the last show was over. Recalled Milton, "We saw it maybe four times in a row and Márcio Borges on that very same day became my first songwriting partner. When I left the movie theater I said to myself that I had to create something. So we went to Márcio's place and started writing songs. All my songs are like a movie—they're all very cinematographic."

Milton and Márcio continued to play together, sometimes performing in the latter's group, Evolussamba. Milton also met Fernando Brant (he and Marcio would become Milton's most frequent songwriting partners), and he struck up a friendship with Márcio's little brother, Lô. It was with Lô that Milton discovered the Beatles, who deeply impressed him: "In my youth my father had a lot of classical music and opera, so I was very given to classical music. And suddenly, with the development of the Beatles, I saw the fusion that George Martin had done with certain [classical] things and what had come with that generation."

Nascimento's singing and composing skills grew rapidly. In 1964 he appeared on a record with composer Pacífico Mascarenhas's quartet, Sambacana, and in 1965 he was invited by TV Excelsior in São Paulo to participate in its first Festival of Popular Music. Milton took fourth place, with his interpretation of Baden Powell and Luis Fernando Freire's "Cidade Vazia" (Empty City), but more important he met a singer by the name of Elis Regina, who—as mentioned in the preceding chapter—won the event with Edu Lobo's "Arrastão."

Milton moved to São Paulo, seeking to establish a career. He recalled, "I spent two years in São Paulo, but they were worth twenty. Some people liked me, like Elis and the Zimbo Trio, but it was very hard to get into the music scene. I played in night clubs when I had the chance, but competition was fierce. There were fifty unemployed musicians for every opening." In 1966 Regina recorded Nascimento's "Canção do Sal" (Salt Song), but his struggles continued and at times he returned to playing clubs in Belo Horizonte. Tiso, meanwhile, had moved to Rio to play in bossa nova groups and to study orchestration with saxophonist-arranger Paulo Moura.

Milton Discovered

Milton became famous in 1967, with a nudge from his friends and the intense spotlight of the second FIC (International Song Festival). His breakthrough almost didn't happen, because he was not inclined to enter his songs in the event, having hated the intense competition of the 1965 TV Excelsior contest. But singer Agostinho dos San-

tos, a popular singer who had sung on the *Black Orpheus* soundtrack, took the shy young musician under his wing. He submitted three of Milton's songs—"Travessia" (Cross), "Morro Velho" (Old Hill), and "Maria, Minha Fé" (Maria, My Faith)—to the FIC without Nascimento's knowledge. All three were accepted, a remarkable achievement that focused great attention on the reticent Milton.

But Nascimento still didn't want to perform his tunes at the event. Enter Eumir Deodato, whom Milton had recently met and who was going to arrange the songs for the festival. Deodato insisted, recalled Milton, "that he'd write the arrangements only if I sang at least two. So I sang 'Travessia' and 'Morro Velho,' and Agostinho sang 'Maria, Minha Fé.'"

On the day of the competition, Milton walked out onto the stage, absolutely terrified, but by the

Keyboardist and producer Eumir Deodato, who helped convince a shy Milton Nascimento to perform at the second International Song Festival in 1967. *Courtesy of Atlantic Records.*

end of the event he had won the award for best performer. "Travessia" was picked as the festival's second-best song and became an instant standard, with its sad acoustic guitar chords, moving melody, and Milton's deep melodious voice soaring powerfully in the song's dramatic chorus. "Morro Velho" took seventh place and "Maria, Minha Fé" also placed among the fifteen finalists.

All three of his songs from the FIC were included that year on Milton's first album, *Milton Nascimento*, arranged by Luis Eça (the record was later reissued with the title *Travessia*). His festival performance and newly issued LP drew both national and international attention. In 1968, Milton was invited to perform in Mexico and the United States, and he recorded the album *Courage* for American label A&M. Included were six songs from *Travessia*. Creed Taylor produced the LP, and Deodato (organ), Herbie Hancock (piano), and Airto Moreira (percussion) participated.

In 1969, Milton returned to the studio to cut two albums for EMI Brazil (*Milton Nascimento* and *Milton*) and wrote songs for director Ruy Guerra's film *Os Deuses e Os Mortos* (The Gods and the Dead). Five of his tunes were included on jazz saxophonist Paul Desmond's *From the Hot Afternoon* LP.

The following year, Milton had a successful one-year run with his musical show *Milton Nascimento e o Som Imaginário*. One of Brazil's best progressive fusion (jazz-rock-Brazilian) groups ever, Som Imaginário (Imaginary Sound), had been formed initially to accompany Milton and would back him on various albums. It went on to record three LPs by itself. Som Imaginário's changing lineup at different times included Tiso (piano); Zé Rodrix (organ and flutes); Toninho Horta, Tavito, and Fredera (guitars); Luis Alves (bass); Robertinho Silva (drums); and Laudir de Oliveira and Naná Vasconcelos (percussion).

Clube da Esquina

In 1971, Milton and his "corner club" pals from Minas rented a house in Piratininga, a beach in Niterói, north of Rio. They stayed there for six months and composed the majority of the songs for Nascimento and Ló Borges's double album *Clube da Esquina*—which was orchestrated by Tiso and Deodato and recorded in 1972 at the EMI-Odeon studios in Rio.

The LP primarily featured compositions by Milton and Ló, with lyrics contributed by Bastos, Brant, and Márcio Borges. Milton and Ló shared lead vocals and played guitar and were joined by Guedes (guitar and backing vocals); Som Imaginário's Horta, Tiso, Alves, Silva, Vasconcelos, and Tavito; and Danilo Caymmi (flute), Novelli (bass), Rubinho (drums), Nelson Ângelo (guitar), and Paulo Moura (several arrangements). It was a sprawling and ambitious work that mixed diverse styles with naturalness and fluency. Ló contributed the dreamy "Mineiro rock" tunes such as "O Trem Azul" (The Blue Train), "Nuvem Cigana" (Gypsy Cloud), and "Tudo Que Você Podia Ser" (All You Could Be) with their strong hints of groups like the Beatles and Procul Harem. Milton's songs on the LP are often more Iberian and South American in flavor, as on "San Vicente"—in which MPB scholar Charles Perrone notes elements of the Chilean *tonada* style (in the guitar accompaniment) and Paraguayan *guarania* (in the bass lines). Brant contributed its surreal lyrics.

> **American heart, I woke from a strange dream**
> **A taste of glass and cut**
> **A flavor of chocolate**
> **In the body and in the city**
> **A taste of life and death**

There were many other memorable songs, including Nascimento's uptempo "Cravo e Canela" (Clove and Cinnamon) and lively "Nada Será Como Antes" (Nothing Will Be Like Before). The album sold well and Milton became commercially viable as a recording artist, as did Guedes, Horta, and Lô Borges. With this success to their credit, they all recorded albums individually or together. The name corner club was used long afterward by the press to describe Milton and his collaborators, even if they weren't from Minas Gerais.

On 1973's Milagre dos Peixes (Miracle of the Fishes) Milton and the Som Imaginário delved into even more experimental territory, casting Milton's lonely voice against dense instrumental soundscapes, as the musicians went all out with electric, percussive, and vocal effects. They had to be especially expressive, since the government censors had banned almost all the lyrics on the album.

Minas to Geraes

Minas in 1975 included Nascimento's two favorite songs: "Saudade dos Aviões da Panair" (Saudades for the Panair Planes) and "Ponta de Areia" (Sand Point). Also that year, Milton was the featured guest on the album *Native Dancer* by jazz saxophonist and composer Wayne Shorter, who had previously covered Milton's "Vera Cruz" on the 1970 album *Moto Grosso Feio* [sic] and in that decade was busy taking jazz into new realms with his group Weather Report.

Native Dancer featured five Nascimento songs— "Ponte de Areia," "Tarde" (Afternoon), "Miracle of the Fishes," "From the Lonely Afternoons," and "Lilia"—and the playing of Herbie Hancock, Airto Moreira, Wagner Tiso, Robertinho Silva, and David Amaro. The interplay between Nascimento's voice, Shorter's sax, and Hancock's piano created a moody, hauntingly beautiful work that profoundly affected many North American

Milton Nascimento and Wayne Shorter in concert a decade after their collaborative *Native Dancer* album, which introduced Milton to a large North American jazz audience for the first time. *Photo by Márcio Ferreira.*

listeners, including a young American keyboardist named Lyle Mays.

"It was a watershed record, a classic, and I think it turned a lot of jazz musicians onto Milton," recalled Mays. "Even to this day it stands as one of the best blends of Brazilian music and American jazz. When I first heard it, I didn't know what to think. It was so different. I thought it was like magic and I just couldn't imagine that music. I simply had to listen again as I couldn't quite grasp it. I had never heard those kinds of tunes [that Milton had composed] before."

On his next album, *Geraes* in 1976, Milton journeyed far into his Brazilian roots and other Latin American folk styles. The album's title comes from an archaic spelling of Gerais, and many of its songs draw on research Tavinho Moura had done in regional music—principally in the Jequitinhonha River valley that winds through the backlands of northern Minas and southern Bahia. One example is "Calix Bento" (Blessed Chalice), which Moura had adapted from a Folia de Reis song. Milton also expanded his explorations of music from other parts of South America: "Volver a Los 17" (Return to 17) was written by Chilean songwriter Violeta Parra, and Milton interprets it in a duet with Argentinean singer Mercedes Sosa. Yet Milton did not

Milton Nascimento and Pat Metheny in concert. *Photo by Márcio Ferreira.*

forget Brazil's contemporary situation: he included the politically charged "O Que Será (Á Flor da Pele)," penned by Chico Buarque, with whom Milton sang the moving duet.

Clube da Esquina 2

In 1978, Milton gathered together with the "clube" for a sequel, another double album. This time it would be more of a pan–South American fusion, with less rock and not as much North American influence. Nascimento, Lô Borges, Beto Guedes, Wagner Tiso, Novelli, Horta, and Nelson Ângelo were joined this time by singer-songwriters Joyce and Flávio Venturini, and guitarist Paulo Jobim (Tom's son). *Clube da Esquina 2* was even more ambitious than its predecessor, and aesthetically more successful. Indeed, the dense album's many outstanding compositions, astonishing variety of instrumentation and styles, consistently excellent arrangements, and wealth of talented musicians participating in the production made it a landmark in both Brazilian and global popular music of the late twentieth century.

The album begins with "Credo," a song that opens and closes with beautiful a cappella singing and includes spirited Andean-style guitar, flute, and vocals backing up Fernando Brant's charged political lyrics.

> **Let's go, walking hand-in-hand with the new**
> **soul**
> **To live planting liberty in each heart**
> **Have faith that our people will awake**
> **Have faith that our people will be shocked**

After that follows one remarkable song after another. Venturini's beautiful "Nascente" features exquisite harmonizing between Venturini and Nascimento. "Paixão e Fé" (Passion and Faith) starts with a Mediterranean atmosphere evoked by Guedes's

mandolin, which is soon overwhelmed by the angelic, soaring vocals of Milton and the Canarinhos de Petrópolis choir, conducted by José Luiz. Another highlight is the moving "O Que Foi Feito Devera," with Elis Regina's superb singing set against the acoustic guitars of Nascimento and Natan Marques, and then joined by Milton's voice; this flows into "O Que Foi Feito de Vera" (What Happened to Vera), which continues an incomparable duet between two of Brazil's greatest singers. The celebratory "Maria Maria" has become yet another Nascimento standard.

Two memorable songs came from his interpretations of compositions by musicians outside

Milton Nascimento and Mercedes Sosa. *Photo by Paulo Ricardo. Courtesy of Sony.*

Brazil. In "Casamiento de Negros" (Marriage of Blacks), adapted from Chilean folk music by Violeta Parra, the Uruguayan Grupo Tacuabé and a large chorus support Milton's lead vocals and guitar. And Nascimento and Chico Buarque join to sing Cuban Pablo Milanés's "Cancion por la Unidad de Latin America" (Song for Latin American Unity), adapted by Buarque.

Nelson Ângelo and Fernando Brant's "Canoa, Canoa" is a showcase for Milton's otherworldly voice, set against a sumptuous backing chorus provided by Nascimento, Novelli, Ângelo, and Lô Borges. Paulo Jobim's melancholy "Valse" (Waltz), recorded by his father on the 1976 *Urubu* album, here acquires lyrics by Ronald Bastos and becomes "Olho d'Agua" (Water Spring). Joyce and Maurício Maestro contributed the beautiful song "Mistérios" (Mysteries), which received an affecting interpretation with Milton's voice. "Tanto" (So Much) is a classic Beto Guedes tune. And the rousing "Reis e Rainhas do Maracatu" (Kings and Queens of Maracatu) alternates exuberant samba with maracatu carried rhythmically by an agogô and triangle.

The *Clube da Esquina* albums profoundly affected American jazz artists Lyle Mays and Pat Metheny. Mays recalled the excitement he felt when he listened to them for the first time with Metheny: "It was an amazing unpredictable combination of cultural influences of the Western classical harmonic sense and the African rhythmic sense, done in a completely different way from jazz. Listening to it gave me the same kind of excitement as when I first heard jazz. I don't think there's any parallel to those records in any music I've come across. The *Clube da Esquina* records have things in common with the Beatles and Miles Davis, a combination of hipness, accessibility, and exoticness."

Sentinela to Anima

Sentinela (Sentinel) in 1980 further mixed contemporary sounds with traditional Mineiro and Latin American influences, all filtered through Milton's transcendental sensibility. In the moving title song, the narrator is standing vigil at a deathbed of a brother or comrade, vowing to keep his spirit alive.

> **Death, candle, I am a sentinel**
> **Of the body of my brother who's departing**
> **In this hour I see again all that happened**
> **Memory will not die**

The dirgelike singing of Milton and haunting vocals of Nana Caymmi are given further emotional power by a full choir of Benedictine monks that backs them. Other songs on the album are livelier and less somber, such as Tavinho Moura's "Peixinhos do Mar" (Little Fishes of the Sea), an adaptation of a *marujada*, a dramatic dance with medieval roots. Nascimento's interpretation of Cuban poet Silvio Rodriguez's "Sueño com Serpientes" (Dream with Serpents) offers another excellent duet, between Milton and Mercedes Sosa. "Peixinhos," "Sueño," and three other tunes feature the classically trained, avant-garde Mineiro group Uakti, which add richly resonant sound colors with instruments fashioned out of wood, glass, and PVC pipe. Other notable songs on the album include "Cantiga Caicó," an adaptation of a Villa-Lobos song, and "Canção da América" (America's Song) which features the backing of vocal group Boca Livre.

Next came Nascimento's most radical concept album to date: 1982's *Missa dos Quilombos* (Mass of the Quilombos), a choral work that combines Afro-Brazilian instruments and rhythms with Catholic hymns and chants. Originally performed before a huge audience in Recife, Pernambuco, and recorded in a colonial church in Caraça, Minas Gerais, this musical mass is an uplifting cry against oppression and servitude, with lyrics written by poet Pedro Tierra and Catholic bishop and liberation theologist Pedro Casaldáliga. At the end of the album, Hélder Câmara, the archbishop of Olinda and Recife, gives a rousing speech against hunger, injustice, and economic exploitation of the poor. It was all too unorthodox for the Vatican, which banned the mass.

The next year, a song from Milton's *Ao Vivo* (Live) album also provided political inspiration. "Coração de Estudante" (Student's Heart), written by Nascimento and Tiso, was adopted as the theme song for the Brazilian movement for democracy in 1984 and sung by thousands of student demonstrators in the streets.

The student's heart
Has to take care of life
Has to take care of the world

Nascimento's albums in the 1980s and 1990s took several different musical and geographic directions. In *Anima* (1982), the percussion of Uakti and the jazz-rock guitar of Ricardo Silveira provide an interesting counterpoint to Nascimento's melodies and elaborate harmonies. *Miltons* from 1989 is a serene work teaming Milton with percussionist Naná Vasconcelos and jazz pianist Herbie Hancock. That year, while Nascimento was on the tour for *Miltons*, he became seriously interested in the plight of the inhabitants of the Amazon rain forest, whose livelihoods were being seriously threatened by deforestation and the illegal invasion of their lands by unscrupulous outsiders.

Nascimento was invited by the Union of Indigenous Nations (UNI) and National Council of Rubber Tappers (CNS) to take an eighteen-day journey by boat up the Juruá River, starting in the town of Cruzeiro do Sul, deep in the heart of the Amazon, meeting with local people along the way. Milton's manager, Márcio Ferreira, along with Roberto Marques and Demerval Filho were part of the trip and the three made field recordings of the songs of the Yanomami, Kayapó, Waiãpi, and other inhabitants of the region. The fruit of this ex-

Milton with his longtime friend and noted keyboardist-arranger Wagner Tiso (*left*) and Manhattan Transfer leader Tim Hauser (*right*) at the Som Livre Studios in Rio, working on Nascimento's "Viola Violar" for the Transfer's 1987 Atlantic album *Brasil*. Photo by Chris McGowan.

pedition was the 1990 album *Txai*, dedicated to the UNI, CNS, and the Alliance for the People of the Forest. Short excerpts of indigenous music are heard throughout the album, in which most of Nascimento's songs are inspired by those he met in the Amazon. Two of *Txai's* most interesting songs are the beautiful duet "Nozani Na," sung by Milton and Marlui Miranda, and "Curi Curi," in which Tsaqu Waiãpi plays flute and the actor River Phoenix reads text protesting the destruction of the Amazon and betrayal of its people.

Milton's songs during this period were widely recorded by international musicians and his albums attracted a legion of accomplished foreign musicians. *Encontros e Despedidas* (Encounters and Goodbyes) in 1985 included Pat Metheny and Hubert Laws; the 1987 album *Yauaretê* (Jaguar) featured Paul Simon, Herbie Hancock, and Quincy Jones; and the 1994 LP *Angelus* had Wayne Shorter, Jon Anderson (of the rock group Yes), James Taylor, and Peter Gabriel. As a vocalist, Nascimento was invited to perform on Paul Simon's *The Rhythm of the Saints*, the Manhattan Transfer's *Brasil*, and Sarah Vaughan's *Brazilian Romance*. The power of Milton's vocals and the enduring appeal of his "world music"—forged in Minas—have made him one of Brazil's most popular performers and composers around the world.

Members of the Club

Milton's overall sound has been inextricably linked to the music of his Mineiro friends and collaborators like Wagner Tiso, Beto Guedes, Toninho Horta, Tavinho Moura, and Lô Borges. Along with co-headlining *Clube da Esquina*, Borges (born in Belo Horizonte in 1952) has released the solo albums *Lô Borges* in 1972, *A Via-Láctea* (The Milky Way) in 1979, and *Nuvem Cigana* (Gypsy Cloud) in 1981, among other works. Tiso, born in Três Pontas in 1945, has been an indispensable part of Nascimento's success. "The two of us together make the cross," said Milton.

Lô Borges. Photo by Cafi. Courtesy of Sire.

Tiso, who played keyboards in the Som Imaginário group, has arranged and orchestrated many Nascimento albums and scored numerous Brazilian movies. His solo albums, including *Assim Seja* (Thus It May Be), *Trem Mineiro* (Minas Train), *Branco e Preto* (Black and White), *Os Passaros* (The Birds), and *Giselle*, have shown off Tiso's sophisticated compositions, as he alternates acoustic piano and electronic keyboards. The 1988 release *Manú Çarué, uma Aventura Holística* is a phantasmagoric pop symphony that mixes rock, baroque, and Brazilian influences and demonstrates Tiso's composing, arranging, and playing skills.

Another corner club standout is Beto Guedes, known for his original songwriting, dexterity with various stringed instruments (guitar, mandolin, and others) and distinctively high, astringent voice. He was born in 1951 in Montes Claros in northern Minas Gerais. As a young musician, Beto forged his own style by mixing Anglo-American 1960s pop styles with his boyhood influences: *música sertaneja* and the *choros* played by his father, Godofredo (a saxophonist-clarinetist).

Beto followed his participation in *Clube da Esquina* by joining with three other alumni of that album to record *Beto Guedes, Novelli, Danilo Caymmi and Toninho Horta* in 1973. In that decade and the next, he continued to contribute songs, vocals, and

Wagner Tiso. *Courtesy of Verve.*

The cover of *Viagem das Mãos*, a 1985 album by Beto
Guedes, who was a key member of the "Corner Club."
Courtesy of EMI.

guitar playing to Nascimento's albums while also
releasing the excellent solo albums *Amor de Índio*
(Indian's Love), *Sol de Primavera* (Spring Sun), *Con-
tos da Lua Vaga* (Stories of the Vague Moon), *Viagem*

das Mãos (Journey of the Hands), and *A Página do
Relâmpago Elétrico* (The Page of Electric Lightning).

The *New York Times* critic Robert Palmer commented about Guedes, "On the best of his albums, the remarkable *A Página do Relâmpago Elétrico*,
he uses what sounds like four or five acoustic guitars, each playing a different rhythmic pattern, to
weave richly detailed sonic tapestries; the disk
contrasts rural string-band styles and jazzy electric music. On 'Novena,' a song from his excellent album *Amor de Índio*, he cushions a ballad's sin-
uously brooding melody with chord voicings
built around minor seconds, creating an astonishing lyricism of dissonances."

Another Mineiro talent who has been an es-
sential part of Milton's albums over the years is
Toninho Horta, born in Belo Horizonte in 1948.
Horta has participated in many of Nascimento's
recordings, including both *Clube da Esquina* releases. In 1980 he cut his first solo album, *Terra dos
Passaros* (Land of the Birds). Toninho is a composer and guitarist who mixes influences from
Minas *modinha* and religious music, jazz musicians
such as Wes Montgomery, and the bossa of João
Gilberto. Forged from such diverse sources,
Horta's composing and playing have had a strong
influence on many musicians outside of Brazil.

"Toninho has emerged as one of the most harmonically sophisticated and melodically satisfying
Brazilian composers of recent times," wrote Pat
Metheny in the liner notes of Horta's 1988 *Diamond
Land* album. "He writes chord progressions that defy
gravity, moving up when you think they're going
down. His melodies stay with you for days; you're
sure you've heard them before, but they're brand
new." Metheny added that Horta, as a guitarist,
plays "great voicings with such a cool time feel."

In the 1980s, Toninho appeared on George
Duke's *Brazilian Love Affair* and released U.S. albums
like *Diamond Land* and *Moonstone* for the Verve label.

Each work was a lyrical, imaginative, free-flying instrumental journey characteristic of Toninho.

Skank

Skank is a band from Belo Horizonte that mixes reggae and ska with *cateretê*, *embolada*, *carimbó*, and *calango*. The quartet is led by vocalist-guitarist-songwriter Samuel Rosa and includes Henrique Portugal (keyboards), Haroldo Ferretti (drums), and Lelo Zaneti (bass). The unofficial fifth member, saxophonist Chico Amaral, writes many of the group's lyrics, which focus mostly on girls, soccer, and cinema. Occasionally they explore serious themes, as in the song "Sem Terra" (Without Land). Skank hit its artistic stride in 1994 with its second album, *Calango*, which achieved a heady blend of Jamaican pop with regional Mineiro styles. Two years later, the band launched the multiplatinum-selling *O Samba Poconé*, which flavored pulsing rhythms with upbeat melodies, Rosa's ebullient vocals, catchy horns, and a slick production.

More Mineiros

Other accomplished contemporary Mineiro musicians include Uakti, keyboardist Túlio Mourão, and singer-songwriters Flávio Venturini, Paulinho Pedra Azul, Sueli Costa, and João Bosco. The groups Sepultura and Overdose are popular in

Toninho Horta. *Photo by Buckmaster. Courtesy of Verve.*

the heavy metal realm, while Pena Branca and Xavantinho, which began performing in the 1960s with the name Peroba e Jabotá, are an acclaimed duo that plays rootsy música sertaneja and gained recognition in the 1980s with albums such as *Cio da Terra*, which was produced by Márcio Ferreira, with musical direction by Tavinho Moura. Their 1988 LP *Canto Violeiro* is a showcase of folk music from Minas, with examples of *toada*, *seresta*, *reisado*, *samba de roda*, and *moda de viola*.

Minas, with its varied heritage and ties to tradition, has given birth to many remarkable musicians who have kept their roots even as they seek to transcend them. They have poured the mysticism and hidden emotion of the region into their music and fashioned a remarkably universal sound.

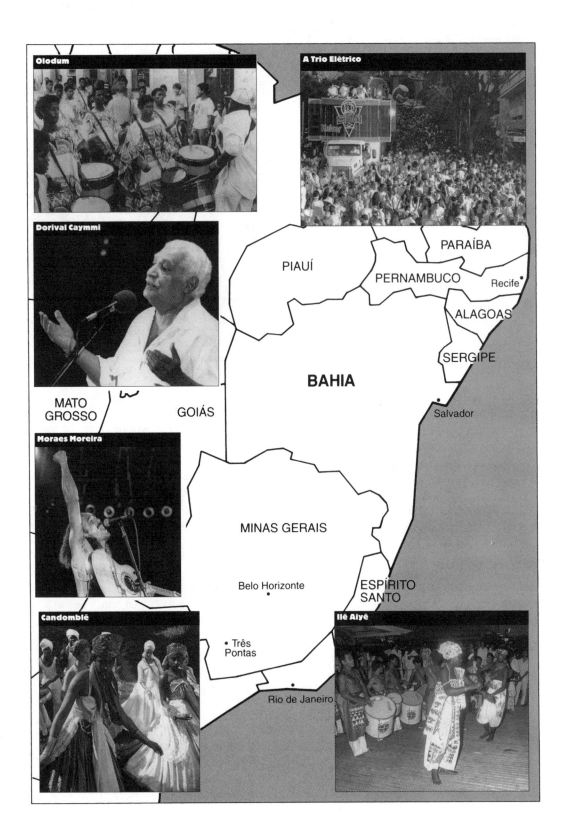

Olodum

A Trio Elétrico

Dorival Caymmi

PIAUÍ

PARAÍBA

PERNAMBUCO

Recife

ALAGOAS

SERGIPE

BAHIA

MATO GROSSO

GOIÁS

Salvador

Moraes Moreira

MINAS GERAIS

Belo Horizonte

ESPÍRITO SANTO

Candomblé

Ilê Aiyê

Três Pontas

Rio de Janeiro

Bahia of All the Saints

Chapter Six

Sun, sun, and rain
Drops of water and light
Yes, we are so many songs
Sambas, ballads, and blues
And the mixture of so many nations
Frevo, choro, and happiness
Reggae, maracatus, and baião
Pernambuco, Jamaica, and Bahia

Moraes Moreira and Zeca Barreto
"Pernambuco, Jamaica e Bahia"

Salvador, the capital of Bahia state, is a port city that looks out across the Atlantic Ocean to West Africa—to Ghana, Nigeria, Angola. Its culture is so different from that of the Northeast's mestizo-populated interior that at times Salvador seems to be spiritually situated on the outskirts of Luanda or Lagos.

Salvador (also often called "Bahia") is like many Portuguese colonial settlements with its narrow cobblestone streets, baroque churches ornamented with gold, and old houses decorated with blue Portuguese tile. Yet it is culturally the most African of all Brazilian cities. It also has the highest concentration of African descendents of any major metropolis in Brazil: an estimated 80 percent of its more than two million inhabitants are black or mulatto. Salvador has retained much of its African heritage, brought to Brazil by the enslaved peoples of past centuries. The white skirts and headdresses worn by many *baianas* (Bahian women) recall West Africa, as does the local food, often cooked in coconut milk or palm oil, and spiced with red pepper.

Nagô Nation

Governor-General Tomé de Sousa established Portugal's colonial government for Brazil in Salvador in 1549. At that time, the city was called São Sal-

A Bahian man in Pelourinho, a historic square in Salvador, once a place where slaves were auctioned and punished but today a center of Afro-Brazilian culture and the headquarters for organizations like Olodum and the Filhos de Gandhi. *Photo by Cláudio Vianna.*

An outdoor candomblé ceremony in Salvador. *Courtesy of Bahiatursa.*

Capoeira. *Courtesy of Bahiatursa.*

vador da Bahia de Todos Os Santos (Savior Saint of the Bay of all the Saints). Over the next three hundred years, plantations of sugar and cocoa were established along the Atlantic coast, and slave traders sold hundreds of thousands of Africans to the Bahian plantation owners. The slaves were of many different ethnic and cultural groups, as discussed earlier, but those who came to dominate Bahia in numbers and culture were the Yoruba and Ewe peoples taken from what are now the countries of Nigeria and the Republic of Benin. In Brazil, the Yoruba were called *Nagô*, a term used by the Fon people; the Nagô included such subgroups as the *Ketu* and Ijexá. The Ewe were called *Gege* (also spelled Jeje) and the fusing of their culture with that of the Yoruba became known as *Gege-Nagô*.

The Nagô worshipped deities called *orixás*

(òrìṣà in Yoruba) in the religion brought from their homeland that became known as *candomblé* in Brazil. *Terreiros* (centers of worship) were established in Salvador as early as 1830. The Bahian government, police, and press looked down on candomblé and persecuted public manifestations of African culture until well into the 1940s.

Yet candomblé thrived in Bahia, with hundreds of terreiros established in Salvador in the nineteenth and twentieth centuries. There have been extremely Yoruba-centric temples (like Ilê Axé Opô Afonjá), Gege-Nagô terreiros, and centers representing other African nations. A particularly famous site is the Terreiro do Gantois, founded in 1849. One of its priestesses, Mãe Menininha (1894–1986), was known throughout Brazil and honored in songs by Caetano Veloso and Dorival Caymmi. By the late twentieth century, candomblé had become acknowledged as a mainstream institution in Salvador.

Candomblé has provided much of the foundation of Afro-Bahian culture, but important elements also came from outside the Gege-Nagô cultural complex, as is the case with *capoeira*.

Capoeira

In the streets of Bahia you will often find a ring of spectators watching two young men—barefoot, shirtless, and wearing loose-fitting white pants—who execute spectacular spins and agile kicks to the astonishment of the crowd. This is done in harmony with an insistent buzzing rhythm played on the *berimbau*, a musical bow with a metal string and a gourd resonator. Berimbaus and additional percussion instruments are played by other participants (*capoeiristas*) who surround the two performers and urge them on by singing traditional songs. The two men perform cartwheels and handstands. They whirl about on their hands and spin their legs faster and faster as the tempo accelerates, coming ever closer with their kicks. Their movements grow increasingly daring, and it becomes obvious how *capoeira*—this spectacular martial art that resembles a dance—is an extremely effective fighting technique. In fact, capoeira is now taught all over Brazil, and in many other countries. And the sounds of capoeira have become a part of Brazil's musical vocabulary.

Two men engaging in capoeira to the accompaniment of songs performed by the capoeiristas around them. *Courtesy of Bahiatursa.*

Capoeira was brought to Brazil by enslaved Bantu peoples from Angola. Many scholars find similarities between it and *n'golo*, an acrobatic dance performed by young males of the Mucope people of Angola. The Angolan martial arts *njinga*, *basula*, and *gabetula* may also have influenced the creation of capoeira. The berimbau that accompanies capoeira during training and performances seems clearly derived from musical bows found in the Congo-Angola region. As it developed in Brazil, capoeira picked up West African elements, such as the use of the *agogô* and references to Yoruba orixás in the songs. Those who practice the art are called *capoeristas*.

There are references to capoeira as early as 1770. During the slavery era, capoeira fighters sometimes attached knives or razors to their feet or shoes, using them to deadly effect when they executed their whirling kicks. This was characteristic of the *maltas*, urban gangs formed of individual slaves and free men of the lower class. The Brazilian government took extreme measures to extinguish capoeira in the nineteenth century and made its practice an offense punishable by death. But on occasion they needed the aid of skilled capoeiristas, such as when they sent them to fight with the front-line troops in the war against Paraguay in the 1860s.

After the abolition, capoeira continued to be outlawed but soon became extremely wide-spread. Many in the lower classes used it for self-defense or intimidation, and for a long time it was identified with hustlers and hard criminals. In *Capoeira: A Brazilian Art Form*, Bira Almeida writes, "In 1920, the capoeiristas from Bahia felt the iron hand of police chief Pedro de Azevedo Gordilho, who placed the full power of his cavalry squadron against outlaws, rodas de capoeira, terreiros de candomblé, and afoxés."

This period saw the opening of the first public academies of capoeira. Manoel dos Reis Machado (1899–1979), known as Mestre Bimba, opened his establishment in 1927, and ten years later it became the first capoeira academy to be registered with the Brazilian government. He created a style called *capoeira regional* that mixed elements of capoeira and *batuque* (an African-based martial dance) and focused on the fighting elements of the martial art. Bimba wanted to de-marginalize capoeira and he encouraged middle-class and upper-class Brazilians to study it. Ultimately, he was successful. Capoeira was legitimized and became popular throughout the country, partly because the repression of Afro-Brazilian culture declined after Getúlio Vargas assumed the presidency in 1930. By 1953, Vargas was calling capoeira "the only true national sport."

Vincente Ferreira Pastinha (1898–1981), known as Mestre Pastinha, was the other major teacher of that time. He advocated a more traditional form called *capoeira angola* that placed its emphasis on the ritualistic, philosophical, and stylistic aspects of capoeira. Musically, capoeira angola can be accompanied by orchestras that include three berimbaus, two pandeiros, one agogô, a reco-reco, and an atabaque.

The key instrument is the berimbau, made of a *verga* (wooden bow), an *arame* (steel wire), and a *cabaça* (hollowed-out gourd). A *dobrão* (large coin) changes the pitch of the wire, which is struck with a thin stick called a *baqueta*. The hand that holds the baqueta also holds a small wicker rattle called a *caxixi*. The berimbaus come in three sizes: the *berimbau gunga* (with the largest gourd and deepest tone), the *berimbau centro* (or *médio*, which maintains the rhythm along with the gunga), and the *berimbau viola* (with the smallest gourd).

In capoeira angola, the singing by the *roda* (the circle of capoeristas surrounding those performing the capoeira moves) has a traditional structure comprised of three parts: the *ladainha*, the *chula*, and the *corrido*. According to Greg Downey, in the liner notes of a 1996 album by the Grupo Capoeira Angola Pelourinho, "The solo ladainha opens the musical sequence. The singer may tell a story, reflect philosophically, or pass messages to listeners paying close attention to the song. These solos are sometimes improvised. They are one of the most important vehicles for the transmission of oral history, political commentary, and traditional wisdom in capoeira angola." The chula follows the ladainha and consists of call-and-response between the soloist and the roda, in which the singer "delivers salutations and pays homage to those that merit such respect, leads prayers, and exhorts the players." Then comes the corrido, call-and-response singing that marks the beginning of the *jogo* (game). Adds Downey, "A good lead singer will improvise calls which comment upon the game being played, address those present at the event, or advise the players."

The roda's singing is an integral part of the art,

"giving energy and feedback to the players and infusing the roda with spirituality and history." Downey adds, "While the supporting instruments move inexorably forward, the berimbaus push and pull on each other, stutter and challenge, and all the players turn to the roda. Different *toques* [rhythms] will call for different games—faster or slower, more aggressive perhaps." There are several dozen toques employed by different capoeira schools, including: São Bento Grande, Iuna, Benguela, Santa Maria, Angola, Jôgo de Dentro, and Cavalaria.

Capoeira rhythms have infiltrated Brazilian popular music in songs like Gilberto Gil's "Domingo no Parque" and Baden Powell and Vinícius de Moraes's "Berimbau." And Naná Vasconcelos and Airto Moreira have incorporated capoeira music into their jazz improvisations and developed the berimbau as a unique solo instrument.

While candomblé and capoeira exist year round, much of Bahia's musical heritage is tied to the annual festivity of *Carnaval*.

Carnaval in Bahia

Today, Salvador vies with Rio for which city has the most popular Carnaval in Brazil. While much of the merrymaking in Rio takes place in private clubs or at the samba school parades in the Sambódromo, the festivities in Bahia are mostly out on the street. Every year, an estimated two million celebrants crowd Salvador's narrow streets to dance, sing, and party to the music of the blocos afro, afoxés, and trios elétricos. Hundreds of thousands of these revelers are from other parts of Brazil or foreign countries. They jam historic squares like the Praça Castro Alves and pack the cobblestone streets in a Carnaval that is chãotic, exhilarating, often violent, and probably pretty close in spirit to the ancient seasonal festivities in Rome like the Bacchanalia.

In the nineteenth century, Salvador had a mixture of indoor and outdoor partying. As early as the 1840s, upper-class Bahians celebrated Carnaval with private aristocratic balls. Outside in the streets, there was the entrudo, the same rough, dirty celebration of the common folk that took place in Rio and had been imported from Portugal. Entrudo was a source of concern in following decades for the press and the police, who had a difficult time trying to repress it. The authorities decided that in order to extinguish entrudo, it would be necessary to introduce another kind of celebration, Carnaval parades, to take its place.

In 1884, when Salvador was a city of 170,000 inhabitants, its first parade took place, emulating pre-Lent celebrations of Venice and Nice. Floats paraded in the cobblestoned streets, bands played polkas and opera overtures, and upper-class revelers dressed in luxurious European-style costumes. A newspaper that year wrote that Salvador's "parade was as elegant and animated as the ones in the court," referring to Rio de Janeiro, then the capital of Brazil.

At this time, middle-class groups like the Clube Carnavelsco Cruz Vermelha, Cavalheiros da Malta, Clube dos Cacetes, Grupo dos Nenês, and Cavalheiros de Veneza were the leading participants, with onlookers awarding their favorites with loud applause. For ten more years, the parades were basically a white festival, until Afro-Brazilians had their first organized participation, with the arrival of the *afoxés*.

A bloco parading through the Campo Grande area during Salvador's Carnaval. *Photo by Artur Ikishima. Courtesy of Bahiatursa.*

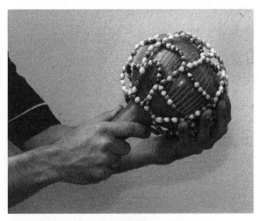

Afoxê. *Photo by Ricardo Pessanha.*

Afoxé

An afoxé is a procession that brings the ceremonial music of candomblé—with its corresponding songs, rhythms, dances, and percussion instruments—into the street in a secular context. Afoxés began in Salvador and have grown into massive groups that parade during Carnaval there and, to a lesser extent, in other cities such as For-

taleza and Recife. Earlier in the century, afoxé members were all candomblé devotees, and usually they would perform a ritual in the temple before heading out onto the street. Today, traditional afoxés still do this, but others have members who do not worship the orixás.

The slow, hypnotic *ijexá* rhythm of afoxé music comes from the rhythm and dance performed for the orixá Oxum in candomblé ceremonies (Ijexá, or Gexá, is also the name of a Yoruba subgroup in Nigeria). Ijexá is played on atabaques of three sizes (the *rum*, *rumpi*, and *lê*), with lots of syncopation on the *gonguê*, a deep-toned type of agogô. Other instruments sometimes used include the ganzá and the *afoxê*, a gourd with strung beads around it otherwise known as the *xequerê*.

The sound of the afoxés is serene, and not frenetic like frevo or thunderous like an escola de samba. Gilberto Gil described listening to the most famous afoxé, the Filhos de Gandhi (Sons of Gandhi), as an experience that "makes you feel like crying. You feel all that tranquility, that shiver running through your body, taking hold of you. This is the spiritual side of Carnaval, its balance."

The first afoxé to parade in Salvador was the Embaixada Africana (African Embassy), in 1895. The following year saw the debut of the Pândegos de África (African Merrymakers). Then others appeared, including the Chegada Africana (African Arrival), and Filhos da África (Sons of Africa). They dressed in African-style clothes and celebrated African themes, honoring Oxalá or heroes like Zumbi, the leader of the Palmares quilombo. With their infectious beat, they were quite a contrast to the staid "floats of the great Societies with their French court themes," as Jorge Amado wrote in his novel *Tenda dos Milagres* (Tent of Miracles).

Amado added, "The *News Journal* called for radical measures: 'What will become of the Carnival of 1902 if the police do not take steps to keep our streets from becoming terreiros, fetishism rampant, with its procession of ogans [male initiates], and its native rattles, gourds, and tambourines?' " There was "an epidemic of sambas and afoxés" in the streets and plazas.

Three years later, the upper class was even more offended. Amado wrote, "Hadn't Dr. Francisco An-

tônio de Castro Loureiro, temporary Chief of Police, expressly forbidden the afoxés to parade anywhere in the city, under any pretext whatever . . . for 'ethnic and social reasons, for the sake of our families, decency, morality, and the public welfare and in order to combat crime, debauchery, and disorder'? Who had dared to disobey the law? The Sons of Bahia had dared. Never had such a majestic carnival pageant, such a constellation of grandeur and beauty, been seen or dreamed of: such rhythmic drumming, such marvelous colors."

The afoxés were banished for nearly fifteen years, not returning until 1918. For the next three decades, Carnaval in Bahia was celebrated in private clubs by the rich and in the streets by *cordões* (which survived much longer in Salvador than in Rio), *blocos* (Carnaval groups, often associated with neighborhoods), small *escolas de samba*, and a few afoxés like the Filhos de Congo (Sons of Congo). Because of persistent repression of Afro-Brazilian culture by police that lasted until the late 1940s, it took much longer for Salvador, compared to Rio, to develop large Carnaval organizations like the latter city's big escolas de samba. Blacks in Salvador had to force their way into the streets during Carnaval, fighting with the police. The situation started to change in 1948 with the founding of the Filhos de Gandhi (Sons of Gandhi), an afoxé that incorporated the pacifist, anticolonialist philosophy of Mahatma Gandhi.

The Filhos de Gandhi

"Antonio Curuzu, a founding member of the Filhos de Gandhi, was responsible for choosing Gandhi to be our patron," recalled one of the group's founding members, in an interview with dance ethnologist Linda Yudin. "The group realized that Gandhi had nothing to do with African or Afro-Brazilian culture, but he was a symbol of world peace. That was what was important to us.

A member of the Filhos de Gandhi. *Photo by Linda Yudin.*

We wanted to demonstrate peacefully that our African heritage was positive for the community." He added, "After our participation, we hoped that the persecution of African manifestations in Bahia would stop occurring."

Their nonviolent approach and use of the name Gandhi gave them respectability in the eyes of the authorities. The new afoxé applied for, and was granted, a permit from the Ministry of Justice to parade during Carnaval. Thus they were protected from police interference and won the right to celebrate peacefully in the streets. The afoxé's roughly one hundred members, dressed in blue and white, made its debut in the Carnaval of 1949 and were warmly received by both the public and the authorities.

The Filhos de Gandhi have become one of the most highly respected institutions in Bahia and helped pave the way for the advent of the blocos afro in later decades. The group became an integral part of Bahian Carnaval, as did another new arrival to the festive Salvador streets the following year.

Dodô and Osmar: The Trio Elétrico

In the Carnaval of 1950, two musicians by the name of Dodô and Osmar appeared in the streets of Salvador in an old Ford pickup truck. Standing in the bed of the truck, they performed with an electrified guitar, electrified cavaquinho, and portable amps. Their style of music was *frevo*, a highly syncopated, fast-tempo marcha that originated earlier in the century in Recife, a large coastal city to the north in Pernambuco state.

Dodô and Osmar created a sensation with their amplified frevo. In 1951, they added a third instrumentalist and the name *trio elétrico* (electric trio) was born. Trio elétrico trucks soon became a common sight in Salvador during Carnaval, winding through the city's old, narrow streets, inciting crowds to dance and sing. The trios grew in size, popularity,

and ability to generate massive decibels. The sound trucks evolved into enormous, custom-built rigs that served as mobile stages, weighted down with numerous musicians and tall, precarious banks of speakers. The sound they generate is deafening, overwhelming, as they lumber through the primary Carnaval areas of Campo Grande, Praça Castro Alves, and Barra. Behind the trios follow thousands of celebrants, dancing and leaping deliriously.

By the 1970s, many Bahian blocos had begun to contract trios elétricos to provide the music for their parades. Some used heavy rope to cordon off a zone of protection around each sound truck. For the price of admission, you received the bloco's costume and could parade in relative safety inside the *cordão*, separated from the often-dangerous chãos in the streets. These days, sound trucks also carry the vocalists of blocos, like Timbalada, that do not identify themselves with the trios elétricos. Many blocos feature celebrity musicians atop the trucks, performing the latest Bahian Carnaval hits. In the mid-1990s, performers like Daniela Mercury, Netinho, Gera Samba, and Chiclete com Banana could be found playing with blocos like Camaleão, Pinel, Crocodilo, and Bizu.

A trio elétrico keeping the crowds dancing. *Photo by Artur Ikishima. Courtesy of Bahiatursa.*

In the 1960s and 1970s, frevo developed into an important vehicle for instrumental improvisation. In Bahia, it became inextricably mixed with the trio elétrico sound, which has come to mean frenetic guitar and cavaquinho soloing coupled with a voracious absorption of musical idioms. Trio elétrico musicians play everything from rock to Rimsky-Korsakov's "Flight of the Bumblebee." Anything that makes the listener jump and dance is incorporated, and this has helped create new musical styles. In addition, many notable Bahian musicians have gotten their start playing with the trios. But by the late 1970s, the trios elétricos would have to share space in the old streets of Salvador with a new cultural manifestation: the *blocos afro*, short for *blocos afrobrasileiros* (Afro-Brazilian Carnaval groups).

Roots of the Afro-Bahian Renaissance

In the 1970s, many Bahian blacks from the lower classes celebrated Carnaval in groups called *blocos índio* like the Apaches de Tororó, which were founded in 1968, and the Comanches, established in 1974. The members of the blocos índio, dressed in Hollywood-style Indian costumes, danced to samba and were notoriously violent. As the rowdy blocos índio grew in popularity, they were regularly met with harassment from the local military police. But in the 1970s and 1980s, with the formation of the blocos afro, poor Afro-Brazilians had a new outlet for their energy and creativity in Carnaval. Consequently, the blocos índio declined in popularity, with many members joining the blocos afro.

The growth of the blocos afro was linked to a renewal of black consciousness then taking place in Salvador and the rest of the country. In the late 1960s and early 1970s, many young black Brazilians were fascinated by the music of James Brown, the Jackson 5, and other African Americans. The wave of black pride that hit the United States ("Black is beautiful") also echoed in Brazil in the favelas of Rio and other large cities. The popularity of American soul music inspired a cultural movement nicknamed "black-rio" in Rio de Janeiro, "black-sampa" in São Paulo, and "black-mineiro" in Minas Gerais. It was panned by many critics as more "cultural imperialism" and "alienation" imposed by the United States. But among many blacks in Brazil, it inspired a renewed pride in African roots, as did the wave of independence movements in Africa in the 1970s. Angola and Mozambique, former Portuguese colonies, were among the many African nations that achieved self-rule in that decade. And in Bahia, Afro-Brazilian pride was further boosted by the popularity of reggae stars Bob Marley, Peter Tosh, and Jimmy Cliff, whose lyrics decried racism and government corruption, while praising Mother Africa.

Ilê Aiyê

The surge of interest in black culture led Vovô and Apolônio—two men who lived in the Curuzu district of the Liberdade neighborhood of Salvador—to have the idea in 1974 of creating a bloco afro to parade during Carnaval. And in their

Drummers and dancers for Ilê Aiyê. *Photo by Fernando Seixas. Courtesy of Eldorado Records.*

group, Ilê Aiyê, only very dark-skinned blacks could be members. Whites and mulattos were excluded. Their policy sparked controversy, which is rather ironic considering the unwritten but obvious boundaries of race and class that already existed in Salvador. It is a city whose governmental leaders and upper class were (and still are) amost entirely light-skinned, even though Afro-Brazilians comprise the vast majority of the population.

There has long been segregation in Bahia's Carnaval both in indoor clubs and outside on the streets, according to Antonio Risério. In his book *Carnaval Ijexá*, he writes, "Put on one side Badauê, Ilê Aiyê, Ara Ketu, etc. On the other side, those that are called 'Class A blocos,' like Barão, Trazos-Montes, Internacionais, etc. And the conclusion is obvious: there exists a relative, but evident, internal racial homogeneity in the blocos, dividing them into two species: those whose racial spectrum goes from black to light mulatto, and those whose spectrum goes from light mulatto to white. It's that simple. Moreover, some blocos of richer people, who don't want to mix with blacks, are contracting small (and lamentable) trios elétricos to play only for them, in the private space of the bloco, staked out by ropes."

Recounting the origin of Ilê, Risério describes how Vovô and Apolônio were drinking and talking one night in Curuzu when the idea came up. Vovô recalled, "It was in that era of that business of black power, and so we thought about making a bloco just for blacks, with African themes." They chose the name Ilê Aiyê (a Yoruba phrase that roughly translates as "house of life") for their bloco afro and quickly attracted many musicians and members. Ilê Aiyê made its Carnaval debut in 1975, with about a hundred people in the bloco and assorted friends trailing after it, according to Vovô.

The local police tended to treat poor blacks as second-class citizens or potential criminals. This meant that an entirely black bloco defiantly af-

firming its *negritude* (blackness) would raise some eyebrows. Vovô told Risério, "There were blacks that didn't leave because they were afraid of being arrested. In that era, we didn't know how it would go, we didn't have the least idea of what would happen. Everyone inexperienced, no big names, no political support. We went to the street just that way, with boldness and heart. It was a major polemic. There were people who asked us if it was a bloco or a protest."

Parading down to the beach, pounding out Afro-Brazilian rhythms on surdos and repiques, Ilê performed raw, unadorned music with just vocals, drums, and percussion, which would set the style for the blocos afro to follow. They created a lot of excitement in Salvador, singing the provocative lyrics of their theme song "Ilê Aiyê," written by Paulinho Camafeu.

> **What bloco is this, I want to know**
> **It's the black world that we have come to**
> **show you**
> **We're crazy blacks, we're really cool**
> **We have kinky hair . . .**
> **White, if you knew the value that blacks**
> **have**
> **You'd take a tar bath and become black too**

The song was later recorded in 1977 by Gilberto Gil on his *Refavela* album, adding to Ilê's renown.

They developed into a Carnaval group with more than two thousand participants by the early 1990s. Each year, they explored a different aspect

Blocos afro have also been founded outside of Salvador. In Rio de Janeiro, four blocos—Agbara Dudu (the oldest in that city, founded in 1982), Dudu Èwe, Òrúnmìlá, and Lemi Ayò—recorded an album together in 1992 titled *Terreiros e Quilombos*. Raimundo Santa Rosa, who produced the LP, applauded the overall importance of the blocos and said, "It's important to open space for new ideas related to blacks, allow for improvement of their living conditions, and stimulate greater awareness." Believing that such roles are no longer fulfilled by organizations like Rio's samba schools, he added, "The music performed by the escolas de samba today is sheer commerce." Of course, the many venerable samba schools that serve as year-round community and cultural

A practice session for Rio's bloco afro Orunmilá. *Photo by Ricardo Pessanha.*

institutions might well take exception to that point.

---

of their African heritage, with costumes researched and woven to match the theme. Without compromise, Ilê Aiyê celebrated *negritude,* urged resistance against Brazil's dominant light-skinned elites, and provocatively used racist or condescending terms against blacks (like *criolos doidos*—crazy blacks—in the above song) in its lyrics. Within just a few years, Ilê became a powerful organization that had a long-lasting impact on Bahia's music and culture.

Muzenza, Malê Debalê, Badauê, and Ara Ketu

The success of Ilê Aiyê triggered the formation of many blocos afro in the late 1970s and 1980s. None of the other blocos imitated Ilê in its policy of excluding those with light skin, but they did follow Ilê's example in tying their identities and Carnaval themes to Africa and Afro-based culture. Each of the larger blocos, with one thousand to three thousand members, has its own unique constellation of percussion, as is the case down south in Rio's samba schools.

Malê Debalê, founded in 1979, paraded one year with its thousands of members dressed as antiapartheid guerillas from Soweto. Badauê (1978) is an afoxé whose members wear costumes of golden-yellow for the orixá Oxum and white for

Oxalá. Ara Ketu (1980) is a bloco afro that usually celebrates Yoruba concepts in its parades. And Muzenza (1982) is a bloco with a special affinity for Jamaica that uses the green, yellow, and black colors of that country's flag.

Linda Yudin told us, "What is so profound about the blocos afro is that they have allowed the young black population of Salvador to identify themselves through the expressions of dance, song, and drumming as opposed to outsiders telling them who they are or what their culture is about."

The blocos afro carried forward the evolution of styles like afoxé and *samba afro* (samba mixed with candomblé rhythms), which is not to be confused with Vinícius de Moraes and Baden Powell's *afro-sambas* played in the bossa nova style. Beginning in 1987, they began performing *samba-reggae,* a fusion of the two styles in which the repiques or surdos take the part of the rhythm guitar in reggae. Samba-reggae boosted the popularity of the blocos and became an essential element of Bahian *axé music* that decade and the next.

The drums and choruses of ten Bahian blocos afro and afoxés, along with the vocals of Luiz Caldas, Margareth Menezes, Gilberto Gil, and other local singers, were heard in 1988 on the album

Afros e Afoxés da Bahia, organized by Durval Ferreira and Paulo César Pinheiro. Many blocos recorded solo albums in the late 1980s and 1990s, and several—most notably Ara Ketu and Olodum—spun off small pop ensembles.

By 1981, an estimated eighty thousand people were parading in blocos afro and afoxés, according to Risério. Two years later, there were sixteen blocos afro and twenty-three afoxés in Salvador, along with eight cordões, five blocos indío, and two samba schools, according to anthropologist Daniel Crowley's *African Myth and Black Reality in Bahian Carnaval*.

By the mid-1990s, participation had shifted and the total number of blocos afro had dropped, with the most successful organizations—Ilê Aiyê, the Filhos de Gandhi, Olodum, Muzenza, and Malê Debalê—drawing members away from the smaller organizations.

Return of the Filhos de Gandhi

Before the advent of Ilê Aiyê, one of the Carnaval groups doing the most to keep Afro-Brazilian identity alive in Bahia was the Filhos de Gandhi. Unfortunately, by the 1960s the popularity of the afoxés was in a sharp decline. The Filhos de Gandhi had paraded with roughly one hundred members during each Carnaval in their first two decades of existence, but by the 1970s they were struggling and in danger of dying out.

Three important factors led to their revival. According to Yudin, one was that the Filhos de Gandhi began a concerted effort to recruit new members. Also, in the early 1970s the municipality of Salvador and Bahiatursa (the state's tourism arm) realized the value to tourism of groups like the afoxés and began to encourage the "re-Africanization" of Bahia's Carnaval, a sharp contrast with earlier government policies. A third

impetus came when MPB star Gilberto Gil returned to Salvador from exile and went in search of the afoxé, hoping to involve himself with their music and culture. He told Risério, "I found about twenty of them, with their drums on the ground, in a corner of the Praça da Sé. They didn't have the resources, nor the will to take a place in the Bahian Carnaval." Gil joined and devoted himself to their music and cultural discipline.

His energy and celebrity helped revitalize the Filhos de Gandhi. In 1976's Carnaval, a year after Ilê Aiyê's debut, Gil paraded with his adopted afoxé, and the next year he recorded the afoxé "Patuscada de Gandhi" (Revelry of Gandhi) on his *Refavela* album, along with "Ilê Aiyê." With the help of Gil and Bahiatursa, and the success of their recruitment efforts, the Filhos de Gandhi were thriving by the next decade, with more than a thousand members (all men) in 1980. The governor of Bahia, Antonio Carlos Magalhães, realizing the political potential of helping the venerable afoxé, gave them a renovated building in the historic Pelourinho to use as their headquarters.

The Filhos continued to grow and by 1996 had more than six thousand members, including children who participated in their parade. Visually, the Filhos de Gandhi are an awesome sight: a shimmering ocean of men dancing to the ijexá rhythm, dressed in costumes of white turbans, tunics, and sandals, royal-blue socks, and blue-and-white sashes and beads. The Filhos de Gandhi and Ilê Aiyê had a major impact on Bahian music and culture, as did a bloco afro formed in 1979: Olodum.

Olodum

It is night in the Pelourinho, the famed historical square in the heart of old Salvador, in the late 1980s. A sultry breeze washes over the large, free-spirited crowd gathered here under a hazy moon.

Olodum. *Courtesy of Sound Wave/WEA.*

Atop a makeshift stage stand singers, percussionists, and dancers from the group Olodum, their backs to the iron balconies, colorful facades, and tile roofs of centuries-old colonial buildings. Near the stage, an unfurled banner reads "África—Olodum—Bahia."

The surdo players begin to generate a solid beat and the caixas add a constant pattern of higher-pitched sixteenth notes, accenting the back beats. The repique kicks in a reggae cadence, other instruments like the African kalimba (thumb-piano) join in, and rhythms build and interact. The music is mesmerizing, as samba meets reggae and creates a heavy, dense, ritualistic sound.

Women start to dance spontaneously in large groups and athletic young men practice capoeira, throwing spinning kicks to the beat. Now the master percussionist appears behind his set of two timbales and adds sharp, rhythmic bursts that contrast with the other instruments, leading and counterpointing them. The lead vocalist and the chorus begin to sing of Egypt and Mozambique and South Africa. The thousands in the audience are carried off into a state of euphoria by the music and dancing.

Olodum (from *Olódùmarè*, the Yoruba supreme deity) has several thousand members and is headquarted in the Pelourinho, once the site of slave auctions and whippings, now a tourist attraction and center of Afro-Brazilian culture. Olodum is the most well known and commercially successful of the blocos afro. It is also a thriving community organization that sponsors courses and workshops for its members and poor youth in Salvador. Its principal goals are to continue the struggle against racism and to seek the recovery and preservation of black culture.

Under the leadership of Neguinho do Samba (Luis Alves de Souza), Olodum has recorded many successful albums using ensembles comprised of the top musicians of the bloco. Neguinho has been largely responsible for shaping Olodum's sound—which at first consisted exclusively of vocals and percussion—and developing its rhythmic innovations.

Olodum is generally credited with having created samba-reggae. According to ethnomusicologist Larry Crook, Olodum introduced the new style during rehearsals for the 1986 Carnaval. In addition, the band augmented their repique-surdo sound with timbales (common in Cuba and Puerto Rico), which further distinguished their music from that of the other blocos. In 1987, Olodum recorded the new samba-reggae rhythm in "Faraó Divinidade do Égito" (Pharoah Egyptian Divinity), written by Luciano Gomes dos Santos. The song paid homage to ancient Egypt and proclaimed that some of the pharoahs were actually black. "Faraó," propelled by the catchy new beat, was the big hit of Carnaval that year and helped the band land a contract with Continental Records.

"Faraó" was featured on Olodum's first album, *Égito Madagáscar* (Egypt Madagascar), which showcased the bloco's seismic drums and unveiled samba-reggae and other rhythmic experiments. Banda Mel also recorded "Faraó" in 1987 and achieved a commercial hit. Another tune on Olodum's LP, Rey Zulu's "Madagáscar Olodum," became a national success for Banda Reflexu's and was included in their best-selling *Da Mãe Africa* album that year.

"Girassol" (Sunflower), "Gira" (Spin), and "Revolta Olodum" (Olodum's Revolt) were popular tunes in the next few years for Olodum.

Dorival Caymmi. *Photo by Wilton Montenegro. Courtesy of EMI.*

Many of the bloco's songs protested Brazilian and global social injustices. Some tunes, like Pierre Onasis-Nêgo's hugely successful 1993 "Requebra" (Shake Your Hips), were just good party music and not political at all. That decade, Olodum's sound on their albums expanded from a percussion-and-vocals base to include guitars and keyboards and mixed their trademark samba-reggae with forró and pop styles.

Olodum gained international fame from music videos, concerts in other countries, and appearances on the albums of famous global pop musicians. They participated in Paul Simon's song "The Obvious Child" from his *Rhythm of the Saints* album, and in the Bill Laswell–produced LP *Bahia Black: Ritual Beating System*. Olodum's percussionists, pounding their trademark red-gold-green-black drums, performed in Simon's concert in New York's Central Park in *Paul Simon's Concert in the Park*, in Michael Jackson's music video "They Don't Really Care About Us," and during festivities for the 1994 World Cup soccer finals (which Brazil won).

Bahian Popular Music

Along with the rich tradition of groups like the blocos and afoxés, many renowned individual artists have come from the city of Salvador or Bahia state, including Gilberto Gil, Caetano Veloso, João Gilberto, Gal Costa, Raul Seixas, Maria Bethânia, and Simone. But one name comes up time and time again when contemporary musicians speak of their influences: Dorival Caymmi, one of the leading figures of the samba-canção era. Caymmi wrote songs marked by a profound simplicity, picturesque lyrics, and unforgettable melodies. His music paints life on the Bahian coast: its fishermen and their *jangadas* (sail-rafts), the beauty and danger of the sea, lush palm-lined shores, and candomblé

temples. It evokes the despair and courage of the poor, the charm and sensuality of the Baiana, and the easy-going tropical pace of Salvador.

Caymmi's samba "Acontece Que Sou Baiano" (It Happens That I'm Bahian) takes the listener into his culture with a reference to a *pai-de santo* (a candomblé priest), whose help he seeks in regard to a woman with an alluring *requebrado*, a voluptuous movement of the hips.

> **I already put a hen's foot in my doorway**
> **I already called a pai-de-santo**
> **To bless that woman**
> **The one with the requebrado**

Caymmi co-wrote "É Doce Morrer no Mar" (It's Sweet to Die in the Sea) with his good friend, the novelist Jorge Amado, also a famed chronicler of the region's folklore. In the sad and hypnotic toada, a woman mourns the loss of her mate—a fisherman who has gone to meet Yemanjá, the candomblé goddess of the sea.

> **In the green waves of the sea**
> **My beloved was drowned**
> **He made his bridegroom's bed**
> **In the lap of Yemanjá**

"Caymmi is timeless. He is specific, the vital force and the poetry of our region," states the Bahian artist Carybe in *Nova História*, adding, "He is the

Pepeu Gomes, former member of Os Novos Baianos.
Courtesy of Pepeu Gomes.

Moraes Moreira. *Photo by José Perderneiras. Courtesy of*
Sony.

saudade of Bahia, the sadness of Bahia, the beaches, the sun."

The group Novos Baianos (New Bahians) played an important role in the evolution of Bahian music in the late 1960s and early 1970s. In their unique sound, Bahian Carnaval met Woodstock rock. One of their most successful al-

bums was *Acabou Chorare* (No More Crying), which was released in 1973 and included the hit single "Preta Pretinha." Os Novos Baianos inspired the trios elétricos to mix rock with frevo—causing what Gilberto Gil later called the *rolling-stonização* of the trios. After the group split up in 1976, bassist Dadi formed the seminal instrumental group Cor de Som (Color of Sound), which played frevo, choro, and samba with jazz-fusion-like arrangements. Guitarist Pepeu Gomes and singer Baby Consuelo (who were then husband and wife) went on to establish solo careers in pop music.

The fourth principal member of Os Novo Baianos, singer-guitarist Moraes Moreira, was Brazil's foremost exponent of frevo in the 1980s. He displayed musical versatility in albums like *Mestiço É Isso* (Mestizo Is This), consistently keeping up with new musical developments such as the advent of the blocos afro. In 1979, he and Antonio Risério composed "Assim Pintou Moçambique" (Thus Arrived Mozambique), a song that fused the ijexá rhythm of the afoxé groups with the trio-elétrico sound. The next year, Moreira dressed in the costume of the afoxé Badauê and performed frevo and reggae-ijexá during Carnaval. He also incorporated reggae into songs like 1986's "Pernambuco, Jamaica e Bahia," which included percussion by rising stars Carlinhos Brown and Tony Mola and guitar by Luiz Caldas. Moreira has written several Carnaval smash hits that celebrate Salvador and Bahian culture. His most famous composition to date is the ecstatic frevo "Festa do Interior" (Party in the Interior), written with Abel Silva, which became a huge success when interpreted by Gal Costa in 1981.

Axé Music

In the 1980s, a new category of popular music emerged in Bahia that fully came of age in the next decade, when it gained the name *axé music*, incorporating the Yoruba word *axé* (life force or positive energy). Olodum, Carlinhos Brown, and Daniela Mercury are among the most notable exponents of axé music, an umbrella term for several different styles, with samba-reggae being the most significant. Primary ingredients in the mix are samba, ijexá, frevo, and reggae, and other elements can include merengue, salsa, soca, and carimbó. Several factors helped local musicians develop the new sound: the influence of the blocos afro, the free-wheeling experimentation of trio-elétrico musicians, access to improved recording technology, and regional support for Bahian music.

By the 1980s, Bahia's musical scene had become thoroughly Africanized. The influence of the Filhos de Gandhi, Olodum, Ilê Aiyê, and other blocos inspired a surge in Afro-Brazilian consciousness. Bahian popular music was suddenly full of Yoruba words, candomblé images, and references to Africa and Jamaica. And the trios elétricos started to present *afro-elétrico* music, to use Antonio Risério's phrase.

Bahian musicians playing in the blocos and the trios began to invent a plethora of new sounds with a strong dance beat. It helped that a number of Brazilian and Caribbean forms mesh quite well together rhythmically. Reggae was an especially big outside influence in the 1980s and fit together well with various Brazilian grooves. Olodum used it to create samba-reggae, the most influential new Brazilian style of the 1980s. Meanwhile, the trio-elétrico groups, the training ground for many young Bahian musicians, were throwing every musical reference they had into their frenetic, high-volume presentations.

The fast-paced creativity going on in Salvador was aided at this time by a regional market that eagerly absorbed locally produced music. Bahians avidly followed their own artists, even as Brazil-

ians in Rio and elsewhere were largely consuming *música sertaneja*, Brazilian rock, and U.S.-U.K. pop music. An article in the September 12, 1990, issue of *Veja* magazine estimated that 95 percent of the music played on the radio was Brazilian music; on weekends 60 percent of it was Bahian. Another factor helping musicians in Salvador was an improvement in technology. Cheaper and better synthesizers became available, and Bahian artists in general had increased access to modern recording studios. In many cases, they didn't wait for deals with the big labels and instead put out their own independent records.

One such example was the singer-songwriter Luiz Caldas, who was born in Feira da Santana in 1963 and had moved to Salvador at age eighteen to play with the Trio Elétrico Tapajós. In 1985,

Luiz Caldas. *Photo by Paulo Ricardo. Courtesy of PolyGram.*

Caldas released his debut album *Magia* (Magic) on a small label, then talked PolyGram into picking up the distribution. The LP included the song "Fricote," which used the *fricote* rhythm (also called *deboche*), in which Caldas concocted his own mixture of ijexá and reggae, juicing up the tempo and creating a new beat. The song was a forerunner of axé music and arguably its first major hit—before the category had a name. Caldas found himself with a platinum-selling album on his hands, with most of the sales coming from record stores in Bahia and the Northeast. He became a major star and scored another commercial success in 1986 with *Flor Cigana* (Gypsy Flower), which featured the fricote tune "Eu Vou Já" (I'll Go Soon).

Chiclete com Banana, Gerônimo, Banda Mel, and Banda Reflexu's were also helping to create the new Bahian sound at this time, which received a further boost from Olodum's introduction of samba-reggae. Shortly thereafter, lambada—a mixture of *carimbó* and merengue—was another element thrown into the simmering musical stew. Sarajane, Abel Duerê, Cid Guerreiro, Lazzo Matumbi, Roberto Mendes, Missinho, Carlos Pita, Djalma Oliveira, Raizes do Pelô, Simone Moreno, Banda Eva, Netinho, Cheiro de Amor, Márcia Freire (former lead vocalist of Cheiro de Amor), and Bragadá (led by Tony Mola) were among the other key artists and groups recording

the emerging styles. For the most part, rhythm has been the key ingredient in their songs, which typically feature simple melodies and harmonies. It is energetic, good-time party music, designed for dancing and Carnaval.

While serious themes have been explored in songs like "Faraó," most axé music tunes feature lyrics that focus on romance, sex, and Carnaval. The Bahian bands Gera Samba and Companhia do Pagode also epitomize this tendency. Both fit more into the sambalanço category, recording pop versions of styles like samba de roda, but their songs were extremely popular in Salvador's Carnaval in the mid-1990s and widely performed by other Bahian artists. Gera Samba's "É o Tchan" sold one million copies throughout Brazil, and a short time later part of the group spun off a second band, É o Tchan, which took the name of the hit song. Companhia do Pagode's "Na Boquinha da Garrafa" was another bestseller. The two songs, with their infectious dance rhythms and sly erotic lyrics, generated the *dança do bumbum* (fanny dance) and the *dança da garrafa* (bottle dance), respectively, which were hit dances in Salvador's Carnaval. They joined other popular Bahian styles like *dança da tartaruga* (turtle dance) to form what some call *axé dance*, the dance movements that accompany axé music. These are drawn from a wide variety of sources, including Brazilian folkloric dances and hip hop, jazz dance, modern dance, and even aerobics.

Daniela Mercury and Margareth Menezes

While axé music was dominating the airwaves in Salvador, it also began to appear on the albums of veteran MPB stars. In the late 1980s Beth Carvalho recorded the afoxé "O Encanto do Gantois" and the Ara Ketu tribute "Majestade Real." At the start of the 1990s, Gal Costa released the samba-reggae "Salvador Não Inerte," "Revolta Olodum" with Raízes do Pelô, and Gerônimo's afoxé "É d'Oxum" with the Filhos de Gandhi. At that time, many MPB singers also covered compositions by Carlinhos Brown. But it was not until the arrival of Daniela Mercury (Daniela Mercuri de Almeida Povoas) that the new music from Bahia really took hold of all of Brazil.

Mercury was born in Salvador in 1965 and began her career singing in bars, favoring MPB standards by her idols Caetano Veloso, Gilberto Gil, Chico Buarque, and Elis Regina. The Bahian singer-songwriter Gerônimo was impressed by her talent, and Daniela sang backup vocals in his band for a year. In 1987 she performed as a singer for the trio elétrico associated with the bloco Eva, then recorded two albums with the group Companhia Clic. Daniela released her debut solo album, *Daniela Mercury*, in 1991. It features the hit song "Swing da Cor" (Swing of Color), written by Luciano Gomes, which Mercury dynamically sings atop the propulsive samba-reggae beat made famous by Olodum. The LP (also referred to as *Swing da Cor*) was a huge national best-seller that took samba-reggae's national popularity to a new level. Radio stations and bars that had previously ignored axé music now played Mercury's music nonstop. The next year, *O Canto da Cidade* (The Song of the City) added to her

Margareth Menezes. *Photo by Livio Campos. Courtesy of Mango/Island.*

success and its title song, co-written by Mercury, was another big hit.

Some Brazilian critics suggested that much of Daniela's popularity was due to her being light-skinned and beautiful. Yet many black performers, including Gilberto Gil and Margareth Menezes, have defended Mercury's success and talent. Daniela is a kinetic performer with a sensual flair and effervescent charisma on stage. She is a fervent vocalist whose abilities have steadily matured, reaching a new level in the 1996 album *Feijão com Arroz* (Beans with Rice), which greatly expanded her musical range. On it, Mercury adeptly interprets well-produced axé music and adds new touches that include "À Primeira Vista" (At First Sight), a romantic ballad by northeastern bard Chico César, and "Vide Gal," a sensational Carlinhos Brown samba with blazing horns and Rio-style percussion. In his article "And Now, the World," critic Bruce Gilman says of Mercury that "her studio recordings never fail to create the sensational energy level of a live performance, one of the widely recognized merits of her work."

Carlinhos Brown. *Photo by Mario Cravo. Courtesy of EMI.*

Even before Mercury conquered Rio with her axé music, the genre was carried overseas by fellow Bahian singer Margareth Menezes (born in 1962). Menezes's deep, powerful voice was well-suited for carrying a tune atop the propulsive drums in samba-reggae. After performing as a vocalist with trios elétricos, she made her solo debut in 1988 with the album *Margareth Menezes*. Her career received a jump start when she was invited by David Byrne (the former leader of the rock group Talking Heads) to accompany him on a world tour. This led to a deal with the Mango label and her first international release, *Elegibô*. Its title song, written by Rey Zulu, is an uplifting hymn to an ancient Yoruba city of the same name and might be described as *samba-reggae-exaltação* (exaltation samba-reggae). Margareth introduced axé music to foreign audiences and helped pave the way for the international success of other Bahian musicians, including Salvador's most influential artist of that era: Carlinhos Brown.

Carlinhos Brown and Timbalada

Mercury, Caldas, Menezes, Marisa Monte, Maria Bethânia, Gal Costa, Caetano Veloso, and Cássia Eller are among those who have recorded songs by Carlinhos Brown (Antonio Carlos Santos de Freitas), an innovative songwriter, bandleader, and percussionist. Brown mixes axé music with funk,

embolada, bossa nova, and other styles in idiosyncratic and rhythmically rich tunes that he describes as "Afro-Brazilian popular music without prejudice. In my sound there's space for everything from Noel Rosa to Pintado do Bongô to Villa-Lobos."

Carlinhos was born in 1963 in Salvador and grew up in Candeal, an area in the Brotas neighborhood. His mother was an evangelical Protestant and his father practiced candomblé. Brown grew up listening to a wide range of music. He favored Luiz Gonzaga, the Beatles, merengue, Tropicália, Jorge Ben (later known as Benjor), and the Jackson 5, and he also absorbed *violeiros* in the streets, candomblé music coming from a *terreiro* near his parents' house, and Gregorian chants echoing out of a Catholic monastery atop a nearby hill.

As a youth, Brown studied with a percussion master named Pintado do Bongô (Osvaldo Alves da Silva), who played with the group Baticum. Carlinhos told us, "Pintado lived near me. At the time I liked to dance and beat my cans and buckets but still hadn't discovered myself as a musician. But when I saw him play I was really impressed. I used to go to his place against my mother's will. As a Protestant, she always connected drum beating to candomblé." As an evangelical, she considered Afro-Brazilian religion to be pagan and evil.

Brown continued, "This was the time of Black Power. I had Afro hair and loved Toni Tornado [a Brazilian funk singer and dancer] and James Brown." The latter also supplied Carlinhos with his stage name. "I was dancing at a party and started to attract everybody's attention. The guy who was throwing the party didn't like it at all. He turned off the stereo and asked, 'Who is that James Brown?' My friends started to make fun of me, calling me Brown, so I became Carlinhos Brown."

Carlinhos continued his lessons with Mestre Pintado, whom Brown described as a "master of *sambão*, a mixture of samba with mambo. The first Caribbean connection in Bahia was sambão, long before fricote. When I played with Luiz Caldas, he didn't know about sambão. He had a fantastic versatility but didn't know what was going on in the streets. When he got in touch with all that, he interpreted it quite well and created those mixtures, the most famous one being fricote. But it all started with sambão." The sambão beat went largely unrecorded, as far as Brown knows, but he did use it in his song "Guia Pro Congal" on the *Bahia Black* album.

Carlinhos performed in bars and at parties with Mestre Pintado, and—as he entered his teenage years—played with the female vocal group Clara da Lua (White of the Moon) and the rock band Mar Revolto (Stormy Sea). Then came a tour of duty with trios elétricos and work as a studio musician. In the 1980s, he played percussion—claves, congas, agogô, pandeiro, timbales, afoxê, and more—on albums by Luiz Caldas, Moraes Moreira, Maria Bethânia, Caetano Veloso, and others. Brown achieved his first radio hit with the song "Visão do Cíclope" (Cyclops Vision) co-written with and recorded by Luiz Caldas, who included the song on his *Magia* album. By the middle of the decade, covers of Brown's tunes were garnering prodigious amounts of radio play on Bahian and northeastern radio stations. He was a part of Caetano Veloso's band in the late 1980s, playing on both *Caetano* and *Estrangeiro*. On the latter album, Veloso sang Brown's "Meia-Lua Inteira" (Entire Half Moon), which was used as the theme song for a novela and was a big hit in Brazil. Carlinhos also toured with Djavan, João Gilberto, and João Bosco.

But after getting his foot in the door of the Brazilian recording industry, Brown decided to head back home to Candeal. "Because I had received so much, I had to do something in re-

turn," he said. Brown started a percussion school for children, and the most musically talented of his students eventually became the band Vai Quem Vem, which would record on several albums with Carlinhos. One of their first appearances was on "Carro Velho" (Old Car), on the album *Os Grãos* by the Paralamas do Sucesso.

In 1992, Brown gained his first major exposure as a recording artist. He appeared on *Bahia Black: Ritual Beating System*, the intriguing group album produced by Bill Laswell that mixed axé music with funk and jazz. The recording largely focused on Carlinhos, featuring five of his songs and teaming him with Olodum and U.S. jazz artists Wayne Shorter and Herbie Hancock (who had created the landmark *Native Dancer* album two decades earlier with Milton Nascimento).

Sérgio Mendes's Grammy-winning *Brasileiro*, released later that same year, also showcased Brown's talent and reached an even wider global audience. Carlinhos and Vai Quem Vem provided the rhythmic underpinnings of *Brasileiro*, an innovative fusion of Rio samba, Bahian axé music, funk, and MPB. Brown wrote and contributed lead vocals to five of the album's songs, which ranged stylistically across the mixture of baião and samba-reggae in "Magalenha," the ijexá rhythm and pop-jazzy chorus of "Barbaré," and the intertwining of samba-reggae and merengue in "Magano." Another interesting sonic adventure was the Bahian-style rap song "What Is This?" composed and sung by Vai Quem Vem's Carmen Alice, with hip-hop rhythms played on berimbau and surdos.

At this time, the always hyperactive Carlinhos was also in the midst of developing another musical entity—Timbalada, a group that began with about thirty musicians and grew to include a few hundred. In 1993, Timbalada released their debut album, *Timbalada*, co-produced by

Carlinhos and Wesley Rangel. It included several Brown tunes, his arrangements, and waves of surging *axé-music* rhythms propelled by *timbau* drums (similar to the pagode *tan-tan*), surdos, and percussion. Most songs featured vocalists Patrícia Gomes, Xexéu, or Augusto Conceição engaging in call-and-response vocals with a male chorus singing in unison. The beautiful northeastern-styled ballad "Filha da Mãe" (Mother's Daughter) featured a special guest on pandeiro: Brown's former teacher Mestre Pintado do Bongô.

The following year, the bloco performed its songs with rousing energy in Salvador's Carnaval. The upper bodies of its musicians (including singer Patrícia's bare breasts) were painted with white dashes, dots, and spirals that recalled the art of Keith Haring, the group's drums were decorated with bright colors, and Carlinhos roamed the percussion section, attracting attention with his unruly dreadlocks, nose rings, and omnipresent sunglasses. Timbalada's next album, *Cada Cabeça É Um Mundo* (Every Head Is a World) again featured a riot of thundering rhythms, but the overall sound was more polished and augmented by a prominent horn section. Several songs had Caribbean or northeastern elements; one of the most unusual was "Convênio com Cristo" (Compact with Christ), which mixed berimbau and percussive effects with the singing of *repentista* Bule-Bule.

Around this time, Brown also started to collaborate with Marisa Monte, whose outstanding albums in the mid-1990s featured several of his songs. Monte's *Cor de Rosa e Carvão* (Rose and Charcoal) in 1994 included "Maria de Verdade" and "Segue o Seco" by Brown and "Na Estrada" by Brown, Monte, and Nando Reis. *A Great Noise*, released two years later, included Brown's "Ar-

repio," "Magamalabares," and "Maraçá," as well as a live version of "Segue o Seco."

In 1996, Carlinhos released his first solo album, *Alfagamabetízado* (AlphaGammaBeta-ized), a singular effort that smoothly combines axé-music drumming, northeastern rhythms, 1970s-type funk, bossa nova, and jazz-fusion sonorities. Wally Badarou and Arto Lindsay produced *Alfa*, which was recorded in Salvador, Paris, and Rio. One can see the progression from Brown's earlier work with Timbalada and the *Bahia Black* collaboration, but overall *Alfa* is a distinctive effort that sounds quite unlike anything previously recorded in Bahia, or Brazil for that matter.

The dense rhythms in the Timbalada style shake the earth in tunes like "O Bode" and "Bog La Bag," but *Alfa* also contains soft ballads, acoustic guitar, cellos, violins, and strange ambient noises. In "Angel's Robot List," Alexandra Theodoropoulou ethereally recites the Greek alphabet while Kouider Berkane idly warms up on violin and dozens of surdos are dragged screeching across a floor. In "Pandeiro-deiro," Brown delivers embolada vocals (that sound like rap to North American ears) atop a driving beat and electric guitar. Brown is joined in "Quixabeira" by Gal Costa, Gilberto Gil, Maria Bethânia, and Caetano Veloso, who add beautiful vocal harmonizing atop a public-domain samba from Bahia's Recôncavo region, performed by a legion of Candeal percussionists and flavored with Maeka Munan's fluid electric guitar. It is the only composition on the album not written by Brown.

On *Alfa*, Carlinhos handles lead vocals and arrangements and plays guitar and a wide variety of percussion instruments. He is backed by an abundance of talented guest artists, such as singer Marisa Monte, guitarist Roseval Evangelista, trombonist

Sérgio Trombone, saxophonists Rowney Scott and Leo Gandelman, and noteworthy African artists like bassist N'Doumbe Djengue, accordion player Cadah Mustapha, and drummer Mokhtar Samba. *Alfa* is a remarkable work, with its excellent musicianship, dense yet subtle textures, and smooth melding of axé music and mellow ballads.

Brown's view of life and art is eclectic, all-embracing. He credited the bloco afro Ilê Aiyê as "the one that opened the road for all the others, but I was never in favor of their racial approach. I cannot admit this separation of blacks and whites. We have to look for understanding.

We're all human beings. People need to go back to the basics, to communicate. That's why we need the drums, our first language. If everybody stopped trying to communicate through different languages, they would find in the drums the rhythm of life, the universal language, the *pulse*."

Carlinhos Brown's philosophical vision is more cosmic than that of the typical musician, but his open-minded musical approach is characteristically *baiano*. Salvador receives the influences of all continents, infuses them with its own special swing, and sends them back out to the world.

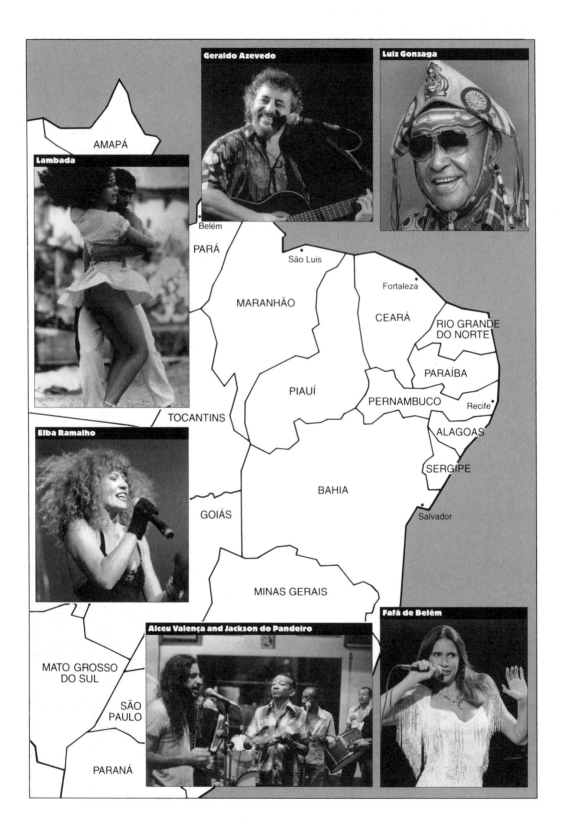

Geraldo Azevedo

Luiz Gonzaga

Lambada

Elba Ramalho

Alceu Valença and Jackson do Pandeiro

Fafá de Belém

AMAPÁ

Belém

PARÁ

São Luis

Fortaleza

MARANHÃO

CEARÁ

RIO GRANDE
DO NORTE

PIAUÍ

PARAÍBA

PERNAMBUCO

Recife

TOCANTINS

ALAGOAS

SERGIPE

BAHIA

GOIÁS

Salvador

MINAS GERAIS

MATO GROSSO
DO SUL

SÃO
PAULO

PARANÁ

North by Northeast

Chapter Seven

Today, many miles away
In a sad solitude
I wait for the rain to fall again
For me to return to my sertão

Luiz Gonzaga and Humberto Teixeira
"Asa Branca"

During the 1940s the most popular music in Brazil consisted largely of either samba-canção songs or imported genres—tangos, boleros, foxtrots, and waltzes. The accordionist Luiz Gonzaga changed all that when he achieved huge commercial success late in the decade with two singles that pulsed with boisterous northeastern rhythms and were charged with a raw poignancy—"Baião" and "Asa Branca."

Gonzaga sang stories about Brazil's Northeast over accordion riffs that were long and melancholy on slow tunes or festive and tumbling over each other on dance numbers. His songs captured the imagination of the country. "Asa Branca" has a haunting melody and lyrics that describe a disastrous drought in the sertão, the vast arid interior of northeastern Brazil. The song's title refers to a type of pigeon that, according to local belief, is the last bird to abandon the sertão during droughts. "Asa Branca" became an unofficial anthem of the Northeast and has been covered by dozens of artists, including Elis Regina, Caetano Veloso, Lulu Santos, Sivuca, Hermeto Pascoal, and Baden Powell.

Gonzaga helped introduce Brazil to the sounds and culture of its Northeast—an area that is rich in folklore and possesses a remarkable musical tradition. It is a region that is quite different from the cosmopolitan urban centers of Rio and São Paulo to the south; in many ways the Northeast is like another country. The region has nearly forty million inhabitants, living in Salvador, Recife, Fortaleza, and other cities on the lush coast, and in towns and farms in the sertão.

The Sertão

Brazil's Northeast is divided by Brazilian geographers into three principal geographic zones: bordering the coast is the *zona da mata*, a lush area once covered by Atlantic rain forest (*mata atlântica*) that is well-suited for sugar-cane fields and cocoa-tree groves; just inland from that is the *agreste*, which receives less rainfall but is still good for farmland; and the *sertão* is the hot, dry interior—an area that covers some 1.5 million square kilometers.

The sertão has a mostly poor, illiterate population who tend their own small plots of land or work for powerful landowners who rule their communities in a feudal manner. Much of this drought-stricken hinterland is covered by a thorny, dense brush called *caatinga*. Cowherds (*vaqueiros*) must wear

Gonzaga, with Dominguinhos in the background. *Photo by Conceição Almeida. Courtesy of BMG.*

head-to-foot leather to protect themselves from the spines and barbs of the caatinga and often cover their horses' chests with cowhide as well. In the sertão, crops are picked by hand, day-to-day existence is hard, and life expectancy is short. Machismo is strong here and blood feuds last for decades. *Sertanejos* (those who live in the sertão) are stoic, passionate, and given to mysticism. Many are strongly religious, attending Catholic church and praying to myriad saints. They are also a generous people. Whether they live in a big ranch house or a dirt-floored hovel, sertanejos are renowned for their warmth and hospitality. It is almost impossible to visit a home there and not be asked to dinner or offered a place to sleep if the hour is late.

Early in this century, some poor sertanejos took to banditry rather than accept the humble misery that was their lot; they would raid towns and farms, then escape on horseback to hiding places in dense tangles of caatinga in the rugged sertão. One such *cangaceiro* (outlaw) was the legendary Lampião (1898–1934), famed for his ruthlessness, sadistic

Lampião (*third from the left in the front row*)—the bandit-hero who was admired by the poor and feared by the rich in the sertão, which he roamed and looted in the 1920s and 1930s—pictured with his gang and (*to his right*) his woman, Maria Bonita. *Public domain image.*

excesses, and fighting skills, and for his courage, generosity, and musical ability. He sang and played the accordion well and often danced all night at parties. According to legend, he and his band of outlaws popularized the *xaxado*, a men's dance. He is revered today by many sertanejos as a bandit-hero and has been the subject of songs, movies, plays, books, and even a TV Globo *novela*.

Roughly every ten years, the usual January-to-May rains fail to refresh the parched sertão. When that happens, the caatinga shrivels in the tropical sun, rivers dry up, cattle drop dead, and hundreds of thousands of people go hungry. Many relocate to overcrowded refugee shantytowns in the northeastern capitals. Countless others emigrate to Rio and São Paulo in search of food and work. There they toil in factories and construction sites, as maids and as doormen, generally discriminated against because of their strong accents and lack of education. They stay in overcrowded *favelas* and wait for rain to return to the sertão so they can go home. Northeasterners in the big southern cities often gather in weekly fairs to eat their own regional specialities, drink *cachaça* (sugar-cane liquor), sell their wares, and dance to the galloping rhythms of earthy, accordion-driven *forró* (a generic term for dance-oriented northeastern styles).

Luiz Gonzaga

Luiz Gonzaga (1912–1989) served as a spokesman for the rural Northeast, its history and its culture, singing tales and woes of the sertão to urban audiences in the industrialized, rapidly growing cities of Rio and São Paulo. Born on the Caiçara ranch just outside the small town of Exu in the Pernambuco sertão, Luiz Gonzaga do Nascimento was the son of a farm worker who was well-respected in the region for his accordion playing. Young Luiz was already tilling the fields at age seven and, soon after, traveling with his father to various local dances, parties, and festivals, where he mastered the accordion and other instruments. As a boy, Gonzaga admired the freedom and audacity of the cangaceiros and his idol was Lampião, then in the prime of his outlaw fame.

At age eighteen, Luiz fell in love with the daughter of Raimundo Delgado, a wealthy and important man in Exu. But when Gonzaga went to ask for the girl's hand in marriage, her father reacted violently to the budding romance. As recounted in *Nova História*, Raimundo seethed, "A devil that doesn't work, that doesn't have farmland, that has nothing, that only plays the accordion, how is it that he wants to marry?" He added a few racist remarks about Gonzaga's dark skin. Enraged, Luiz left and returned to defend his honor (with a knife, by some accounts). But Raimundo managed to talk him down and then later told all to Santana, Gonzaga's mother. Furious, she whipped Luiz until he collapsed onto a stool. Humiliated, he decided to give up his romance and leave for Ceará, where he joined the army.

He remained an enlisted man for nine years, until 1939. Gonzaga played the cornet in the army band and studied accordion with Domingos Ambrósio, who taught Luiz the popular music of the Southeast: polkas, waltzes, and tangos. After leaving the military, Gonzaga moved to Rio and survived by playing his accordion in clubs and bordellos. He got on the radio but did not make much of an impression until one night a group of Cearense students asked him to play some music from the sertão. So, on Ary Barroso's show, Gonzaga played a *chamego* he had written, "Vira e Mexe" (chamego is described by Luiz in *Nova História* as a choro with northeastern inflections in the rhythm and harmony). It won first prize, and

Luiz Gonzaga in his trademark outfit. *Courtesy of BMG.*

he was asked by an enthusiastic audience to do an encore. That year (1941) he recorded two 78-rpm singles for RCA and was on his way.

Over the next five years Luiz cut around seventy singles, most of them waltzes, polkas, mazurkas, and chamegos. Then came the chance to bring the musical heritage of his home state to the forefront, when Gonzaga achieved a breakthrough that transformed his career and had a huge impact on Brazilian popular music.

In 1946, Gonzaga recorded the revolutionary "Baião," whose title became the name of a new genre. Written by Gonzaga and Humberto Teixeira, a lawyer from Ceará, the tune exhorts listeners to try the new dance.

> **I'm going to show all of you how you dance a baião**
> **Whoever wants to learn please pay attention**

Gonzaga and Teixeira's baião derived from an older, folkloric baião or *baiano*, a northeastern circle dance of African origin. In the interior of

Pernambuco, this dance would be performed as a prelude to a *desafio*, a sung poetic contest, between two sertanejo singer-guitarists. The instrumental musical introduction that accompanied the dance came to be called baião or *rojão*.

Gonzaga and Teixeira urbanized the baião, taking its syncopated 2/4 rhythm and expanding it into an entire song form of its own. They added a steady beat from beginning to end, making it easier to dance to. They changed the instrumentation, replacing the guitar with an accordion, and adding a triangle and *zabumba* bass drum. And they introduced a melody that used a natural scale with a raised fourth and flattened seventh, sometimes mixing this with a minor scale.

The flat seventh is referred to by some as the *sétima nordestina* (northeastern seventh) and is usually attributed to African influences, as are the flattened third and flattened fifths or sevenths in the North American blues. Other tonal peculiarities of the baião are thought by some scholars, such as the conductor Júlio Medaglia, to resemble medieval modes utilized in Gregorian chant.

Gonzaga had created a vivid new dance music, whose accordion-bass-drum-triangle instrumentation gave it a rocking, earthy sound, akin to Louisiana zydeco. He followed "Baião" with a string of hits—performed by himself as well as others—and within a few years the baião style was heard as often as the samba on the radio throughout Brazil. One Gonzaga-Teixeira success from 1950 was the lively "Paraíba," which is the name for a woman from Paraíba state. The song paid tribute to the courage and stoicism of a wife left behind in the sertão when her man traveled south to find work. It would be recorded by many artists in that era and became a standard that was given a great interpretation four decades later by Chico César, on his *Aos Vivos* album.

When the mud turned to stone and the mandacaru cactus dried up
When the dove became thirsty, beat its wings and left
It was then that I went away, carrying my pain
Today I send a hug to you, little one
Manly Paraíba woman, very macho, yes sir

Around this time, Gonzaga's songwriting partnership with Teixeira ended, when Humberto was elected a federal deputy and became busy with governmental matters. Luiz had written "Vem Morena" with Zé Dantas, a doctor from Pernambuco, and they continued to collaborate in the 1950s, as Gonzaga's success continued. Besides the baião, Gonzaga popularized the xaxado (the dance favored by Lampião), and xote (another very danceable 2/4 rhythm).

Nowadays, much of Gonzaga's music is often referred to as *forró*, a word that originally meant a party or place to play dance music. Its etymology is the subject of much speculation, but forró probably derives from *forrobodó*, a word for revelry or a party that may have been in use as early as 1833, according to Luis da Câmara Cascudo's *Dicionário do Folclore Brasileiro*. Forró came to be used as a generic tag for danceable northeastern styles such as *coco, xote, and xaxado*. According to some, forró refers specifically to a faster, livelier type of baião, introduced by Gonzaga in tunes such as "O Forró de Mané Vito" and "O Forró de Zé Antão."

By the 1960s, Gonzaga's songs had fallen out of favor with the critics and the urban public, who were more interested in bossa nova and the new artists emerging from the music festivals. But Luiz's career was revived when he was championed by the young new stars Gilberto Gil and Caetano Veloso, both of whom recorded covers of Gonzaga songs. Veloso startled his hip fans by proclaiming the out-of-style Gonzaga "a genius." Their support helped to revive his career, and many of his tunes were covered by MPB artists in following years. "Vem Morena" reappeared in two superb new renditions—by Gil in 1984 and by Gonzaga himself with Fagner in 1988.

Late in his life, Gonzaga became a musical legend in Brazil, and even more than that for the Northeast. Once incident aptly illustrates his almost mythic stature in the region of his youth. In June 1978, a member of the Sampaio clan killed Zito Alencar, the mayor of Exu, reigniting a twenty-year-old war between the two families. Gonzaga, armed only with his accordion, decided to be a peacemaker. He returned to his native city for the first time in almost fifty years and succeeded in calming the tensions there between the Sampaios and the Alencars. It was something perhaps only Gonzaga could have done, for he had now become as famous in the sertão as the idol of his youth, the bandit Lampião.

When Luiz died in 1989, his body lay for two days in an open coffin in the legislative assembly hall of Recife. Thousands came to pay their respects, and all of Brazil mourned his passing. At the vigil, Dom Hélder Câmara, the archbishop of Olinda and Recife, was quoted in the *Jornal do Brasil* as saying, "I have certainty that with so good a soul, with such an understanding of the common people, that Gonzaga was received with a great party there in heaven."

Jackson do Pandeiro

While Luiz Gonzaga brought the rural sounds of the Northeast to the attention of all Brazil, his contemporary Jackson do Pandeiro (José Gomes Filho, 1919–1982) did much to popularize the North-

Jackson do Pandeiro. *Photo by Hugo. Courtesy of Agência JB.*

east's coastal and urban sounds, especially the *coco*. Jackson is mentioned repeatedly by contemporary Brazilian artists as an important influence. Born in Alagoa Grande, the singer-percussionist played good-time music with an uncanny rhythmic sense. He was a master of the coco, a merry and lively Afro-Brazilian song style and circle dance known to have been present on the northeastern littoral as far back as the eighteenth century. It has a stanza-and-refrain structure and pulls the listener along with a fast tempo and irresistible syncopation. In the coco, singers and dancers form a ring, with solo dancers sometimes inside it, sometimes not. The coco can include the *umbigada* movement, the navel-touching invitation to the dance.

Singer-songwriter Manezinho Araújo believed that the coco originated in the Palmares *quilombo* in the backlands of Alagoas in the seventeenth century, from a work song sung by African-Brazilians breaking coconuts on rocks. Its rhythm is typically in 2/4 time and can be maintained by the clapping of hands, the clacking of coconut shells, or with ganzá, pandeiro, and atabaque. Depending on the rhythmic variations and instrumentation, there many variations: *coco de praia* (beach coco), *coco de roda* (circle-dance coco), *coco de sertão* (sertão coco), and others.

Many of Jackson's biggest hits were recorded in the 1950s and 1960s. They include "Sebastiana," "Forró em Limoeiro" (Forró in Limoeiro), "Cantiga do Sapo" (Song of the Toad), "Um a Um" (One By One), "Vou Gargalhar" (I'm Going to Laugh), and "O Canto da Ema" (Song of the Rhea). Some were interpretations of tunes by Gordurinha, João do Vale, and others. Jackson also co-wrote many of his own successes but registered them in the name of his wife, Almira Castilho. One such tune was the famed "Chiclete com Banana" (Bubblegum with Banana), co-written with Gordurinha and recorded by Jackson in 1959. It is a clever jab at American cultural attitudes and rather prophetic. The song was covered by many artists in later years and provided the name for a popular Bahian axé music band in the 1980s.

> **I'll only put bebop in my samba**
> **When Uncle Sam plays tamborim**
> **When he gets a pandeiro and zabumba**
> **When he learns that samba isn't rumba**
> **Then I'll mix Miami with Copacabana**
> **I'll mix bubblegum with banana**

Besides being a great musician, Jackson was a funny guy and could make audiences laugh at his crazy dance steps and his humorous facial expressions while he sang.

Embolada and Desafio

Jackson was also a master of another important northeastern song form, the *embolada*, which is structurally quite similar to the coco (indeed, many scholars consider it to be essentially a more sophisticated form of the coco). The embolada is typically accompanied by pandeiro and ganzá. With a rapid tempo and small musical intervals, it rolls on at a breathless pace. Whereas the coco usu-

ally tells a simple, intelligible story, the embolada often employs improvised, tongue-twisting lyrics.

The embolada has set refrains that allow the singer to organize his next improvised stanza. Alliterative and hard-to-prounounce words are often used, and the lyrics may be comical, satirical, or descriptive. The tempo is gradually increased until the singer's words are pronounced so fast that they are almost unintelligible: they become *emboladas* (mixed together). Manezinho Araújo (1910–1993), born in Cabo, Pernambuco, was one of the greatest performers of the genre, known as the "king of the embolada" from the 1930s to the 1950s.

An embolada can be sung by a soloist, or used by two vocalists for poetic song duels called *desafios*. Desafios share long improvisations, extended rhyming, and a spirit of bravado with American rap music, yet they are a more demanding poetic form. Such "song challenges" are also present in Venezuela (*porfias*), Argentina (*contrapunto*), Chile (*payas*), Spain, and Portugal, and have been around for centuries.

In public squares in the cities of the Northeast, crowds gather round embolada singers who are engaged in a desafio. One keeps the rhythm with a pandeiro, the other with a ganzá, as the improvised vocals fly back and forth. One singer poses a question, challenge, or insult; the other responds, trying to top his opponent, always in the same rigidly observed poetic form. The words are sung rather flatly, almost in a monotone. Sometimes riddles are posed; in *Dicionário do Folclore Brasileiro*, Luis da Câmara Cascudo quotes a famous stanza sung by João Izidro as a riddle to his desafio challenger (it rhymes in Portuguese).

> **To say you were never imprisoned**
> **Is a well-known lie**
> **You passed nine months**

In an oppressive prison
A prison with only one entrance
Where was the exit?

Gathered around the singers, the audience admires the verbal dexterity and laughs at the better jokes and insults hurled by the two. Afterward, a hat is passed to collect some coins.

Desafios are also performed with both singers playing guitar, and they can last hours or even entire nights. The participants are sometimes illiterate but demonstrate an astonishing capacity for wordplay and a remarkable grasp of regional culture. Their improvisations must follow certain rules, with the number of verses and syllables determined by the poetic form used. For example, the *martelo* has ten syllables per verse, and a *galope* is a martelo with six verses per stanza. Desafios may use the embolada song style as a structure or employ other musical forms.

The singers in the desafio are called *repentistas*, and they strive to come up with an improvised verse (a *repente*) that will break the concentration of their opponent and leave him unable to respond. The first repentista who is not able to invent and pronounce a fast response loses the desafio. An example of the repentista style wedded to a modern dance beat is found on Daúde's eponymous 1995 album, in the song "Quatro Meninas" (Four Girls), in which singer Daúde and repentista Miguel Bezerra try to outdo each other in reciting strings of girls' names.

João do Vale

While repentistas express themselves through improvised performance, João do Vale worked for decades crafting popular songs that were brought to life in the recording studios by other artists. But for all the many famous tunes João has written, few

João do Vale with Gonzaguinha (the son of Luiz Gonzaga).
Photo by Frederico Mendes. Courtesy of Sony.

people in the country know his name. For example, when Brazilians gather to play guitar at someone's house, they sometimes sing a beautiful, mysterious tune called "Na Asa do Vento" (On the Wing of the Wind), which was recorded by Caetano Veloso in 1975. But they probably won't know who wrote it, although they might guess that it was Caetano or maybe—if they're older—Dolores Duran, who sang the intriguing lyrics in 1956.

Love is a bandit
It can even cost you money
It's a flower that has no scent
That all the world wants to smell

João (1933–1996), born in Pedreiras, Maranhão, co-wrote that song with Luis Vieira and composed hundreds of other recorded tunes, dozens of them standards. A few examples include "Carcará," "Sina do Caboclo" (Fate of the Mestizo), "Pisa na Fulo" (Step on the Flower), "A Voz do Povo" (The Voice of the People), "Coroné Antonio Bento," and "O Canto da Ema" (The Rhea's Song). João's tunes were covered heavily from the 1950s through the 1970s by artists such as Veloso, Duran, Bethânia, Nara Leão, Ivon Curi, Marlene, Alayde Costa, Tim Maia, Gilberto Gil, and Jackson do Pandeiro.

Although comparatively unknown, João had a

huge impact with his prolific songwriting. He was an important popularizer of northeastern song styles, along with Luiz Gonzaga and Jackson do Pandeiro, as well as a great lyricist. He told the story of his life and of the poor people of Maranhão in concise, poignant narratives filled with vivid images and the vernacular of the sertão (a dialect sometimes difficult for urban Brazilians to fathom). He could indulge in earthy good humor—as in the lascivious "Peba na Pimenta" (Armadillo in the Pepper), a playful tune full of lewd double-entendres—or meditate lyrically about love and nature, as in "Na Asa do Vento."

In the 1960s, João stepped into the limelight for a few years. Early in that decade, Zé Keti took him to a hip musician's hangout—the restaurat Zicartola, run by the sambista Cartola and his wife, Zica. João began performing there and was invited to play a role in the 1964 musical theater piece *Opinião*, alongside Keti and Nara Leão. The play was a success, and one of its songs, João's stirring anthem "Carcará," launched Maria Bethânia (who replaced Leão) to fame the next year when she recorded it as a single. "Carcará" was about the *carcará* bird-of-prey that never goes hungry, even when millions of northeasterners are starving to death in the sertão during one of the region's frequent droughts. Another song, "Sina de Caboclo," concisely summarizes another fate of many northeasterners.

> **I am a poor mestizo, I earn my living with a hoe**
> **What I harvest is divided with he who plants nothing**
> **If it it continues thus, I will leave my sertão**
> **Even with eyes full of tears and with pain in the heart**
> **I will go to Rio to carry mortar for the bricklayer**

João did not have a great voice and achieved his success through his songwriting. By the late 1970s he had fallen out of the public eye, but this peers never forgot him. In 1981, his many friends (Tom Jobim, Chico Buarque, and Leão among them) gathered with João to record the album *João do Vale*, a star-studded retrospective of his greatest hits. And his home town of Pedreiras named a street and a school after him.

Beside João, Luiz, and Jackson, other important northeastern musicians of their era who sang embolada, coco, baião, frevo, and other regional styles included: Beija-flor and Oliveira, Catulo de Paula, Luis Bandeira, Patativa do Assaré, Otacílio and Lourival Batista, Cego Aderaldo, Zé Limeira, Zé do Norte, Gordurinha, João Pernambuco, Jararaca and Ratinho, Venâncio and Corumbá, and Lauro Maia.

Northeastern Musical Traditions

The history and folklore of the Northeast is kept alive in its music, in the *literatura de cordel* (handbound booklets of folk stories and moral tales in rhymed verse), and in its many processional and dramatic dances. Its culture derives from the usual Brazilian roots from Portugal, Africa, and the native Amerindians. But in the Northeast, this heritage mixed together for centuries in a relative isolation, especially in the backlands, far from the cosmopolitan influences of Rio and São Paulo. The Northeast created its own traditions, some of which include archaic traits from Africa or Portugal that no longer exist in their places of origin.

Ancient Iberian musical elements often turn up in folk music from the region. Both Arabic scales (the Moors occupied Portugal for centuries) and medieval modes and harmonies have been noted in many northeastern songs by scholars such as Antonio José Madureira, co-founder of the 1970s group

Quinteto Armorial. That band explored northeastern roots in a meticulously elaborated context in LPs such as *Do Romance ao Galope Nordestino*. The Northeast's rich musical heritage was also adeptly recapitulated by Quinteto Violado in the 1970s and by troubadours Xangai, Elomar, Vital Farias, and Geraldo Azevedo in their 1980s albums *Cantoria* (Song Feast) and *Cantoria 2*.

One of the Northeast's most important genres is *maracatu*, an Afro-Brazilian processional dance performed during Carnaval in Recife, Fortaleza, and other northeastern cities. In maracatu, participants sing and dance to a heavy, slow, almost trance-inducing rhythm, played usually on zabumbas, tambores, chocalhos, and gonguês. Performers dress up as a king, queen, baianas, and the *dama de passo*, a woman who carries the *calunga* cloth doll, a figure of a black woman dressed in white. Some scholars think that maracatu may derive from an early form of the Afro-Brazilian processional dances *congo* and *congada*.

Congos are found in the North and Northeast, while congadas are typical of central and southern Brazil. They derive from a mixture of African, Portuguese, and Spanish practices. Congos feature characters dressed as African royalty and their courts and ministers. Participants enact various scenarios of war and peace, singing their lines to an accompaniment of drums, chocalhos, pandeiros, and violas.

Caboclinho groups have been active in the Northeast since at least the late nineteenth century. Inspired by the legacy of the Brazilian Indian, caboclinhos parade during Carnaval in Pernambuco, Bahia, Ceará, and other northeastern states. Their performers dress as stylized Indians and dance in the street to the sound of flutes, fifes, and arrows banging on bows. They perform dramatic dances, with

assorted characters and a varied choreography that illustrate stories taken from Brazil's colonization era.

Other important exponents of northeastern folkloric music are the fife-and-drum ensembles called *bandas de pífano* (fife bands), which typically perform forró for dance events as well as devotional music for *novenas* (prayer sessions devoted to saints) and religious processions.

Frevo is a musical genre first developed in the Northeast that has become an important part of Brazilian popular music and a Carnaval mainstay in states like Bahia, Ceará, and Pernambuco. Frevo originated in 1909 when Zuzinha (Captain José Lourenço da Silva), the director of the Pernambuco Military Brigade band, decided to transform the polka-marcha into a frevo by heightening the syncopation, increasing the tempo, and creating a vigorous new form that lent itself well to instrumental improvisation. It began to be played in clubs in Recife during Carnaval in 1917 and derived its name from the verb *ferver*, which means to boil. "Frevo is full of nuances," singer-songwriter Alceu Valença told us. "It was the most sophisticated invention of the Pernambucano people."

All these traditions and musical styles provided the roots for contemporary musicians who would mix their northeastern culture with modern influences and instruments to add a fresh new sound to Brazilian popular music.

The Northeastern Wave

At the beginning of the 1970s, a new and more cosmopolitan generation of singers and musicians swept down to Rio from Fortaleza, Recife, and other points close to the equator. Inspired by bossa, rock, and Tropicália, this generation of northeastern artists added keyboards, electric guitars, pop arrangements, and other influences to

Alceu Valença recording with his hero, Jackson do Pandeiro.
Photo by Ronaldo Theobald. Courtesy of Agência JB.

baião, xote, maracatu, and embolada. Among these musicians were Alceu Valença, Geraldo Azevedo, Fagner, Elba Ramalho, Zé Ramalho, Belchior, Amelinha, and Ednardo. "After bossa nova and Tropicália, there was a strong northeastern movement. It didn't have a name, but I think it was as important," recalled singer-songwriter Geraldo Azevedo.

Alceu Valença

Alceu Valença was one of the key figures in the northeastern musical invasion. Some music critics called his kinetic style *forróck*, to describe Alceu's driving mixtures of forró and embolada with electric guitar and drums. On stage, Alceu often takes on a trickster's persona and dresses as a court jester. His visceral, imaginative music and theatrical presenations made him one of MPB's biggest stars and a popular performer overseas.

Alceu was born in 1946 to a middle-class family in São Bento do Una, a small village in Pernambuco, located between the sertão and the agreste. His father was a farmer, lawyer, and politician. Valença was heavily influenced musically by Luiz Gonzaga and Jackson do Pandeiro; he absorbed Jackson's clownish spirit and would later record cocos in the latter's style. Alceu also absorbed the unrecorded but vital music played by local groups and troubadours. "Maracatu, Xangô de Pernambuco, violeiros, bandas de pífanos, frevos de bloco, frevos de rua, caboclinhos, coco, xote, xaxado, baião. I saw a lot of theater of the street, such as bumbameu-boi, chegança, clowns," recalled Alceu, whose family was also musical. "My grandfather played guitar, he was more or less a repentista and influenced me with the sonority of the region. He passed this taste for popular music to me, and then on the coast I observed the black culture."

At age nine, Alceu and his family moved to Recife, the capital of Pernambuco, and five years later he began to play guitar. "In the big city, Recife, a million folkloric things passed by on my street, Rua das Palmares. But on the radio they didn't play that kind of music. What they played came from Rio, as well as international music." Two foreign singers made a deep impact on the young Valença: Ray Charles and Elvis Presley.

Alceu's career began in Recife, where he liked

Four northeastern troubadours—Xangai, Geraldo Azevedo, Vital Farias, and Elomar—in concert. *Courtesy of Kuarup.*

to play the northeastern music that was out of fashion with his well-off peers. "The middle class was ashamed of the baião. They wanted what was imported, canned," he told us. Valença attended college and obtained a law degree but was unenthusiastic about entering the legal profession. He made the obligatory pop musician's journey to Rio in 1970 and began to enter his songs in the music festivals. In 1972 he and Geraldo Azevedo recorded an album together, with Rogério Duprat (who had often worked with the Tropicalistas) handling the orchestration. Then Alceu made his solo debut with *Molhado de Suor* (Wet with Sweat) in 1974, chosen by critics as one of the year's top three albums. Alceu's spirited blend of blues, rock, and northeastern styles began to win great acclaim. His 1978 rock-embolada "Agalapado" displayed the vivid romanticism of his lyrics.

> **I sing the pain, the love, the disillusion**
> **And the infinite sadness of lovers**
> **Don Quixote free of Cervantes**
> **I discover that the windmills are real**
> **Between beasts, owls, jackals**
> **I turn to stone in the middle of the road**
> **I turn into a rose, path of spines**
> **I ignite these glacial times**

In 1982 came perhaps his finest work to date, *Cavalo de Pau* (Stick Horse), and an appearance at the Montreux Jazz Festival in Switzerland.

Mixing Luiz Gonzaga and Elvis Presley, maracatu with synthesizers, coco with electric guitar, Alceu concocts exhilarating musical blends. Atop them, he sings vivid lyrics in which he seeks to create what he describes as "a hybrid language, urban and rural." In his concerts, he strives for an "almost operatic" climate in which he improvises a great deal and assumes many roles. He commented, "I have the clown side and the more cool

Alceu in concert at La Scala in Rio in 1988. *Photo by Fernando Seixas. Courtesy of BMG.*

side. I have various persons inside me, faces, masks, and my music is this—frevo to maracatu to something totally romantic."

Geraldo Azevedo

Another key figure in the "northeastern wave" was Alceu's partner on his first album: singer-songwriter Geraldo Azevedo. His light, clear songs center on his voice and guitar, with lyrics evoking the beaches, jangadas, and coconut trees of the northeastern coast. Azevedo bases his songs in styles such as toada, xote, and reggae, which he augments with bossa vocal influences and modern arrangements. The result is suave, carefully constructed music that is gentle, romantic, and reflective.

Born in 1945 in Petrolina, Pernambuco, on the banks of the São Francisco River, Geraldo grew up in a musical household where everyone played instruments or sang. "The folklore of the region—maracatu, coco, repentistas—it's in all of us without our perceiving it," remarked Azevedo. As a teenager, he listened to Luiz Gonzaga and Jackson do Pandeiro, as well as such diverse musicians as Johann Sebastian Bach, classical guitarist Andrés Segovia, bossa guitarist Baden Powell, and romantic crooner Nelson Gonçalves. But it was the bossa nova singer João Gilberto who inspired Geraldo to become a professional musician. "He made me more serious about looking into harmony. We didn't have those [bossa nova] harmonies in Petrolina."

Geraldo Azevedo. *Photo by Livio Campos. Courtesy of BMG.*

At eighteen he traveled to Recife to attend college, and while there he performed with the members of Grupo Construção, which included Naná Vasconcelos, Teca Calazans, and Paulo Guimarães. Five years later, in 1968, Geraldo moved to Rio and formed the group Quarteto Livre (Free Quartet) with Vasconcelos and others to back up singer-songwriter Geraldo Vandré, the aforementioned hero of the 1960s song festivals who sang protest lyrics against social problems and the dictatorship.

Then the infamous Institutional Act No. 5 clamped down hard on dissent and made it impossible for Vandré and Quarteto Livre to record. Vandré left the country and Azevedo went to prison. Azevedo was not politically militant, but his friendship with loudly dissenting musicians and artists caused him to be clandestinely seized and placed under arrest in 1969. When he came out of prison, after staying for forty-one days, he felt depressed and beaten down and almost gave up music for good. The next year was a bleak year for Azevedo, but near its end he re-encountered Alceu Valença, who gave Geraldo "a force, a strong push."

Azevedo made his debut in 1972 with the aforementioned *Alceu Valença e Geraldo Azevedo*, which included one of his most memorable songs, the haunting "Novena," a toada written with Marcus Vinícius. In it, Azevedo poetically evoked the intense Catholicism of his childhood.

While the family prays
Someone follows the novena into the chasm
Of owed prayers
Of the whisper of an agony without end

Placing songs on numerous television novelas over the next few years brought him great attention, as it did Alceu. In 1976, he released his first solo LP, *Geraldo Azevedo*, which included the beautiful and melancholy Azevedo-Valença tune "Caravan."

Life is a gypsy woman, it's a caravan
It's a stone of ice in the sun
Thaw your eyes
They are alone in a sea of clear water

Since then, Azevedo has recorded a number of excellent albums that show off his superb songwriting, including *Bicho de Sete Cabeças* (Seven-Headed Animal), *De Outra Maneira* (Another Way), and *Eterno Presente* (Eternal Present).

Elba Ramalho

Born in 1951 in Conceição do Piancó, Paraíba, Elba Ramalho is one of the foremost vocalists to come from the Northeast. She was a national-class handball player, a drummer in an all-girl rock band, and a sociology student before journeying to Rio as a singer for the northeastern group Quinteto Violado. Also an actress, she has appeared on stage and screen, in plays such as *Lampião no Inferno* (directed by Azevedo) and in the Ruy Guerra film *Ópera do Malandro*.

Ramalho launched her first album on CBS in 1979, *Ave de Prata* (Silver Bird). With her ability to interpret a wide range of northeastern styles, her high-energy performing style, and her flamboyant, theatrical concerts, she soon became a national and international star. Her popularity

soared in the 1984 with the smash album *Do Jeito Que a Gente Gosta* (The Way We Like It), with its infectious forrós and maracatus, and the biting, politicized repentista-style track "Nordeste Independente" (An Independent Northeast). In subsequent years, Ramalho continued to expand her repertoire, adding Caribbean and other new rhythms to her song list. Elba and her backup group "Banda Rojão" have done much to expand the vocabulary of northeastern pop, mixing keyboards, wind instruments, and new vocal arrangements with forró and other regional styles.

Elba Ramalho. *Photo by Livio Campos. Courtesy of PolyGram.*

Also from the Northeast

Along with Elba and the late Gonzaga, Dominguinhos has been one of the top forrozeiros (forró-makers) of Brazil in recent years. Born in 1941 in Garanhuns, Pernambuco, Dominguinhos has written standards such as "Só Quero um Xodo" and is one of Brazil's greatest accordionists. He has made numerous appearances on other artists' albums (including many of Luiz Gonzaga's) when the perfect accordion touch was required.

Also important in the 1970s northeastern wave were singer-songwriters Marcus Vinícius and Zé Ramalho. Vinícius has been described as "a popular composer of the vanguard." His sophisticated music is a meeting of northeastern roots with modern classical music and other influences. Ramalho combines sertanejo-style guitar, Dylanesque stylings, and esoteric images into an usual northeastern pop hybrid.

The so-called *Pessoal do Ceará* (People of Ceará) included Fagner, Ednardo, Belchior, and Amelinha, all of whom began their musical careers in Fortaleza, the capital of Ceará state. Fagner (born in 1950 in Orós, Ceará) has ventured far into inter-

A 1988 album by Luiz Gonzaga (*right*) and Fagner. *Courtesy of BMG.*

national pop at times but also has been an excellent interpreter of local styles, especially on his albums in the 1970s and in later works such as the 1988 release *Gonzagão & Fagner*. Other noteworthy northeastern musicians include accordion virtuosos Baú

Chico César. *Courtesy of PolyGram.*

dos 8 Baixos and Pinto do Accordeon, producer-flutist Zé da Flauta, Trio Nordestino, singer-songwriter Nando Cordel, and vocalists Genival Lacerda, Anastácia, Jorge de Altinho, Clemilda, and Amelinha.

The Next Generation: Chico César

The musical achievements of Valença, Azevedo, and their peers from the Northeast have been integrated in the 1990s into the music of Chico César, who combines his regional heritage with influences from Tropicalismo and the Caribbean.

César was one of Brazil's two most popular songwriters in recent years—the other being Carlinhos Brown. César's tunes have been recorded by Daniela Mercury, Maria Bethânia, João Bosco, Elba Ramalho, and Zizi Possi, among others. But the best interpretations of his work so far have been by Chico himself, on his acclaimed albums *Aos Vivos* (1995) and *Cuscuz Clã* (1996).

Francisco César Gonçalves was born in 1964 in Catolé do Rocha, a town of twelve thousand inhabitants located in the sertão of Paraíba state. Chico started early, forming his first band, Supersom Mirim, when he was ten. He wrote his first song, "Quando Chega o Carnaval" (When Carnaval Comes), two years later, and joined the group Jaguaribe Carne in his teen years. All the while, from age eight to fifteen, he worked in a record store, listening to Secos & Molhados, Pink Floyd, Luiz Gonzaga, Quinteto Violado, and everything else that came through the shop.

Chico moved to São Paulo, where he worked as a journalist and continued to develop his musical abilities. Recognition arrived around the time he was turning thirty. Rave reviews of his club appearances led to his debut album *Aos Vivos* for the Velas

Chico César. *Courtesy of PolyGram.*

label. Recorded before a live audience the previous year, it features César singing and playing acoustic guitar, accompanied on some songs by guitarists Lenine and Lanny Gordon (who co-produced). His follow-up effort, *Cuscuz Clã*, features a full band, strong dance rhythms, and a big production coordinated by veteran hitmaker Marco Mazzola. Chico initially drew attention in part because of his bright, heavily embroidered clothes and a shock of hair that springs straight up from an otherwise shaved head. But it was his music that overwhelmed the public.

He has a high, expressive voice and at times can sound remarkably similiar to Caetano Veloso. On the whole though, César's vocals are quite distinctive, with great emotion and versatility. Along with being an excellent singer, Chico writes powerful, well-crafted songs. His beautifully poetic lyrics explore personal and profound themes with clever wordplay and verbal invention. He fuses diverse musical elements in ways that seem utterly natural and harmonious; his work presents a smooth fusion of MPB, reggae, bossa, soca, and jazz with reisado, carimbó, embolada, and repente. "Mulher Eu Sei" (I Know Woman), "À Primeira Vista" (At First Sight), and "Mama África" (Mother Africa) are some of his most popular songs.

Chico Science and the Mangue Beat

Another promising contemporary artist from the Northeast was Chico Science, whose life was cut short by an automobile accident. Franciso de Assis França (1966–1996) and his band Nação Zumbi (Zumbi Nation) hailed from Recife and introduced a sound called *mangue* (mangrove swamp), or *mangue beat*, in their debut album *De Lama ao Caos* (From Mud to Chaos) in

1994. Their mixture of maracatu, embolada, and hard rock is not mellifluous like the music of César; rather, it is aggressive, harsh, and driving. The fans of Chico Science and Nação Zumbi consider their second album, 1996's *Afrociberdelia*, to be their masterpiece. It takes its name from the words Africa, cybernetics, and psychedelica. The lyrics are written by Chico, who shares credit on the music-writing side with the rest of the band. *Afrociberdelia* follows a line that leads from Alceu Valença straight into acid jazz, hip-hop, heavy metal, and cyber culture. In most of the songs, booming maracatu rhythms bolster raging electric guitars and the flat, embolada-style vocals growled out by

Nazaré Pereira, who has established a career in Europe singing carimbó and other musical styles from Belém and Brazil's North. *Photo by Evandro Teixeira. Courtesy of Sire.*

Two dancers from the Brazilian-European band Kãoma performing lambada. *Courtesy of Epic.*

Chico. There are strange looping effects, and tracks embellished by baião and ciranda, rap and funk, psychedelic guitar and space-age bachelor-pad music. The album's twenty-three tracks are an encyclopedia of mangue-beat experiments and drew great praise from critics. Sadly, Chico's life ended later that year, when his car struck a pole on the highway between Recife and Olinda.

Carimbó, Lambada, and the North

Like the Northeast, Brazil's North is a region of rich folklore and musical invention. It is a hot and humid area, covered mostly by tropical rain forest, and includes much of the Amazon Basin. Some of the musical styles there include *carimbó* (a native Afro-Brazilian song and dance form that can be heard on Nazaré Pereira's *Ritmos da Amazô-*

nia), *siriá* (played with the marujada and boi-bumbá dramatic dances), and *sirimbó* (a mix of siriá and carimbó). And deep in the vast rain forest there is the indigenous music of Amerindian tribes.

The northern state of Pará is where lambada was created in the 1970s, in and around the capital city of Belém. The latter is a bustling port of nearly one million inhabitants, located just upstream from where the huge Tocantins River converges with the even mightier Amazon, as both rivers spill into the Atlantic Ocean. Marajó Island, around which the estuaries of the Tocantins and Amazon flow as they reach their ocean destination, is the size of Switzerland. Belém receives cultural influences from the Guyanas, located just a few hundred miles away, and from the Caribbean. In the 1970s the city's radio stations were heavily programming merengue, salsa, and rumba, as well as electrified versions of carimbó. According to a series of articles on lambada in the newspaper *Folha de São Paulo,* Belém disc jockey Haroldo Caraciolo of the Clube AM station began in 1974 to call all such music "lambada," which in Portuguese means "slap" or "shot of cachaça."

In 1976, the guitarist Joachim de Lima Vieira applied the name "lambada" to a new musical hybrid that he had popularized: a fusion of merengue, electric carimbó, and hints of other Caribbean flavors. Syncopated with a 2/4 time signature, it had a fast tempo and simple, insistent riffs on the electric guitar or sax, with drums and bass accompanying (congas came later). Vieira recorded *Lambada das Quebradas,* considered the first lambada album, that same year, although it was not released until 1978.

The lambada dance was also a new hybrid, mixing elements of the merengue, maxixe,

Fafá de Belém

Early on, lambada had a booster in Fafá de Belém (Maria de Fátima Palha de Figueiredo), who has long been a sort of cultural ambassador from Brazil's North to the rest of the country. Born in 1957, she has a strong, appealing voice with which she interprets a wide variety of popular songs, with a focus on romantic ballads. But her regionality has set her apart; she was probably the first major MPB star to record carimbó (an example can be found on *Tamba-Tajá* in 1976) and lambada (*Atrevida* in 1986 has a lambada medley that clearly shows its carimbó roots).

Adding to the complexity of lambada's musical identity is that the big lambada stars, such as Beto Barbosa, often augmented the genre with cumbia, salsa, and other Caribbean genres, as well as spicing it (especially in the late 1980s) with additions of Bahian samba-reggae and fricote. Still, the sound of lambada from Pará generally retains a lighter, more upbeat sound than lambada from Bahia, which has more synthesizers and is more Afro-Brazilian.

samba, and forró dances. In it, couples press tightly together, the right thigh of each between the other's legs, and dip and swirl sensually to up-tempo, high-energy rhythms. The lambada's popularity grew quickly. In Belém, the rhythm was spread through *festas de aparalhagem*—"sound parties" in which DJs would set up enormous sound systems for one-night dances—and then by radio. The new rhythm and dance spread to Manaus, the capital of Amazonas state, and Salvador, and eventually to Fortaleza, where it is said that the dance grew more erotic. In the late 1980s it hit São Paulo, where numerous dance clubs called *lambaterias* opened.

Teixeira de Manaus was a popular saxophonist from the state of Amazonas who was recording lambadas in the early 1980s. In that decade, saxophonist Manezinho do Sax and vocalists Beto Barbosa, Betto Douglas, Carlos Santos, Alípio Martins, Márcia Rodrigues, and Márcia Ferreira were successful lambada performers from Pará. Ferreira had a big hit with "Chorando Se Foi," which would later gain global fame as "Lambada," performed by Kaoma.

Márcia Rodrigues was the most popular female lambada vocalist at the end of the decade. Often called the "muse of lambada," she melted audiences with her powerful voice and provocative style. When she performed for miners at the Amazonian gold-rush town of Laranjal do Jari in 1989, several rough-and-tumble fans approached her after the show. They pointed revolvers at the

sixteen-year-old star and demanded she sleep with them. But Márcia was able to talk them out of it. "I beat them with my sweetness," she told *Folha de São Paulo*, and escaped unharmed, ready to continue her lambada tour of the northern backlands.

In 1989 the daring, sexy lambada dance emerged in the nightclubs of Europe. On the continent that year, especially in France and Germany, lambada seemed the essence of tropical passion. The international lambada fad was ignited through marketing by two French music

A record cover of a lambada compilation issued by French label Carrere. *Courtesy of Carrere.*

155

entrepreneurs named Jean Karakos and Olivier Lorsac (Olivier Lamotte d'Incamps). While visiting Brazil in 1988, the two visited the Bahian resort town of Porto Seguro and first heard and saw the exotic new style. At the time, lambada was a regional success—like the *fricote* of Luiz Caldas—popular in the North and Northeast.

Karakos and Lorsac knew they were on to something, and back in France they organized a multinational group called Kaoma to sing lambada songs in Europe (Kaoma's lead singer was a Brazilian named Loalwa Braz). Kaoma recorded a cover of Márcia Ferreira's hit "Chorando Se Foi," which was her Portuguese adaptation of "Llorando Se Fue," a Bolivian *saya* tune written by the brothers Gonzalo and Ulises Hermosa. They had recorded it originally in 1982 with their group Los Kjarkas, on the album *Canto a la Mujer de mi Pueblo*. Karakos and Lorsac renamed the Ferreira version, and Lorsac registered it with SACEM (the French performing rights society) under a pseudonym, "Chico de Oliveira." They filmed a music video for the tune

that served as a commercial for the soft drink Orangina, which got them lots of television exposure, and arranged a record deal with CBS.

"Lambada" was the sensation of the summer and fall on the continent. It hit number 1 on the charts in fifteen countries, was number 1 on the *Music & Media* Pan-European pop chart for months, and sold five million units (the album sold two million copies). Kaoma's smash hit single was actually a hybrid, mixing a Bolivian folk theme with lambada, and having a pronounced "northeastern" feel as well. The issue of what was and was not "lambada" became even more confused when record labels started sticking the "lambada" label to anything that was Brazilian—even bossa nova.

By 1990, nightclubs in New York and Los Angeles offered "lambada" nights, and Kaoma's album (called *World Beat* in the United States) went gold and hit number 1 on the Billboard Latin music chart. Publicists outdid themselves in the hype department, spreading ridiculous stories about how lambada had been banned as "immoral" in

Kaoma, the band that hit it big with lambada in the European summer of 1989. *Courtesy of Epic.*

Brazil in the 1930s. Two lamentable low-budget exploitation movies (*The Forbidden Dance* and *Lambada: Set the Night on Fire*) attempted to cash in on the craze.

All the international attention helped turned lambada into a national craze in Brazil. Rio de Janeiro embraced the dance. Many leading Brazilian pop artists, especially those from Bahia, added at least one lambada to their albums in 1989 and 1990. Meanwhile, the publishing scheme hatched by Lorsac and Karakos finally backfired on them, and they were sued by EMI Music, which represented the interests of the Hermosa brothers. The two Frenchmen came to an agreement with EMI and relinquished the authors' earnings from "Lambada." Lorsac received a reprimand from SACEM, the French performing rights society. Ulises Hermosa never benefited financially from his global hit, because he died in 1992.

Lambada soon disappeared from the international spotlight, a victim of hype and exploitation. But it didn't take long for music from the North to find its way back onto the European charts. Every year in the city of Parintins in Amazonas state, a musical festival called Boi de Parantins is staged that features the local *boibumbá* style (a variation of bumba-meu-boi) and other regional sounds, and attracts crowds of more than twenty thousand people. One of the popular acts there, the group Carrapicho, released their song "Tic Tic Tac" in France in the summer of 1996, selling more than one million copies according to *Veja* magazine. The single was included in their album *Fiesta de Boi-Bumbá*. Most Brazilians heard about Carrapicho for the first time in reports filed by European correspondents.

Rather unexpectedly, both lambada and boibumbá helped introduce Europeans to the music of Brazil and Brazilians to the music of their own northern regions.

PARÁ

PIAUÍ

PARAÍBA

PERNAMBUCO

Recife

ALAGOAS

TOCANTINS

BAHIA

SERGIPE

GOIÁS

Naná Vasconcelos

Hermeto Pascoal

Airto, Flora, and jazz friends

Belo Horizonte

ESPÍRITO SANTO

MINAS GERAIS

Eliane Elias

SÃO PAULO

Três Pontas

RIO DE JANEIRO

São Paulo

Rio de Janeiro

Egberto Gismonti

SANTA CATARINA

Uakti

Brazilian Instrumental Music and Jazz

Instrumental music has always been a richly varied and important part of the Brazilian sound, from Pixinguinha's elegant and lively compositions to Uakti's primordial chamber music played on specially designed instruments. And part of the instrumental spectrum in Brazil is jazz, which its musicians have absorbed and expressed in their own way. Conversely, many of the world's leading jazz and instrumental artists have been heavily influenced by Brazilian music. Before we delve into such subjects, it is necessary to take a side trip back to the late nineteenth century, to explore the origins of one of Brazil's most important genres, which provides the backbone of much of its instrumental music. It is called choro.

Choro

In the late nineteenth century in Rio a new musical style emerged that would become one of the most creative musical manifestations in Brazil. Choro is primarily an instrumental form, and to a North American ear might sound a little like a small Dixieland jazz combo playing with strange rhythms, extreme melodic leaps, unexpected modulations, and occasional breakneck tempos. Choro and jazz are both characterized by their use of improvisation and mixtures of African and European musical elements. Interestingly, choro's early development arguably predates that of both ragtime, which first appeared in the 1890s, and jazz, which emerged at the start of the twentieth century.

The first chorões (groups that played choro) began to play in Rio around 1870. In its early days, choro was less a genre than a style, with Afro-Brazilian syncopation and a Brazilian flair added to fashionable European dance music of the time,

including waltzes, polkas, schottishes, quadrilles, and mazurcas. The pioneering figure Joaquim Antônio da Silva Calado (1848–1880) founded the group Choro Carioca in 1870, the same year that he was appointed a teacher at Rio's Imperial Conservatory of Music. Choro Carioca, the most popular chorão of that decade, was an ensemble that initially consisted of flute, two guitars, and a cavaquinho.

Calado was a virtuoso flutist, whose solos often featured spectacular octave leaps and mercurial key changes. He could create the "illusion of two flutes playing simultaneously an octave apart," according to musicologist David Appleby in *The Music of Brazil*. Another aspect of his performance style was the *ganha-tempo*, a "stalling for time" in which a melodic or rhythmic passage would be played languidly, with a "deliberate indolence and indeterminancy." Few of Calado's many compositions were published but those that were exerted a great influence on his peers. Other key figures from the first generation of chorões included the flutist-composers Viriato da Silva, Virgílio Pinto da Silveira, and Luizinho.

The first choro musicians were usually not professionals. They didn't mind playing all night long at parties providing there was a lot of food and drinks present. Between 1870 and 1919, there were hundreds of chorões in Rio that spent nights moving from house to house, party to party. When these ensembles played a song with vocals, it was usually termed a *seresta* (serenade), whereas an instrumental piece was called a *choro*. José Ramos Tinhorão writes in *Pequena História da Música Popular* that the new style may have gained its name from the common use of low guitar notes and "plaintive tones." Choro also means "the act of weeping, crying, or sobbing" in Portuguese. Others think the name derives from *xolo*, a word used long ago by some Afro-Brazilians for their parties or dances.

The early chorões usually followed Choro Carioca's format of flute, guitar, and cavaquinho. The flute acted as the soloist, the guitar supplied the lowest tones with its bass strings, and the cavaquinho handled the rhythm. Other instruments would be added later. Choro musicians improvised upon European rhythms and melodies and developed a dialogue between the soloist and other instruments in which the objective was the *derrubada* (drop)—the moment in which the accompanying musicians could no longer follow the soloist's creative and unpredictable riffs.

The popular "Caiu, Não Disse?" (Didn't I Say You Fell?) was a popular choro-type song composed in 1880 by Viriato da Silva (1851–1883). It was a polka with prominent derrubada sections that emphasized the virtuosity of the flute soloist. This competitive characteristic of choro would be reflected in later choro titles such as Ernesto Nazaré's "Apanhei-Te Cavaquinho" (I Got You, Cavaquinho) and Pixinguinha and Lacerda's "Cuidado, Colega" (Careful, Pal).

Another early composition in the choro style was Chiquinha Gonzaga's 1877 polka "Atraente" (Attractive), which some critics later termed a *choro-polca*. Appleby notes that "Atraente" was Gonzaga's "first successful attempt to write in the improvisational style of the chorões." It included some chromaticism and a few wide leaps and repeated notes in the melodic line characteristic of Calado's compositions, observes Appleby, adding, "The use of alternation of melodic elements among flute, clarinet, and cavaquinho also is suggestive of the style of the choros."

Gonzaga was the colorful daughter of Marshall José Basileu Neves Gonzaga, a high-ranking mili-

tary official. A prolific and brilliant composer in nearly every idiom, she was a tremendously influential figure in Brazilian popular music, which at that time was almost exclusively a male domain. In 1889, Chiquinha published a composition called "Só no Choro" (Only in Choro) that seemed to give the new genre "proof of existence," according to Tinhorão. She went on to write many choros, including the classic "Forrobodó" in 1912. Chiquinha, known for her independent spirit and disregard for convention, was the first woman in Brazil to conduct a military band and a theater orchestra and the author of the landmark *marcha* "Ô Abre Alas," the first song composed especially for Carnaval. She was also politically active and, when young, worked for both the abolitionist and the republican causes in Brazil.

By the turn of century, choro had developed into an independent genre with its own basic characteristics, although choros were still labeled according to the polkas and other dances that provided the underlying rhythm. Each choro was typically divided into three parts, in three different tonalities, repeated in the sequence ABACA, with a medium to fast tempo. Only one instrumentalist in choro performed the solos, a marked contrast with jazz. The flute took the solos in choro's early years, and later the clarinet or guitar could assume this role. The new genre also displayed the derrubada and other characteristics mentioned earlier.

Ernesto Nazaré (1863–1934) took the style pioneered by Calado, Gonzaga, and others and developed it further, penning sophisticated compositions with strong melodies. Ernesto was classically trained like Gonzaga and wrote in various popular styles for the piano. He authored many classic choros and maxixes that were usually designated as "Brazilian tangos." Nazaré (the old spelling of his name is "Nazareth") will always be remembered for "Odeon" (1909) and "Apanheite Cavaquinho" (1913), which became standards in the choro repertoire. Zequinha de Abreu (1880–1935) was another important composer from this era and in 1917 wrote the scintillating "Tico-Tico no Fubá" (Tico-Tico Bird in the Cornmeal), one of Brazil's all-time most popular songs. It hit Hollywood in 1947, when it was sung by Carmen Miranda in the film *Copacabana*.

Pixinguinha and Os Oito Batutas
The legendary Pixinguinha (Alfredo da Rocha Vianna, Jr., 1898–1973) was both a founding father of samba and a superb choro flutist-composer. Many consider him the greatest choro musician of all time. Pixinguinha wrote many of the most famous standards in the genre, including "Carinhoso" (Affectionate), "Rosa," and "Sofre Porque Queres" (You Suffer Because You Want

An album of Pixinguinha standards released by Brazilian independent label Kuarup. *Courtesy of Kuarup.*

To). He was a pioneer in taking Brazilian music overseas, touring Europe and South America.

Pixinguinha was the son of a government functionary who worked in the department of telegraphs and liked to play flute at home with friends. The Vianna household was always packed with friends and often was the site of all-night choro sessions. Pixinguinha showed musical talent as a boy, and his father bought him a beautiful flute imported from Italy. He began studying with the music teacher Irineu de Almeida, who stayed for a while with the Vianna family. By the age of twelve, the young prodigy had already composed his first choro, "Lata de leite" (Milk Can), and played with the Carnaval group Filhas da Jardineira. His development continued and, as a teenager in 1915, he made his first recording—interpreting Irineu's *tango brasileiro* "São João debaixo d'água" (St. John Under the Water) with the group Choro Carioca.

By 1917, the nineteen-year-old Pixinguinha had his own band, Choro Pixinguinha. The talented young musician also played with the Carnaval bloco Grupo do Caxangá, which included friends who often jammed with Pixinguinha at Tia Ciata's legendary house. Several members of the bloco would subsequently join Pixinguinha's next group, which he formed when the manager of the movie theater Palais asked him to organize a small orchestra to play in the foyer. At first the flutist was a little incredulous, since it was unheard of to have a black band play in such an elegant setting. But he went ahead and recruited several of his most talented colleagues from Grupo do Caxangá. In 1919 his instrumental ensemble Os Oito Batutas (The Eight Masters) made its debut at the Palais, playing various popular styles including choros, maxixes, lundus, and modinhas. The Batutas were extremely well received and even Ernesto Nazaré came to hear them play after he was done with his own gig at the Odeon theater.

The Oito Batutas was the first ensemble of its type to incorporate the percussion instruments ganzá, pandeiro, and reco-reco. The early formation of the band included Nelson Alves (cavaquinho), José Alves (mandolin), Raul Palmieri (guitar), Luís Silva (mandolin and reco-reco), China (Pixinguinha's brother Otávio Viana, on piano, guitar, and vocals), Jacó Palmieri (pandeiro), and Donga (Ernesto dos Santos, on guitar), co-author of the first recorded samba, "Pelo Telefone."

With a slightly different lineup, Pixinguinha and the Batutas took a boat to Paris for a highly successful six-month stay playing choros, sambas, and maxixes. They accompanied Duque (the Bahian ex-dentist Antônio Lopes de Amorim Diniz) and Gaby (a French ballerina), a pair of dancers who had already become famous performing maxixe in Europe in the previous decade. Once in Paris, the Oito Batutas were greatly influenced by the foxtrot orchestras they heard there; they returned home and added saxophone, clarinet, trombone, and trumpet to their instrumentation and foxtrots, shimmys, and ragtime to their repertoire. With new members in the group, the Batutas continued playing until around 1928 and left a musical legacy that had a tremendous impact on the development of choro and Brazilian popular music. A few years later, Pixinguinha founded another influential group, Grupo da Guarda Velha, which included Donga, Luís Americano, and João da Baiana in its formidable lineup.

New Choro Generations

The guitarist Garoto (Annibal Augusto Sardinha, 1915–1955), advanced the choro genre in the 1930s and 1940s with his songwriting and innovative playing. Born in São Paulo, Garoto was adept with guitar, banjo, mandolin, and cavaquinho. He played with chorões as a young man and became known for the challenging harmonies that he added to the music. In 1939, Garoto journeyed to the United States to join Carmen Miranda's Bando da Lua. He performed with them on stage and in the film *Down Argentine Way*. Twenty-four of his compositions can be heard on Paulo Bellinati's 1991 album *The Guitar Works of Garoto*.

Choro's popularity had waned somewhat by the start of the 1940s, but a new generation of choro musicians appeared in that decade to ensure the continuation of the genre. Flutists Benedito Lacerda and Altamiro Carrilho, mandolin virtuoso Jacó do Bandolim, clarinet and alto saxophonist Abel Ferreira, bandleader Severino Araújo, and cavaquinho master Valdir Azevedo were responsible for a short-lived but important choro revival. Another chapter in choro's story that decade occurred when Pixinguinha, apparently out of financial necessity, joined Lacerda's group, concentrating on sax while Lacerda handled the flute. This was a subordinate role for Pixinguinha, but the collaboration popularized several of his compositions, including "Um a Zero" (One to Zero), "Ingênuo" (Naive), and "Segura-ele" (Grab Him). Unfortunately, he had to split their authorship with Lacerda. They were among the many choro standards composed in the 1940s; another example is the beloved "Brasileirinho" (Little Brazilian) by Azevedo from 1947.

Choro's fortunes again declined, but another revival would occur in the mid-1970s, stimulated by musicians like Paulo Moura, Turíbio Santos, Arthur Moreira Lima, Raphael Rabello (1962–1995), Marcos Ariel, Paulinho da Viola, Hermeto Pascoal, and the Novos Baianos, all of whom included choros on their records. Nó em

Luís Americano (1900–1960): É do que há, Lágrimas de Virgem (Virgin's Tears), "Numa Serestra" (In a Serenade).

Severino Araújo (b. 1917): "Espinha de Bacalhau" (Cod Spine), "Um Chorinho em Aldeia," "Compassivo."

Valdir Azevedo (1923–1980): "Carioquinha" (Rio Girl), "Carinho e Amor" (Love and Tenderness), "Você" (You), "Arrasta-Pé."

Jacob Bittencourt (Jacó do Bandolim), 1918–1969: "Noites Cariocas" (Rio Nights), "Assanhado" (Provocative), "Vibrações" (Vibrations), "Doce de Côco" (Coconut Candy), "Gostosinho" (Tasty Little One), "Encantamento" (Enchantment).

Altamiro Carrilho (b. 1924): "Aleluia" (Hallejulah), "Misterioso" (Mysterious), "Fogo na Roupa" (Fire in the Clothes).

Abel Ferreira (1915–1980): "Chorando Baixinho" (Crying Softly).

Radamés Gnattali (1906–1988): "Chiquinha Gonzaga," "Remexendo," "Garoto Amoroso" (Amorous Boy), "Bate-Papo" (Conversation), "Bolacha Queimada."

Paulinho da Viola (b. 1942): "Inesquecível" (Unforgettable), "Sarau Para Radamés" (Soirée for Radamés), "Choro Negro" (Black Choro).

Annibal Sardinha (Garoto), 1915–1955: "Amoroso" (Amorous), "Caramelo" (Caramel), "Desvairada" (Deceived), "Nosso Choro" (Our Choro), "Enigmático" (Enigmatic).

Pingo D'Água (Knot in a Drop of Water) was an instrumental group founded in 1978 that modernized choro in several eclectic albums.

One of the best choro albums in recent years was 1988's *Noites Cariocas,* in which Altamiro Carrilho (flute), Chiquinho (accordion), Joel Nascimento (mandolin), Paulinho da Viola (cavaquinho), Paulo Moura (clarinet), and Paulo Sérgio Santos (clarinet and sax) perform seventeen choro standards. Classic choros were also covered on numerous albums in the 1980s and 1990s by Laurindo Almeida, Carlos Barbosa-Lima, Arthur Lima, Charlie Byrd, Paulo Moura, Raphael Rabello, Richard Stoltzman, and other notable musicians. And U.S. mandolin player David Grisman released two volumes of Jacó do Bandolim choros on his own label.

Although its mass appeal has gone up and down in cycles, choro remains a fundamental part of the musical vocabulary for most Brazilian intrumentalists.

Paulo Moura

Paulo Moura is a good example of how Brazilian musicians have dexterously woven choro together with a variety of other styles. Moura is a virtuoso on both saxophone and clarinet, from which he can coax refined, raucous, or soulful sounds, depending on the occasion. He is a master of many idioms besides choro, including jazz, bossa, classical music, and *samba de gafieira,* an orchestrated style performed in dance halls.

Born in 1933, Moura began as a classical clarinetist with the Municipal Theater Orchestra of Rio and later ventured into jazz-bossa with Sérgio Mendes's Sexteto Bossa Rio. Since the 1960s, Paulo

Clara Sverner and Paulo Moura performing choros at Rio's Mistura Up club in 1989. *Photo by Chris McGowan.*

has been a highly influential force in Brazilian popular music. He has taught music theory to the likes of Wagner Tiso and Mauro Senise, arranged albums by Elis Regina, Fagner, and Milton Nascimento, and appeared as a sideman on many important recordings, including Marisa Monte's debut album in 1989. And he has recorded several exceptional solo albums, such as *Confusão Urbana, Suburbana e Rural* (Urban, Suburban and Rural Confusion) in 1976.

Confusão is a masterful guided tour through landscapes of modern and traditional Brazilian music. In the Severino Araújo choro "Espinha de Bacalhau" (Cod Spine), Moura's capricious soprano sax leaps and winds spectacularly across the strumming of cavaquinho and guitar. The samba "Notícia" (News) swells with a big band sound, as Paulo's sax follows the slow and sentimental arrangements, while an insistent cuíca yelps, calls, and whoops amidst the orchestration. "Bicho Papão" (Bogeyman) features a wild, fast beating of bass and hand drums, a rather unsettling jazzy sax solo, and an urban traffic jam of a horn section. "Tema do Zeca do Cuíca" (Cuíca Zeca's Theme) is a variegated montage of electric guitar riffs, cuíca gasps, wistful flute-playing, and intermittent Gil Evans–like strings, all coalescing into a rolling, breathless batucada. "Carimbó do Moura" balances Paulo's joyful clarinet playing with the rollicking carimbó rhythm from Pará. And "Se Algum Dia" (If One Day) is an earthy, tender reading of a sentimental samba by Martinho da Vila. With such variety and virtuosity, *Confusão* was one of the most creative and accomplished Brazilian albums of the 1970s.

Moura continued to weave together jazz, choro, and samba in subsequent decades. One of his more traditional works came in 1988 when he and a pianist friend paid homage to choro's greatest exponent with the album *Clara Sverner & Paulo Moura Interpretam Pixinguinha.*

Laurindo Almeida

Laurindo Almeida was from an older generation than Moura but also displayed a great facility for meshing old and new instrumental styles. Laurindo José de Araújo Almeida Nobrega Neto (1917–1995) was born in the village of Prainha, near São Paulo. He was a guitarist known for his harmonic mastery, subtle dynamics, rich embellishments, and adept improvisatory skills with a variety of idioms. Even though he never was a household name in Brazil or abroad, his playing was ultimately heard by millions around the

Laurindo Almeida in 1951 on the cover of *BMG* magazine. *Courtesy of Laurindo Almeida.*

world, thanks to decades of studio work in Hollywood for film and television.

Almeida's career spanned several decades. In the 1930s, the self-taught young musician formed a guitar duo with Garoto, playing choros and sambas while adding chords that were harmonically advanced for the time. In 1947, Almeida left for the United States and began his career there. He was invited to play with Stan Kenton's orchestra and was its featured guitarist for three years.

Laurindo settled in Los Angeles and began a recording career. In 1952 he led a trio that added jazz edges to choro, baião, and samba. He teamed with saxophonist Bud Shank to cut *Laurindo Almeida Quartet Featuring Bud Shank*, in sessions that took place in April 1953. A pair of ten-inch records on the Pacific Jazz label were released in 1954 and then combined in 1961 into a twelve-inch World Pacific disc called *Brazilliance*. On that innovative work, he mixed cool jazz with Brazilian idioms.

Almeida and Shank's "jazz-samba" was not bossa nova, as some have claimed; it lacked the characteristic João Gilberto beat, the harmonic stamp of Jobim and others, and the economy of expression achieved by bossa. Quite simply, it had a different mood and sound. But Almeida and Shank's work was certainly valuable in its own right. They continued their jazz-samba collaborations with *Holiday in Brazil* and *Latin Contrasts*. On other albums, Almeida linked a variety of Brazilian genres to jazz and classical forms. For example, he explored modinha, choro, maracatu, and boi-bumbá in *Duets with the Spanish Guitar* in 1957. He also covered Villa-Lobos and Radamés Gnattali in *Impressões do Brasil* and played guitar transcriptions of Debussy, Ravel, and Bach in the Grammy-winning *Spanish Guitars of Laurindo Almeida*.

Though Almeida was several thousand miles away from the burgeoning bossa nova movement in Rio in the late 1950s, he adapted that to his own style when it was carried to American shores by Getz, Gilberto, Byrd, Jobim, and others. His 1962 album *Viva Bossa Nova!* was a commercial success; it hit the number 9 spot on the charts. Almeida won five Grammy awards, most of them coming in the late 1950s and early 1960s, and received an additional eleven Grammy nominations throughout his career.

In 1974, he and Shank formed the L.A. Four with bassist Ray Brown and drummer Chuck Flores, and the group recorded numerous albums together (Flores's place would be taken by Shelly Manne, then by Jeff Hamilton). Their varied repertoire included jazz, classical, and Brazilian-oriented material. Almeida also recorded with pianist George Shearing, singer Sammy Davis, Jr., the Modern Jazz Quartet, and guitarists Sharon Isbin, Charlie Byrd, and Larry Coryell. And he arranged, scored, and played on hundreds of scores for films and television shows. His electric guitar, mandolin, and lute playing could be heard in Elvis Presley films, *The Godfather*, *A Star Is Born*, *Camelot*, *Funny Girl*, and *The Agony and the Ecstasy*, and the television shows "Bonanza," "Rawhide," and "The Fugitive."

Egberto Gismonti

Of Brazil's best instrumental musicians, few have followed as singular a path as Egberto Gismonti, who had formal training in the conservatory and also absorbed musical lessons in the Amazon jungle. Gismonti (born in 1945 in Carmo, a small city in Rio de Janeiro state) has been engaged in a life-long search for new musical languages. He started by taking fifteen years of classical piano lessons in Rio and then studying orchestration and composition in Paris with Nadia Boulanger and Jean Barraqué. But Egberto's interest in all

Egberto Gismonti at the keyboard in 1986. *Photo by Mabel Arthou. Courtesy of Agência JB.*

kinds of popular music—jazz, samba, choro, baião, bossa—took him out of the conservatory and into a new musical world of his own making.

Gismonti can be intensely lyrical, sounding something like a highly rhythmic Ralph Towner on guitar or Keith Jarrett on piano, improvising atop baião and frevo patterns. He has written beautiful melodies that have been covered by many musicians; for example, "Sonho" (Dream) has been recorded by Henry Mancini, Paul Mauriat, and more than a dozen others. Then again, his music can be jarring, strange, and difficult. Nevertheless, Egberto is one of Brazil's most popular musicians internationally. *Danca das Cabeças* (Dance of the Minds), recorded with percussionist Naná Vasconcelos, has been released in eighteen countries and has sold over two hundred thousand copies, an im-

pressive sum for nonvocal experimental music. Egberto is quite popular in Europe, where his work is released on the ECM label, and well respected by jazz and classical musicians around the globe.

Egberto plays acoustic and electric keyboards, eight- and ten-string guitar, sitar, accordion, violoncello, all kinds of flutes, and numerous other instruments he has come across in his world travels. Sometimes he records solo, other times in ensembles. He collaborated with bassist Charlie Haden and saxophonist Jan Garbarek on *Mágico* and *Folk Songs*, and flutist Paul Horn on *Altitude of the Sun*. And Gismonti released *Academia de Danças* (Academy of Dances) and *Corações Futuristas* (Future Hearts) with Robertinho Silva (drums), Nivaldo Ornellas (sax and flute), and Luis Alves (bass).

Egberto has also recorded without accompaniment. *Solo* (1979) is a beautiful, lyrical effort that features him on acoustic piano and guitar. And in 1982's *Fantasia*, Gismonti used sound samplers to simulate an entire orchestra. The opening two cuts on that album—"Overture" and "Infância"—demonstrate the range Egberto may explore in just a few minutes. The overture begins with a foundation of sustained chords over which dissonant harmonic clusters are juxtaposed with nervous rhythmic patterns. This anxious mood then mellows as "Infância" begins; the main theme is introduced and worked through many variations, and the composition ends up with a rambunctious baiãolike feeling that evokes images of children dancing and playing.

"For me personally Egberto has been a kind of model in that he is willing to use a child singing one minute and then have a chamber orchestra the next, then a whole bank of synthesizers," keyboardist Lyle Mays told us. "He has a raw edge that sometimes puts people off, but to me the vision behind his music is just astounding."

Gismonti on guitar. *Courtesy of ECM.*

Hermeto Pascoal in 1988. *Courtesy of Som da Gente Records.*

Another adventurous Gismonti album, *Sol do Meio Dia* (Noonday Sun), released in 1978, was influenced by his friendship with Sapain, a shaman from the Yawalapiti tribe in the Amazon jungle near the Xingu River. Egberto stayed with the Yawalapiti for several weeks in 1977 and learned much about their music from Sapain. Because of the experience, Gismonti sought to make his own music more spontaneous and to find a perfect integration between musician, music, and instrument.

Watching Egberto play live is an unforgettable experience. On guitar, he plays with blinding speed and superb precision and can elicit a wide range of timbral effects. Sometimes he plays the guitar like a piano or percussion instrument, using his left hand to pluck and "hammer" the strings. His improvisations on guitar and on piano (on which he is equally proficient) are consistently surprising and imaginative. He also sings in a gentle voice, often with lyrics composed by the poet Geraldo Carneiro. However, words in Gismonti's music are primarily part of the sound, functioning like another instrument.

Gismonti has scored films, and in 1985 produced the soundtrack of the Hector Babenco film *Kiss of the Spider Woman*. ECM has a large catalog of much of Gismonti's best work, and several of his most experimental albums have been released on his own label, Carmo.

Hermeto Pascoal

One of Brazil's most colorful musical figures is Hermeto Pascoal, born in 1936 in Lagoa da Canoa, a neighborhood in the town of Arapiraca in Alagoas. When he performs, Hermeto cuts a striking figure. He is an albino with a flowing white beard and long luminous white hair, and he tends to dart from instrument to instrument on stage, full of energy and

inspiration as he follows each musical impulse wherever it leads him. His music is not for those with a lazy ear: he may shift from a merry frevo played by horns and guitars to a droning, dolorous toada on the accordion, then swing between xaxado and maxixe, plunge into a free-jazz piano interlude, and finish with a cuíca and saxophone giddily chasing each other all over the scales.

Like Gismonti, Pascoal has an uncanny ability to create new sounds. But while Egberto will often accomplish that by playing conventional instruments in unusual ways, Hermeto will do it by making ordinary household objects into instruments. He can elicit interesting and uncanny tones from pots, pans, jars, whatever is available.

On the 1984 composition "Tiruliruli" he took a phrase from a Brazilian soccer announcer's on-air play-by-play report and repeated it over and over, gradually adding more and more harmonium embellishments until he had created a quirky but strangely affecting short piece. In Hermeto's world, everything has musical possibilities. Percussionist Airto Moreira has called him "the most complete musician I ever met in my life. A genius."

Pascoal was a child musical prodigy. He started with a flute and then at the age of seven learned to play the accordion. By eleven he was already playing at the dances and *forrós* in the region around Arapiraca. When he was fourteen, his family moved to Recife, and Hermeto began to earn money performing on radio programs there. At sixteen, he moved to Caruaru, a city famous for its regional music. There Hermeto played his accordion on the local radio and at dances, returning to Recife a few years later. Although he was self-taught, Hermeto's musical development continued at a rapid pace: the piano came next, followed by various wind and percussion instruments. Pascoal moved south and struggled to make a living by playing any and all types of music in Rio and São Paulo in the late 1950s and early 1960s.

In 1964, he formed the Sambrasa Trio with bassist Humberto Claiber and percussionist Airto Moreira, who recalled, "We would often stay up all night talking about music." Later, Airto was in a band called Trio Novo with guitarists Heraldo do Monte and Théo de Barros. Hermeto joined them and the group changed its name to Quarteto Novo (New Quartet) and dedicated itself to a progressive re-invention of northeastern song styles. "We played baião, xaxado, other northeastern Brazilian rhythms, but the arrangements were very jazzy, in 4/4 time with modern harmonies," recalled Airto. The band released just one LP, *Quarteto Novo*, in 1967.

After the group split up, Hermeto journeyed to the United States. He was invited to record by jazz legend Miles Davis. Hermeto played piano on Miles's *Live-Evil* LP (1970). That same year, Pascoal cut the acclaimed solo album *Hermeto* on Buddha Records. While in North America, the multi-instrumentalist drew raves for his extraordinary improvisational abilities in concert and his idiosyncratic and original compositions. Gil Evans

and the Berlin Symphony recorded his material at this time. Pascoal's songs explored choro, frevo, maxixe, baião, jazz, and many other forms, mixing them freely and in unusual combinations. He included surprising modulations, eccentric instrumentation, and multiple rhythms within individual songs. Hermento's singularity was especially evident in his 1976 album *Slaves Mass*, in which he included the grunts of little piglets in his music and employed the human talents of Airto, Flora Purim, Laudir de Oliveira, Raul de Souza, David Amaro, Ron Carter, and Alphonso Johnson.

In the years since, Pascoal's own recordings have continued to be freewheeling and uninhibited, incorporating an ever-expanding array of found instruments, animate or inanimate: parrots, chickens, teapots, and bowls of water. In concert, Hermeto has always been unpredictable. He may stalk off the stage in a rage if the sound is inadequate or the audience is clinking their cocktail glasses and talking too loudly. But more than likely he will give a unique performance—unique because his group has a large repertoire of tunes and on any given night may perform any number of them in any order, always enlivened with improvisation, humorous between-song comments, and the unpredictable results of Hermeto's ability to make music with almost any animate or inanimate object on this earth.

Because of his eclecticism and radical experimentations, Hermeto became a cult figure and mentor to many musicians. Lyle Mays finds him "worth listening to just for his wild creativity. His music tends to show me that there are possibilities that I should try to open myself up to explore. He has a real devotion to the making of music and it comes across—let's go for it, let's do everything we can!"

Airto Moreira (*center*), flexing his muscles backstage, with Cannonball Adderley and Flora. *Photo by Phil Bray. Courtesy of Fantasy.*

Airto Moreira

While Sérgio Mendes was the biggest Brazilian name in the United States in the late 1960s, husband-and-wife musicians Airto Moreira and Flora Purim took the spotlight in the next decade, adding their Brazilian spirit to the burgeoning jazz fusion scene of those years. Airto spearheaded the Brazilian "percussion invasion" of the late 1960s and 1970s that infused American jazz with new rhythms, percussive textures, and tone colors. Although drummers Milton Banana and Hélcio Milito had recorded with Americans during the bossa era, and Dom Um Romão and João Palma had played with Mendes in the mid-1960s, Airto would have the biggest impact outside his country of any Brazilian drummer or percussionist.

Airto was born in 1941 in Itaiópolis, Santa Catarina, and grew up in the city of Curitiba. After playing with the bossa group Sambalanço Trio in the early 1960s, he was part of the aforementioned Sambrasa Trio and Quarteto Novo with Hermeto Pascoal. Airto was interested in both jazz and progressive interpretations of traditional Brazilian styles, and he was a multi-talented instrumentalist who didn't fit into any one niche. "At that time, percussionists in Brazil were usually specialists," he recalled. "One guy would play pandeiro really well, another guy would be a cuíca player, another would play surdo. But I mixed instruments and played everything."

In Rio, Airto had met and fallen in love with a young singer by the name of Flora Purim. In 1968, she decided to travel to the United States to pursue a jazz career, and Airto chose to follow her there, convinced he could eventually persuade her to return to Brazil with him. That was not to be, but he and Flora did stay together, marrying in 1972 and settling permanently in California.

When he first came to the United States, Airto was prepared to work. "I brought all the hand percussion instruments I had, and the fact is that I came at the right time." Jazz was especially ready for him in the late 1960s: Miles Davis, Larry Coryell, Herbie Hancock, Tony Williams, Chick Corea, Weather Report, and other artists were creating new musical hybrids by mixing free jazz and bebop with funk, rock, and Latin styles. Brazil offered an alternative to Cuban music, which had heavily influenced many jazz musicians in the 1940s and 1950s with rumba, charanga, and mambo rhythms, and congas, maracas, timbales, and bongos (following the Fidel Castro revolution in 1959, the American-Cuban interchange had slowed somewhat).

Airto spent his first several months in the United States studying with composer-arranger Moacir Santos, then began integrating himself into the American jazz scene, playing first with Paul Winter, one of the few Americans familiar with Brazilian hand percussion instruments. Later, he did session work with Wayne Shorter, Cannonball Adderley, and others.

Airto astonished the American musicians and producers with his vast array of percussion pieces—cuíca, berimbau, agogô, afoxê, ganzá, pandeiro (his strongest solo instrument), *pau de chuva* (rain stick), and various other rattlers, shakers, and drums, as well as musical devices that he had invented. Each instrument had different tones and textural possibilities, and their sum total—especially in Airto's dexterous hands—was all rather staggering for Americans who were seeing him perform for the first time.

When he would show up at a recording studio with all his gear in tow "the producers would go crazy," Airto remembered. "They would go up to the pile of percussion instruments and say, 'I like this one. Play this.'"

Moreira played the berimbau on albums by Paul Desmond and others. He added cuíca to Paul Simon's "Me and Julio Down by the Schoolyard," a salsa-flavored hit single in 1972. About Simon, Airto recalled, "He said he wanted something different, like a human voice. I had the cuíca and he said, 'That's it!'"

Airto caught the attention of Miles Davis, who used him on the albums *At Fillmore* and *Live-Evil*, both recorded in 1970. He also played with Weather Report on their groundbreaking eponymous first album in 1971. He was invited to join the group permanently but was unable to because of his commitment with Miles; Dom Um Romão would replace him on Weather Report's next LP, *Mysterious Traveller*.

Airto commented that Miles "really didn't want me to play rhythm all the time. He wanted me to play colors and sounds more than rhythm. I would play the cuíca to kind of tease him and he would feed off that and play more." By focusing on "atmosphere" with Miles, Airto greatly expanded the role of the percussion. This would ultimately change his own musical direction and influence almost all jazz drummers and percussionists to follow.

"He was playing stuff that couldn't be played by anybody else," recalls jazz keyboardist George Duke. "I'd never heard a percussionist play like that, that free, and understanding how to play the right thing at the right moment." Airto's success would trigger a northerly migration: "After I

played for Miles, a lot of Brazilian percussionists started coming to the States and bringing all kinds of stuff and making their own instruments."

Meanwhile, in between gigs with Davis, Airto found time for his first solo albums, *Natural Feelings* (1970) and *Seeds on the Ground* (1971). The next year, he and Flora joined bassist Stanley Clarke, saxophonist-flutist Joe Farrell, and keyboardist Chick Corea for Corea's seminal fusion LP *Return to Forever* (the album's name would become the group's moniker). "When Chick heard the rhythms I was playing, it was a whole new thing for him. Brazilian music has a very different beat, and he really liked the way Flora was singing and phrasing. It was different from both jazz and Latin music." In the band, Airto had an uncharacteristic role, playing only drums, while Flora handled the percussion. Airto and Flora also played on Return to Forever's 1973 album *Light as a Feather*, and they gave both albums a strong Brazilian edge.

Airto then left the group because "Chick wanted to go more into electronics and I didn't want to do that, to play loud." Instead, with producer Creed Taylor's backing, Airto formed his own band, Fingers, which included David Amaro on guitar and lasted for two years. In 1975 came Airto's tour-de-force solo effort, *Identity*, considered one of the finest fusion albums. It inspired musicologist John Storm Roberts to effuse in *The Latin Tinge*, "The texture of *Identity* was extraordinarily dense. Driving Afro-Brazilian percussion, berimbau musical bow, bossa nova vocals, almost purely Congo-Angola melodies, Amerindian wooden flutes, rich strings, rock drumming and guitar, shimmering free-rhythm bells and strikers, a kind of manic avant-garde scatting, were interwoven through multiple tracking in a series of compositions so rich in their references that they took on deeper meaning on every listening."

After Moreira's performances with Miles Davis, Weather Report, and Chick Corea, many bands added a percussionist, and percussive coloration became standard procedure in jazz and fusion. In fact, because of Airto, *down beat* magazine added a percussion category to its annual awards in 1972. Moreira took top honors that year and in many following years.

In 1979, Airto went to Brazil with George Duke, Ndugu Chancler, Stanley Clarke, Raul de Souza, Roland Batista, and other fusion stars to give a concert in Rio. Recalls George, "It was the first time Airto had been back to Brazil in a long time. He was nervous, because everybody was waiting to hear him. And he played a solo that night by himself that was the most incredible, magnificent percussion solo I've ever heard, bar none. It was an experience."

Concerts given by Moreira are always vivid experiences. Audiences are fascinated by his vast array of musical objects, the strange new sounds he can generate, the virtuoso solos Airto offers on pandeiro, the Amerindian-like chanting he weaves into his music, and the near-trance intensity with which he creates his exotic, incredibly rhythmic musical atmospheres. During the 1980s and 1990s, Airto and Flora have teamed on joint albums, and Moreira has recorded and toured with the Crusaders, Freddie Hubbard, Carlos Santana, Herbie Hancock, Gil Evans, Mickey Hart, and Babatunde Olantunji.

Naná Vasconcelos

Naná Vasconcelos is another creative and influential percussionist who has left his mark on global music of the last three decades. Naná, whom Airto calls "the best berimbau player in the world," has gained international critical acclaim

Naná Vasconcelos with a berimbau slung over his shoulder. Photo by Nick White. *Courtesy of Antilles/Island.*

with his work with Egberto Gismonti, Codona, and the Pat Metheny Group.

Naná (born in Recife in 1945) was part of Quarteto Livre with Geraldo Azevedo in the late 1960s, then lived in Europe throughout much of the 1970s. There he toured with saxophonist Gato Barbieri and also spent a few years in Paris working with disturbed children in a psychiatric hospital, using music as a form of creative therapy. Back in Brazil, he was part of the notable Som Imaginário band, then toured and recorded with Egberto Gismonti. In 1979, he formed Codona with trumpeter Don Cherry and percussionist Collin Walcott. The trio released three highly regarded albums that mixed free jazz and cross-cultural improvisation.

Naná next played percussion and sang with the Pat Metheny Group, adding a significant amount of rhythmic density and atmosphere to the albums, especially 1981's *As Falls Wichita, So Falls Wichita Falls*, on which Naná was part of a trio with guitarist Metheny and keyboardist Lyle

International musical travelers (*left to right*): Airto, Ndugu Chancler, Raul de Souza, Miroslav Vituous, Flora Purim, George Duke, and Cannonball Adderley. *Photo by Phil Bray. Courtesy of Fantasy.*

Mays. "He was a total joy to work with," said Mays. "One of the things that I most enjoyed about playing with Naná was that he was interested in working with me as a synthesizer player to come up with combination textures that neither of us could do alone. He took things a step further, using his voice together with his instrument and with my instruments. Naná broadened our soundscape, and he added charisma, another focal point of attention on stage."

Like Airto, Naná can create a dense musical atmosphere of rustles, rattles, whispers, and rumbles, moving with irresistible rhythm or clashing in unearthly cacophony. And, as Airto notes, Naná can wield the berimbau like no other, turning it into a unique solo voice. His best works, among them the 1989 solo album *Rain Dance*, are like sound encyclopedias, beautiful elaborations of rhythmic and textural possibilities.

Flora Purim

Airto's wife, Flora Purim, was the most successful jazz-fusion singer of the 1970s, both artistically and commercially. Many were the jazz fans in that decade who tuned in one of Flora's songs on the radio and were astonished and delighted by what they heard. She sang with great passion in Portuguese and accented English, with a sensuous voice that was alternately smooth and husky. Flora used an amazing array of vocal effects: squeaks, moans, cries, electronic distortions, free-form scat-

ting, and precipitous glissandi. A new type of jazz singer, she could serve as a lead vocalist or as another instrument interacting with the flute, guitar, and percussion. Flora was ideally suited to collaborate with the creative talents of Airto, George Duke, Chick Corea, Hermeto Pascoal, and Stanley Clarke.

Born in 1942, Flora grew up listening to jazz and blues, as well as samba and classical music. She sang in various clubs in and around Rio in the 1960s, during which time she met Hermeto Pascoal, who suggested she try wordless vocal improvisations. After moving to New York in 1968, she sat in on jam sessions with the likes of Herbie Hancock and Thelonious Monk. Her first gigs involved singing jazz-bossa in Europe with Stan Getz and recording with Duke Pearson and Gil Evans.

Then Corea invited Purim and Moreira to play on the *Return to Forever* album, and she stayed with that band for two years, singing and writing lyrics for songs such as "Light as a Feather." Commented George Duke, "She was so free melodically that she sounded like a horn player. It was absolutely new music. I don't think there's anybody that sings quite like her. Free as a bird."

In 1973, she recorded her solo debut, *Butterfly Dreams*. The album's opening notes—Airto's cuíca and Stanley Clarke's funky bass playing off each other—gave the listener a hint of the jazz-fusion feast that follows. The album's personnel also included keyboardist Duke, guitarist Amaro, flutist Joe Henderson, and zither-player Ernie Hood. Collectively they mixed funk-Brazilian grooves with uninhibited free-form soloing to create one of the era's most noted works. Highlights included Purim's lovely rendition of Jobim's beautiful "Dindi" and the ballad "Love Reborn," with its bossalike guitar, Flora's romantic vocals, and Henderson's languid sax.

Flora cut a live album in Montreux, finished another studio work, *Stories to Tell*, and then was awarded *down beat* magazine's 1974 award for best female jazz vocalist. In 1976, she recorded *Open Your Eyes, You Can Fly*, whose title song became one of her most popular standards. That LP included Duke, Airto, Pascoal, Gismonti, bassist Alphonso Johnson, and drummers Ndugu and Robertinho Silva.

In later decades, Flora released several more albums and was a frequent performer at events such as the Montreux Jazz Festival. Some of the time she was part of a band that included Airto, saxophonist-flutist Gary Meek, and acoustic guitarist José Neto. She teamed with Mickey Hart and Airto on the intriguing *Dafos* (1989) and added her atmospheric vocals to Hart's world-music drumming-and-percussion fest *Planet Drum* (1991).

The Brazilian Wave

Of the prolonged interchange between Brazilian and American music, Sérgio Mendes told us, "It's interesting for me today to see Herbie Hancock doing things with Milton Nascimento. It's a kind of mutual curiosity between two different worlds. I still listen to Horace Silver and Bud Powell. And Stevie Wonder, Henry Mancini, Burt Bacharach, Pat Metheny—who has not been influenced by Brazilian music?"

Latin American and Caribbean music have strongly influenced American jazz and popular music throughout the twentieth century, as was painstakingly documented by musicologist John Storm Roberts in *The Latin Tinge*. Jelly Roll Morton used the habanera rhythm in many songs, Cole Porter incorporated the rumba, and Professor Longhair and Fats Domino both had Latin-influenced piano styles. Rocker Bo Diddley's trademark beat was a pounding rumba rhythm, with Jerome Green on maracas. Jazz musicians

Dizzy Gillespie, Duke Ellington, Stan Kenton, George Shearing, and Bud Shank experimented with Latin (especially Cuban) rhythms, percussion, and song styles in the 1940s and 1950s. And Machito, Gato Barbieri, Tito Puente, Willie Bobo, Cal Tjader, Mongo Santamaria, Paquito D'Rivera, Daniel Ponce, Jorge Dalto, and Eddie Palmieri were all important figures in the Latin-jazz interchange from the 1950s through later decades.

The Brazilian Percussion Invasion

Brazilian music—its rhythms, instruments, harmonies, melodies, and textures—would have an enormous influence on American music from 1962 on. Percussionists were a large part of that impact. Brazilian music helped create a new rhythmic emphasis in jazz and became an important element in the emerging style called "jazz fusion." Airto Moreira, as noted above, led the way in this rhythmic revolution. Other influential Brazilian drummers and percussionists in the 1960s and 1970s were Don Um Romão, Édison Machado, Milton Banana, Naná Vasconcelos, Laudir de Oliveira, Guilherme Franco, and Paulinho da Costa, all of whom recorded and toured with numerous jazz, rock, and pop artists in the United States.

"In all fusion bands, the drummers slip into a jazz-Brazilian groove almost automatically," observed jazz flutist Herbie Mann. And, in the 1970s, "it became almost matter of fact for every band to have a percussionist. But all the colors were Brazilian-influenced. Before that, the Latin drummers just played congas, timbales, and bongos."

Sambas have been recorded by many North Americans, including Joni Mitchell ("Dreamland" in 1978), Earl Klugh and George Benson ("Brazilian Stomp" in 1988), John Patitucci ("Our Family" in 1988), and David Byrne ("Office Cowboy" in 1989), among others. George

Brazilian Rhythm Masters and International Music

Brazil turns out great drummers and percussionists the way it turns out great soccer players. Some of the best who have made their careers primarily within Brazil include Robertinho Silva, Pascoal Meirelles, Jorginho do Pandeiro, Wilson das Neves, Paulinho Braga, Chico Batera, Dom Chacal, Gordinho, Sidinho, Marcos Suzano, Jurim Moreira, Marcelo Costa, Toninho Pinheiro, Ovídio Brito, Simone Soul, and Firminho. Other Brazilian rhythm masters have performed a great deal overseas, and the following is a sampling of their recording and touring activity in recent decades. The name of the Brazilian artist (or ensemble) is followed by some of the international artists with whom they toured or recorded.

Waltinho Anastacio: JoAnne Brackeen, Gerry Mulligan.

Ara Ketu: Jimmy Cliff.

Mingo Araújo: Paul Simon.

Milton Banana: Stan Getz.

Cyro Baptista: Paul Simon, David Byrne, Ambitious Lovers, Herbie Mann, Paula Robison, Ryuichi Sakamoto.

Carlinhos Brown: Bill Laswell, Wayne Shorter, Herbie Hancock.

Café: Elements, Adela Dalto, Sadão Watanabe, Roberta Flack, David Byrne, Herbie Mann, Larry Coryell, Michael Brecker, Randy Brecker, Richard Stoltzman, Paul Winter.

Djalma Correa: Peter Gabriel, the Manhattan Transfer.

Mayuto Correa: Charles Lloyd, Gabor Szabo, Hugh Masakela, Freddie Hubbard, Donald Byrd.

Paulinho da Costa: Dizzy Gillespie, Milt Jackson, Ella Fitzgerald, Joe Pass, Michael Jackson, Madonna, Barbra Streisand, Lionel Richie.

Alyrio Lima Cova: Webster Lewis, Weather Report.

Duduka da Fonseca: JoAnne Brackeen, Herbie Mann.

Guilherme Franco: Gato Barbieri, Keith Jarrett, McCoy Tyner, Elvin Jones, Don Pullen, Paul Winter.

Téo Lima: Yutaka, Hendrik Meurkens, Toots Thielemans.

Hélcio Milito: Herbie Mann, Kenny Durham.

César Machado: Hendrik Meurkens.

Édison Machado: Herbie Mann, Stan Getz.

Armando Marçal: the Pat Metheny Group.

Airto Moreira: Miles Davis, Weather Report, Return to Forever, Stan Getz, Paul Simon, George Duke, Paul Desmond, Mickey Hart.

Sidinho Moreira: Paul Simon.

Carlinho de Oliveira: Herbie Mann.

Laudir de Oliveira: Chicago, Nina Simone.

Olodum: Paul Simon, Bill Laswell, Herbie Hancock, Wayne Shorter.

João Parahyba: Michel LeGrand.

Roberto Pinheiro: Al Di Meola.

Carlos Pinto: Al Di Meola.

Portinho: Hendrik Meurkens.

Dom Um Romão: Cannonball Adderley, Paul Horn, Weather Report.

Jorge da Silva: John Zorn, Arto Lindsay, David Byrne.

Naná Vasconcelos: Codona, Ralph Towner, Gato Barbieri, the Pat Metheny Group, Paul Simon, B. B. King, the Talking Heads.

Duke commented, "I think you can find these Brazilian rhythms everywhere; they've gone into TV and film scoring. And percussion has become so strong in dance music; all that stuff on top is Brazilian stuff that sounds like a batucada—shakers, agogôs, and those kind of rhythms. In a strange sort of way, it infiltrated the modern pop world without them even knowing it."

The Pat Metheny Group is an example of a band that consciously incorporated many Brazilian elements into its sound. "During the first half of the group's history, one hundred percent of the music we did had that straight-eighth rhythm, which comes from Brazilian music," observed Lyle Mays, noting that most jazz has the characteristic "swing eighth note." Mays was the keyboardist for the group and co-wrote its material with Metheny. He continued, "You can hear it in 'San Lorenzo,' 'Phase Dance,' and then it is even more evident in the album *Watercolors*. We played on electric guitar and keyboards, but under the surface the actual rhythms had a whole lot to do with Brazilian music. I don't mean that to sound like we were pioneers. It was a thing happening in jazz in general, such as with Gary Burton, which is where Pat got it from. There was some Latin influence going around too, all the way back to Dizzy Gillespie. But the Brazilian rhythms are a little more subtle and translated into a music that sounded like a hybrid. It wasn't so obvious it was Brazilian based."

While such influences were "covert," as Lyle saw it, a more "overt" impact began when Brazilian musicians began to join American bands. A good example is the effect Vasconcelos had on the Pat Metheny Group. In 1981, Metheny and Mays started to work with Naná, who stayed with them through *Travels* (1983). He made a vivid atmospheric contribution to their sound; and, rhythmically, some of their tunes, such as "Are You Going With Me?" and "Straight on Red," became more obviously samba-based.

Vasconcelos left the group after a few years but would later play on Lyle Mays's 1986 eponymous solo album and Pat Metheny's 1992 solo effort *Secret Story*. The latter album also featured Brazilian percussionist Armando Marçal, who took Naná's

place in the Pat Metheny Group in the mid-1980s and appeared on albums such as *Still Life (Talking)* and *Letter from Home*.

"I think that Naná was more interested in sounds and textures, while Armando is more interested in rhythms. Armando is almost like an entire samba school," said Mays. "He has maybe the strongest rhythmic clock of anybody I've ever heard, just relentless, incredible. He does everything from rock tamborine parts to more traditional samba."

Keyboardist-composer Don Grusin and his brother Dave Grusin have both been inspired by the Brazilian sound. "It started in the 1960s when I first heard Astrud Gilberto and Stan Getz and João Gilberto," recalled Don, who over the next two decades produced and arranged albums for Gilberto Gil, Simone, Rique Pantoja, and other Brazilian artists. He sees Brazilian music as having strongly influenced contemporary jazz. "I hear a kind of hybrid sound in my music and that of Dave, Lee Ritenour, Ronnie Foster, Harvey Mason.

In recent decades, Brazilian rhythms have been prominently incorporated into the music of international jazz and pop artists such as Michael Franks, Sade, Basia, and countless others (see Discography, pages 233–236).

The Melodic-Harmonic Impact

"I think Brazilian music has affected jazz musicians and songwriters a lot, including how they melodically approach their music," George Duke told us. "I know that when I was in Brazil in 1970, I bought every Milton, Ivan Lins, Edu Lobo, and Simone record I could find. I brought them back and played them for my friends. And then I sat down and tried to emulate those songs, to compose in that area, and you can hear that on some of my early records. The same way I learned to play jazz, I learned to play Brazilian music; you have to learn the fundamentals first. And I know that Cannonball Adderley was totally immersed in that music before he died. He felt the same way."

Duke collaborated on many recordings with Brazilian musicians. His album *A Brazilian Love Affair*, from 1977, featured Milton, Airto, and Flora Purim. Duke, like many jazz artists, turned to Brazil in the 1970s and 1980s for great melodies to cover, because so much of the music sounded fresh and original. It is arguable that in recent decades American composers have not been writing popular songs that have the melodic-harmonic quality of the standards produced by the likes of George Gershwin, Duke Ellington, Cole Porter, and Billy Strayhorn earlier in the century. "The U.S. is be-

coming more of a rhythm nation than a melodic nation," noted Duke. "Brazil is both."

In recent years, the songs of Tom Jobim, Milton Nascimento, Ivan Lins, Gilberto Gil, Djavan, and other composers from Brazil have been covered extensively overseas. Numerous jazz musicians have also been mining the musical treasures of the choro and samba-canção eras, recording the standards of Pixinguinha, Jacó do Bandolim, and Ary Barroso.

Over the past few decades, noteworthy international artists who have covered Brazilian songs include Bud Shank, Stan Getz, Charlie Byrd, Paul Winter, Herbie Mann, Paul Desmond, Frank Sinatra, the Crusaders, George Benson, Joe Pass, Carmen McRae, Diane Schuur, Sadao Watanabe, Al Jarreau, Al Di Meola, Willie Bobo, Larry Coryell, Quincy Jones, Ella Fitzgerald, Toots Thielemans, the Manhattan Transfer, Mark Murphy, Lee Ritenour, Ernie Watts, Patti Austin, Hendrik Meurkens, Sarah Vaughan, Wayne Shorter, Herbie Hancock, Terence Blanchard, Joe Henderson, and Richard Stoltzman.

Keyboards and Accordion

One of the most influential Brazilian musicians in North America in the 1970s was Eumir Deodato, a pianist-arranger born in Rio in 1943. Eumir scored a smash hit with his funky-jazzy rendition of Richard Strauss's "Also Sprach Zarathustra" in 1973 (which at the time was on the public mind because of Stanley Kubrick's film *2001, a Space Odyssey*). Deodato's hip version went to number 2 on *Billboard's* pop singles chart, and the album it was from, *Prelude* (1972), hit number 3.

Deodato also played an important part in launching Milton Nascimento's career in Brazil by arranging Milton's songs for his debut at the International Song Festival in Rio. In the United States, Eumir helped shape the pop sound of the

Eliane Elias. *Photo by Paul D'Inmocenzo. Courtesy of Blue Note.*

The cover of Sivuca's *Som Brasil* **album.** *Courtesy of Sonet Records.*

1970s and 1980s through his work as a producer or arranger for acts such as Kool and the Gang; Earth, Wind and Fire; Roberta Flack; Bette Midler; Stanley Turrentine; and Aretha Franklin.

Singer-songwriter-pianist Tania Maria (born in 1948) was a familiar figure on jazz radio in the 1980s, achieving great success with a spicy combination of Brazilian and Cuban rhythms, funk and rock influences, a percussive piano attack, and vigorous vocalese. Tania started her career in France by launching several albums there, then moved to the United States. She released her first album there in 1981, *Piquant*, produced by Latin-jazz legend Cal Tjader. Later came a string of hit LPs, notably *Come with Me* and *Love Explosion*, that established her as a compelling new jazz voice.

Pianist-composer Eliane Elias established her career in the 1980s, with a style steeped in traditional jazz. She has been lauded for her impressive piano technique, harmonic inventiveness, and compositional skill. Born in 1960 in São Paulo, Eliane was a child prodigy who at the age of twelve could play jazz standards by Wynton Kelly, Bud Powell, Red Garland, Art Tatum, and Bill Evans. At seventeen, she started playing behind Vinícius de Moraes and Toquinho and stayed with their group for three years. In 1981, in Paris, she met bassist Eddie Gomez, then a member of the fusion group Steps Ahead. She subsequently moved to New York and began a one-year stint with the band. She married American trumpet-player Randy Brecker, with whom she recorded *Amanda* (named for their daughter) in 1985. On her first solo album, *Illusions* (1987), Elias delved into bebop, ballads, and choro, backed by Gomez, Al Foster, Stanley Clarke, Lenny White, and Toots Thielemans. *Cross Currents* (1988) was also heavily jazz-oriented, while *So Far, So Close* (1989) included more samba, choro, and bossa.

Antonio Adolfo started his career in the mid-

1960s with the trio 3-D and went on to become a leading keyboardist, songwriter, and music teacher. His song "Sá Marina" was given English lyrics by Marilyn and Alan Bergman, and—as "Pretty World"—was recorded by Stevie Wonder, Sérgio Mendes, Herb Alpert, Earl Klugh, and Yutaka, among others. In 1977, frustrated with the indifference of major record companies in Brazil to instrumental music, Adolfo financed and released his own LP, *Feito em Casa* (Homemade), and its success proved there was a small but eager market for such works. Many other artists subsequently launched their own albums, triggering a boom in independent recording. Later, Adolfo released the accomplished LPs *Cristalino* (1989) and *Jinga* (1990).

Sivuca (Severino D'Oliveira) is an accordion virtuoso who also sings and plays piano and guitar. Born in 1930 in Itabaiana, Pernambuco, he has recorded numerous albums featuring forró, choro, waltzes, and other genres interpreted with a folksy, jazzy style and embellished with rich improvisation. He has been a fixture on the international jazz scene since the 1960s and has toured and recorded with Miriam Makeba, Harry Belafonte, Oscar Brown, Jr., Airto, and Toots Thielemans.

Other notable contemporary Brazilian piano and synthesizer players not mentioned elsewhere include: João Carlos Assis Brasil, Amilson Godoy,

Bola Sete (guitar), Paulinho (drums), and Sebastião Neto (bass) on the cover of an album recorded for Fantasy in the 1960s. *Courtesy of Fantasy.*

The guitar trio D'Alma in 1988 (*left to right*): Andre Geraissati, Ulisses Rocha, and Marco Pereira. *Photo by Paulo Vasconcellos. Courtesy of Som da Gente Records.*

Amilton Godoy, Manfredo Fest, Dom Salvador, Cido Bianchi, César Camargo Mariano, Nelson Ayres, Gilson Peranzzetta, João Carlos Assis Brasil, Marcos Ariel, Tulio Mourão, Lincoln Olivetti, Hugo Fattoruso, Luiz Avellar, Ricardo Leão, Marcos Silva, Rique Pantoja, Guilherme Vergeiro, Paulo Calasans, Paulo Braga, Jota Morais, Marcio Miranda, William Magalhães, and Marinho Boffa. A few of Brazil's many outstanding accordion players are Dominguinhos, Renato Borghetti, Chiquinho do Acordeon, Baú dos Oito Baixos, Orlando Silveira, and Severo.

Guitar and Strings

If there is a musical instrument that most typifies Brazil, it is the guitar. Brazil has produced many greats on that instrument, from Garoto to Baden Powell, Luiz Bonfá to Toquinho. Bola Sete (Djalma Andrade, 1923–1987) was a guitarist who was adept at mixing jazz and samba, and playing choro and bossa nova. Born in Rio, he studied classical music at the National School of Music and was influenced early in his career by Andres Segovia, Django Reinhardt, and Charlie Christian. He developed a versatile repertoire, playing in samba groups and composing choros ("Cosminho no Choro," for example). In 1959 he moved to the United States and lived there for the rest of his life, developing his own jazz-samba fusion. Bola toured with Dizzy Gillespie and recorded several albums for Fantasy Records (one of the best was *Autêntico!*).

Heraldo do Monte (born in Recife in 1935) was a member of Quarteto Novo with Airto Moreira and Hermeto Pascoal. Heraldo is a master of the guitar and has a command of many other stringed instruments as well, including the mandolin and cavaquinho. In the 1980s, Heraldo recorded the excellent solo albums *Cordas Vivas* (Live Strings) and *Cordas Mágicas* (Magic Strings), which show off his dazzling electric and acoustic guitar work and mix baião, xaxado, and other regional styles with choro and Tal Farlow influences.

André Geraissati, Ulisses Rocha, and Marco Pereira have recorded together in the acoustic guitar trio D'Alma and have released outstanding solo efforts. Pereira's *Círculo das Cordas* (Circle of Strings) in 1988 was a compelling meeting of classical guitar and jazz improvisation. Ricardo Silveira has added his impressive jazz-fusion guitar licks to albums and shows by Milton Nascimento, Herbie Mann, Sonny Fortune, Don

Guitarist Torcuato Mariano, who released the Windham Hill album *Paradise Station* in 1994. *Courtesy of Windham Hill Records.*

Grusin, and Jon Hassell and has cut instrumental solo LPs like *Long Distance* and *Sky Light*.

Torcuato Mariano was born in Argentina in 1963 and moved to Brazil at the age of fourteen. In the 1980s, he played guitar on the albums or in the shows of Johnny Alf, Ivan Lins, and Marina and later arranged songs for saxophonist Leo Gandelman, co-wrote songs for pop performers Xuxa, Angélica, and Rosana, and produced Brazilian funk and R&B albums. His debut solo LP *Paradise Station* incorporated these disparate influences in a collection of appealing crossover songs.

Other noteworthy Brazilian guitarists of recent decades include Nonato Luis, Cristóvão Bastos, Olmir "Alemão" Stocker, Hélio Delmiro, Victor Biglione, Almir Sater, Fredera, Francisco Mario, Carlos Barbosa-Lima, Turíbio Santos, Paulinho Soledade, Natan Marques, Paulo Bellinati, Romero Lubambo, João Lyra, Nelson Faria, Dino 7 Cordas, Luiz Brazil, Eduardo Gudin, Raphael Rebello, Canhoto da Paraíba, Francisco Soares de Araújo, Tavinho Bonfá, Jaime Alem, Luiz Brasil, Heitor T.P. (who joined the Simply Red band in 1980s), Oscar Castro-Neves (discussed in Chapter Three), and the remarkable siblings Sérgio Assad, Odair Assad, and Badi Assad.

On the bass guitar, some of the best are Luis Alves, Nico Assumpção, Jorge Degas, Zeca Assumpção, Pedro Ivo, Arismar do Espírito Santo, Nilson Matta, Rubão Sabino, Yuri Popoff, and Jamil Joanes. Henrique Cazes is a renowned cavaquinho player. And Jaques Morelenbaum is a cellist who has appeared on many albums.

Wind Instruments and Combos

Pixinguinha was not the last notable Brazilian wind musician to come from Brazil. Cláudio Roditi, a trumpeter who has been part of the international jazz scene since the early 1970s, has appeared on albums by Charlie Rouse, Slide Hampton, Herbie Mann, and Paquito D'Rivera. His solo albums *Gemini Man* and *Slow Fire* display his unique bebop-Brazilian blends. Raul de Souza is a trombonist who was a strong presence in the jazz world in the 1960s and 1970s, recording with the Crusaders and Sonny Rollins, among others.

Moacir Santos, who taught music theory to both Airto and Flora Purim, has been an influential music professor and mentor for many young Brazilian musicians since he moved to the United States in 1969. He scored a big hit in Brazil with "Naná" in 1964, and in the United States recorded three LPs for Blue Note in the early 1970s (including *Maestro*, for which he received a Grammy nomination). He is known for his esoteric mixes of jazz and Brazilian idioms, and his complicated rhythms.

Saxophonist Leo Gandelman's smooth, swinging playing style and mixing of jazz, techno-pop,

Moacir Santos, as pictured on the cover of one of his albums.

Saxophonist Leo Gandelman, a popular instrumental recording artist. *Courtesy of Verve.*

and Brazilian genres made him the most popular Brazilian instrumental artist of the late 1980s and early 1990s—voted into that position four years running by the Brazilian press. Gandelman's solo albums *Solar, Visions,* and *Made in Rio*—featuring both standards and songs written by Leo and keyboardist William Magalhães—have reached a wide national audience.

Trumpeter Márcio Montarroyos has been a

valued session man, and his solo albums like *Samba Solstice* have found an international audience. Other notable Brazilian wind musicians include harmonica players Mauricio Einhorn and Rildo Hora; saxophonist-flutists Nivaldo Ornellas, Roberto Sion, Mauro Senise, Dirceu Leitte, Marcelo Martins, and Raul Mascarenhas; saxophonist-pianist Zé Nogueira; clarinetist Paulo Sérgio dos Santos; flutists Danilo Caymmi and Andrea Dias; trumpeters Guilherme Dias Gomes and Bidinho; flutist-pianist Jovino Santos; and flutist-guitarist Edson Alves.

In terms of combos, the trio Azymuth was a popular international act in the eighties that blended jazz, samba, and funk. The members of the band are José Roberto Bertrami on keyboards, Ivan Conti on drums, and Alex Malheiros on bass (all three were born in 1946). In 1979, they released *Light As a Feather,* and its single "Jazz Carnival" went gold in England. *Telecommunication,* in 1982, was a top 10 jazz album for the group. Azymuth went on

Progressive-jazz band Azymuth (*left to right*): Ivan Conti, José Roberto Bertrami, and Alex Malheiros. *Courtesy of Milestone Records.*

to record many more LPs and the threesome also released numerous solo works on their own.

Cama de Gato (Cat's Cradle) released compelling Brazilian "fusion" albums in the 1980s and was composed of four talented instrumental artists—bassist Arthur Maia, saxophonist-flutist Mauro Senise, drummer Pascoal Meirelles, and keyboardist Rique Pantoja—all of whom have recorded solo albums.

Nó Em Pingo D'Agua (Knot in a Drop of Water) is an exceptional instrumental combo that augments choro with samba, jazz, tango, and salsa with inspired creativity. Its founder, flutist-saxophonist Mario Seve, is also a member of Aquarela Carioca (Rio Watercolor), which moves fluidly and passionately through the above styles and maracatu, pop, and reggae. Other accomplished instrumental groups from recent years include Orquestra de Cordas Dedilhadas de Pernambuco (Plucked String Orchestra of Pernambuco), Pau Brasil (Brazilwood), Orquestra de Música Brasileira, ZonAzul (BlueZone), and Homem de Bem (Man of Good).

Uakti

In many respects, the most innovative Brazilian instrumental group of the past twenty years has been Uakti, named after a mythological figure of the Toucan tribe in the Amazon rain forest. His story was recounted in the liner notes of the band's eponymous U.S. debut album. Uakti's body was perforated with holes and when the wind blew through them an irresistible sound was produced that attracted all the Toucan women. Jealous, the men killed Uakti, burying his body in the ground in a place where tall palms later grew. From the wood of the palms, the Indians fashioned instruments that could produce melodious and seductive tones like those once made by the wind passing through Uakti's body. Naturally, it was absolutely forbidden to play these flutes outside of secret male ceremonies.

The group Uakti, which also makes its own instruments, was formed in the mid-1970s by Marco Antonio Guimarães, who had studied at

Jazz ensemble Cama de Gato performing at the Jazzmania club in Rio (*left to right*): Rique Pantoja, Arthur Maia, Mauro Senise, and Pascoal Meirelles. *Photo by Chris McGowan.*

the University of Bahia with the legendary com-poser Walter Smetak, a sort of Swiss-Brazilian Harry Partch who created new musical systems and instruments. One of Smetak's creations was *A Grande Virgem* (The Big Virgin), a giant flute played by twenty-two persons.

When Guimarães returned home to Belo Hor-izonte, Minas Gerais, he gathered together a group of like-minded, adventurous musicians, each of whom had classical training: Paulo Sérgio dos Santos, Artur Andres Ribeiro, and Décio de Souza Ramos. The foursome designed an orches-tra of wholly original string, wind, and percus-sion instruments. Among them are the *planetário* (planetarium), a wooden box strung with latex bands; the *marimba de vidro*, a two-octave glass marimba; and the *trilobita* (trilobite), a cluster of tuned PVC tubes topped with drum skins. The sounds that come from them are as mesmerizing as what might have come from their mythologi-cal namesake. The Manhattan Transfer's Tim Hauser, who worked with the quartet in 1987 on the Transfer's *Brasil* album, found their sounds

"very spiritual" and added, "It makes you feel like you're in a band two thousand years ago."

Uakti also made appearances on albums by Milton Nascimento—most notably on *Anima*—in the 1980s and can be heard on Paul Simon's *The Rhythm of the Saints*. But it is their solo work that is most remarkable, on such outstanding works as *Tudo e Todas As Coisas* (All and Every-thing), *Mapa* (Map), and *I Ching*. They mix to-gether maracatu, samba, jazz, minimalism, and elements of medieval, Hindu, and Andean mu-sic; all this is then played upon their strange-looking and beautiful-sounding instruments. Uakti's songs sound like chamber music from some lost Asian civilization.

The International Impact

Looking at the profound influence of Brazilian rhythms, songwriting, and percussion on global music, it is fitting to reiterate Sérgio Mendes's rhetorical question: "Who has not been influ-enced by Brazilian music?" A significant inter-

Uakti in concert. *Photo by Cristiano Quintino. Courtesy of Verve.*

change has been going on for an entire century and has accelerated over the past few decades. Herbie Mann added, "It gets to the point where you have Djavan recording in Los Angeles, and Manhattan Transfer in Brazil, and they are all using people who have been listening to Herbie Hancock and Ivan Lins. That is, it all gets so crossed that each in turn re-influences the other."

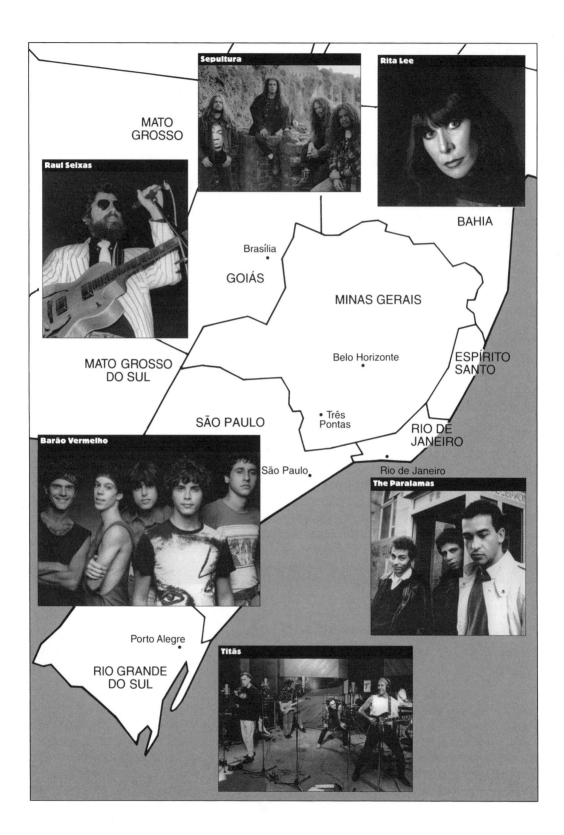

Sepultura

Rita Lee

Raul Seixas

MATO
GROSSO

BAHIA

Brasília

GOIÁS

MINAS GERAIS

MATO GROSSO
DO SUL

Belo Horizonte

ESPÍRITO
SANTO

SÃO PAULO

Três
Pontas

Barão Vermelho

RIO DE
JANEIRO

São Paulo

Rio de Janeiro

The Paralamas

Porto Alegre

RIO GRANDE
DO SUL

Titãs

Tropical Rock

Chapter Nine

Oh, my God, what happened to MPB?
Everybody is serious
Everyone takes it seriously
But this seriousness sounds like a game to me

Rita Lee and Paulo Coelho
"Arrombou a Festa" (Crashed the Party)

Over the past several decades, rock has under-gone as complex an evolution in Brazil as it has in the United States, its country of origin. Brazilian musicians have produced their own versions of bubble-gum rock, Beatles-styled pop rock, hard rock, punk rock, folk rock, and heavy metal. They have also fused rock with Brazilian genres such as frevo, baião, samba, and embolada, inventing new musical hybrids. Rock and roll has also met with sharp criticism from Brazilians who have resented the encroachment of American pop music into MPB territory. The band Os Mutantes, of which Rita Lee was a member, was an early target of nationalistic wrath.

As a whole, Brazilian rock came of age in the 1980s. One reason for this, perhaps, was that the new generation of *roqueiros* (rockers) had grown up listening to rock—American, English, and Brazilian—their entire lives. "It was like our generation was eating the whole rock history," commented singer Paulo Ricardo, ex-leader of RPM, the first rock act to sell more than two million units of a single album. "We had all that information in our minds and we couldn't wait to put it all together. We felt we were equal in some sense with rock in the rest of the world."

Starting in that decade, Brazilian *roqueiros* had access to high-quality electric guitars and keyboards and high-tech recording equipment, and they demonstrated a greater degree of profes-sionalism in staging shows. They also began to benefit from increased music company support. These changes helped the leading Brazilian rock acts to realize their potential, producing innovative music of high technical quality. And the best Brazilian rock wordsmiths carried on the MPB tradition of great lyric writing, albeit with an angrier, more outspoken edge. Cazuza, the Titãs, the Engenheiros, the Paralamas, Legião Urbana, and other bands from the new generation became enormously successful in Brazil.

Two other factors may have also contributed to producing so many notable rock artists in that decade: the lifting of censorship imposed by the government and the arrival of the socioeconomic crisis that slammed Brazil in the 1980s. During the military dictatorship's heaviest repression, roughly between 1968 and 1978, lyrics had to be free of political content or heavily coded, and MPB artists crafted elegant and metaphoric verses to voice their discontent. But in the next decade, songwriters were by and large free to question the government and critique Brazil. Many rock groups used raw, direct, openly aggressive language to express their generation's dismay with Brazil's horrific problems.

And those problems were serious indeed, as Brazil plunged into the worst economic and moral crisis of its history. Hyper-inflation struck (topping 1,700 percent in 1989), widespread corruption continued in all levels of government and society, and quality of life took a tremendous drop for both the poor and the middle class. Crime skyrocketed, as did the numbers of abandoned children, homeless people, and starving poor.

Brazilians in the 1980s were cynical and bitter. People had the feeling that the government had been making fools of everyone for quite a long time and no one had noticed. They were impatient for a return to democracy; they were sick and tired of governmental corruption and repression. This feeling was strongest among the youth, and the form of art that best expressed it, for the middle class, was rock. One such angry song was "Estado Violência" (State of Violence), by Titãs.

> **Violent state, hypocritical state**
> **The law that isn't mine, the law I didn't**
>   **want . . .**
> **Man in silence, man in prison**
> **Man in darkness, future of the nation**

Yet, diversity was also a hallmark of Brazilian rock at that time. Not all rock was full of outrage. After all, Brazilians have a remarkable capacity to make do with new circumstances, as well as to

Jovem Guarda—Erasmo Carlos, Wanderléia, and Roberto Carlos—at the microphone in 1968. *Photo by Wilson Santos. Courtesy of Agência JB.*

seize the moment and leave their sorrows behind, at least for a night of partying or an afternoon of soccer. And because Brazil has absorbed so many influences, national and international, there is not one Brazilian rock style, but many.

From Copacabana to the Underground

Brazilian rock dates to 1957, when Cauby Peixoto recorded the first domestically composed rock tune, "Rock 'n' Roll 'em Copacabana." The next year, Celly Campello recorded Fred Jorge's giddy "Banho de Lua" (Moonlight Bath), which in its innocence seems light years away in attitude from the angry lyrics of rock artists such as Titãs and Cazuza in the 1980s.

> **I take moonlight showers**
> **And turn snow-white**
> **Moonlight is my friend**
> **No one dares to reproach me**
> **It's so good to dream about you**
> **Oh, what a pure moonlight**

During the next few years, Campello, Demetrius, Sérgio Murilo, Ronnie Cord, and others recorded a string of Portuguese-language covers of American and European rock tunes. In 1965, the Jovem Guarda (Young Guard) movement arrived, led by Roberto Carlos and Erasmo Carlos. Roberto, a singer and composer, had established a rock career two years earlier with "Calhambeque" (Old Heap) and a cover of "Splish Splash." By that time, bossa nova musicians had largely turned to social and political themes, singing about the poverty and suffering of poor Brazilians. But a large portion of urban youth did not care about droughts in the Northeast or peasants without

Roberto Carlos in concert in the 1980s. *Photo by Mircea Dordea. Courtesy of Sony.*

land. They worried about more immediate things in their own lives: cars, romance, clothes, and school. Jovem Guarda's rock and roll reflected these concerns.

Roberto Carlos (born in 1943) started out singing bossa nova but then met Erasmo Carlos (Erasmo Esteves, born in 1941), a true Carioca rocker, and a long and fertile songwriting partnership was born. Roberto's romanticism blended perfectly with Erasmo's naive aggressiveness, shaping the format of Jovem Guarda music: upbeat, simple rock and roll. They recorded separately and together, but most of their many successes came through Roberto singing their co-written tunes.

Fame resulted from the "Jovem Guarda" show on the TV Record network, a massive success that lasted from 1965 to 1968. Recorded live in São Paulo, the show was watched all over the country by millions of curious and emraptured fans. On videotape the nation saw girls crying hysterically, boys dancing madly, and, on stage—under Roberto and Erasmo's command—young singers like Wanderléia, Eduardo Araújo, Rosemary, Ronnie Von, and Jerry Adriani.

Roberto and Erasmo scored hits with "Parei na Contramão" (I Parked the Wrong Way), "É Proibido Fumar" (No Smoking), "Garota do Baile" (Dance Girl), and Jovem Guarda's anthem, "Quero que Tudo Mais Vá Pára o Inferno" (I Want All the Rest to Go to Hell). It was a reply to the more nationalistic critics and other musicians who did not accept any mixture that defiled the "purity" of Brazilian music.

By 1969, the music business phenomenon of the "Jovem Guarda" television show was over, and each artist went off on his or her own path. In the 1970s, Roberto made a transition from roqueiro to romantic singer and has since typically had mostly boleros and ballads on his albums. He achieved success with sentimental songs like "Detalhes" (Details), "Proposta" (Proposal), "Eu Disse Adeus" (I said Goodbye), all written with his old partner and friend Erasmo.

Roberto was the best-selling recording artist in Brazil in the 1970s and 1980s. He sold an annual average of one million units (quadruple-platinum) with *each* new album in Brazil alone. Roberto also achieved success in Europe and Latin America, his foreign releases commonly hitting the top 10 in many countries. His main international competition as a crooner has come from Spanish ballad-singer Júlio Iglesias, the most popular global star of his time. But in Brazil, Roberto was number one.

The Jovem Guarda movement translated and adapted rock to Brazil, to its language and culture. Jovem Guarda had taken American rock and reformulated it with Brazilian singers, composers, arrangers, and instrumentalists.

Os Mutantes

The next big step for Brazilian rock came with Tropicália, which mixed rock freely with domestic genres. The rock side of the movement was represented by the group called Os Mutantes (The Mutants). Sérgio Dias Baptista (guitar and vocals), his brother Arnaldo Dias Baptista (bass, key-

Os Mutantes in 1968 (*left to right*): Sérgio Dias Baptista, Rita Lee, and Arnaldo Dias Baptista. *Courtesy of Agência JB.*

Sérgio Dias and Phil Manzanera in 1990, while collaborating on the album *Mato Grosso*. *Courtesy of Black Sun.*

boards and vocals), and Rita Lee (flute and vocals) formed the basic lineup of the first artistically important rock band in Brazil.

Founded in 1966, the Mutantes made occasional appearances on the "Jovem Guarda" television show before teaming up with Gilberto Gil, who would show them how they could mix rock and roll with Brazilian culture. His song "Domingo no Parque," with its dazzling conjunction of influences, especially inspired the young band. The Mutantes backed Gil in 1967 when he performed the song in the TV Record song festival, and their appearance—three long-haired kids playing electric instruments—provoked controversy. They outraged even more people when they wore plastic clothes and accompanied Caetano Veloso in 1968, as he sang "É Proibido Proibir" at the International Song Festival in São Paulo. Many irate nationalists wrote petitions to the event organizers asking them to ban the Mutantes, who enjoyed the role of provocateur.

In 1968, the group participated in the seminal 1968 recording *Tropicália ou Panis et Circensis* with Gil, Veloso, Tom Zé, and Rogério Duprat and released their debut album, *Os Mutantes*. In it, they fused rock and roll with baião, mambo, música sertaneja, and irreverent, sometimes surrealistic lyrics. A mixture of Bosch and Salvador Dali is how Arnaldo reportedly described it.

Many critics remained hostile toward the group. "In the beginning they called our music imperialistic, North American. We spent a lot of time proving it was Brazilian, putting Brazilian rhythms into rock and roll," recalled Lee.

Good humor was always part of the group's personality: their philosophy was yes to nonconformism, no to anger. This spirit was maintained in their next several albums, as evidenced by the titles: *A Divina Comédia ou Ando Meio Desligado* (The Divine Comedy or I'm Kind of Spaced-Out) in 1970, *Jardim Elétrico* (Electric Garden) in 1971, and *Mutantes e Seus Cometas no País dos Bauretz* (The Mutants and Their Comets in Bauretz Country) in 1972.

The band's song "Caminhando Noturno" (Night Walker) illustrates the band's Tropicalista tendency to create musical salads: it opens with a fanfare leading into a waltz. Then a strong bass enters, introducing a rock pulse. The melody takes surprising twists and turns, the vocals sometimes natural and at other times quite artificially pinched, and the waltz rhythm comes and goes. A Mexican-flavored interlude is introduced by a Herb Alpert Tijuana Brass–like arrangement. The song keeps throwing out surprises until it ends in a burst of sonorous paraphernalia that includes a soccer-stadium crowd chant and the voice of the robot in the "Lost in Space" TV series repeating (in Portuguese): "Danger, danger . . ."

Rita Lee had already recorded two solo albums before she left the band in 1973 to follow her own path, and Arnaldo departed the next year. But Sérgio Dias, one of the best Brazilian guitarists of his time, stayed, added new players, and kept the band going. This new incarnation of Os Mutantes, with a bassist named Liminha, had nothing to do with the old band. They made two more albums, then broke up in 1978. Os Mutantes had a short career, but they had a tremendous impact on the next generation of roqueiros. They also had many foreign fans; among them were the popular Seattle rock bands Nirvana and the Posies, both of which discovered the Mutantes' recordings in later years.

Liminha went on to become one of Brazil's top producers, working with domestic acts, including Os Paralamas do Sucesso, Gilberto Gil, Jorge Benjor, and Titãs, and foreign artists like Sigue Sigue Sputnik. Meanwhile, Sérgio Dias embarked on an international career as a studio musician. He toured and recorded with violinist L. Shankar and was a member of the jazz-rock band Unit. In 1990, he teamed with Roxy Music veteran Phil Manzanera on *Mato Grosso*, in which the duo combined their guitar, keyboard, and production skills to create a rock-driven, New Age, Brazilian-flavored album of exotic soundscapes.

Rita Lee

Rita Lee (Rita Lee Jones, born in São Paulo in 1947) was a successful solo artist in the 1970s and early 1980s whom the press labeled Brazilian rock's first lady. As she had with the Mutantes,

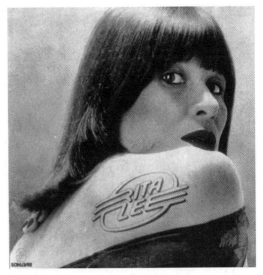

A 1979 Rita Lee album. *Courtesy of Som Livre.*

Rita continued packing her lyrics with irony and irreverence. Little by little, she moved in the direction of an upbeat, light pop-rock sound flavored with various Brazilian rhythms and touches. She had her first solo hits in 1976 with "Ovelha Negra" (Black Sheep) and "Arrombou a Festa" (Crashed the Party).

Babilônia in 1978 was a major seller, and her following albums went consistently gold and platinum. Her many hits included "Chega Mais" (Get Closer), "Lança Perfume" (named for an ether-laden perfume frequently sniffed during Carnaval), "Saúde" (Health), "Baila Comigo" (Dance with Me), and the typically playful "Mania De Você" (Mania for You).

> **Baby, you make my mouth water**
> **Making up fantasies, taking your clothes off**
> **We make love through telepathy**
> **On the ground, in the sea, in the street, in the melody**

By this time, Rita had begun to write songs with her new husband, guitarist Roberto de Carvalho. Rita and Roberto combined the sensuous and the sarcastic, mixing catchy melodies with Brazilian rhythms, boleros, and rock beats. But there was often a serious undertone to their playfulness, as shown in the 1987 tune "Brazix Muamba"

Rita Lee in 1980s. *Photo by Bob Wolfenson. Courtesy of EMI.*

("Brasix" is a made-up word; *muamba* means contraband). In the song, they bemoan Brazil's many problems and criticize Angra I and II, the nuclear power plant reactors built outside of Rio.

Long live Brazix
Dying of pain
AIDS for those who make love
Angra I, Angra II, III, and afterward
The exterminating angel

The Underground

In the 1960s, rock artists were not considered real Brazilian musicians, and they didn't care. But then Tropicália came and absorbed the rock attitude (iconoclastic and free) and some of its musical characteristics into "authentic" Brazilian music. All of a sudden rock had lost its niche in the music scene.

At the time, rock musicians were very radical about their musical convictions. Like samba musicians, they desired to keep their musical "purity," and so they hid. Their hideout was the underground, where it was good to be anyway during the 1970s because of government repression and brutal censorship. Recording companies and radio stations did not like to take risks with a musical genre that didn't fit the taste of the rulers.

With all doors closed, rock became music for afficionados. Groups played for small audiences at small theaters. Many never had access to recording. Most of these groups—O Terço (led by Flávio Venturini), O Som Nosso de Cada Dia, Vímana, and A Barca do Sol, for example—fell into the broad genre of "progressive rock."

In terms of public recognition, only two rock acts were really successful in the seventies. One was the short-lived but very popular Secos e Molhados (Dry Ones and Wet Ones), which existed from 1972 to 1974 and decorated its faces with black-and-white makeup. Their androgynous lead singer, Ney Matogrosso, commanded attention with his unusual high-pitched voice and provocative dancing style. He sang lyrics and poems by the likes of Vinícius de Moraes, Manuel Bandeira, and Oswald de Andrade, surrounded by progressive rock that often used unusual fusions—for example, the tune "O Vira" mixed rockabilly with *vira*, a syncopated, high-spirited Portuguese folk style played on the accordion. After the group split up, Matogrosso became one of MPB's most popular vocalists.

Raul Seixas

Raul Seixas (1945–1989), born in Salvador, was a tragic figure who broke many musical boundaries. As a teenager, he was fascinated with metaphysics, philosophy, and religion. He was not interested in music until he heard the Beatles on the radio, then decided he wanted to write songs instead of books.

He formed a rock-and-roll band called Raulzito e os Panteras (Little Raul and the Panthers). Dressing in a black leather jacket, he performed with total abandon, dancing, quivering, throwing himself on the stage, sometimes imitating the flamboyant Little Richard. The band cut their first record in 1968.

Ney Matogrosso. *Photo by Mircea Dordea. Courtesy of Sony.*

In the 1970s, living in Rio, Raul began recording as a solo artist, releasing albums such as *Krig-Ha Bandolo!* (1973) and *Gita* (1974). He co-composed some tunes with Paulo Coelho, who later wrote best-selling mystical novels (*The Alchemist* is one famous example) that were tremendously successful in Brazil and translated into many languages abroad. Raul was still a rocker, but—like many Brazilian musicians of his generation—one with no use for boundaries or limitations. He was the first, along with Alceu Valença and Gilberto Gil, to mix 1950s American-style rock and Beatles-type pop with the northeastern styles baião, xote, and repente. His tunes often started in one rhythm and finished in another. Raul's first hit, "Ouro de Tolo" (Fool's Gold), was recorded in 1973.

Far from the fences adorned with flags
That separate backyards
A flying saucer's sonorous shadow lands
On the calm summit of my seeing eye

Raul's lyrics were full of imagery of the occult, religion, and bizarre situations. Always he strove to provoke and challenge, as in the lyrics for "Metamorfose Ambulante" (Walking Metamorphosis), also from 1973.

I want to say now
The opposite of what I said before
I'd rather be a walking metamorphosis
Than to have that old fixed opinion about
everything

Seixas was capable of extremely provocative performances. Marcelo Nova, in the liner notes of PolyGram's boxed-set collection *Raul*, recalled how in 1976, when Raul was performing in the Teatro Castro Alves in Salvador, he took off all his clothes on stage during a show. Proclaiming, "This is my homeland, and here I will be as I want," Raul or-

Raul Seixas. *Photo by André Barcinski. Courtesy of Agência JB.*

dered the audience to throw away their identity cards (as important in Brazil as a driver's license in the United States) and stated, "There do not exist frontiers on earth that transform human beings into numbers." This, recalled Nova, "provoked a true shower" of identity cards and "a terrible headache for those who needed them the next day."

Seixas was committed to freedom and nonconformity. He ran for Congress in 1978 and dreamed of building a utopian city in Minas

Gerais, but neither goal was achieved. He recorded seventeen albums in a career cut short by an early death from alcoholism. But his work would inspire many Brazilian rock artists who followed him.

The Eighties: The Third Wave

During Brazilian rock's underground period (1972–1981), its place in the hearts and minds of the youth was usurped by MPB musicians like Alceu Valença, Belchior, Fagner, Zé Ramalho, and others who incorporated rock attitudes and instrumentation into their northeastern-rooted music. Most of these artists even had former rock musicians in their bands.

Considering Jovem Guarda and Os Mutantes as the first generation of Brazilian rock and the un-

derground groups the second, the 1980s saw the birth of the third wave: the strongest and most creative generation of rock musicians Brazil has ever seen. It was a generation that grew up listening, not only to Anglo-American rock, but also to modern MPB, which had already begun incorporating elements of rock and jazz.

There were also a few veterans from the 1970s who found success in the next decade. Two of them—Lobão and Lulu Santos—played together in a 1970s progressive-rock group called Vímana, along with non-Brazilians Patrick Moraz (who had previously played keyboards for Yes) and singer-songwriter Ritchie. After Vímana broke up, English expatriate Ritchie briefly hit the top of the Brazilian charts with his pop-rock. Lulu Santos went on to a successful solo career, recording his own style of "Brazilianized, tropicalized, Latinized rock" (as he termed it) that incorporated boleros, ballads, bossa nova, reggae, and samba. His appealing tunes had fluid melodies and high energy; a few examples are "De Repente California" (Suddenly California), "Tesouro da Juventude" (Treasure of Youth), and "De Leve" (Lightly). Lobão was another Vímana alumnus who went on to establish a solo career, but first he had a stint in an unusual group called Blitz.

Blitz

Underground-theater actor Evandro Mesquita and guitarist Ricardo Barreto got together in the early 1980s to create Blitz, and the band's massive success opened the Brazilian market for many new native rock groups. Evandro defined Blitz's sound as *rock de breque*, a mixture of rock and *samba de breque*. The latter type of samba, made popular by Moreira da Silva, generally tells a story in which the singer is also an actor. He stops the song in the middle—the

Evandro Mesquita, former leader of Blitz. *Photo by Livio Campos. Courtesy of PolyGram.*

Baby Consuelo, an ex-Novo Baiano, who mixed rock with other styles in the eighties and also found time to nurse several babies. *Courtesy of Sony.*

breque (break)—to dramatize the song's story, then resumes singing from where he stopped.

Most of Blitz's songs were sung dialogues between Evandro and the two sexy female vocalists Fernanda Abreu and Marcia Bulcão, woven into bouncy reggae, funk, rock, or pop ballads. Blitz created a theatrical and ludicrous atmosphere on stage and in their records. Their themes were colloquial, quotidian situations described with heavy Caroica slang, laden with mocking irony, and presented in a fast, comic-book style. Blitz's first and biggest hit was the 1982 single "Você Não Soube me Amar" (You Didn't Know How to Love Me), which sold 700,000 copies. Then came the hits "Weekend" and "Betty Frígida" (Frigid Betty).

The band's debut album from that year, *Aventuras da Blitz* (Adventures of Blitz), went platinum. They performed all over the country, including the important concert hall in Rio: Canecão, considered an MPB temple. Blitz was the first rock group allowed to play there. Their commercial success opened record-company doors for other new Brazilian bands and suddenly rock was mainstream. Soon came gold and platinum albums by Ritchie, Lulu Santos, Barão Vermelho, Marina, and Kid Abelha. Talented new groups like Os Paralamas do Successo (The Mudguards of Success) and Ultraje a Rigor (Formal Outrage) were also appearing on the scene. Rock wasn't underground any longer.

Rock in Rio

But its biggest boost was yet to come—a ten-day music festival called Rock in Rio that drew 1.38 million fans in 1985 and featured Blitz as one of its acts. Staged by entrepreneur Roberto Medina and his advertising-promotion agency, Artplan, Rock in Rio took place in January in the Barra da Tijuca neighborhood on the outskirts of Rio. It was the biggest multi-day rock event to date (a fact that

Barão Vermelho at the start of their career, with Cazuza on the far left. *Photo by Frederico Mendes. Courtesy of Sony.*

went largely unreported in the North American press that year) and featured international acts James Taylor, Rod Stewart, Yes, Al Jarreau, George Benson, Ozzy Osbourne, Iron Maiden, the Go-Gos, Whitesnake, AC/DC, Scorpions, the B-52s, Nina Hagen, and Queen. Playing with them were Blitz and fellow Brazilian artists Erasmo Carlos, Ney Matogrosso, Ivan Lins, Gilberto Gil, Elba Ramalho, Blitz, Baby Consuelo and Pepeu Gomes, Rita Lee, Lulu Santos, Moraes Moreira, Eduardo Dusek, Kid Abelha, Alceu Valença, Barão Vermelho, and the Paralamas do Sucesso.

Lobão. *Courtesy of BMG.*

At Rock in Rio, Brazilian rock lost its inferiority complex for good. Brazilian and foreign bands playing together on the same bill made comparisons possible, and some Brazilian bands gave better performances than the foreign acts. And the festival popularized native rockers in their own country via network television and heavy press coverage. Recalled André Midani, managing director of WEA Brazil, "Rock in Rio helped break acts in a big way and life has never been the same since for the music business. I think that this new generation of Brazilian youth needed a new language, something to identify with." WEA, along with EMI Brazil, signed many of these acts in the 1980s. The middle-class and upper-class youth of Brazil began to tune in to their own country's rock, listening more to it than to the North American or U.K. variety.

Lobão

Blitz cut two more LPs following their auspicious debut album and then broke up in 1986. Band member Lobão (João Luis Woerdenbag, born in 1957) had left after the group's first record and established a solo career. He sings, plays drums and guitar, and writes the songs on his albums, which mix hard rock and bittersweet ballads. Lobão's

sound is heavy, percussive, and energetic. He sings in a rough, growling voice, never forgetting he was a drummer: he rhythmically knocks out the words in bursts rather than fully enunciating them. Commented Lobão, "When I sing I think percussion. I'm a musician not a singer. My syllabic division is percussive." His guitarwork shows influences of both Led Zeppelin's Jimmy Page and Spanish flamenco. Lobão added, "I love rock, but my music is a big mixture." For instance, his hard rock is permeated by subtle samba-percussion influences. He has played *tamborim* for Mangueira, one of the most important samba schools in Rio. That's unusual because samba and rock musicians generally don't mix.

Lobão broke the invisible barrier separating the two genres by recording with samba singers like Elza Soares and Ivo Meirelles. With Ivo (who went on to found the band Funk'n Lata) he co-wrote the hard-driving funk tune "Cuidado" (Caution) in 1988. In it, the two sing a duet and several Mangueira musicians add heavy samba percussion to close the song. On 1989's *Sob o Sol de Parador* (Under the Parador Sun), he employs pandeiros, repiques, congas, and afoxês in the percussive mix of the album, which ranges expertly through hard rock, punk, rockabilly, and ballads. American jazz keyboardist Ronnie Foster is a guest on two cuts. The title is an ironic reference to the Paul Mazursky film *Moon over Parador*, about a dictator in a fictional South American country called Parador.

One of Lobão's biggest hit tunes to date is the sad, melancholy "Me Chama" (Call Me), covered by singers from pop star Marina to bossa nova pope João Gilberto. Lobão has also penned songs charged with ironic, political criticism. In the song "O Eleito" (The Elected), he and co-writer Bernardo Vilhena castigate the ineffectual and unpopular Brazilian president José Sarney, who fought against free elections when the populace demanded them in 1984.

The palace is his most perfect refuge
For his most secret desires
There he thinks of himself as the elected
Without any elections nearby

Cazuza

Also from Rio, Cazuza (Agenor de Miranda Araújo Neto, 1958–1990) was one of the most incensed and incendiary songwriters and vocalists of his time in Brazil. He started out as the vocalist and leader of Barão Vermelho (Red Baron), perhaps the only Brazilian rhythm-and-blues band to achieve widespread popularity. Two of their biggest hits came in 1984: "Maior Abandanado" and "Bete Balanço." The latter was the theme song to a popular movie of the same name, in which the group also performed. Cazuza stayed with the band until 1985, then left to pursue a solo career.

In subsequent albums, it was his lyrics that stood out, placed against a background of boleros and bossa mixed with blues and rock. In romantic songs, he displays a bitter and desperate lyricism, as in "O Nosso Amor a Gente Inventa" (We Invent our Love).

Your love is a lie
That my vanity wants
My love is a blind man's poem
That you can't see

Other songs are vivid attacks against deception and hypocrisy. In the electrifying "Brasil," Cazuza sums up the injustice of his country.

They didn't invite me to this lousy party
That the men put on to convince me
To pay, before seeing, for this entire *droga*
That already was cut before I was born

Here, "droga" has the double meaning of "bummer" and "drug," while "cut" means to weaken a drug by adulteration. "Brasil" is one of Cazuza's most corrosive songs, and its lyrics evoke the situation of most everyone in Brazil except the privileged upper class. The narrator of the song (the average Brazilian) has to stay outside the walls of the party (the good life from which he is excluded)—which he is taught to crave, to yearn for, to support, but will never have. Cazuza asks who was paid off, who put Brazil in its terrible present state. The lyrics continue: "Will it be that my fate is to watch color TV in the village of an Indian programmed only to say yes?"

Cazuza discovered he had AIDS in 1987. Between treatments over the next two years, he continued recording in the studio and performing in concert, even as his health deteriorated. He won prestigious Sharp Awards for his album *Ideologia* (Ideology) and song "Brasil." And he continued to compose songs, his natural irony and sarcasm becoming even more bitter and biting. In 1989, Cazuza achieved the greatest public acceptance of his career. His last two works, the live album *O Tempo Não Para* (Time Doesn't Stop) and the double album *Burguesia* (Bourgeoisie) both achieved critical adulation and multi-platinum sales. He died the next year.

Os Paralamas do Sucesso

Perhaps the most musically innovative Brazilian rock group of the 1980s was Os Paralamas do Sucesso (The Mudguards of Success), which

The Paralamas in 1989 (left to right): Bi Ribeiro, João Barone, and Herbert Vianna. Photo by Mauricio Valladarez. Courtesy of Intuition/Capitol.

managed to build solid musical bridges connecting Brazil, North America, Africa, and the Caribbean. Their music is upbeat party music with an edge, a seamless weaving together of rock energy, reggae soul, and world-beat fusion. It is wrapped up in a tight pop format and delivered with infectious energy, a driving rhythmic sense, and a pinch of irony. Their sound, said leader Herbert Vianna, is "a collage that has created a style. Caribbean music, ska, reggae, samba. Lots of swing, very Latin, very Brazilian."

The Paralamas, based on a simple trio format, were formed in Rio de Janeiro in 1982. João Barone (drums) and Bi Ribeiro (bass) are Cariocas; Herbert Vianna (guitar and lead vocals) is from Paraíba. Early influences included the Specials, Madness, the English Beat, and the Clash. Their first two albums, *Cinema Mudo* (Silent Cinema) in 1983 and *Passo do Lui* (Lui's Step) in 1984, feature Herbert's raw, bittersweet vocals riding atop fast, compelling rock and ska riffs and rhythms. The latter LP, coupled with exposure from the Rock in Rio festival, helped the Paralamas achieve commercial success. Herbert recalled, "With Rock in Rio we went to the top of the charts. We were known [before] in Rio, but not in the rest of Brazil."

Selvagem? (Wild?), released in 1986, was a creative leap forward for the trio, as they succeeded in infusing their rock and ska with a distinctively Brazilian accent, be it through suave arrangements or percussive touches. Veteran *roqueiro* Liminha produced and played keyboards on several songs. A notable tune was "Alagados," a Caribbean-Brazilian fusion that mixes elements of reggae, samba, and northeastern xaxado. It was a hint of things to come, both in its deft and natural mixing of genres and in Vianna's hard-hitting lyrics about the Alagados and Favela da Maré slums (in Salvador and Rio, respectively).

> **Alagados, Trench Town, Favela da Maré**
> **Hope comes neither from the sea nor from**
> **the TV antennas**
> **Art is to live out of faith**
> **One just doesn't know what to have faith in**

The LP sold 700,000 units in Brazil alone, and they followed it up the next year with a live album recorded at the Montreux Jazz Festival. Their 1988 album *Bora Bora* was even more accomplished, a bold expansion of their world-beat experiments. "We used a horn section for the first time, and with that we could make our intentions clear and play the kind of music we wanted to play. It allowed us to use other rhythms, many from Brazil such as lambada, afoxé, coco, congada," explained Vianna. With the added instrumentation, the Paralamas' new Caribbean-Brazilian blends grew heady indeed.

"Um a Um" (One to One) is an infectious cover of a classic Jackson do Pandeiro tune, in which Vianna carries the coco rhythm in his voice while he plays reggae chords on his guitar. "Sanfona" (Accordion), according to Herbert, is "a fusion of lambada with baião." Other highlights included the reggae-dub "Don't Give Me That," in which Jamaican deejay Peter Metro adds vocals in English, and the delirious Caribbean-Brazilian instrumental

Legião Urbana in 1987 with lead singer Renato Russo (second from right). Photo by Isabel Garcia. Courtesy of EMI.

"Bundalelê," which incorporates the Haitian *compas* rhythm. "Bora Bora" is a rhythmic tour-de-fource, a masterful fusion of Afro-based styles and an innovative rethinking of Brazilian genres.

More outstanding LPs followed, including 1989's *Big Bang*, 1991's *Os Grãos*, and 1994's *Severino*, which included Tom Zé, Egberto Gismonti, and Phil Manzanera among the guest artists. The Paralamas made their most memorable political comment in 1995 with the tune "Luiz Inácio (300 Picaretas)." The song was inspired by presidential candidate Luiz Inácio da Silva ("Lula")'s accusation two years earlier that there were three hundred *picaretas* (charlatans) in the Brazilian Congress. Vianna's tune takes this as its theme and attacks corruption in Brasília. Federal judge Ionilda Maria Carneiro Pires censored the song, banning it from radio airplay and public shows.

Legião Urbana

Brasília, the capital of Brazil, is only three years younger than Brazilian rock, but it is already a metropolis. Inaugurated in 1960, Brasília was an instant city, designed by architect Oscar Niemeyer and built out in the middle of a high deserted plateau in Goiás state. Today, it is the cosmopolitan home of around one million inhabitants and culturally isolated from the rest of the country. Teenagers there, more than in other parts of the country, have tended to move toward the international youth language of the late twentieth century: rock. So, in 1978, while the rest of Brazil was dancing to disco music or listening to MPB, Brasília already had its punks.

The best-known punk bands in the capital were Aborto Elétrico (Electric Abortion) and Dado e o Reino Animal (Dado and the Animal Kingdom). Members from these two bands—Renato Russo (guitar and vocals), Dado Villa-Lobos (guitar), Renato Rocha (bass), and Marcelo Bonfá (drums)—formed Legião Urbana (Urban Legion). They came to Rio in 1983 and conquered the public with their poetic lyrics, driven by enraged energy.

Legião Urbana's songs had a hard strong beat, guitar chords reminscent of U2, and vocals influenced by the Cure. In concert, they wore jeans and T-shirts, and disheveled, unshaven lead-singer Renato Russo would whirl around on stage in a strange tribal dance, as if being stung by a thousand bees. Inspired by Legião Urbana's antifashion style and Dylanesque protest anthems, crowds went into frenzies.

Singing about unemployment, the army, urban violence, and social disillusion, Legião summed up the life of Brazilian youth with honesty and passion, in songs such as "Geração Coca Cola" (Coca-Cola Generation).

> **Ever since we were kids**
> **We've been eating commercial and industrial trash**
> **Now it's our time, we'll spit it all back on you**

By 1989, they had released three LPs. The second one, called simply *Dois* (Two), was a tremendous commercial success, selling 700,000 copies. Legião's third album was an anthology of their first ten years and one of its tracks became their biggest radio hit—the nine-minute song "Faroeste Caboclo" (Mestizo from the Far West)—an epic of a northeastern immigrant in Brasília who is oppressed by society. The band's career was cut short when leader Russo (Renato Manfredini Junior) died of AIDS in 1996 at the age of thirty-six. At the time, he was Brazil's most popular rock star. Veteran music journalist José Emilio Rondeau called Russo one of the two biggest talents in the history of Brazilian rock, along with Arnaldo Baptista of the Mutantes.

Titãs

São Paulo has long been a center of Brazilian rock and roll. It is a huge metropolis (more than fifteen million people in greater São Paulo) with immigrants from all over Brazil and the world: *sertanejos* from the Northeast, Bolivians, Italians, Lebanese, Portuguese, and Japanese. Accordingly, in terms of *paulistano* rock, there is no dominant style. Punk, experimental, progressive, rockabilly, techno-pop, and even Japanese-influenced bands are found there.

One Paulistano band that made it big in Brazil for a while was RPM, a techno-pop band led by vocalist-composer-bassist Paulo Ricardo and keyboardist-arranger Luis Schiavon. In 1986, they produced the biggest-selling Brazilian rock album to date, *Radio Pirata Live* (Live Pirate Radio), which sold more than two million copies. But their career was short-lived. In 1988, they cut the musically more ambitious album *Os Quatro Coiotes* (The Four Coyotes), which included Milton Nascimento and sambista Bezerra da Silva, but broke up the next year.

As RPM was fading away, another Paulistano band was emerging that would be the most critically acclaimed rock group of its generation: Titãs (Titans). A group with multiple personalities, Titãs was comprised of eight individuals who all wrote songs, five of whom were lead singers. Their pluralistic music went from romantic ballads to two-chord punk to reggae to funk to rap. Lyrics were evocative and often aggressively critical. During their dynamic shows, they took turns being up front on the stage. The band had no leader. "We are not a band with only one aesthetical choice. We are not reggae, nor funk, nor heavy. We are nothing. We kind of confiscate everything in a free and sincere way," said Nando Reis (vocals and bass). According to drummer Charles Gavin, the band recorded "everything from angry, aggressive songs to romantic, tacky ballads. We inspire feelings that range from pure romanticism to repugnance." Their song "Sonífera Ilha" (Somniferous Island) is a romantic-existential lament.

> **I can't stay at your side anymore**
> **So I stick my ear to the radio**
> **To get in tune with you**
> **Alone on an island**

"Bichos Escrotos" (Disgusting Pests) is one of their "repugnant" numbers, a rough-edged rock-

Titãs inside São Paulo's Transamérica Studios. *Courtesy of WEA.*

Sepultura: Heavy Metal from Minas Gerais

Heavy-metal band Sepultura (Grave) is Brazil's most popular recording act internationally since the heyday of Sérgio Mendes and Brasil '66 in the late 1960s. The quartet—Max Cavalera (vocals and rhythm guitar), his brother Igor Cavalera (drums), Andreas Kisser (leader guitar), and Paulo Jr. (bass)—come from Belo Horizonte and released their first full-length album, *Mortal Visions*, in 1986. Their apocalyptic intensity generated a cult following abroad, and their international audience was expanded by their 1989 album *Beneath the Remains* (released by an American label) and an appearance at Rock in Rio II (the 1991 follow-up to the first event). *Arise*, launched that year, sold more than one million copies worldwide. Two years later, their album *Chãos A.D.* addressed social problems in Brazil and elsewhere. The song "Kaiowas" was about a tribe of Amazonian Indians who had committed suicide rather than be moved out of their rain forest home by the Brazilian government. "Manifest" was inspired by a revolt of inmates in the Carandiru prison in São

Sepultura, the most popular Brazilian act in the United States since Sérgio Mendes and Brasil '66. *Photo by Gary Monroe. Courtesy of Epic.*

Paulo, in which more than one hundred prisoners were massacred by police. "Biotech is Godzilla" included lyrics by Jello Biafra, founder of the punk band Dead Kennedys.

funk piece that says that only the pests will inherit the earth.

> **Animals, come out of the filth**
> **Cockroaches, let me see your paws**
> **Rats, get in the shoes of civilized citizens**
> **Fleas, come live in my wrinkles**

On their third album, the acclaimed *Cabeça Dinossauro* (Dinosaur Head), the Titãs consolidated their musical and thematic language. The album assaults modern societal institutions with acidic fury. In "Porrada" (Punch), they ridicule all those who uphold hypocritical society.

> **A mark of ten for the girls of the opposing**
> **team**
> **Congratulations to the academics of the**
> **association**
> **Salutations to those graduating in law**

> **All due respect to the ladies**
> **A punch in the face of those who do nothing**

In 1989, the writer and law professor Willis Guerra Filho commented on the band's lyrics: "The words of the songs are like a critical register of the Brazilian way of life, of our society nowadays, with its great insecurity where the people are attacked from all sides, from bandits and the police, from insects and DDT, from the state and social agencies."

Besides Gavin and Reis, the other members of the hydralike band were Arnaldo Antunes (vocals), Toni Bellotto (guitar), Paulo Miklos (bass, vocals), Sérgio Britto (keyboards, vocals), Branco Mello (vocals), and Marcelo Fromer (guitar). In 1989, *Cabeça Dinossauro* was chosen as the best Brazilian album of the 1980s by a poll in the Rio daily newspaper *Jornal do Brasil*. The Titãs broke up in the early 1990s. Reis and Antunes both released solo works in the 1990s and went on to become prominent songwriters, their tunes recorded by Marisa Montes and others.

More Brazilian Rock

Another popular and outspoken band that emerged in the 1980s was Engenheiros do Hawaii (Hawaiian Engineers), whose members came from Porto Alegre, the capital of Brazil's southernmost state, Rio Grande do Sul. An art-school band that performed together at college parties, they were influenced by Caetano Veloso, Led Zeppelin, and Pink Floyd and created a style they call "garage MPB." Bassist and bandleader

Singer Marina. *Photo by Flávio Colker. Courtesy of World Pacific.*

Humberto Gessinger grounded philosophical ideas in long ballads with descriptive lyrics that build to a heavy climax (they sound something like the rock group Rush). In some cities the Engenheiros were invited to give lectures. In Fortaleza, at the end of one particular concert, the crowd chanted, "Philosophy!"

The wide spectrum of Brazilian pop in the 1980s and 1990s also includes blues artists Celso Blues Boy, André Christovam, and Blues Etilicos. Other artists and groups that deserve mention are Robertinho de Recife (who mixes frevo and rock); Fausto Fawcett, a bard of Copacabana low-life; Eduardo Dusek, a theatrical, satirical crooner who fuses rock, MPB, and tacky love songs; and Marina, a talented interpreter of pop and rock material, with a sensual, husky voice.

Vinícius Cantuária, Ritchie, Leo Jaime, Capital Inícial (Startup Capital), Ultraje a Rigor (Formal Outrage), Ira! (Anger), Camisa de Vênus (Condom) led by Marcelo Nova, Os Mulheres Negras (The Male Negresses), Kid Abelha (Kid Bee), Herois da Resistência (Heroes of the Resistance), and Overdose are other rock and pop artists of recent years. Mamonas Assassinas (Killer Breasts) was a rock band from São Paulo that surged to the top of the charts in 1996 with an album of crass, crude parody songs that appealed greatly to Brazilian preteens; all members of the group died in a plane crash that same year. Two other bands that gained fame in the mid-1990s were Skank (see Chapter Five) and Chico Science and Nação Zumbi, both of which mixed heavy amounts of rock into their overall sounds. Karnak is a noteworthy band that made its recording debut in 1995 and incorporates Brazilian genres and world-music samples into its rock and roll fusion.

Though rock is a genre that was imported from elsewhere, in Brazil it has gained many interesting new elements. It may be a different kind of percussion, a blend with Brazilian rhythms, or an original way of placing words in the melody. In the hands of artists like Os Mutantes, Raul Seixas, and the Paralamas, rock has assumed a distinctly Brazilian character.

Marisa Monte

Grupo Fundo de Quintal's Bira

RORAIMA

AMAPÁ

Belém

São Luis

Fortaleza

AMAZONAS

Manaus

PARÁ

MARANHÃO

CEARÁ

RIO GRANDE DO NORTE

PARAÍBA

PIAUÍ

PERNAMBUCO

Recife

ACRE

TOCANTINS

ALAGOAS

SERGIPE

RONDÔNIA

BAHIA

Salvador

MATO GROSSO

GOIÁS

Brasília

Zizi Possi

MINAS GERAIS

Belo Horizonte

ESPÍRITO SANTO

MATO GROSSO DO SUL

SÃO PAULO

Três Pontas

RIO DE JANEIRO

São Paulo

Rio de Janeiro

PARANÁ

SANTA CATARINA

Naná Vasconcelos parading with Olodum

Porto Alegre

RIO GRANDE DO SUL

Xuxa

Chitãozinho and Xororó

More Brazilian Sounds

From the 1980s through the mid-1990s, several trends took Brazilian music in new directions. *Música sertaneja, brega* romantic ballads, *pagode* samba, *sambalanço*, children's music, Brazilian rock, and international pop led record sales, while Brazilian rap, funk, and *axé music* grew in popularity.

Música sertaneja, a type of Brazilian country music, surged in national popularity and was the single biggest category in terms of record sales. It is a pop-music version of *música caipira*, the rural folk music from Brazil's South, Southeast, and Central regions. Most sertaneja artists are *duplas* (duos) who strum guitars and ten-string *violas*, harmonizing plaintively as they croon about romance and rural life. Frequently they mix the rural idioms *toada, moda de viola, cana-verde*, and *catira* with musical influences from Bolivia, Paraguay, Mexico, Nashville, and Brazil's Northeast.

Música caipira was an unrecorded folk music until the 1920s and 1930s, when it began to be commercialized by artists such as Cornélio Pires (and his band, the Turma Caipira Cornélio Pires). Later, Jararaca and Ratinho, Alvarenga e Ranchinho, and Tonico & Tinoco continued the development of *sertaneja*. Chitãozinho e Xororó (who record in Spanish as José Y Durval), Leandro e Leonardo, Milionário e José Rico, João Mineiro e Marciano, and Zezé Camargo e Luciano were among the most popular sertaneja duplas in the eighties and nineties. Roberta Miranda and Sérgio Reis are successful solo singers, while Almir Sater is a noteworthy guitarist-vocalist. Pena Branca e Xavantinho form a duo that has kept close to their caipira roots and won many awards.

Música sertaneja is especially popular in the states of São Paulo, Minas Gerais, Mato Grosso, Mato Grosso do Sul, Goiás, Paraná, Rio Grande do Sul, and Santa Catarina. In terms of regional artists, the South has also produced the notable accordionists Gaúcho da Fronteira and Renato Borghetti. The latter has fused *músic gaúcha* (gau-cho music) with forró, samba, and other styles in many imaginative blends.

The music of the indigenous peoples of the Amazon rain forest is explored in Marlui Miranda's 1995 *Ihu: Todos Os Sons*. On the album, Miranda sings and plays guitar and *kukuta* (an Indian bamboo flute). She is joined by Gilberto Gil, Uakti, and other artists as she interprets the music of the Yanomâmi, Kayapó, Jaboti, and other Indian peoples. Traditional music recorded in the Amazon can be heard in its pure form on CDs issued by various European labels (see Discography).

Romantic ballads were commercially successful

Sertaneja stars Chitãozinho and Xororó. *Photo by Renato Aguiar. Courtesy of EMI.*

Accordion wizard Renato Borghetti, from the South of Brazil. *Courtesy of BMG.*

Xuxa on the cover of her fourth album, released in 1989. *Courtesy of Som Livre.*

in the 1980s and early 1990s in Brazil, sung by vocalists such as Amado Batista, Wando, Fabio Jr., Rosana, Joana, and Roberto Carlos. These slow, sentimental, tear-jerking tunes were pejoratively nicknamed *brega* (tacky) by journalists, and the term stuck as a label for the genre. Brazilian rock bands such as Legião Urbana, RPM, Titãs, and the Paralamas were also popular in the 1980s; and in the next decade heavy metal band Sepultura achieved the most international success of any Brazilian artists since Sérgio Mendes in the late 1960s. One of Brazil's most innovative rock bands of recent years is Karnak, led by André Abujamra.

The group mixes rock and world music in their eponymous 1995 album, with its heavy sampling and eccentric fusions of global and Brazilian styles.

Children's music is also a big part of Brazil's record business, and Xuxa (Maria da Graça Meneghel) has been its most successful figure. Born in 1963 in Santa Rosa, Rio Grande do Sul, Xuxa was a blonde model who gained fame as soccer star Pelé's girlfriend. She moved on to host a hugely successful TV Globo children's show, much of which was devoted to musical numbers. In 1986 Xuxa began releasing her own albums. Featuring catchy songs written by top pop songwriters, they were slickly produced and heavily promoted by Globo on her show and elsewhere. Over the next several years, she often sold more than two million copies of each new album just in Brazil, and massive merchandising campaigns peddled Xuxa videos, comics, dolls, clothes, toys, and notebooks. In the early 1990s, a Spanish-language edition of her show aired in many countries, and she was the biggest-selling recording artist in Latin America at that time. Xuxa had a major impact on the Brazilian record industry, which increased its production of albums for children. A direct imitator was Angélica, another cute blonde singer who hosted a rival television show for children. Xuxa has become one of Brazil's most famous international figures and the subject of an academic critique: Amelia Simpson's *Xuxa: The Mega-Marketing of Gender, Race, and Modernity.*

Funk music is also popular in Brazil. *Bailes funk* (funk dances) have been around since the end of the 1960s, and over the past ten years have attracted big crowds to large clubs and gymnasiums on the outskirts of Rio and São Paulo. The *funkeiros* are typically poor blacks and mulattos from the suburbs. Security is heavy as *galeras* (groups from different neighborhoods) compete on the dance floor, exchange taunts, and sometimes start huge

Daúde. *Courtesy of Tinder Records.*

brawls. Soul Grand Prix, Furacão 2000, and DJ Marlboro are among the most successful of those who have released dance remixes for these events.

Contemporary Brazilian funk-oriented musicians include Ed Motta, Sandra de Sá, Cláudio Zoli, Luni, Skowa e Mafia, and Hanói Hanói. Fernanda Abreu, a Blitz alumnus, took the funk-dance music route with her much lauded 1995 album *Da Lata*. And Mangueira sambista Ivo Meirelles, a longtime collaborator with rocker Lobão, created a percussion-loaded group called Funk'n Lata that combines funk, rock, and heavy samba.

Bahian vocalist Daúde (Maria Waldelurdes Costa de Santana), in her eponymous 1995 debut album, immerses northeastern styles like repente, embolada, and forró into a heavy dance mix that incorporates hip hop, funk, and acid jazz with booming bass lines by Arthur Maia and a thick, multi-layered production by Celso Fonseca, formerly of Gilberto Gil's band. With a deep, cool voice, Daúde takes a repente duet with Miguel Bezerra, and tunes by Fonseca, Lenine, Jorge Benjor, and Caetano Veloso to the international dance floor. One of her best songs is Celso Fonseca and Carlinhos Brown's "Véu Vavá," which gained a lively dance remix by Soul II Soul's Will Mowatt.

Brazilian rap music was being recorded in the late 1980s but became widely popular only in the next decade with the arrival of Gabriel o Pensador (Gabriel the Thinker), a Carioca rapper. He garnered instant fame at the age of nineteen in 1992 with the song "Tô Feliz (Matei o Presidente)" (I'm Happy [I Killed the President]), which was directed at the corrupt and soon-to-be-impeached President Fernando Collor de Mello. The song was banned from the airwaves and the newly notorious Gabriel signed a contract with Sony. He has had many hit songs since then, attacking poverty, bigotry, and domestic violence in Brazil. Two other leading Brazilian rap acts are Racionais MC's and Sampa Crew.

Sandra de Sá, a vocalist who specializes in funk and ballads. *Courtesy of BMG.*

Reggae was a major influence from abroad that widely infiltrated Brazilian music beginning in the 1980s. Early in the decade, artists like Gilberto Gil

Singer Zizi Possi, who released several outstanding albums in the 1990s, including *Valsa Brasileira* on the Velas label. *Courtesy of PolyGram.*

and Moraes Moreira included reggae songs on their albums. Reggae and ska provided the base for the music of the Paralamas do Sucesso and (later) Skank, both of which combined Jamaican rhythms with rock and Brazilian genres. Reggae was a pervasive influence in the creation of Bahia's axé music; an early example was its incorporation into the fricote style of Luiz Caldas. And the samba-reggae fusion created by Olodum became the prominent style of most Bahian blocos afro and axé music bands. In addition, reggae could be heard in a more straightforward form in the music of Cidade Negra, Bernardo, Nadegueto, O Rappa, and Papas da Língua.

Carlinhos Brown, Chico César, and Chico Science and Nação Zumbi were other noteworthy artists to gain national recognition. And Brazilian women dramatically increased their presence in the Brazilian music scene, with vocalists Marisa Monte, Daniela Mercury, Daúde, Vania Bastos, Cássia Eller, Leila Pinheiro, Monica Araújo, and

Selma Reis coming into prominence. In addition, veteran Brazilian vocalist Zizi Possi hit her artistic stride with outstanding albums like 1994's *Valsa Brasileira* (Brazilian Waltz).

In prior decades, few Brazilian female vocalists composed their own material; Joyce and Rita Lee were among the exceptions. In recent years, however, a whole generation of talented female singer-songwriters has arrived, including Rosa Passos, Zélia Duncan, Adriana Calcanhoto, Junia Lambert, Fernanda Abreu, and Marisa Monte. Daniela Mercury also writes some of her own songs.

Batacotô was an outstanding new Brazilian group of the 1990s, formed of veteran musicians and led by drummer-producer Téo Lima. Its debut album, *Batacotô*, revised samba, jongo, catira, congada, and maracatu with jazzy arrangements and instrumentation, stirring vocals, and dynamic drums and percussion from Lima, Café, and Pirulito. The group also includes Sizão Machado (bass), Claudio Jorge (guitar), Itamar Assiere (keyboards), Jorjão Barreto (vocals), and Suzana Bello (vocals). Batacotô's 1994 LP *Semba dos Ancestrais* (Samba of the Ancestors) explores Afro-Brazilian roots and a wide range of old and new sambas.

In the 1990s, the increased growth of *axé* music—most notably performed by Carlinhos Brown, Timbalada, Olodum, and Daniela Mercury—was a significant development in Brazilian popular music. As ever, Brazil absorbed foreign musical styles, altered them, and used them to create something new. A century ago, this process resulted in the creation of *choro* and *maxixe*. Later it produced *bossa nova* and *Tropicália*. And in the past two decades, it has given birth to *samba-reggae*, *lambada*, *fricote*, *mangue*, and *sambalanço*.

As it moves into the twenty-first century, Brazilian music is still as playful, open, vibrant, imaginative, and self-renewing as ever.

Glossary

aboio: wordless song used by cowboys of the *sertão* to call cattle.

acalanto: lullaby (from Portugal).

afoxé: *Carnaval* group that performs music and dance derived from candomblé ritual music; the music an afoxé performs.

afoxê: a gourd with beads strung on cords or on wire wrapped around it.

afro-samba: *samba* mixed with additional candomblé musical elements.

agogô: double bell (each bell is a different size) struck by a wooden stick.

ala (alas): one of the units into which an *escola de samba* is divided during its *Carnaval* parade.

ao vivo: live performance.

apito: any whistle; whistle used by the *bateria's* director in an *escola de samba*.

arame: steel wire attached to the *verga* of a *berimbau*.

atabaque: generic name for conical single-headed drums played with the hands, similar to Cuban conga drum.

auto: dramatic form (often processional) that includes dances, songs, and allegorical characters. Autos are performed during December and January. They came to Brazil from Portugal, where they date to medieval times. Jesuits introduced religious-themed autos as a method of instruction and conversion, but over the years autos incorporated local themes and musical elements. Examples of autos include *bumba-meu-boi* and *chegança*.

axé: Yoruba word for positive energy or life force.

axé music: general term for Afro-Bahian pop styles, such as *samba-reggae*.

Bahia: state in northeastern Brazil; common nickname for Salvador, the capital of Bahia state.

Baiano (Baiana): someone or something from Bahia state; archaic, Afro-Brazilian circle dance.

baião: northeastern song style with syncopated melody; instrumental refrains in short arpeggios; and often, raised fourth and flattened seventh.

baixo: bass

balanço: swing.

banda: group of people who celebrate *Carnaval* together, especially with *marchas*, attempting to bring the atmosphere of club festivities out onto the street; any musical group.

bandolim: mandolin.

baqueta: thin stick that is struck against the wire string of a *berimbau*.

bateria: drums; drum-and-percussion section of an *escola de samba*.

batucada: *samba*-drumming or percussion-playing involving different instruments.

batuque: archaic Afro-Brazilian music and dance observed as early as the eighteenth century; generic name for Afro-Brazilian drumming and dances; type of Afro-Brazilian religion; type of drum used in jongo.

berimbau: wooden bow with metal string and gourd resonator, common in Bahia and used especially to accompany *capoeira*.

bloco: group of people who parade together during *Carnaval*.

bloco afro (blocos afro): Afro-Brazilian *Carnaval* group, primarily in Salvador.

bloco de empolgação: *Carnaval* group whose members wear the same costume and parade to *samba* music.

bloco de enredo: *Carnaval* group structured like a small *escola de samba*.

boi-bumbá: variation of *bumba-meu-boi* in the Amazonian region.

boi-de-mamão: variation of *bumba-meu-boi* in southern Brazil.

boi-surubi: variation of *bumba-meu-boi* in Ceará state.

bolero: Cuban song form that has become a slow, sentimental international style for romantic ballads.

bombo (or **bumbo**): the largest Brazilian bass drum.

bossa nova: genre of music developed in Rio de Janeiro in late 1950s that includes rhythmic elements of *samba*, a highly syncopated style of guitar playing, a generally subdued vocal style (when sung), and harmonic influences from cool jazz and classical music.

brega: pejorative word for sentimental, commercial romantic songs, used especially in the 1980s.

bumba-meu-boi: processional dance (an *auto*) of Portuguese origin with added Brazilian elements. It celebrates the death and resurrection of a bull and involves elaborate costumes and choreography.

cabaça: hollow gourd that is part of a *berimbau*.

caboclinho: northeastern *Carnaval* group that parades in stylized Indian costumes and plays flutes and *pífanos*.

cachaça: Brazilian sugar-cane liquor.

caixa: snare drum.

calango: popular dance in Minas Gerais and Rio de Janeiro states, performed by couples with simple steps and 2/4 meter.

calunga: fetishistic doll carried by *dama de passo* in a *maracatu* procession.

canção praieira: fisherman's song.

candomblé: Afro-Brazilian religion primarily of Gege-Nagô derivation. Its ritual music uses three different *atabaques* (the rum, rumpi, and lê) and pentatonic and hexatonic scales.

cantador: troubador of northeastern and central Brazil who sings improvised or memorized songs.

cantiga: generic term for ballad or popular song.

canto: song.

cantoria: singing; act of performing a *desafio*.

capoeira: Afro-Brazilian martial art brought to Brazil by Bantu slaves from Angola, practiced and performed publicly to singing and the playing of *berimbaus*, *pandeiros*, and other instruments.

capoerista: someone who performs or practices capoeira.

carimbó: Afro-Brazilian song and dance from Pará that dates from at least the nineteenth century. The song has a 2/4 rhythm, fast tempo, and heavy percussion dominated by the carimbó drum (a hollow tree-trunk section covered with deer skin). The dance is a circle dance, with couples taking turns soloing in the center of the circle.

Carioca: someone or something from the city of Rio de Janeiro.

Carnaval: Carnival, four days of celebration before Ash Wednesday, observed primarily in Roman Catholic countries. Mardi Gras is the U.S. version.

cateretê: rural dance of probable Amerindian origin, performed by couples who are accompanied by a singer and two *violas*.

catimbó: a type of *umbanda* in northeastern Brazil.

catira: common alternate name for *cateretê*.

cavaquinho: a four-stringed instrument similar to a ukelele, with seventeen frets and usually tuned D-G-B-D.

caxambu: Afro-Brazilian song and dance accompanied by drums and handclapping; type of drum used in it.

caxixi: small, closed wicker basket filled with seeds, used as a shaker in *capoeira*.

Cearense: someone or something from Ceará state.

chamego: a *choro* with northeastern inflections in the rhythm and harmony, as in Luiz Gonzaga's "Vira e Mexe."

cheganças: popular dramatic procession (an *auto*) about the Christians fighting the Moors; lascivious and sensual Portuguese dance from the eighteenth century. Variations include chegança-de-mouros and cristãos-e-mouros.

chocalho (or **xocalho**): wooden or metal shaker in the shape of two cones united at the base.

choro: instrumental genre of music that features rapid modulations, melodic leaps, and improvisation, developed in the late nineteenth century in Rio.

chorões: *choro* ensembles.

chula: dance of Portuguese origin dating from at least the eighteenth century in Brazil, and accompanying rhythm, most common in Rio Grande do Sul; one of three sections in a *capoeira* song.

cinema novo: Brazilian film movement in the 1950s and 1960s that sought to create an authentically Brazilian cinema.

ciranda: children's circle dance of Portuguese origin; rural *samba* in Rio de Janeiro state; folkloric song and dance from Pernambuco.

coco: Afro-Brazilian song/dance in 2/4 from northeastern littoral.

congada (or **congo**): processional dances that incorporate both African traditions and Iberian elements and often include characters who represent African royalty. *Congada* is found in southern and central Brazil, while *congo* is generally found in northern and northeastern Brazil.

conjunto: musical group.

cordão (cordões): originally an all-male group that danced and celebrated *Carnaval* to the accompaniment of *batucada* and first appeared in the late nineteenth century; heavy rope that demarcates a *bloco*'s parading area in Salvador's Carnaval.

cozinha: bass, drums, and assorted percussion; rhythmic mix.

cuíca: small friction drum with a thin stick inside attached to the drumskin. The drummer rubs the stick with a moistened cloth and with one hand applies pressure to the drumskin, producing grunting, groaning, and squeaking noises.

dama de passo: the woman who carries the *calunga* doll in a *maracatu* procession.

dança: dance.

desafio: poetic improvisational contests between two vocalists. The question-and-answer exchanges are sung, usually without accompaniment, and are interrupted by short instrumental passages.

desfile: *Carnaval* parade.

dobrão: large coin with which musicians change the pitch of a *berimbau*.

dupla: musical duo.

embolada: poetic-musical form from northeastern littoral with stanza-and-refrain structure, 2/4 meter, fast tempo, declamatory melody, short note values, small musical intervals, and stanzas that are often improvised.

enredo: theme.

entrudo: rude, chaotic style of celebrating *Carnaval* that originated in Portugal and was popular in Brazil until the late nineteenth century.

escola de samba: samba school, an organization that plans and puts on *samba* parades during *Carnaval*. It typically has many other social functions and may serve as the community center in its neighborhood (usually a poorer area of the city).

fado: melancholy, guitar-accompanied Portuguese ballad that derived from lundu. Some scholars believe it actually originated in Brazil but was fully developed in Portugal.

fandango: generic name in southern Brazil for circle dances and accompanying music; also refers to gathering at which these dances are performed.

favela: slum, shantytown.

Fluminense: someone or something from Rio de Janeiro state.

fofa: voluptuous Portuguese dance of the eighteenth century.

folia de reis: groups that perform religious music in the streets, in December and January; another name for *reisado*.

forró: generic name for dance-oriented northeastern styles or dance at which they are played; also used by some to signify a certain variation of the *baião*.

frevo: fast, syncopated *marcha* that originated in Recife.

fricote: song form that mixes *ijexá* and *reggae*.

frigideira: percussion instrument shaped like a frying pan and played with a stick.

galope: six-verse *martelo* (same as *agalopado* or *martelo-agalopado*).

ganzá: single, double, or triple tubular metal shaker; wooden or metal square with cymbals.

Gaúcho (Gaúcha): someone or something from Rio Grande do Sul state.

Gege (or **Jeje**): Brazilian word for Ewe people who came from Dahomey, now the People's Republic of Benin.

Gege-Nagô: combined cultural systems of *Gege* and *Nagô* peoples in Brazil.

guitarra: electric guitar.

habanera: slow Cuban song and dance in duple time.

heavy samba: term used by some Brazilian critics to describe fusion of *samba* and hard rock.

ijexá: rhythm of *afoxé* song form; also a subgroup of the Yoruba people.

Jeje: see *Gege.*

jogo: game; the playing of *capoeira.*

jongo: type of rural *samba* from southeastern Brazil.

Ketu: subgroup of Yoruba people.

lambada: a fusion of *merengue* and *carimbó* with other Caribbean accents, featuring 2/4 rhythm, syncopation, and a fast tempo; a close, sexy dance for two partners that incorporates elements of *merengue, maxixe,* and *forró* dances.

lundu (or **lundum**): song and dance of Angolan origin, brought to Brazil by Bantu slaves; ancestor of many urban Brazilian song forms.

maculelê: Afro-Brazilian stick-fighting war dance.

macumba: generic name for various Afro-Brazilian religions (*candomblé, umbanda, Xangô, catimbó, batuque,* etc.).

malandro: man who makes his living by exploiting women, gambling, or playing small confidence tricks; scoundrel, vagabond, loafer.

maltas: urban lower-class gangs in pre-abolition Brazil.

mangue: fusion of hard rock and hip hop with northeastern styles such as *maracatu,* popularized in Recife in the 1990s.

maraca: hollow gourd with dried seeds or pebbles inside, commonly used musically by Brazilian Indians.

maracatu: slow, heavy Afro-Brazilian processional music and accompanying dance from northeastern Brazil, featuring many characters including a king, a queen, a *dama de passo,* and other characters.

marcha: merry Afro-Brazilian form with strong accent on downbeat and fast, influenced in the 1920s by one-step and ragtime.

marcha-rancho: slower and more melodically developed variations of the *marcha.*

martelo: northeastern poetic form with ten syllables to a line, and six to ten lines to a stanza.

marujada: popular dramatic procession (an *auto*) with maritime themes and men dressed as sailors.

maxixe: song and dance that was a fusion of *lundu* with polka, habanera and (later) tango. It was created in the late-nineteenth century and was the first original Brazilian urban dance.

merengue: Caribbean song/dance in 2/4 time that originated in the Dominican Republic in the early nineteenth century.

mestre-sala: master of ceremonies who symbolically protects the *porta-bandeira* in an *escola de samba* parade.

Mineiro (Mineira): someone or something from Minas Gerais state.

moda: sentimental song from Portugal.

moda de viola: rural folk song with simple melody, often performed by two guitarist-vocalists singing in thirds, found in central and southeastern Brazil.

modinha: sentimental Brazilian song style derived from *moda* and *lundu.*

morro: in Rio used to mean one of the hills around the city upon which are located poor neighborhoods (the *favelas*); any hill.

MPB: acronym for *música popular brasileira* (Brazilian popular music); common term for post-bossa Brazilian urban popular music that combined many different musical elements and whose artists did not fall into individual categories such as *samba, forró,* jazz, or rock.

mulato (mulata): mulatto.

música caipira: folk music from interiors of southern, southeastern, and central Brazil.

música gaúcha: generic name for music from Rio Grande do Sul.

música gaúchesca: rural music from Rio Grande do Sul.

música sertaneja: popular "country" music from

southern, southeastern, and central Brazil that derives from *música caipira*.

Nagô: name for Yoruba descendents in Brazil.

nordestino (nordestina): someone or something from northeastern Brazil.

nueva canción: folk music style that emerged in the 1960s in Chile and Argentina, incorporating indigenous regional song forms and instruments and lyrics that protested poverty and injustice; called nueva trova in Cuba.

one-step: American dance in simple duple time.

orixá: deity in Afro-Brazilian religions.

pagode: party or gathering where *samba* is played; type of samba popularized in 1980s by composers who gathered in Ramos, a neighborhood in Rio's Zona Norte.

pandeiro: similar to tambourine, but with jingles inverted.

Paraense: someone or something from Pará state.

partido alto: type of *samba* with short, light refrains that the singers must follow with improvised verses.

passista: person who masters samba steps.

Paulista: someone or something from São Paulo state.

Paulistano (Paulistana): someone or something from city of São Paulo.

pífano (or **pífaro**): fife.

polka: a round dance and musical form in uptempo 2/4 time that originated in Bohemia around 1830.

pontos de candomblé: invocation song for deities in *candomblé* religion.

pontos de umbanda: invocation songs for deities in *umbanda* religion.

porta-bandeira: standard-bearer (always a woman) in *escola de samba* parade.

pratos: cymbals.

preto: black; a black person.

quadrilha: quadrille, a square dance popular in France in the early nineteenth century.

quilombo: settlements established by runaway slaves in colonial Brazil.

rancho: *Carnaval* group that parades to *marcha-ranchos*. Highly influential on early *escolas de samba*.

reco-reco: a notched instrument (often made of bamboo or metal) that is scraped with a stick and produces a crisp sound.

rei: king.

reisado: a popular dramatic procession that celebrates the Epiphany; a January 6 Catholic commemoration of the manifestation of Christ to the Wise Men of the east; the songs sung by those participating.

repente: improvised stanza sung by a *repentista*.

repentista: a troubador, generally of northeastern Brazil, who sings improvised stanzas as he tells stories or performs in a *desafio*.

repique (or **repinique**): two-headed tenor drum in *samba*.

rock tupiniquim: nickname, often pejorative, for Brazilian rock.

roda: circle; the ring of musicians or bystanders surrounding *capoeira* participants.

rojão: synonym for *baião*; sometimes refers to a faster-tempo *baião*.

roqueiro: a rock-and-roll musician.

samba: the most famous Brazilian song and dance, musically characterized by 2/4 meter and interlocking, syncopated lines in melody and accompaniment.

samba-canção: slower, softer type of *samba* in which melody and lyrics are emphasized more than the rhythm.

samba de breque: type of *samba* with a "break" during which singer dramatizes situation or improvises dialogues.

samba de gafieira: a dance-hall style of *samba*, generally instrumental and with horn arrangements influenced by American big-band jazz.

samba de morro: name used by Brazilian media in 1940s and 1950s to characterize samba that kept essential characteristics of style developed by Estácio composers such as Ismael Silva and Bide, and to differentiate this style from *samba-canção*, *sambolero*, etc.

samba de roda: circle-dance *samba*, accompanied by hand-clapping and *batucada*.

samba do partido alto: see *partido alto*.

samba-enredo (or **samba de enredo**): theme samba, performed by an *escola de samba* and written for *Carnaval*.

sambalada: *samba* mixed with a ballad.

sambalanço: pop music played with a *samba* rhythm by groups like Raça Negra.

sambanejo: pejorative term for *sambalanço* music in which *música sertaneja* hits were re-recorded with a *samba* rhythm.

samba-reggae: mixture of *samba* and reggae developed in Salvador in 1980s.

sambista: someone who sings, writes, plays, or dances *samba* almost exclusively.

sambolero: a mixture of *samba* and bolero.

sanfona: accordion; button-accordion.

saudade: longing or yearning for someone or something.

saya: Bolivian musical genre.

schottische: ballroom dance similar to polka introduced to England in the mid-nineteenth century, also called "German polka."

seresta: serenade.

sertaneja: *música sertaneja*; someone or something from the *sertão*.

sertanejo: someone or something from *sertão*.

sertão: general name for remote interior regions of Brazil; arid backlands of northeastern Brazil.

sétima nordestina: the northeastern flattened seventh note.

siriá: folkloric music from Cametá region of Pará played in *marujada* and *boi-bumbá* dramatic dances; a couples' dance with elements of *maxixe* and *forró*.

soca: dance-oriented mixture of soul, funk, and calypso introduced by musicians from Trinidad in the 1970s.

som: sound; tone.

surdo: drum in *samba* played with a wooden stick that has a velvet-covered wooden head, it comes in three sizes and functions as the bass in the *bateria* of an *escola de samba*.

tambor: any drum.

tamborim: small tambourine without jingles played with single or double stick.

tango: dance and song form that developed in Argentina at the start of the twentieth century and derived its rhythm from the Cuban *habanera* and Argentinian *milonga*.

tan-tan: deep drum similar to an *atabaque*, substitutes for the *surdo* in *pagode*.

tarol: shallow two-headed drum with strings across skin and played with two wooden sticks.

teclados: keyboards.

terreiro: place of worship in *candomblé* or *umbanda*.

toada: generic term for a stanza-and-refrain song with a simple, often melancholy melody and short, romantic or comical lyrics.

toque: rhythm or tempo, refers especially to rhythms played on the *berimbau* during *capoeira*.

triângulo: triangle.

trio elétrico: musicians playing electrified instruments; the decorated truck atop which they play during *Carnaval*.

Tropicália: arts movement in the late 1960s, led in the musical area by Gilberto Gil, Caetano Veloso, and others.

Tropicalismo: see *Tropicália*.

umbanda: Afro-Brazilian religion developed in the twentieth century that has considerable influence from Spiritist beliefs.

umbigada: movement in *lundu*, *samba*, and other Afro-Brazilian dances in which dancer touches navels with another as an invitation to the dance.

vanerão (vaneirão): accordion-accompanied musical style from southern Brazil.

verga: wooden bow that is part of a *berimbau*.

viola: guitarlike instrument whose number of strings (five, seven, eight, ten, twelve, or fourteen) varies according to the region.

violão: guitar.

violeiro: guitarist; especially, troubadors of rural Brazil who play guitar or viola and perform improvised or memorized songs.

violino: violin.

virada: change in percussion pattern.

Xangô: *orixá* of fire, thunder, and justice; Afro-Brazilian religion most widely practiced in Pernambuco state.

xaxado: northeastern song and dance.

xerém: song and dance from northeastern Brazil, similar to polka and *xote*, generally accompanied by accordion.

xique-xique: a type of cactus; a type of *chocalho*.

xote: a northeastern dance in 2/4 derived from the *schottische*.

Yoruba: an African people from Nigeria; also their language.

zabumba: bass drum in northeastern music.

Zona Norte: northern zone of Rio that includes neighborhoods such as Estácio, Tijuca, Vila Isabel, and Ramos.

Zona Sul: southern zone of Rio close to the beaches, includes neighborhoods such as Flamengo, Botafogo, Copacabana, Ipanema, Leblon, Jardim Botânico, and Gávea.

Select Bibliography

Almeida, Bira. *Capoeira: A Brazilian Art Form*. Berkeley, Calif.: North Atlantic Books, 1986.

Almeida, Laurindo. *Latin Percussion Instruments and Rhythms*. Sherman Oaks, Calif: Gwyn, 1972.

Alvarenga, Oneyda. *Música Popular Brasileira*. Rio de Janeiro: Editora Globo, 1950.

Amado, Jorge. *Tent of Miracles*. New York: Alfred A. Knopf, 1971.

Andrade, Mário de. *Danças Dramaticas do Brasil*. São Paulo: Livraria Martins Editora, 1959.

———. *Dicionário Músical Brasileiro*. 2d ed. São Paulo: Editora da Universidade de São Paulo, 1989.

Appleby, David P. *The Music of Brazil*. Austin: University of Texas Press, 1983.

Assumpção, José Teixeira de. *Curso de Folclore Musical Brasileiro*. Rio de Janeiro: Livraria Freitas Bastos, 1967.

Bahiana, Ana Maria. *Nada Será Como Antes*. Rio de Janeiro: Editora Civilização Brasileira, 1980.

Barsante, Cassio Emmanuel. *Carmen Miranda*. Rio de Janeiro: Editora Europa, 1985.

Behague, Gerard. *Music in Latin America: An Introduction*. Englewood Cliffs, N.J.: Prentice-Hall, 1979.

Bello, José Maria. *A History of Modern Brazil: 1889–1964*. Stanford, Calif.: Stanford University Press, 1968.

Bramly, Serge. *Macumba*. New York: St. Martin's Press, 1977.

Brown, Diana DeG. *Umbanda: Religion and Politics in Urban Brazil*. New York: Columbia University Press, 1994.

Browning, Barbara. *Samba: Resistance in Motion*. Bloomington: Indiana University Press, 1995.

Burns, E. Bradford. *A History of Brazil*. 2d ed. New York: Columbia University Press, 1980.

Cabral, Sérgio. *As Escolas de Samba: O Que, Quem, Como, Quando e Por Que*. Rio de Janeiro: Fontana, 1974.

Calado, Carlos. "Lambada Vai Dividir Com 'Negões' a Folia Baiana." *Folha de São Paulo*, Feb. 11, 1990, E-4.

Campos, Augusto de. *Balanço da Bossa e Outras Bossas*. São Paulo: Editora Perspectiva, 1978.

Carvalho, José Jorge de. "Aesthetics of Opacity and Transparence: Myth, Music and Ritual in the Xangô Cult and in the Western Art Tradition." *Latin American Music Review* 14, no. 2 (1993): 202–31.

———. "Music of African Origin in Brazil." *Africa in Latin America*. New York: Holmes and Meier, 1984.

Cascudo, Luis da Câmara. *Dicionário do Folclore Brasileiro*. 5th ed. Belo Horizonte: Editora Itatiaia Limitada, 1984.

Castro, Ruy. "Bossa fora da Capsula." *Veja*, May 30, 1990, 48–54.

———. *Chega de Saudade*. São Paulo: Companhia das Letras, 1990.

Caúrio, Rita, ed. *Brasil Musical*. Rio de Janeiro: Art Bureau, 1988.

Caymmi, Dorival. *Cancioneiro da Bahia*. 5th ed. Rio de Janeiro: Editora Record, 1978.

Céspedes, Gilka Wara. "Huayño, Saya, and Chuntunqui: Bolivian Identity in the Music of 'Los Kjarkas.'" *Latin American Music Review* 14, no. 1 (1993): 52–101.

Civita, Victor. *Nosso Século*. São Paulo: Abril Cultural, 1980.

Crowley, Daniel J. *African Myth and Black Reality in Bahian Carnaval*. Monograph series no. 25. Los Angeles: UCLA Museum of Cultural History, 1984.

Damante, Hélio. *Folclore Brasileiro*. São Paulo. Rio de Janeiro: FUNARTE, 1980.

Daniel, G. Reginald. "Multiethnic Populations in the United States and Brazil." *UCLA ISOP Intercom* 14, no. 7 (Jan. 15, 1992): 1–5.

Dawson, C. Daniel. "Capoeira: An Exercise of the Soul." *Icarus*, no. 13 (1994): 13–28.

Draeger, Alain, and Amado, Jorge. *Bahia Mystery Land*. Paris: Editions d'Art Yvon, 1984.

Dunn, Christopher. "Afro-Bahian Carnival: A Stage for Protest." *Afro-Hispanic Review* 11, nos. 1–3 (1992): 11–20.

Feather, Leonard. *The Encyclopedia of Jazz in the Sixties*. New York: Horizon, 1966.

Feather, Leonard, and Ira Gitler. *The Encyclopedia of Jazz in the Seventies*. New York: Bonanza, 1976.

Fonseca, Heber. *Caetano: Esse Cara*. Rio de Janeiro: Editora Revan, 1993.

Frade, Cascia. *Folclore Brasileiro: Rio de Janeiro*. Rio de Janeiro: FUNARTE, 1979.

Freyre, Gilberto. *The Mansions and the Shanties*. 2d ed. Westport, Conn.: Greenwood Press, 1980.

Galemba, Phyllis. *Divine Inspiration: From Benin to Bahia.* Albuquerque: University of New Mexico Press, 1991.

Gilman, Bruce. "Carlinhos Brown: Planetary Minstrel." *Brazzil*, Sept. 1996, 41–44.

———. "Chico César: The King of Ditties." *Brazzil*, Nov. 1996, 42–44.

———. "Daniela Mercury: And Now, the World." *Brazzil*, Jan. 1997, 40–43.

———. "Pure Samba." *Brazil*, Feb. 1997, 40–43.

Giron, Luis Antonio. "Carnaval de 90 Promete 'Lambadear'." *Folha de São Paulo*, Feb. 11, 1990, E-1.

———. "Obra de Câmara Cascudo Omitiu Ritmos do Pará." *Folha de São Paulo*, Feb.11, 1990, E-3.

Goes, Fred de. *O País do Carnaval Elétrico.* Salvador: Editora Corrupio, 1982.

Goldfeder, Sonia. "Farra Européia: Grupo Amazonense É a Febre do Verão Francês." *Veja*, Aug. 14, 1996, 134.

Gontijo, Ricardo. "Oi . . . Milton." *Canja*, Oct. 1, 1980.

Gonzalez, Lélia. *Festas Populares no Brasil.* 2d ed. Rio de Janeiro, Editora Index, 1989.

González-Wippler, Migene. *Santería: The Religion.* New York: Harmony Books, 1989.

Graham, Richard. "Technology and Culture Change: The Development of the Berimbau in Colonial Brazil." *Latin American Music Review* 12, no. 1 (1991): 1–19.

Graham, Ronnie. *The Da Capo Guide to Contemporary African Music.* New York: Da Capo Press, 1988.

Gridley, Mark C. *Jazz Styles.* Englewood Cliffs, N.J.: Prentice-Hall, 1978.

Hess, David J. *Samba in the Night: Spiritism in Brazil.* New York: Columbia University Press, 1994.

Kernfield, Barry, ed. *The New Grove Dictionary of Jazz.* New York: Macmillan, 1988.

Lacerda, Regina. *Folclore Brasileiro: Goiás.* Rio de Janeiro: FUNARTE, 1977.

Lewis, J. Lowell. *Ring of Liberation: Deceptive Discourse in Brazilian Capoeira.* Chicago: University of Chicago Press, 1992.

Ligiero, Zeca, and Galembo, Phyllis. "Iemanjá, The Sea Queen Mother." *Icarus*, no. 13 (1994): 13–28.

Lima, João Gabriel de, and Bosco, Silvania Dal. "O Brasileiro Everardo." *Veja*, Aug. 14, 1996, 110–14.

Lockhart, James, and Schwartz, Stuart B. *Early Latin America: A History of Colonial Spanish America and Brazil.* Cambridge: Cambridge University Press, 1984.

Lody, Raul Giovanni. *Cadernos de Folclore: Afoxé.* Rio de Janeiro: FUNARTE, 1976.

Marcondes, Marco Antonio, ed. *Enciclopédia da Música Brasileira: Erudita, Folclórica e Popular.* São Paulo: Art Editora, 1977.

Mariz, Vasco. *A Canção Brasileira.* 5th ed. Rio de Janeiro: Editora Nova Fronteira, 1985.

Máximo, João. "O Quixote do Chapéu de Couro." *Jornal do Brasil*, Aug. 3, 1989, B1.

Máximo, João, and Carlos Didier. *Noel Rosa: Uma Biografia.* Brasília: Editora Universidade de Brasília, 1990.

McGowan, Chris. "Brazilian Instrumental Music." *Billboard*, Nov. 7, 1987, special supplement, "Viva Brazil," B6.

———. "Brazilian Music Industry: Challenging the Cross-Currents of a Volatile World Market." *Billboard*, Nov. 7, 1987, special supplement, "Viva Brazil," B-4.

———. "Brazilian Talent: A Deep Reserve of Musical Greatness to Come." *Billboard*, Nov. 7, 1987, special supplement, "Viva Brazil," B-3.

———. "The Brazilian Wave Comes Ashore. *Billboard*, Nov. 7, 1987, special supplement, "Viva Brazil," B-1.

———. "Fourteen Acts Ready to 'Rock in Rio.' "*Billboard*, Sept. 29, 1984, 36.

———. "Gilberto Gil: Cultivator of the Spirit." *The Beat* 10, no. 2 (1991): 48.

———. "Industry Struggles Uphill Against Four-Year Recession, Aided by Strong Musical Heritage." *Billboard*, Jan. 26, 1985, special supplement, "Viva Latino," VL-22.

———. "In Quotes: Perspectives on Brazilian Music." *Billboard*, Nov. 7, 1987, special supplement, "Viva Brazil," B-4.

———. "The Latest Brazilian Wave." *Pulse*, Feb. 1992, 92.

————. "Monte's Ante." *Billboard*, Sept. 7, 1991.

————. "Música Brasileira: Spirit and Soul." *The Beat* 10, no. 2 (1991): 26.

————. "A Nation of Cannibals." *The Beat* 10, no. 4 (1991): 24.

————. "Olodum: Bahian Powerhouse." *Pulse*, Aug. 1991, 43.

————. "Rhythms of Resistance." *Pulse*, Dec. 1990, 112.

————. "The Road to Rio." *The Beat* 10, no. 6 (1991): 25.

Mello, José Eduardo Homem de. *Música Popular Brasileira*. São Paulo: Editora da Universidade de São Paulo, 1976.

Moffett, Matt. "A Racial 'Democracy' Begins Painful Debate on Affirmative Action." *Wall Street Journal*, Aug. 6, 1996, A1.

Moore, Zelbert. "Reflections on Blacks in Contemporary Brazilian Popular Culture in the 1980s." *Studies in Latin American Popular Culture* 1, no. 1 (1988): 213–25.

Moraes Filho, Mello. *Festas e Tradições Populares do Brasil*. São Paulo: Livraria Itatiaia Editora, 1979.

Motta, Nelson. *Música, Humana Música*. Rio de Janeiro: Salamandra, 1980.

Moura, Roberto M. *Carnaval: Da Redentora a Praça do Apocalipse*. Rio de Janeiro: Jorge Zahar, 1986.

Navarro, Jesse, Jr., ed. *Nova História da Música Popular Brasileira*. 2d ed. São Paulo: Abril Cultural, 1977.

Nettl, Bruno. *Folk and Traditional Music of the Western Continents*. Englewood Cliffs, N.J.: Prentice-Hall, 1973.

Neves, Guilherme Santos. *Folclore Brasileiro: Espírito Santo*. Rio de Janeiro: FUNARTE, 1978.

Nketia, J. H. Kwabena. *The Music of Africa*. New York: W.W. Norton, 1974.

Omari, Mikelle Smith. *The Art and Ritual of Bahian Candomblé*. Los Angeles: UCLA Museum of Cultural History, Monograph Series no. 24, 1984.

Palmer, Robert. "Eastern Brazil Exports Influential Pop to the World." *New York Times*, May 4, 1986.

Pareles, Jon, and Stephen Holden. "Rock's Own Generation Gap." *The New York Times*, Dec. 24, 1989, Arts and Leisure section, 29.

Perrone, Charles A. "Axé, Ijexá, Olodum: The Rise of Afro- and African Currents in Brazilian Popular Music. *Afro-Hispanic Review* 11, nos. 1–3 (1992): 42–48.

————. *Letras e Letras da Música Popular Brasileira*. Rio de Janeiro: Elo Editora, 1988.

————. *Masters of Contemporary Brazilian Song: MPB, 1965–1985*. Austin: University of Texas Press, 1989.

————. "Os Outros Rômanticos." *Los Ensayistas: Brazil in the Eighties*, nos. 28–29 (1990): 79–97.

Pessanha, Ricardo. "Margareth Menezes: She's Not the Girl from Ipanema." *The Beat* 10, no. 2 (1991): 46.

————. "Street Urchins of São Paulo." *The Beat* 11, no. 4 (1992): 28.

Pessanha, Ricardo, and Ana Paula Macedo. "The New Afro Beat of Rio." *The Beat* 11, no. 6 (1992): 26.

Pinto, Tiago de Oliveira. "Making Ritual Drama: Dance, Music, and Representation in Brazilian Candomblé and Umbanda." *The World of Music* 33, no. 1 (1991): 70–88.

Popovic, Pedro Paulo, ed. *Rock, a Música do Seculo XX*. Consultores Editoriais Ltda. Rio de Janeiro: Rio Grafica, 1983.

Poppino, Rollie E. *Brazil—the Land and People*. 2d ed. New York: Oxford University Press, 1973.

Rawley, James. *The Transatlantic Slave Trade*. New York: W.W. Norton, 1981.

Ribeiro, Maria de Lourdes Borges. *Cadernos de Folclore: O Jongo*. Rio de Janeiro: FUNARTE, 1984.

Risério, Antonio. *Carnaval Ijexá: Notas sobre a Re-africanização do Carnaval Baiano*. Salvador: Editora Corrupio, 1982.

Roberts, John Storm. *Black Music of Two Worlds*. New York: William Morrow, 1974.

————. *The Latin Tinge*. Oxford: Oxford University Press, 1979.

Rocca, Edgard. *Ritmos Brasileiros e Seus Instrumentos de Percussão*. Rio de Janeiro: Europa Editora, 1986.

Rotella, Sebastian. "Singer Finds Race Issue No Laughing Matter in Brazil." *Los Angeles Times*, Sept. 5, 1996, A1.

Sabanovich, Daniel. *Brazilian Percussion Manual*. Van Nuys, Calif.: Alfred Publishing Company, 1988.

Seraine, Florival. *Folclore Brasileiro: Ceará*. Rio de Janeiro: FUNARTE, 1978.

Simpson, Amelia. *Xuxa: The Mega-Marketing of Gender, Race, and Modernity*. Philadelphia: Temple University Press, 1993.

Sousa, José Geraldo de, Padre. *Cadernos de Folclore: Características da Música Folclórica Brasileira*. Rio de Janeiro: FUNARTE, 1969.

Souza, Tárik de. *O Som Nosso de Cada Dia*. Porto Alegre: L&PM, 1983.

Souza, Tárik de, and Elifas Andreato. *Rostos e Gostos da Música Popular Brasileira*. Porto Alegre: L&PM, 1979.

Tenenbaum, Barbara, ed. *Encyclopedia of Latin American History and Culture*. New York: Charles Scribner's Sons, 1996.

Tereza, Irany. "Os Deuses do Olimpo." *Revista da Mangueira*, 1997, 20–23.

Tinhorão, José Ramos. *Pequena História da Música Popular: Da Modinha ao Tropicalismo*. 5th ed. São Paulo: Art Editora, 1986.

Vasconcelos, Ary. *Raízes da Música Popular Brasileira*. Rio de Janeiro: Rio Fundo Editora, 1991.

Ventura, Zuenir. *1968, o Ano que não Terminou*. Rio de Janeiro: Nova Fronteira, 1988.

Verger, Pierre Fatumbi. *Orixás*. Salvador: Corrupio, 1981.

Vieira, Marceu. "É Nota 1000." *Revista da Mangueira*, 1997, 20–23.

Wafer, Jim. *The Taste of Blood: Spirit Possession in Brazilian Candomblé*. Philadelphia: University of Pennsylvania Press, 1991.

Yudin, Linda K. "Filhos de Gandhi Afoxé: Afro-Bahian Dance Traditions in the Carnaval of Salvador da Bahia, Brazil." Master's thesis, University of California at Los Angeles, 1988.

Select Discography

The following albums are a representative list of contemporary popular Brazilian music, with an emphasis on titles that are mentioned in the book, or CDs that have recently become available. This is not a complete listing of all Brazilian artists and their releases. Instead, this discography is a starting point for listeners interested in exploring Brazilian sounds.

If titles were released in both Brazil and the United States, the U.S. release is listed in most instances; the date of the U.S. release is often one or more years after the original Brazilian release. The list is alphabetized by group name and artist's last name or stage name (such as Jackson do Pandeiro or Zeca Pagodinho). Only full-length albums are included. Reprint years can refer to either date of reprint or date of original release.

If no country abbreviation is listed, the album was released in the United States.

Abbreviations: (rpt.), reprint; INF, Instituto Nacional do Folclore; BR, Brazilian release; GE, Germany; JP, Japan; FR, France; UK, United Kingdom; NO, Norway.

Abreu, Fernanda. *Da Lata*. EMI 834616, 1995.
Adolfo, Antonio. *Jinga*. Happy Hour 5011, 1990.
———. *Antonio Adolfo Abraça Ernesto Nazaré e Chiquinha Gonzaga*. BR/Imagem 1023, 1991.
Agepê. *Minha História: Agepê*. BR/PolyGram 518 215, 1994.
Alcione. *A Voz do Samba*. BR/PolyGram 518 904, 1975 (rpt.).
———. *A Cor do Brasil*. BR/RCA 103.0627, 1984.
———. *Fruto e Raiz*. BR/RCA 103.0673, 1986.
———. *Nosso Nome: Resistência*. BR/RCA 130.0015, 1987.
———. *Personalidade: Alcione*. BR/Philips 836 440, 1988.
Alf, Johnny. *Diagonal*. BR/RCA BBL 1271, 1964.
———. *Ele É Johnny Alf / Nós*. BR/EMI 8290302, 1971, 1974 (rpt.).
———. *Johnny Alf*. BR/Abril Cultural MPB-43, 1972.
———. *O que é Amar*. BR/RCA 1300059, 1989.
Almeida, Laurindo. *Outra Vez*. Concord CCD-4497, 1992.
Almeida, Laurindo, and B. Shank. *Artistry in Rhythm*. Concord CJ-238, 1984.

———. *Brazilliance, Vol. 1*. World Pacific CDP796339, 1991 (rpt.).
———. *Brazilliance, Vol. 2*. World Pacific CDP796102, 1991 (rpt.).
Almeida, Laurindo, and C. Barbosa-Lima, C. Byrd. *Music of the Brazilian Masters*. Concord CCD-4389, 1989.
Almeida, Laurindo, and C. Byrd. *Brazilian Soul*. Concord CJP-150, 1981.
Alves, Ataulfo. *Ataulfo Alves*. BR/Abril Cultural HMPB-29, 1977.
———. *Ataulfo Alves: 80 Anos*. BR/EMI 062 792602, 1989.
Alves, Lúcio. *A Bossa é Nossa*. BR/Philips 630410, 1960.
Alves, Tania. *Amores e Boleros*. BR/PolyGram 523 406, 1995.
Alvim, Maria, and Rick Udler. *Rhythm & Romance*. Malandro MAL 71001, 1996.
Amelinha. *Só Forró*. BR/PolyGram 523 166, 1994.
Andrade, Leny. *A Arte Maior de Leny Andrade*. BR/Polydor 4097, 1964.
———. *Luz Neon*. BR/Eldorado 130.88.0536, 1988.
———. *Maiden Voyage*. Chesky JD113, 1994.
Antunes, Arnaldo. *Nome*. BR/BMG M30.072, 1993.
———. *Ninguém*. BR/BMG 74321-26593, 1995.
Aquarela Carioca. *Aquarela Carioca*. BR/Visom 5016, 1989.
Aquinho, João de. *Patuá*. BR/Leblon 001, 1991.
Ara Ketu. *The Best of Ara Ketu*. BR/Continental 45099812, 1995.
Araújo, Severino. *12 Ritmos Brasileiros*. BR/Phonodisc 34-405-124, 1983 (rpt.).
Ariel, Marcos. *Terra de Índio*. Tropical Storm/WEA WH 55942, 1989.
Assad, Sérgio and Odair. *Alma Brasileira*. Elektra/Nonesuch 79179, 1988.
Assumpção, Itamar. *Intercontinental!* GE/Messidor 15590, 1988.
Augusto, José. *Corpo & Coração*. BR/PolyGram 528 493, 1995.
Ayres, Nelson. *Mantiquera*. BR/Som da Gente SDG 009, 1981.
Azevedo, Geraldo. *A Luz de Solo: Geraldo Azevedo*. BR/Barclay 827 904, 1985.

————. *Minha História: Geraldo Azevedo*. BR/Polygram 514 442, 1994.

Azevedo, Geraldo, and N. Vasconcelos. *De Outra Maneira*. BR/RCA 109.0157, 1986.

Azuma, Cristina. *Contatos*. GSP 1009, 1995.

Azymuth. *Telecommunication*. Milestone M-9101, 1982.

————. *Rapid Transit*. Milestone M-9118, 1983.

Babo, Lamartine. *Lamartine Babo*. BR/Abril Cultural HMPB-09, 1977.

Banda Black Rio. *Gafieira Universal*. BR/RCA 103 0268, 1978.

Banda de Pífano de Caruaru. *Zabumba Caruaru*. BR/CBS 104 233, 1972.

Banda Eva. *Hora H*. BR/PolyGram 529 215, 1995.

Banda Mel. *Força Interior*. Continental 1-01-404-317, 1987.

————. *Banda Mel do Brasil*. BR/Continental 1.01.404.376, 1989.

Banda Reflexu's. *Da Mãe Africa*. BR/EMI 062 748 544, 1987.

Barão Vermelho. *Maior Abandonado*. BR/CBS 412.082, 1984.

Barbosa, Adoniran. *Adoniran Barbosa*. BR/EMI 364-789726, 1980.

Barbosa, Beto. *Beto Barbosa*. BR/Continental 1.73.405.016, 1988.

Barbosa-Lima, Carlos. (w. G. Thiago de Mello). *Chants for the Chief*. Concord CCD-4489, 1991.

————. *Music of the Americas*. Concord CCD-4461, 1991.

————. *Ginasteria's Sonata*. Concord CCD-42015, 1993.

Barbosa-Lima, Carlos, and S. Isbin. *Brazil, with Love*. Concord CCD-4320, 1987.

Barros, João de (Braguinha), and Alberto Ribeiro. *João de Barros & Alberto Ribeiro*. BR/Abril Cultural HMPB-24, 1977.

Barroso, Ary. *Ary Barroso*. BR/Abril Cultural HMPB-14, 1977.

Bastos, Vânia. *Canta Mais*. BR/Velas 11-V022, 1994.

Batacotô. *Batacotô*. U.S./Triloka 7196, 1993.

————. *Semba dos Ancestrais*. BR/Velas 11-V043, 1994.

Bau dos 8 Baixos. *Bucho com Bucho*. BR/Som da Gente SDG 011, 1982.

Belchior. *Alucinação*. BR/Philips 634 9160, 1976.

————. *Melodrama*. BR/PolyGram 832 377, 1987.

————. *Belchior Ao Vivo e Acústico*. BR/PolyGram 512 125, 1995.

Bellinati, Paulo. *The Guitar Works of Garoto*. GSP 1002, 1991.

————. *Serenata: Choros & Waltzes of Brazil*. GSP 1005, 1992.

Ben, Jorge (a.k.a. Jorge Benjor). *Samba Esquema Nova*. BR/Philips 632 161, 1963.

————. *Ben*. BR/PolyGram 518 1122, 1972 (rpt.).

————. *Personalidade: Jorge Ben*. BR/Philips 832 806, 1987.

————. *Grandes Successos de Jorge Ben*. BR/Som Livre 402.0012, 1988.

————. *Benjor*. BR/WEA 670 8067, 1989.

————. *Live in Rio*. Tropical Storm/WEA 90214, 1992.

————. *23*. Tropical Storm/WEA 94199, 1994.

————. *Grandes Nomes: Jorge Ben (4 CDs)*. BR/PolyGram 528 086, 1995.

Bethânia, Maria. *Recital na Boite Barroco / Maria Bethânia*. BR/EMI 827 027, 1968, 1969 (rpt.).

————. *Alibi*. BR/Philips 836 001, 1978 (rpt.).

————. *Maria*. RCA 8585, 1988.

————. *Memória Da Pele*. BR/Philips 838 928, 1989.

————. *Canto do Pajé*. Verve 848 508, 1990.

————. *As Canções Que Você Fez Pra Mim*. BR/Philips 314 518 214, 1993.

————. *Grandes Nomes: Bethânia (4 CDs)*. BR/PolyGram 522 971, 1995.

————. *Maria Bethânia Ao Vivo*. BR/PolyGram 526 719, 1995.

————. *Ambar*. Metro Blue 2243-8-54171-2-9, 1996.

Biglione, Victor. *Baléia Azul*. Tropical Storm/WEA WH 55999, 1989.

————. *Biblioteca*. BR/Leblon LB017, 1993.

Blanco, Billy. *Músicas de Billy Blanco na Voz do Próprio*. BR/Elenco 29, 1965.

Blitz. *As Aventuras do Blitz*. BR/EMI 064 422 919, 1982.

Boca Livre. *Minha História: Boca Livre*. BR/PolyGram 518 668, 1994.

Bonfá, Luiz. *Amor!* Atlantic 8028, 1959.

————. *The Gentle Rain*. Mercury 61016, 1967.

————. *Luiz Bonfá*. Dot 25804, 1967.

————. *Non-Stop to Brazil*. Chesky JD29, 1989.

————. *The Bonfá Magic*. Milestone MCD-9202, 1993.

Borges, Ló. *Ló Borges*. BR/EMI SC 10112, 1977 (rpt.).

————. *A Via-Láctea / Nuvem Cigana*. BR/EMI 789 367, 1979, 1981 (rpt.).

Borghetti, Renato. *Renato Borghetti*. BR/RCA 103.0705, 1987.

Bosco, João. *João Bosco*. BR/RCA 103 0062, 1973.

————. *Caça a Raposa*. BR/RCA 103 0112, 1975.

————. *Galos de Briga*. BR/RCA 103 0171, 1976.

————. *Bandalhismo*. BR/RCA 110 0022, 1980.

————. *Gagabirô*. BR/Barclay 823 694, 1984.

————. *Ai Ai Ai de Mim*. BR/CBS 138 292, 1986.

————. *Bosco*. BR/CBS 231 218, 1989.

————. *João Bosco ao Vivo: 100a. Apresentação*. BR/Philips 817 282, 1989 (rpt.).

————. *Zona da Fronteira*. BR/Columbia 860.001/2-464184, 1991.

————. *Acústico*. BR/Columbia 852024, 1992.

————. *Na Onda Que Balança*. BR/Sony 6692 67210, 1994.

Bossa Três. *The Bossa Três*. Audio Fidelity 1988, 1963.

Braga, Leandro. *E Por Que Não?* Arabesque Jazz AJ0104, 1992.

Brandão, Leci. *Attitude*. BR/RGE 342-6181, 1993.

Brasil, João Carlos Assis. *Jazz Brasil*. BR/Kuarup KLP-022, 1986.

Brown, Carlinhos. *Alfagamabetizado*. BR/EMI 7243-8-41441-2-8, 1996.

Buarque, Chico. *Sinal Fechado*. BR/PolyGram 518 217, 1974 (rpt.).

————. *Meus Caros Amigos*. BR/Philips 6349 189, 1976.

————. *Chico Buarque*. BR/EMI 5182182, 1978 (rpt.).

————. *Vida*. BR/Philips 6349 435, 1980.

————. *Almanaque*. BR/PolyGram 510 010, 1981 (rpt.).

————. *Chico Buarque*. BR/PolyGram 510 032, 1984 (rpt.).

————. *Ópera do Malandro*. BR/PolyGram 838 516, 1985 (rpt.).

————. *Francisco*. RCA 9628, 1987.

————. *Personalidade: Chico Buarque*. BR/Philips 832 220, 1987.

————. *A Arte de Chico Buarque*. BR/PolyGram 836 241, 1988.

————. *Construção*. BR/Philips 836 013, 1989 (rpt.).

————. *Chico 50 Anos* (5 CDs). BR/PolyGram 522 802, 1994.

————. *Grandes Nomes: Chico* (4 CDs). BR/PolyGram 522 956, 1995.

Calazans, Teca. *Mina do Mar*. BR/Eldorado 8884 0438, 1984.

Caldas, Luiz. *Magia*. BR/PolyGram 826 583, 1985.

————. *Flor Cigana*. BR/Polydor 831 268, 1986.

Cama de Gato. *Guerra Fria*. BR/Som da Gente SDG 036, 1988.

Camisa de Vênus. *Camisa de Vênus ao Vivo*. BR/PolyGram 528 047, 1996.

Candeia. *Candeia*. BR/Abril Cultural HMPB-18, 1977.

Canhoto da Paraíba. *Walking on Coals*. Milestone 9230, 1993.

Capital Inícial. *O Melhor do Capital Inícial*. BR/PolyGram 521 787, 1994.

Caram, Ana. *Amazônia*. Chesky JD 45, 1990.

Cardoso, Elizeth. *Canção do Amor Demais*. BR/Festa 6002, 1958.

————. *Elizeth Cardoso no Japão*. BR/ABW 81605, 1992.

Cariocas, Os. *A Bossa dos Cariocas*. BR/Philips 632 152, 1962.

Carlos, Erasmo. *Mulher*. BR/Polydor 2451-176, 1981.

————. *Minha História: Erasmo Carlos*. BR/PolyGram 523 856, 1994.

Carlos, Roberto. *Roberto Carlos*. BR/Abril Cultural MPB-18, 1971.

————. *Roberto Carlos*. BR/CBS 230 105, 1986.

————. *Roberto Carlos*. BR/Columbia 879015/2-482302, 1996.

Carneiro, Nando. *Topázio*. BR/Visom LPVO 019, 1988.

Carrapícho. *Fiesta de Boi Bumba*. FR/BMG 74321 39990, 1996.

Carrilho, Altamiro, and Chiquinho et al. *Noites Cariocas*. BR/Kuarup KCD-040, 1988.

Cartola. *Cartola*. BR/Abril Cultural HMPB-18, 1977.

————. *70 Anos*. BR/RCA 103 0278, 1978.

Carvalho, Bete. *Beth Carvalho Ao Vivo*. BR/RCA 713 0018, 1987.

————. *Alma do Brasil*. BR/Philips 836 695, 1988.

————. *Saudades da Guanabara*. BR/Philips 842 084, 1989.

————. *Ao Vivo no Olympia*. BR/Som Livre 400 1052, 1991.

Carvalho, Bete, and Martinho da Vila. *O Carnaval de Beth Carvalho e Martinho da Vila*. BR/BMG 10085, 1990.

Cassiano. *Cedo ou Tarde*. BR/Sony 860003-464194, 1991.

Castro-Neves, Oscar. *Oscar!* Living Music LM 0010, 1987.

Caymmi, Dori. *Dori Caymmi*. BR/EMI 0644 22874, 1980.

————. *Dori Caymmi*. Elektra Musician 60790, 1988.

————. *Kicking Cans*. Qwest/Warner 945184, 1993.

————. *If Ever . . .* Qwest/Warner 9 45604, 1995.

Caymmi, Dorival. *Caymmi e Seu Violão / Eu Não Tenho Onde Morar*. BR/EMI 789014, 1959, 1961 (rpt.).

————. *Dorival Caymmi*. BR/Abril Cultural HMPB-02, 1976.

————. *Saudades da Bahia*. BR/EMI 036 422.593, 1985.

————. *Caymmi in Bahia*. BR/PolyGram 522 041, 1994.

Caymmi, Dorival, and A. C. Jobim. *Caymmi Visita Tom*. BR/PolyGram 848 966, 1994 (rpt.).

Caymmi, Nana. *Atrás da Porta*. BR/CID 8014, 1977.

————. *Nana*. BR/PolyGram 526 956, 1995 (rpt.).

Caymmi, Nana, and Dori, Danilo, and Dorival Caymmi. *Caymmi's Grandes Amigos*. BR/EMI 064 422.963, 1986.

————. *Família Caymmi*. BR/EMI 064 748 788, 1987.

Cazes, Henrique, et al. *Orquestra Brasília: Pixinguinha*. BR/Kuarup 035, 1989.

Cazuza. *Burguesia*. BR/Philips 838 447, 1989.

————. *O Tempo Não Para*. BR/PolyGram 836 839, 1989.

————. *Grandes Nomes: Cazuza* (4 CDs). BR/PolyGram 528 242, 1995.

César, Chico. *Aos Vivos*. BR/Velas 11-V080, 1995.

————. *Cuscuz Clã*. BR/PolyGram 001 068, 1996.

Cezar, Caio. *Caio Cezar Interpreta João Pernambuco*. BR/Carrilhões CAR 001, 1992.

Cheiro de Amor. *Agitando Todas*. BR/PolyGram 529 335, 1995.

Chiclete com Banana. *Tambores Urbanos*. BR/Continental 1.01.404.360, 1988.

Chico Science, and Nação Zumbi. *Da Lama ao Caos*. BR/Sony 850224, 1994.

Chiquinho do Acordeon. *Chiquinho do Acordeon*. BR/Visom 026, 1989.

Chitãozinho and Xororó. *Nacimos Para Cantar*. EMI H2H 42645, 1991.

————. *Chitãozinho & Xororó*. BR/PolyGram 528 917, 1995.

Cidade Negra. *Negro no Poder*. BR/Sony 850158-464276, 1992.

Clementina de Jesus, and Pixinguinha, João da Bahiana. *Gente da Antiga / Marinheiro Só*. BR/EMI 780 915, 1968, 1973 (rpt.).

Companhia do Pagode. *Na Boquinha da Garrafa*. BR/PolyGram 529 763, 1995.

Consuelo, Baby. *Sem Pecado e Sem Juízo*. BR/CBS 138272, 1985.

Costa, Alayde. *Alayde Canta Suavemente*. BR/RCA 1030, 1960.

Costa, Gal. *Aquarela do Brasil*. BR/Philips 836 017, 1988 (rpt.).

————. *Fantasia*. BR/Philips 836 015, 1988 (rpt.).

————. *Gal Canta Caymmi*. BR/Philips 836 014, 1988 (rpt.).

————. *Tropical*. BR/Philips 836 016, 1988 (rpt.).

————. *Plural*. BR/RCA 2214-RL, 1990.

————. *Gal*. BR/RCA 150 0024, 1992.

————. *Grandes Nomes: Gal* (4 CDs). BR/PolyGram 522 966, 1995.

————. *Mina D'Agua do Meu Canto*. BR/BMG 74321 26323, 1995.

Creuza, Maria. *Maria Creuza e os Grandes Mestres de Samba*. BR/RCA 1030156, 1975.

Cruz, Arlindo, and Sombrinha. *Da Música*. BR/Velas 11-V158, 1996.

D'Alma. *D'Alma*. BR/Som da Gente SDG 019, 1983.

Daúde. *Daúde*. Tinder Records. 42841102, 1995.

———. *Véu Vavá*. Natasha NAT042, 1996.

Delmiro, Hélio. *Chama*. BR/Som da Gente SDG 020, 1984.

Deodato, Eumir. *Inútil Paisagem*. BR/Fontana 6485108, 1964 (rpt.).

———. *Prelude*. CTI 6021, 1972.

Deodato, Eumir, and A. Moreira. *Deodato/Airto In Concert*. CTI 6041, 1974.

Deodato, Eumir, and Silvino Jr., C. Soares, A. Carrilho, D. Ferreira. *Nova Geração em Ritmo de Samba*. BR/Copacabana 11158, 1960.

Djavan. *Luz*. BR/CBS 138.251, 1982.

———. *Meu Lado*. JP/Epic-Sony 32 8P-144, 1986.

———. *Bird of Paradise*. Columbia CK 44276, 1988.

———. *Seduzir*. World Pacific 48206, 1990 (rpt.).

———. *Alumbramento / Djavan*. World Pacific CDP7 96865, 1992 (rpt.).

Dodô and Osmar. *O Melhor do Trio Elétrico*. BR/Continental 1.04.405.266, 1979.

———. *Carnaval da Bahia*. FR/NTI 307 3GLO 121, 1990.

Dominginhos. *Nas Quebradas do Sertão*. BR/Continental 995552, n.d.

Donato, João. *Chá Dancante*. BR/Odeon 3037, 1956.

———. *Muito à Vontade*. Polydor 4085, 1963.

———. *Coisa Tão Simples*. World Pacific CDP 7243-8-36008, 1995.

Donato, João, and E. Deodato. *João Donato*. Muse MR 5017, 1973.

Donga. *Donga*. BR/Abril Cultural HMPB-36, 1978.

Dougllas, Betto. *O Rei da Lambada*. BR/Continental 1.73.405.017, 1988.

Duboc, Jane. *Jane Duboc*. BR/Som da Gente SDG 101, 1982.

Duncan, Zelia. *Zelia Duncan*. BR/Warner M995570, 1994.

Duran, Dolores. *Dolores Duran*. BR/Copacabana 80695, 1973 (rpt.).

Eça, Luis. *Luiz Eça, Piano e Cordas*. BR/PolyGram 526 960, 1995 (rpt.).

Elias, Eliane. *Illusions*. Blue Note 46994, 1987.

———. *So Far So Close*. Blue Note 91141, 1989.

———. *Eliane Elias Plays Jobim*. Blue Note 93089, 1990.

———. *A Long Story*. Manhattan CDP7 95476, 1991.

———. *Fantasia*. Blue Note 96146, 1992.

———. *Paulistana*. Blue Note 89544, 1993.

Eller, Cássia. *Cássia Eller*. BR/PolyGram 522 500, 1996.

———. *Cássia Eller: Ao Vivo*. BR/PolyGram 529 687, 1996.

Elomar, and A. M. Lima, P. Moura, H. do Monte. *Con-Sertão*. BR/Kuarup KLP 008/9, 1981.

Elomar, and G. Azevedo, V. Farias, Xangai. *Cantoria*. BR/Kuarup KLP-018, 1984.

———. *Cantoria 2*. BR/Kuarup KLP-032, 1987.

Engenheiros do Hawaii. *Alívio Imediato*. BR/RCA 150.0004, 1989.

Espindola, Tetê. *Tetê Espindola*. BR/Som da Gente SDG 012, 1982.

Fafá de Belém. *Tamba-Tajá*. BR/Polydor 2451 073, 1976.

———. *Atrevida*. BR/Som Livre 530 032, 1985.

Fagner. *Raimundo Fagner*. BR/CBS 137.964, 1976.

Falcão, Fernando. *Memória das Águas*. BR/Poitou 001, 1981.

Farney, Dick. *Dick Farney Especial: 30 Successos*. BR/EMI 162 421194/5, 1978.

———. *Feliz de Amor*. BR/Som da Gente SDG 017, 1983.

———. *Dick Farney & Orquestra Gaya*. BR/PolyGram 526 954, 1995 (rpt.).

Ferreira, Abel, and Os Chorões. *Chorinhos da Pesada/Chorando Baixinho*. BR/EMI 829031, 1971, 1962 (rpt.).

Fest, Manfredo. *Jungle Cat*. DMP CD-470, 1989.

———. *Oferenda*. Concord CCD-4539, 1993.

———. *Fascinating Rhythm*. Concord Picante 4711, 1996.

Fredera. *Aurora Vermelha*. BR/Som da Gente SDG 006, 1981.

Gabriel o Pensador. *Gabriel o Pensador*. BR/Sony 850.202/2-464423, 1993.

———. *Ainda é Só o Começo*. BR/Sony 850.249/2-479069, 1995.

Galo Preto. *Só Paulinho da Viola*. BR/Leblon LB036, 1994.

Gandelman, Leo. *Visons*. One Globe 60001, 1992.

Gaúcho da Fronteira. *Pelo Duro*. BR/Continental 207405-359, 1992.

Geraissati, André. *Dadgad*. Tropical Storm/WEA WH 55998, 1989.

Gera Samba. *É o Tchan*. BR/PolyGram 529 216, 1995.

———. *Grupo Gera*. BR/PolyGram 527 737, 1995.

Gerônimo. *Gerônimo*. Continental 1-01-404-357, 1988.

Gilberto, Astrud. *The Astrud Gilberto Album*. Verve 68608, 1965.

Gilberto, Astrud, and Stanley Turrentine. *Gilberto with Turrentine*. CTI 527, 1973.

Gilberto, Gil. *Louvação*. BR/Philips R 765 005L, 1967.

———. *Gilberto Gil*. BR/Philips R765 024L, 1968.

———. *Expresso 2222*. BR/Philips 6349 034, 1972.

———. *Refazenda*. BR/Philips 6349 152, 1975.

———. *Refavela*. BR/Philips 6349 329, 1977.

———. *UmBandaUm*. BR/WEA BR26.063, 1982.

———. *Extra*. BR/WEA BR36.198, 1983.

———. *Raça Humana*. BR/WEA BR 36.201, 1984.

———. *Em Concerto*. BR/WEA 670.9001, 1987.

———. *Parabolic*. Tropical Storm/WEA 76292, 1992.

———. *Gilberto Gil Acoustic*. Atlantic 82564, 1994.

Gilberto, Gil, and Jorge Ben. *Gil e Jorge*. Verve 314 512 067, 1975 (rpt.).

Gilberto, João. *Chega de Saudade*. BR/Odeon 3073, 1959.

———. *O Amor, o Sorriso e a Flor*. BR/Odeon 3151, 1960.

———. *João Gilberto*. BR/Odeon 3202, 1961.

———. *João Gilberto*. BR/Polydor 2451037, 1973.

———. *Amoroso*. BR/WEA 36022, 1977.

———. *Brasil*. BR/WEA 3613, 1981.

———. *Interpreta Tom Jobim*. BR/EMI 052 422005, 1985.

———. *João Gilberto: Live in Montreux*. Elektra 9 60760, 1987.

———. *O Mito*. BR/Odeon 16479 1115, 1988.

———. *The Legendary João Gilberto*. World Pacific 93891, 1990.

———. *João*. Verve 848 507, 1991.

Ginga Pura. *Todo Seu*. BR/PolyGram 527 278, 1995.

Gismonti, Egberto. *Carmo*. BR/EMI 064 422830, 1977.

———. *Sol do Meio Dia*. ECM 1116, 1978.

———. *Solo*. ECM 1136, 1979.

———. *Sanfona*. ECM 1203, 1981.

———. *Alma*. BR/EMI 064 422965, 1986.

———. *Dança dos Escravos*. ECM 1387, 1989.

———. *Kuarup* [soundtrack]. BR/Kuarup 037, 1989.

———. *ZigZag*. ECM 78118-21582, 1996.

Gismonti, Egberto, and N. Vasconcelos. *Dança das Cabeças*. ECM 1089, 1977.

———. *Duas Vozes*. ECM 1279, 1984.

Godoy, Amilson. *Amilson Godoy*. BR/Som da Gente SDG 040, 1989.

Gomes, Manoel, et al. *Brasil, Flauta, Cavaquinho e Violão*. BR/Marcus Pereira 9301, 1975.

Gomes, Pepeu. *Energia Positiva*. BR/CBS 138 284, 1985.

Gonzaga, Luiz. *De Fia Pavi*. BR/RCA 109 0159, 1987.

———. *Ai Tem*. BR/RCA 103 0730, 1988.

———. *O Melhor de Luiz Gonzaga*. BR/RCA 10032, 1989.

Gonzaga, Luiz, and Fagner. *Gonzagão & Fagner*. BR/RCA 130 0050, 1988.

Gonzaga, Luiz, and Humberto Teixeira. *Luiz Gonzaga & Humberto Teixeira*. BR/Abril Cultural HMPB-11, 1977.

Gonzaguinha. *É*. World Pacific 91688, 1990 (rpt.).

Grupo de Capoeira Angola Pelourinho. *Capoeira Angola from Salvador, Brazil*. Smithsonian/Folkways 40465, 1996.

Grupo Fundo de Quintal. *Samba Brazil*. One Globe Music 60002, 1993.

Grupo Raça. *Pura Emoção*. BR/BMG 74321 32363, 1995.

Gudin, Eduardo, and Vania Bastos. *Eduardo Gudin & Vania Bastos*. BR/Eldorado 14589 0552, 1989.

Guedes, Beto. *A Página do Relâmpago Elétrico*. BR/EMI EMCB 7021, 1977.

———. *Viagem das Mãos*. BR/EMI 06431C 422935, 1985.

———. *Amor de Índio*. BR/EMI 364 748141, 1987 (rpt.).

———. *Andaluz*. BR/EMI 796 853, 1991.

Guineto, Almir. *Almir Guineto*. BR/RGE 308.6118, 1986.

Guinga. *Simples e Absurdo*. BR/Velas 11V001, 1991.

———. *Delírio Carioca*. BR/Velas 11V008, 1994.

Hora, Rildo. *Espraiado*. Milestone 9222, 1992.

Horta, Toninho. *Toninho Horta*. World Pacific CDP7 93865, 1981 (rpt.).

———. *Diamond Land.* Verve Forecast 835 183, 1988.

———. *Moonstone.* Verve Forecast 839 734, 1989.

———. *Toninho Horta.* World Pacific 93865, 1990 (rpt.).

———. *Once I Loved.* Verve 314 513 561, 1992.

Ilê Aiyê. *Canto Negro.* BR/Eldorado 16789 0577, n.d.

Ingênuos, Os. *Os Ingênuos Play Choros From Brazil.* Nimbus NI5338, 1992.

Jackson do Pandeiro. *Jackson Pandeiro e os Nordestinos.* BR/Abril Cultural HMPB-63, 1979.

———. *Isso É Que É Forró!* BR/PolyGram 2494 622, 1981.

———. *A Popularidade de Jackson do Pandeiro.* BR/PolyGram 523 454, 1994.

Jacob do Bandolim. *Jacob do Bandolim: Original Classic Recordings, Vol. 1.* Acoustic Disc ACD-3, 1991.

———. *Jacob do Bandolim: Original Classic Recordings, Vol. 2.* Acoustic Disc ACD-13, 1994.

João do Vale. *João do Vale.* BR/Abril Cultural HMPB-33, 1977.

———. *João do Vale.* BR/CBS 138237, 1981.

Jobim, Antonio Carlos. *The Composer of "Desafinado" Plays.* Verve 2304 502, 1963.

———. *Wave.* A&M SP-9-3002, 1967.

———. *Tide.* A&M SP-9-3031, 1970.

———. *Stone Flower.* CTI 6002, 1971.

———. *Tom Jobim.* BR/Abril Cultural HMPB-27, 1977.

———. *Terra Brasilis.* WB 3409, 1980.

———. *Tom Jobim e Convidados.* BR/Philips 826 665, 1985.

———. *Urubu.* BR/WEA 610 7044, 1985 (rpt.).

———. *Passarim.* Verve 833 234, 1987.

———. *Antonio Brasileiro.* BR/Columbia 419 058, 1994.

———. *The Girl from Ipanema: The Antonio Carlos Jobim Songbook.* Verve 314 525 472, 1995.

———. *Grandes Nomes: Tom (4 CDs).* BR/PolyGram 528 071, 1995.

———. *Matita Perê.* BR/PolyGram 826 856, 1996 (rpt.).

———. *Wave: The Antonio Carlos Jobim Songbook.* Verve 314 535 528, 1996.

Jobim, Antonio Carlos, and Billy Blanco. *Sinfónia do Rio de Janeiro.* BR/Continental 1000, 1956.

Jobim, Antonio Carlos, and Gal Costa. *Rio Revisited.* Verve 841 286, 1989.

Jobim, Antonio Carlos, and Vinícius de Moraes. *Orfeu da Conceição.* BR/Odeon 3056, 1956.

Jongo Trio. *Jongo Trio.* BR/Farroupilha 407, 1965.

Jovelina Pérola Negra. *Pérola Negra.* BR/RGE 738.6107, 1986.

Joyce. *Feminina / Agua e Luz.* BR/EMI 364 789 626, 1980, 1981 (rpt.).

———. *Joyce/Jobim.* BR/CBS 106002, 1987.

———. *Negro Demais no Coração.* BR/CBS 320005, 1988.

———. *Revivendo Amigos.* BR/EMI 828 967, 1994.

Karnak. *Karnak.* BR/PolyGram 527 813, 1995.

Kenia. *Initial Thrill.* MCA ZBC 5967, 1987.

Keti, Zé. *Zé Keti.* BR/Abril Cultural HMPB-41, 1978.

Kleiton and Kledir. *Minha História: Kleiton & Kledir.* BR/PolyGram 518 664, 1994.

Lacerda, Genival. *A Popularidade de Genival Lacerda.* BR/PolyGram 523 466, 1994.

Lambert, Junia. *Ar de Rock.* BR/PolyGram 526 757, 1995.

Lauria, Nando. *Points of View.* Narada 63026, 1994.

Leandro e Leonardo. *Leandro e Leonardo.* BR/Continental 207405335, 1990.

Leão, Nara. *Opinião de Nara.* BR/Philips 632 732, 1964.

———. *Nara Leão.* BR/PolyGram 848 970, 1967 (rpt.).

———. *The Girl from Ipanema.* Philips 826 348, 1985.

———. *Meus Sonhos Dourados.* BR/Philips 832 639, 1988.

———. *Grandes Nomes: Nara (4 CDs).* BR/PolyGram 528 352, 1995.

Leão, Nara, and Zé Keti, João do Vale. *Opinião.* BR/PolyGram 522 400, 1994 (rpt.).

Lee, Rita. *Rita Lee.* BR/EMI 834 093, 1980.

———. *Rita Lee.* BR/Som Livre 530 035, 1986 (rpt.).

———. *Tratos à Bola.* BR/Philips 830 374, 1986.

Lee, Rita, and R. de Carvalho. *Flerte Fatal.* BR/EMI 064 422971, 1987.

Legião Urbana. *Dois.* BR/EMI 064 422961, 1986.

———. *Que Pais É Este?* BR/EMI 068 748 8201, 1987.

Leitte, Dirceu. *Leitte de Coco.* Milestone 9231, 1994.

Lenine and Susano. *Olho de Peixe.* BR/Velas 11-V018, 1994.

Lima, Arthur Moreira. *Brazilian Nights: The Tangos of Ernesto Nazareth*. Pro-Arte CDD 512, 1990.

Lima, Arthur Moreira, and A. Ferreira. *Chorando Baixinho*. BR/Kuarup KLP 005, 1979.

Lins, Ivan. *Juntos*. BR/Philips 822 672, 1984.

———. *Amar Assim*. BR/Philips 836 613, 1988.

———. *Mãos*. BR/Philips 832 262, 1988.

———. *Love Dance*. Reprise 9 25850, 1989.

———. *Awa Yiô*. Reprise 9 26499, 1991.

———. *Anjo de Mim*. BR/Velas 11-V076, 1995.

Lobão. *Cuidado*. RCA 9633, 1988.

———. *Sob o Sol de Parador*. BR/RCA 150.0001, 1989.

Lobo, Edu. *Edu Lobo por Edu Lobo*. BR/PolyGram 848 967, 1967 (rpt.).

———. *Camaleão*. BR/Philips 6349 350, 1978.

———. *Personalidade: Edu Lobo*. Verve 314 514 133, 1987.

———. *Corrupião*. BR/Velas 11-V012, 1993.

———. *Meia-Noite*. BR/Velas 11-V090, 1995.

Lobo, Edu, and A. C. Jobim. *Edu e Tom*. BR/Philips 6328 378, 1981.

Lobo, Edu, and Maria Bethânia. *Edu & Bethânia*. BR/PolyGram 512 053, 1967 (rpt.).

Lubambo, Romero, and Drummond, Weber. *Face to Face*. GSP 5003, 1993.

———. *Two*. GSP 5004, 1994.

Luis, Nonato, and D. Corrêa, L. Alves. *Gosto do Brasil*. Milestone 9204, 1991.

Luis, Nonato, and Túlio Mourão. *Carioca*. Milestone 9214, 1991.

Luiz Melodia. *Pérola Negra*. BR/Fontana 6488 151, 1982 (rpt.).

———. *Claro*. BR/Continental 1.35.404.032, 1987.

———. *Pintando o Sete*. BR/PolyGram 510 705, 1991.

———. *Minha História: Luiz Melodia*. BR/PolyGram 518 669, 1994.

Lyra, Carlos. *Bossa Nova*. BR/Philips 630 409, 1960.

———. *Carlos Lyra*. BR/Philips 630 430, 1961.

———. *O Sambalanço de Carlos Lyra*. BR/Philips 630 492, 1962.

———. *Pobre Menina Rica*. BR/CBS 37360, 1964.

———. *Carlos Lyra, 25 Anos de Bossa Nova*. BR/3M 900006, 1987.

Macalé, Jards. *Jards Macalé*. BR/Philips 6349 045, 1972.

Maia, Tim. *Minha História: Tim Maia*. BR/PolyGram 510 474, 1994.

Malheiros, Alex. *Atlantic Forest*. Milestone M-9131, 1984.

Mamonas Assassinas. *Mamonas Assassinas*. BR/EMI 835 082, 1995.

Marçal, Nilton Delfino. *A Incrível Bateria do Mestre Marçal*. BR/Polydor 835 123, 1987.

Maria, Tania. *Come With Me*. Concord CCD-200, 1983.

———. *Love Explosion*. Concord CJP-230, 1984.

Mariano, Cesar Camargo. *Solo Brasileiro*. BR/PolyGram 518 874, 1994.

Mariano, Torcuato. *Paradise Station*. Windham Hill 11137, 1994.

Marina. *Fullgas*. BR/Philips 818 380, 1984.

———. *Próxima Parada*. BR/Philips 838 298, 1989.

———. *Marina Lima*. World Pacific 97728, 1992.

Mário, Francisco. *Retratos*. Milestone 9232, 1994.

Martinho da Vila. *Canta Canta, Minha Gente*. BR/RCA 110.0002, 1974.

———. *Batuqueiro*. BR/RCA 103.0678, 1986.

———. *Coração Malandro*. BR/RCA 130.0011, 1987.

———. *Festa da Raça*. BR/CBS 138.310, 1988.

———. *O Canto das Lavadeiras*. BR/Sony 850084-464120, 1989.

———. *Tá Delicia, Tá Gostoso*. BR/Columbia 850.257/2-479164, 1995.

Martins, Alípio. *Eu Chego Lá*. BR/Continental 2.73.405.157, 1989.

Mascarenhas, Raul. *Raul Mascarenhas*. Tropical Storm/WEA WH 56214, 1989.

Matogrosso, Ney. *Personalidade: Ney Matogrosso*. BR/Philips 833 696, 1987.

———. *Ney Matogrosso Ao Vivo*. BR/CBS 231.222, 1989.

———. *Estava Escrito*. BR/PolyGram 526 316, 1995.

———. *Grandes Nomes: Ney* (4 CDs). BR/PolyGram 528 066, 1995.

Matogrosso, Ney, and Aquarela Carioca. *As Aparências Enganam*. BR/PolyGram 514 688, 1993.

Maysa. *Maysa*. BR/PolyGram 526 957, 1995 (rpt.).

Melodia, Luis. *Luis Melodia*. BR/Polygram 518 669, 1994.

Mendes, Sérgio. *Dance Moderno.* BR/Philips 630 491, 1960.

———. *Sérgio Mendes & Bossa Rio.* BR/Philips 632 701, 1964.

———. *Sérgio Mendes & Brasil '66.* A&M 4116, 1966.

———. *Bossa Nova York.* BR/PolyGram 526 953, 1967 (rpt.).

———. *Arara.* A&M SP 5250, 1989.

———. *Brasileiro.* Elektra 9 61315, 1992.

———. *Grandes Nomes: Sérgio Mendes* (4 CDs). BR/Poly-Gram 525 994, 1995.

———. *Oceano.* Verve 714 532 441, 1996.

Menescal, Roberto. *Bossa Nova.* BR/Imperial 30060, 1962.

———. *A Bossa Nova de Roberto Menescal.* BR/Elenco ME-3, 1963.

Menezes, Margareth. *Elegibô.* Mango 539 855, 1990.

———. *Kindala.* Mango 162 539 917, 1991.

———. *Luz Dourada.* BR/Verve 519 537, 1993.

Mercury, Daniela. *O Canto da Cidade.* BR/Sony 80998-20-464348, 1992.

———. *Música da Rua.* BR/Epic 758209, 1994.

———. *Feijão com Arroz.* BR/Epic 758 290, 1996.

Mestre Suassuna e Dirceu. *Capoeira: Cordão de Ouro.* BR/Warner 997157, 1975.

Milito, Hélcio. *Kilombo.* Antilles 90629, 1987.

Milton Banana Trio. *Milton Banana Trio.* BR/Odeon 3417, 1965.

Miranda, Carmen. *Carmen Miranda.* BR/RCA 103 0651, 1989.

——— (w. Lamartine Babo). *Carmen Miranda.* FR/Milan Sur CD CH 524, 1990.

Miranda, Marlui. *Ihu: Todos Os Sons.* Blue Jackel 5005, 1995.

Miúcha. *Miúcha.* BR/Continental 1.35.404.035, 1988.

Miúcha, and A. C. Jobim. *Falando de Amor.* BR/RCA 130 0060, 1989 (rpt.).

Mocidade Independente de Padre Miguel. *Batucada.* FR/JSL 003, 1990.

Mola, Tony. *Bragadá.* Blue Jackel 5006, 1996.

Monsueto. *Monsueto.* BR/Abril Cultural HMPB-31, 1977.

Montarroyos, Márcio. *Terra Mater.* Black Sun 15004, 1989.

Monte, Heraldo do. *Cordas Vivas.* BR/Som da Gente 015, 1983.

———. *Cordas Mágicas.* BR/Som da Gente SDG 030, 1986.

Monte, Marisa. *Marisa Monte.* BR/EMI 791 761, 1988.

———. *Mais.* World Pacific CDP 7 96104, 1991.

———. *Rose and Charcoal.* Metro Blue/Capitol CDP 7243-8-30080-2-5, 1994.

———. *A Great Noise.* Metro Blue CDP 7243-8-53353-2-7, 1996.

Montenegro, Oswaldo. *Oswaldo Montenegro.* BR/Som Livre 401 0035, 1988.

Moraes, Vinícius de. *Vinícius de Moraes.* BR/PolyGram 526 959, 1967 (rpt.).

———. *Vinícius de Moraes.* BR/Abril Cultural HMPB-19, 1977.

———. *A Arte de Vinícius de Moraes.* BR/Philips 834 654, 1988.

———. *Minha História: Vinícius de Moraes.* BR/PolyGram 510 457, 1994.

Moraes, Vinícius de, and Dorival Caymmi. *Vinícius & Caymmi no Zum Zum.* BR/PolyGram 848 969, 1995 (rpt.).

Moraes, Vinícius, and Odette Lara. *Vinícius + Odette Lara.* BR/PolyGram 512 057, 1995 (rpt.).

Moraes, Vinícius de, and Toquinho. *Vinícius and Toquinho.* BR/Philips 6349 090, 1985.

Moreira, Airto. *Identity.* Arista 4068, 1975.

———. *Free.* CTI 8000, 1979 (rpt.).

Moreira, Airto, and Flora Purim. *The Colours of Life.* GE/In + Out 001, 1988.

Moreira, Moraes. *Mancha de Dendê Não Sai.* BR/CBS 138264, 1984.

———. *Mestiço É Isso.* BR/CBS 138294, 1986.

———. *Terreiro do Mundo.* BR/PolyGram 510 4562, 1993.

Moreira, Moraes, and Pepeu Gomes. *Moraes & Pepeu Live in Japan.* Tropical Storm/WEA 90216, 1991.

Moreira, Wilson. *Peso Na Balança.* BR/Kuarup KLP-026, 1986.

Motta, Ed. *Entre e Ouça*. BR/Warner 990269, 1992.

Moura, Paulo. *Gafieira, Etc. & Tal*. BR/Kuarup 992 320, 1986.

——. *Confusão Urbana, Suburbana e Rural*. Braziloid 4013, 1988 (rpt.).

——. *Mistura e Manda*. Braziloid 4012, 1988 (rpt.).

Moura, Paulo, and Raphael Rabello. *Dois Irmãos*. Milestone 9203, 1992.

Moura, Tavinho. *Tavinho Moura*. BR/RCA 103.0334, 1980.

MPB-4. *Deixa Estar*. BR/PolyGram 526 956, 1995 (rpt.).

Mutantes, Os. *Jardim Elétrico*. BR/PolyGram 825 887, 1971 (rpt.).

——. *Minha História: Mutantes*. BR/PolyGram 523 859, 1994.

Muzenza. *Muzenza do Reggae*. BR/Continental 1-01-404-332, 1988.

——. *Som Luxuoso*. BR/Continental 1-01-404-359, 1988.

Nascimento, Milton. *Clube da Esquina*. BR/EMI MOAB 6005-6, 1972.

——. *Minas*. BR/EMI 064 82325, 1975.

——. *Gerais*. BR/EMI 064 422806D, 1976.

——. *Clube da Esquina 2*. BR/EMI 164 422831-32, 1978.

——. *Travessia*. BR/Sigla 403 6152, 1978 (rpt.).

——. *Sentinela*. BR/Ariola 201 610, 1980.

——. *Anima*. Verve 813 296, 1982 (rpt.).

——. *Missa dos Quilombos*. BR/Ariola 201 649, 1982.

——. *Milagre dos Peixes*. Intuition/Capitol C1-90790, 1988 (rpt.).

——. *Miltons*. Columbia FC 45239, 1989.

——. *Txai*. Columbia CK 46871, 1990.

——. *Angelus*. Warner 9 45499, 1994.

——. *Amigo*. Quilombo/Warner 9 46428, 1996.

——. *Nascimento*. Warner 46492, 1997.

Nazaré, Ernesto, and Chiquinha Gonzaga. *Ernesto Nazaré & Chiquinha Gonzaga*. BR/Abril Cultural HMPB-20, 1977.

Negril. *Negril*. BR/PolyGram 531 168, 1996.

Neguinho da Beija-Flor. *Quem Te Ama Sou Eu*. BR/PolyGram 531 312, 1996.

Nelson Cavaquinho. *Nelson Cavaquinho*. BR/Abril Cultural HMPB-40, 1978.

Netinho. *Netinho*. BR/PolyGram 528 613, 1995.

Nó em Pingo D'Água. *Receita de Samba*. BR/Visom 219, 1990.

Novos Baianos. *Acabou Chorare*. BR/Som Livre 400.1162, 1992 (rpt.).

Nunes, Clara. *O Canto da Guerreira*. BR/EMI 066 792177, 1989.

——. *The Best of Clara Nunes*. World Pacific CDP7 96866, 1992.

Obina Shok. *Obina Shok*. BR/RCA 103 0691, 1986.

Oficina de Cordas. *Pernambuco's Music*. Nimbus NI5398, 1994.

Oito Batutas. *Oito Batutas*. BR/RCA RVCD-064, 1993 (rpt.).

Oliveira, Coaty de. *Saudades do Brasil*. FR/Arion ARN 64165, 1991.

Oliveira, Silas, and Mano Décio da Viola. *Silas de Oliveira & Mano Décio da Viola*. BR/Abril Cultural HMPB-21, 1977.

Olodum. *Égito Madagáscar*. BR/Continental 1-01-404-325, 1987.

——. *Núbia Axum Étiopia*. BR/Continental 1-01-404-362, 1988.

——. *10 Anos: Do Nordeste do Saara ao Nordeste Brasileiro*. BR/Continental 1-01-404-383, 1989.

——. *O Movimento*. BR/Warner 107800521, 1993.

Orquestra da Cordas Dedilhadas de Pernambuco. *Orchestra da Cordas Dedilhadas de Pernambuco*. Som da Gente SDG 031, 1987.

Oswaldinho. *Ceu e Chão*. BR/Som da Gente SDG 016, 1983.

Pantoja, Rique. *Rique Pantoja*. Sound Wave/WEA WH 56325, 1989.

Pantoja, Rique, and Chet Baker. *Rique Pantoja & Chet Baker*. Tropical Storm/WEA WH 55155, 1989 (rpt.).

Parahyba, João. *The New Lambadas*. Happy Hour 5010, 1990.

Paralamas do Sucesso. *Selvagem?* BR/EMI 062 421 273, 1986.

——. *Big Bang*. BR/EMI 364 793548, 1989.

————. *Bora Bora.* Intuition/Capitol CDP 7 90554, 1989.

————. *Arquivo.* BR/EMI 364 795667, 1990.

————. *Os Grãos.* BR/EMI 7979782, 1991.

————. *Severino.* BR/EMI 829 405, 1994.

Pascoal, Hermeto. *Slave's Mass.* WEA BS 2980, 1977.

————. *So Não Toca Quem Não Quer.* BR/Som da Gente SDG 034, 1987.

————. *Lagoa da Canoa.* Happy Hour 5005, 1988.

————. *Por Diferentes Caminhos.* BR/Som da Gente SDG 039, 1988.

————. *Brasil, Universo.* Happy Hour 5007, 1989.

————. *Hermeto Pascoal & Grupo.* Happy Hour 5009, 1989.

————. *A Música Livre de Hermeto Paschoal* [sic]. Verve 824 621, 1990 (rpt.).

Passira, Duda da, et al. *Pé de Serra Forró Band, Brazil.* GE/Welt Musik SM 1509 281509, 1992.

Passos, Rosa. *Pano Pra Manga.* BR/Velas 11-V145, 1996.

Pau Brasil. *Cenas Brasileiras.* BR/Continental 1.01.404.316, 1987.

————. *Babel.* Blue Jackel, BJAC 5009, 1995.

Paulinho da Viola. *Eu Canto Samba.* BR/RCA 104 0010, 1989.

————. . *20 Years de Samba.* BR/EMI 052 792040, 1989.

Paulinho da Viola, and E. Medeiros. *Samba na Madrugada.* BR/RGE 341.6007, 1968 (rpt.).

Paulinho Pedra Azul. *Quarenta.* BR/Velas 11-V037, 1994.

Pena Branca, and Xavantinho. *Canto Violeiro.* BR/Continental 1-71-405-657, 1988.

Pereira, Marco. *Círculo das Cordas.* BR/Som da Gente SDG 038, 1988.

Pereira, Marco, and Cristóvão Bastos. *Bons Encontros.* Milestone 9213, 1992.

Pereira, Nazaré. *Ritmos da Amazônia.* FR/Playa Sound PS 65030, 1988.

Perelman, Ivo. *Children of Ibeji.* Enja/ENJ-7005, 1992.

Pinheiro, Leila. *Benção Bossa Nova.* BR/Philips 842 036, 1989.

————. *Coisas do Brasil.* BR/PolyGram 518 137, 1994.

————. *Isso É Bossa Nova.* BR/EMI 830 979, 1994.

Pixinguinha. *Pixinguinha.* BR/Abril Cultural HMPB-07, 1976.

Popoff, Yuri. *Catopê.* BR/Leblon LB009, 1992.

Possi, Zizi. *Sobre Todas as Coisas.* BR/Eldorado ELD 7074, 1991.

————. *Valsa Brasileira.* BR/Velas 11-V020, 1994.

Powell, Baden. *Afro Sambas.* BR/Philips FE 1016, 1966.

————. *Baden Powell À Vontade.* BR/PolyGram 848 968, 1967 (rpt.).

————. *Baden Powell Swings with Jimmy Pratt.* BR/PolyGram 528 042, 1967 (rpt.).

————. *A Arte de Baden Powell.* BR/Fontana 6470 533, 1975.

————. *Estudos.* GE/MPS 821 855, 1979.

————. *Felicidade.* FR/Adda 581011, 1987 (rpt.).

————. *Mestres da MPB.* BR/WEA M995353, 1994.

Purim, Flora. *Butterfly Dreams.* Fantasy OJC-315, 1973 (rpt.).

————. *500 Miles High.* Milestone 9070, 1976.

————. *Open Your Eyes, You Can Fly.* Milestone 9065, 1976.

Quarteto em Cy. *Quarteto em Cy.* BR/PolyGram 526 955, 1968 (rpt.).

Quarteto Negro. *Quarteto Negro.* BR/Kuarup KLP 031, 1987.

Quarteto Novo, and Radamés Gnattali. *Quarteto Novo / Radamés Gnattali Sexteto.* BR/EMI 8274972, 1967, 1975 (rpt.).

Quinteto Armorial. *Do Romance ao Galope Nordestino.* BR/Marcus Pereira MPL 9306, 1975.

Quinteto Violado. . . . *Até a Amazônia?* BR/Philips 6349 362, 1978.

———— (w. Nana Rocha). *O Guarani.* Braziloid BRD 4021, 1992.

14 Bis. *Sete.* BR/EMI 064 422972, 1987.

Rabello, Raphael. *Raphael Rabello Interpreta Radamés Gnattali.* BR/Visom VO 006, 1987.

Rabello, Raphael, and Dino 7 Cordas. *Raphael Rabello & Dino 7 Cordas.* Milestone 9221, 1991.

Raça Negra. *Raça Negra, Vol. 2.* BR/RGE 3206161, 1992.

Ramalho, Elba. *Do Jeito Que a Gente Gosta.* BR/Barclay 823 030, 1984.

————. *Remexer*. BR/PolyGram 510 114, 1986 (rpt.).

————. *Elba ao Vivo*. BR/Philips 842 336, 1989.

————. *Felicidade Urgente*. BR/PolyGram 848 688, 1991 (rpt.).

————. *Devora-Me*. BR/PolyGram 519 901, 1994.

————. *Grandes Nomes: Elba Ramalho* (4 CDs). BR/Poly-Gram 528 347 (4 CDs), 1995.

Ramalho, Zé. *Zé Ramalho*. BR/Epic 44231, 1978.

Regina, Elis. *Samba Eu Canto Assim*. BR/Philips 632 742, 1963.

————. *Elis*. BR/Philips 836 009, 1972 (rpt.).

————. *A Música de João Bosco e Aldir Blanc*. BR/Fontana 6488 106, 1981.

————. *Personalidade: Elis Regina*. BR/Philips 832 218, 1987.

————. *Essa Mulher*. WEA WH 55900, 1988 (rpt.).

————. *Falso Brilhante*. BR/Philips 836 010, 1988 (rpt.).

————. *Fascination: The Best of Elis Regina*. Verve 836 844, 1990.

————. *No Fino da Bossa* (3 CDs). BR/Velas 11-V030, 1994.

————. *Grandes Nomes: Elis* (4 CDs). BR/PolyGram 522 951, 1995.

Regina, Elis, and A. C. Jobim. *Elis & Tom*. Verve 824 418, 1974.

Regina, Elis, and Jair Rodrigues. *Dois na Bossa, No. 3*. BR/PolyGram 522 663, 1994 (rpt.).

Regina, Elis, and Zimbo Trio. *O Fino do Fino*. BR/Poly-Gram 830 060, 1994 (rpt.).

Reis, Mário. *Mário Reis Canta Suas Criações em Hi-Fi*. BR/Odeon 3177, 1960.

Reis, Nando. *12 de Janeiro*. BR/Warner M450999002, 1995.

Reis, Selma. *Selma Reis*. BR/PolyGram 518 066, 1994.

Reppôlho. *Em Perfeita Vibração*. BR/Leblon LB025, 1994.

Ribeiro, Roberto. *Arrasta Povo / Roberto Ribeiro*. BR/EMI 827 6132, 1976, 1978 (rpt.).

Ricardo, Sérgio. *A Bossa Romântica de Sérgio Ricardo*. BR/Odeon 3168, 1960.

Robertinho de Recife. *Satisfação*. BR/Philips 6328 342, 1981.

Rocha, Ulisses. *Alguma Coisa a Ver Com o Silêncio*. BR/Visom VO 002, 1986.

Roditi, Cláudio. *Slow Fire*. Milestone M-9175, 1989.

Rodrigues, Jair. *Minha História: Jair Rodrigues*. BR/Poly-Gram 518 663, 1994.

Rodrigues, Lupicínio. *Lupicínio Rodrigues*. BR/Abril Cultural HMPB-05, 1976.

Romão, Dom Um. *Dom Um Romão*. Muse MR 5013, 1974.

————. *Spirit of the Times*. Muse MR 5049, 1975.

Rosa, Noel. *Noel por Noel*. BR/Imperial 30.205, 1971.

————. *Noel Rosa*. BR/Abril Cultural HMPB-08, 1977.

Roupa Nova. *Minha História: Roupa Nova*. BR/PolyGram 518 667, 1994.

RPM. *Rádio Pirata Ao Vivo*. BR/CBS 144.500, 1986.

Sá, Wanda. *Wanda Vagamente*. BR/RGE 5248, 1964.

Sambacana. *Conjunto Sabacana*. BR/Odeon 3375, 1964.

Sambalanço Trio. *Sambalanço Trio*. Audio Fidelity 6010, 1964.

Santiago, Emilio. *Minha História: Emilio Santiago*. BR/Poly-Gram 518 659, 1994.

Santos, Agostinho dos. *A Popularidade de Agostinho dos Santos*. BR/Polygram 523 458, 1994.

Santos, Lulu. *Tudo Azul*. BR/WEA BR 26126, 1984.

————. *Amor a Arte*. BR/RCA 140.0009, 1988.

Santos, Moacir. *Coisas*. BR/Forma FM-8, 1963.

————. *Maestro*. Blue Note LA007-F, 1972.

Santos, Turíbio. *Valsas e Choros*. BR/Kuarup KLP 001, 1980.

Sargento, Nelson. *Encanto da Paisagem*. BR/Kuarup KLP-025, 1986.

Sater, Almir. *Instrumental*. BR/Som da Gente SDG 025, 1985.

————. *Varandas*. BR/RGE 303 6199, 1990.

————. *Instrumental Dois*. BR/Velas 11-V102, 1995.

Secos e Molhados. *Secos & Molhados*. BR/Continental 1-01-800-007, 1973 (rpt.).

Seixas, Raul. *Krig-Ha, Bandolo!* BR/PolyGram 848 938, 1973 (rpt.).

————. *Gita*. BR/PolyGram 838 288, 1974 (rpt.).

————. *Grandes Nomes: Raul* (4 CDs). BR/PolyGram 522 976, 1995.

Sepultura. *Chãos A.D.* Epic 57458, 1993.

⸻. *Roots.* Road Runner RR8900, 1996.

Sete, Bola. *Autêntico!* Fantasy OJC 290, 1987 (rpt.).

⸻. *Bossa Nova.* Fantasy OJC 286, 1987 (rpt.).

Severo. *Machucando Gostosinho.* BR/EMI 036 422 636, 1987.

Silva, Bezerra da. *Justiça Social.* BR/RCA 103 0701, 1987.

Silva, Ismael. *Ismael Silva.* BR/Abril Cultural HMPB-16, 1977.

Silva, Orlando. *O Cantor das Multidões: 1935-1942.* BR/BMG 74321-23238, 1995.

Silva, Robertinho. *Speak No Evil.* Miletone 9220, 1991.

Silveira, Ricardo. *Sky Light.* Verve 837 696, 1989.

⸻. *Storyteller.* Kokopelli 1307, 1995.

Simonal, Wilson. *Wilson Simonal Tem Algo Mais.* BR/Odeon 3370, 1963.

Simone. *Cigarra.* BR/EMI 064 421089, 1978.

⸻. *Amar.* BR/CBS 138.247, 1981.

⸻. *Corpo e Alma.* BR/CBS 138.267, 1982.

⸻. *Delírios e Delícias.* BR/CBS 138.277, 1983.

⸻. *The Best of Simone.* World Pacific CDP7 96867, 1992.

⸻. *25 de Dezembro.* BR/PolyGram 528 948, 1995.

Sinhô. *Sinhô.* BR/Abril Cultural HMPB-26, 1977.

Sivuca. *Sivuca.* Vanguard VMD 79337, 1974 (rpt.).

⸻. *Cabelo de Milho.* BR/Copacabana 12528, 1980.

⸻. *Forró e Frevo.* BR/Copacabana 12859, 1984.

⸻. *Som Brasil.* NO/Sonet SNTF-942, 1985.

⸻. *Crazy Groove.* Milan/BMG 73138 35641, 1993.

Skank. *Calango.* BR/Sony 758.214/2-476429, 1994.

⸻. *O Samba Poconé.* BR/Sony CDZ-82090/2-479351, 1996.

Soares, Claudette. *Claudette.* BR/Imagem 2003, 1987 (rpt.).

Só Preto sem Preconceito. *Outras Viagens.* BR/BMG 1300150, 1992.

Souza, Raul de. *Colors.* Milestone 9061, 1974.

Stocker, Olmir (Alemão). *Alemão Bem Brasileiro.* Happy Hour 5008, 1988.

⸻. *Longe dos Olhos.* Happy Hour 5006, 1989.

Sverner, Clara, and Paulo Moura. *Clara Sverner & Paulo Moura Interpretam Pixinguinha.* BR/CBS 177040, 1988.

Tamba Trio. *20 Anos de Sucessos.* BR/RCA 103 0548, 1984.

Tapajós, Sebastião. *Painel.* BR/Visom VO 0001, 1986.

Telles, Sylvia. *Sylvia.* BR/Odeon 3034, 1958.

⸻. *Amor de Gente Moça.* BR/Odeon 3084, 1959.

⸻. *Bossa, Balanço, Balada.* BR/PolyGram 512 054, 1995 (rpt.).

Teixeira, Renato, and Pena Branca and Xavantinho. *Ao Vivo em Tatui.* BR/Kuarup KLP 053, 1993.

Timbalada. *Timbalada.* BR/Philips 314 518 068, 1993.

⸻. *Cada Cabeça É Um Mundo.* BR/PolyGram 522 813, 1994.

⸻. *Andei Road.* BR/PolyGram 528 919, 1995.

⸻. *Timbalada Dance.* BR/PolyGram 526 779, 1995.

Tiso, Wagner. *Os Pássaros.* BR/EMI 064 422948, 1985.

⸻. *Giselle.* Verve 831 819, 1987.

⸻. *Manú Çaruê, Uma Aventura Holística.* BR/Philips 834 632, 1988.

⸻ (w. Salif Keita). *Bãobab.* Antilles 422 848 959, 1990.

⸻. *Wagner Tiso's Brasil.* BR/Caju 843 837, 1990.

Titas. *Cabeça Dinossauro.* BR/WEA 6106014, 1986.

⸻. *Õ Blésq Blom.* BR/WEA 22925 7032, 1989.

⸻. *Titanomaquia.* BR/WEA M993050, 1993.

Tonico and Tinoco. *Coração do Brasil.* BR/PolyGram 521 984, 1994.

Toquinho. *A Luz de Solo.* BR/Barclay 827 823, 1985.

⸻ (w. Sadão Watanabe). *Made in Coração.* BR/RCA 140 0007, 1988.

⸻. *A Sombra de um Jatobá.* BR/RCA 150 0002, 1989.

Toquinho and Vinícius. *Dez Anos de . . .* BR/Philips 634 940, 1979.

Trio da Paz. *Trio da Paz.* Concord CCD-4524, 1992.

Trio Esperança. *Segundo.* BR/PolyGram 526 577, 1996.

Trio 3-D. *Trio 3-D Convida.* BR/RCA 1332, 1965.

Uakti. *Uakti.* Verve 831-705, 1987.

⸻. *Mapa.* Point/Philips 432 965, 1992.

⸻. *I Ching.* Point/Philips 442 037, 1993.

Ultraje a Rigor. *Nós Vamos Invadir Sua Praia.* BR/WEA 28128, 1985.

Unidos da Vila Isabel. *Vila Isabel: Martinho da Vila.* BR/Columbia 850.216/2-464449, 1994.

Valença, Alceu. *Espelho Cristalino*. BR/Som Livre 403 6140, 1977.

———. *Cavalo de Pau*. BR/Ariola 201 647, 1982.

———. *Mágico*. BR/Barclay 823 693, 1984.

———. *Ao Vivo*. BR/Barclay 825 738, 1986 (rpt.).

———. *Rubi*. BR/RCA 103 0687, 1986.

———. *Alceu Valença*. BR/RCA 130 0012, 1987.

———. *Oropa, França e Bahia*. BR/RCA 130 0068, 1989.

Valle, Marcos. *Samba Demais / O Cantador e o Compositor*. BR/EMI 829370, 1964, 1965 (rpt.).

———. *The Essential Marcos Valle*. UK/Mr. Bongo MR-BCD003, 1993.

Vandré, Geraldo. *Hora de Lutar*. BR/Phonodisc 03040 4063, 1964.

———. *Cinco Anos de Canção*. BR/Som Maior 3013 2001, 1965.

———. *Geraldo Vandré*. BR/Abril Cultural MPB-34, 1971.

Various Artists. *A Arte da Cantoria*. BR/INF-1002, 1984.

———. *A Bossa no Paramount*. BR/RGE 3206017, 1989.

———. *Afro Brasil*. Verve 834 326, 1992.

———. *Afro-Brazilian Religious Songs*. Lyrichord LLST 7315, n.d.

———. *Afros e Afoxés da Bahia*. BR/Polydor 837 658, 1988.

———. *Amazônia: Festival & Cult Music of Northern Brazil*. Lyrichord LYRCD 7300, 1993 (rpt.).

———. *Asa Branca: Accordion Forró from Brazil*. Rykodisc 20154, 1990.

———. *Ataulfo Alves: Leva Meu Samba . . .* BR/Som Livre 407 0006, 1989.

———. *Axé Bahia 96*. BR/PolyGram 529 826, 1996.

———. *Axé Brasil: Samba-Reggae*. BR/EMI 781040, 1992.

———. *Axé Brazil: The Afro-Brazilian Music of Brazil*. World Pacific CDP7 95057, 1991.

———. *Berimbau e Capoeira*. BR/INF-46, 1988.

———. *Black Orpheus* [soundtrack]. Verve 830 783, 1990 (rpt.).

———. *Bossa Nova*. BR/CBS 231 083, 1988.

———. *Bossa Nova*. BR/Fontana 826 666, 1985.

———. *Bossa Nova Story*. FR/Carrere CA 96-405, 1986.

———. *Bossa Nova: Trinta Anos Depois*. BR/Philips 826 870, 1987.

———. *Brazil: A Century of Song* (4 CDs). Blue Jackel 5000, 1995.

———. *Brazil: Forró—Music for Maids and Taxi Drivers*. Rounder 5044, 1989.

———. *Brazil Classics 1: Beleza Tropical*. Fly/Sire 9 25805, 1989.

———. *Brazil Classics 2: O Samba*. Luaka Bop/Sire 9 26019, 1989.

———. *Brazil Classics 3: Forró Etc.* Luaka Bop/Sire 9 26323, 1991.

———. *Brazilliance! The Music of Rhythm*. Rykodisc 20153, 1990.

———. *Brazil-Roots-Samba*. Rounder 5045, 1989.

———. *Bresil En Fete: Batucadas et Musique do Nordeste*. FR/Playa Sound PS65098, 1992.

———. *Cartola: Bate Outra Vez*. BR/Som Livre 406 0034, 1988.

———. *Clássicos do Choro*. BR/EMI 364 793 308, 1990.

———. *Cururu e Outros Cantos das Festas Religiosas*. INF-45, 1988.

———. *Festival da Bossa*. BR/RGE 3426019, 1989.

———. *Forró Mania*. BR/PolyGram, 1995.

———. *Grandes Autores: Ary Barroso*. BR/Philips 838 337, 1989.

———. *Grandes Autores: Dorival Caymmi*. BR/Philips 838 336, 1989.

———. *Grandes Autores: Noel Rosa*. BR/Philips 838 335, 1989.

———. *Lambada*. Epic 46052, 1990.

———. *Música Popular do Norte*. BR/Marcus Pereira MP-10046, 1976.

———. *Nordeste Brasil*. Verve 845 327, 1992.

———. *O Melhor da Bossa*. BR/RGE 3206020, 1989.

———. *O Melhor dos Festivais*. BR/EMI 364 793278, 1990.

———. *Os Melhores Carnavais da Sua Vida: Sambas de Enredo 1973/1984*. BR/Top Tape 011027, 1995.

———. *Raça Brasileira*. BR/RGE 308.6087, 1987.

———. *Samba!* MetroBlue 7243-8-53343-2-0, 1996.

———. *Samba de Enredo 95*. BR/BMG 74321 24542, 1994.

——— *Samba de Enredo 96: Grupo Especial*. BR/BMG 74321 33261, 1995.

———. *Samba de Roda no Recôncavo Baiano.* BR/Funarte CFCP-47, 1994.

———. *Som Especial—Clube da Esquina.* BR/EMI 052 422 158, 1985.

———. *Sounds of Bahia, Vol. 1.* Sound Wave/WEA 89003, 1991.

———. *Sounds of Bahia, Vol. 2.* Sound Wave/WEA 89007, 1991.

———. *30 Anos de Jovem Guarda* (5 CDs). BR/PolyGram 529 098, 1995.

———. *Voyage Musical Brésil: La Région Nordeste.* FR/Auvidis YA 225707, 1995.

———. *Yelé Brazil.* EMI 7243 8 31153 27, 1994.

Vasconcelos, Naná. *Saudades.* ECM 1147, 1980.

———. *Rain Dance.* Island 91070, 1989.

———. *Storytelling.* IRS/EMI 10771, 1995.

Vaz, Célia. *Célia Vaz.* Leblon LB033, 1994.

Velha Guarda da Portela. *Velha Guarda da Portela.* BR/Kuarup KLP-027, 1986.

Veloso, Caetano. *Caetano Veloso.* BR/Philips R765 026L, 1968.

———. *Araçá Azul.* BR/PolyGram 824 691, 1972 (rpt.).

———. *Cinema Transcendental.* BR/Philips 6349 436, 1979.

———. *Cores, Nomes.* BR/PolyGram 838 464, 1982 (rpt.).

———. *Uns.* Verve 314 512 022, 1983 (rpt.).

———. *Velô.* BR/PolyGram 824 024, 1984 (rpt.).

———. *Totalmente Demais.* Verve 833 237, 1987.

———. *Estrangeiro.* Elektra Musician 60898, 1989.

———. *Circuladô.* Elektra Nonesuch 9 79277, 1991.

———. *Grandes Nomes: Caetano* (4 CDs). BR/PolyGram 522 961, 1995.

———. *Pura Estampa.* BR/PolyGram 528 918, 1995.

Veloso, Caetano, and Gal Costa. *Domingo.* BR/Philips R765 007P, 1967.

Veloso, Caetano, and Gilberto Gil. *Tropicália 2.* BR/Poly-Gram 518 178, 1993.

Veloso, Caetano, and Gilberto Gil, Os Mutantes, Gal Costa, Tom Zé, et al. *Tropicália ou Panis et Circensis.* BR/Philips R765 040L, 1968.

Veloso, Caetano, and Jaques Morelembaum. *O Quatrilho.* Blue Jackel 5007, 1996.

Venturini, Flávio. *Ao Vivo.* BR/Som Livre 400 1103, 1987 (rpt.).

Vianna, Herbert. *Ê Batumare.* BR/EMI 781127, 1992.

Vieira. *Lambada.* UK/Stern's 2001, 1988.

Vinícius, Marcus. *Trem dos Condenados.* BR/Marcus Pereira 9351, 1976.

Wanderley, Walter. *Samba É Samba.* BR/Odeon 3285, 1959.

———. *Rain Forest.* Verve 8658, 1966.

Wando. *Dança Romantico.* BR/PolyGram 524 090, 1995.

Xangai (Eugenio Avelino). *Mutirão da Vida.* BR/Kuarup KLP-019, 1984.

Xangai and Elomar. *Xangai Canta Elomar.* BR/Kuarup KLP-023, 1986.

Zé, Tom. *Brazil Classics 4: The Best of Tom Zé.* Luaka Bop/Sire 26396, 1990.

———. *The Return of Tom Zé—The Hips of Tradition.* Luaka Bop/Warner 9 45118, 1992.

Zeca Pagodinho. *Zeca Pagodinho.* BR/RGE 308.6104, 1986.

———. *Samba Pras Moças.* BR/PolyGram 527 738, 1995.

Zil. *Zil.* Verve 841 929, 1990.

Zimbo Trio. *Zimbo Trio.* BR/RGE 5253, 1964.

Music of Indigenous Peoples in Brazil

Brazil: The Bororo World of Sound. FR/Auvidis-UNESCO D8201, 1989.

Brésil: Assurini et Arara. FR/Ocora C560084, 1995.

Brésil: Enquené-Naué et Nhambiquara du Mato Grosso. FR/VDE 875, 1995.

Etenhiritipá. BR/Quilombo/Warner M996997, 1994.

Music of the Upper Amazon: The Iawa and Bora Indians. Olympic 6116, 1975.

Musiques du Haut Xingu. FR/Ocora C580022, 1992.

International Artists: Releases with Brazilian Influence

The titles listed below are a sampling of the many international albums that guest Brazilian musicians, or have a pronounced Brazilian influence on two or more songs.

Adderley, Cannonball (w. Sérgio Mendes). *Cannonball's Bossa Nova*. Landmark 1302, 1985 (rpt.).

Ambitious Lovers. *Greed*. Virgin 90903, 1989.

Anderson, Arild, and R. Towner, N. Vasconcelos. *If You Look Far Enough*. ECM 1493, 1993.

Anderson, Jon. *Deseo*. BMG 01934 11140, 1994.

Baker, Chet. *Chet Baker & The Boto Brazilian Quartet*. Dreyfus FDM 36511, 1991 (rpt.).

Barbieri, Gato. *The Third World Revisited*. RCA 6995, 1988 (rpt.).

Barron, Kenny (w. T. Horta). *Sambão*. Verve 314 514 472, 1993.

Basia. *Time and Tide*. Epic EK 40767, 1987.

Benson, George. *Give Me the Night*. WB HS 3453, 1980.

Blanchard, Terence (w. Ivan Lins). *The Heart Speaks*. Columbia CK67415, 1996.

Brackeen, Joanne. *Breath of Brazil*. Concord CCD-4479, 1991.

———. *Take a Chance*. Concord CCD-4602, 1994.

Brasilia. *River Wide*. Kokopelli 1304, 1995.

Brecker, Randy, and Eliane Elias. *Amanda*. Passport 88013, 1986.

Byrd, Charlie. *Brazilian Byrd*. Legacy 52973, 1973.

———. *Sugar Loaf Suite*. Concord CJP-114, 1980.

———. *Brazilville*. Concord CJP-173, 1982.

———. *The Bossa Nova Years*. Concord 4468, 1991.

———. *Aquarelle*. Concord CCD-42016, 1993.

Carter, Joe. *Um Abraço no Rio*. Empathy E1008, 1996.

Choro Club. *Choro Club II*. JP/Fun house FHCF-1126, 1991.

Cliff, Jimmy. *Breakout*. JRS 35808, 1992.

Codona. *Codona*. ECM 1132, 1978.

———. *Codona II*. ECM 1177, 1980.

———. *Codona III*. ECM 1243, 1982.

Corea, Chick. *Return to Forever*. ECM 811 978, 1972.

Corea, Chick, and Return to Forever. *Light As a Feather*. Polydor 827 148, 1973.

The Crusaders (w. I. Lins). *Life in the Modern World*. MCA 42168, 1988.

Dalto, Adela. *Papa Boco*. Milestone MCD-9253-2, 1994.

Davis, Miles (w. A. Moreira). *Live-Evil*. Columbia G 30954, 1970.

Desmond, Paul (w. Edu Lobo). *From the Hot Afternoon*. A&M 0824, n.d.

DiMeola, Al. *Tirami Su*. Manhattan MLT-46995, 1987.

D'Rivera, Paquito. *Tico! Tico!* Chesky JD34, 1989.

Duke, George. *A Brazilian Love Affair*. Epic EK53032, 1994 (rpt.).

Elements (w. Café, A. Moreira). *Spirit River*. Novus 3089, 1990.

Fitzgerald, Ella. *Ella Abraça Jobim*. Pablo 2630-201, n.d.

Franks, Michael. *Sleeping Gypsy*. Warner BS 3004, 1977.

Fygi, Laura. *The Lady Wants to Know*. Verve 314 522, 1994.

Gable, Bill. *There Were Signs*. Private Music 2031, 1989.

Getz, Stan. *Big Band Bossa Nova*. Verve 68494, 1962.

——— (w. L. Bonfá). *Jazz Samba Encore*. Verve 68523, 1963.

——— (w. A. Gilberto). *Getz Au Go Go*. Verve 68600, 1964.

——— (w. C. Corea, S. Clarke, A. Moreira). *Captain Marvel*. Columbia KC 32706, 1972.

——— (w. Miúcha). *The Best of Two Worlds*. CBS PC 33703, 1976.

———. *The Girl from Ipanema: The Bossa Nova Years* (4 CDs). Verve 823 611, 1989.

Getz, Stan, and Charlie Byrd. *Jazz Samba*. Verve 68432, 1962.

Getz, Stan, and João Gilberto. *Getz/Gilberto*. Verve 68545, 1964.

Getz, Stan, and L. Almeida. *Stan Getz/Laurindo Almeida*. Verve 68665, 1966.

Grusin, Dave, and L. Ritenour (w. I. Lins). *Harlequin*. GRP 9522, 1986.

Grusin, Don. *Raven*. GRP 9602, 1990.

Guaraldi, Vince. *Cast Your Fate to the Wind*. Fantasy 607 8089, 1965.

Guaraldi, Vince, and Bola Sete. *Vince Guaraldi, Bola Sete and Friends*. Fantasy 8356, 1963.

Guedes, Carlos, and Desvio. *Churun Meru*. Oxymoron 3006, 1990.

Haden, Charlie and J. Garbarek, E. Gismonti. *Mágico.* ECM 1151, 1980.

———. *Folk Songs.* ECM 1170, 1981.

Hart, Mickey, and A. Moreira, F. Purim. *Dafos.* Rykodisc RCD 10108, 1989.

Hawkins, Coleman. *Desafinado.* Impulse LP AS-28, 1962.

Henderson, Joe. *Double Rainbow: The Music of Antonio Carlos Jobim.* Verve 527 222, 1995.

Horn, Paul, and E. Gismonti. *The Altitude of the Sun.* Black Sun 15002, 1989 (rpt.).

Kaoma. *World Beat.* Epic EK 40610, 1989.

L.A. Four. *The L.A. Four Scores!* Concord CJ-8, 1975.

———. *Zaca.* Concord CCD-4130, 1993.

———. *Executive Suite.* Concord 1343-14215, 1995.

Laswell, Bill and C. Brown, W. Shorter, H. Hancock. *Bahia Black: Ritual Beating System.* Axiom 314 510 856, 1992.

Lawrence, Steve, and Eydie Gormé, L. Bonfá. *Steve and Eydie, Bonfá and Brazil.* CBS 9530, 1966.

Lettau, Kevyn. *Braziljazz.* JVC 6002, 1995.

Mandala. *Watercolor of Brazil.* Igmod 49601, 1996.

The Manhattan Transfer (w. Uakti, Djavan, M. Nascimento). *Brasil.* Atlantic 81803, 1987.

Mann, Herbie, (w. S. Mendes, A. C. Jobim). *Do the Bossa Nova with Herbie Mann.* Atlantic 1397, 1962.

——— (w. C. Roditi). *Jasil Brazz.* RBI 1401, 1987.

———. *Caminho de Casa.* Chesky JD 40, 1990.

——— (w. R. Silveira). *Opalescence.* Kokopelli 1298, 1994 (rpt.).

Marshall, Mike. *Brasil Duets.* Earthbeat R271674, 1996.

Mays, Lyle (w. N. Vasconcelos). *Lyle Mays.* Geffen 24097, 1986.

Meurkens, Hendrik. *Sambahia.* Concord CCD-4474, 1991.

———. *Clear of Clouds.* Concord CCD 4531, 1992.

———. *Poema Brasileiro.* Concord 1343-14728, 1996.

Modern Jazz Quartet (w. L. Almeida). *Collaboration.* Atlantic 1429, 1964.

Montoliu, Tetê. *Temas Brasilenos.* Ensayo 3951, n.d.

Mulligan, Gerry and J. Duboc. *Paraiso.* Telarc CD-83361, 1993.

Murphy, Mark. *Brazil Song (Canções do Brasil).* Muse MR 5297, 1984.

——— (w. Azymuth). *Night Mood.* Milestone M-9145, 1987.

Pass, Joe (w. P. da Costa). *Tudo Bem.* Pablo 2310-824, 1977.

Pat Metheny Group. *Pat Metheny Group.* ECM 1114, 1978.

——— (w. N. Vasconcelos). *As Falls Wichita, So Falls Wichita Falls.* ECM 1190, 1981.

——— (w. N. Vasconcelos). *Offramp.* ECM 1216, 1982.

——— (w. N. Vasconcelos). *Travels.* ECM 1252, 1983.

——— (w. A. Marçal). *Still Life (Talking).* Geffen 24145, 1987.

——— (w. A. Marçal). *Letter from Home.* Geffen 24245, 1989.

——— (w. A. Marçal). *The Road to You.* Geffen 24601, 1993.

Pearson, Duke (w. F. Purim). *It Could Only Happen to You.* Blue Note LA317, 1970.

Pisano, John. *Among Friends.* Pablo 2310 956, 1995.

Puente, Tito (w. João Donato). *Vaya Puente!* Philips 1085, 1959.

Pullen, Don. *Kele Mou Bana.* Blue Note CDP7 98166, 1992.

———. *Ode to Life.* Blue Note 89233, 1993.

Ritenour, Lee. *Rio.* GRP 1017, 1979.

———. *Portrait.* GRP GRD-9553, 1987.

——— (w. J. Bosco). *Festival.* GRP GR-9570, 1988.

Robison, Paula. *Brasileirinho.* Omega OCD 3016, 1993.

Rogers, Shorty, and X. Cugat, G. McFarland (w. L. Almeida et al). *Brazil.* Saludos Amigos 62031, 1993.

Sade. *Diamond Life.* CBS FR 39581, 1985.

Schifrin, Lalo. *Bossa Nova em Nova York.* Audio Fidelity 1981, 1962.

Shank, Bud (w. M. Silva). *Tomorrow's Rainbow.* Contemporary C-14048, 1989.

Shearing, George. *Bossa Nova.* Capitol 1873, n.d.

Shorter, Wayne, and M. Nascimento (w. H. Hancock). *Native Dancer.* Columbia PC 33418, 1975.

Simon, Paul. *The Rhythm of the Saints.* WB26098, 1990.

———. *Paul Simon's Concert in the Park.* Warner 9 26737, 1991.

Sinatra, Frank (w. A. C. Jobim, E. Deodato). *Sinatra & Company.* Reprise 2019, 1969.

Sinatra, Frank, and A. C. Jobim. *Francis Alpert Sinatra & Antonio Carlos Jobim*. Reprise FS-1021, 1967.

Slagle, Steve (w. R. Silveira). *Rio Highlife*. Atlantic 81657, 1986.

Steps Ahead (w. E. Elias). *Steps Ahead*. Elektra 9 60168, 1983.

Stoltzman, Richard. *Brasil*. RCA 60708-2-RC, 1991.

Tempo, Nino. *Nino*. Atlantic 7 82471, 1993.

Thielemans, Toots. *The Brasil Project*. Private Music 01005-82101, 1992.

———. *The Brasil Project II*. Private Music 01005-82110, 1993.

Thielemans, Toots, and Elis Regina. *Aquarela do Brasil*. Philips 830 931, 1969.

Thielemans, Toots, and Sivuca. *Chiko's Bar*. NO/Sonet SNTF-944, 1985.

Thomas, Michael Tilson. *Alma Brasileira: Music of Villa-Lobos*. BMG 09026-68538, 1996.

Tjader, Cal (w. J. Donato). *Solar Heat*. Skye SK-1, 1968.

Tupi Nagô. *Tupi Nagô do Brasil*. FR/Celluloid 66926, 1993.

Various Artists. *Blue Note Plays Jobim*. Blue Note CDP 7243 8 3528325, 1996.

———. *Red Hot + Rio*. Antilles/Verve 314 533 183. 1996.

———. *A Twist of Jobim*. Verve/PolyGram 3 4533 893, 1997.

———. *Wild Orchid* [soundtrack]. Sire 9 26127, 1990.

Vaughan, Sarah. *I Love Brazil!* Pablo 2312-101, 1979.

——— (w. D. Caymmi). *Brazilian Romance*. CBS FM 42519, 1987.

Vaughan, Sarah, and H. Delmiro. *Copacabana*. Fantasy 2312 137, 1987 (rpt.).

Warwick, Dionne. *Aquarela do Brasil*. Arista 07822-18777, 1994.

Watanabe, Sadao. *Bossa Nova Concert*. JP/Denon DC8556, 1967 (rpt.).

———. *Birds of Passage*. Elektra 9 60748, 1987.

——— (w. Toquinho). *Elis*. Elektra 9 60816, 1988.

———. *Sadao Meets Brazilian Friends*. JP/Denon DC8557, 1989.

———. *Sadao in Tempo*. Verve 314 527 221, 1994.

Watts, Ernie (w. Gilberto Gil). *Afoxé*. CTI R2/4 79479, 1991.

Weather Report (w. A. Moreira). *Weather Report*. Columbia 30661, 1971.

——— (w. D. U. Romão). *Mysterious Traveller*. Columbia 32494, 1974.

Winter, Paul. *Jazz Meets the Bossa Nova*. Columbia CS 8725, 1962.

———. *The Winter Consort*. A&M SP-4170, 1968.

——— (w. L. Bonfa, R. Menescal, L. Eça). *Rio*. Columbia JCS 9115, 1973 (rpt.).

——— (w. O. Castro-Neves). *Common Ground*. A&M SP-4698, 1978.

——— (w. O. Castro-Neves). *Missa Gaia: Earth Mass*. Living Music LMR-2, 1982.

——— (w. O. Castro-Neves). *Earthbeat*. Living Music 0015, 1987.

——— (w. Thiago de Mello). *Earth: Voices of a Planet*. Living Music 0019, 1990.

Winter, Paul, and Carlos Lyra. *The Sound of Ipanema*. Columbia CL 2272, 1964.

Woods, Phil. *Astor & Elis*. Chesky JD146, 1996.

Xiame. *Xiame*. GE/Traumton LC 5597 1995.

Yutaka (w. O. C. Neves). *Brazasia*. GRP GRD 9616, 1990.

Index